Human Rights in International Relations

This new edition of David Forsythe's successful textbook provides an authoritative overview of the place of human rights in international politics in an age of terrorism. The book focuses on four central themes: the resilience of human rights norms, the importance of "soft" law, the key role of non-governmental organizations, and the changing nature of state sovereignty. Human rights standards are examined according to global, regional, and national levels of analysis with a separate chapter dedicated to transnational corporations. This second edition has been updated to reflect recent events, notably the creation of the ICC and events in Iraq and Guantanamo Bay, and new sections have been added on subjects such as the correlation between world conditions and the fate of universal human rights. Containing chapter-by-chapter guides to further reading and discussion questions, this book will be of interest to undergraduate and graduate students of human rights, and their teachers.

DAVID P. FORSYTHE is Charles J. Mach Distinguished Professor of Political Science at the University of Nebraska, Lincoln. He is the author of numerous International Relations titles including *The Humanitarians: The International Committee of the Red Cross* (2005) and *Human Rights and US Foreign Policy: Congress Reconsidered* (1988) which won the Manning J. Dauer Prize.

Themes in International Relations

This new series of textbooks aims to provide students with authoritative surveys of central topics in the study of International Relations. Intended for upper level undergraduates and graduates, the books will be concise, accessible and comprehensive. Each volume will examine the main theoretical and empirical aspects of the subject concerned, and its relation to wider debates in International Relations, and will also include chapter-by-chapter guides to further reading and discussion questions.

Human Rights in International Relations

Second Edition

David P. Forsythe

CAMBRIDGE
UNIVERSITY PRESS

CAMBRIDGE UNIVERSITY PRESS
Cambridge, New York, Melbourne, Madrid, Cape Town, Singapore, São Paulo

Cambridge University Press
The Edinburgh Building, Cambridge CB2 2RU, UK

Published in the United States of America by Cambridge University Press, New York

www.cambridge.org
Information on this title: www.cambridge.org/9780521684279

First published 2000, second edition 2006

Printed in the United Kingdom at the University Press, Cambridge

A catalogue record for this publication is available from the British Library

ISBN-13   978-0-521-86560-9 hardback
ISBN-10   0-521-86560-3 hardback

ISBN-13   978-0-521-68427-9 paperback
ISBN-10   0-521-68427-7 paperback

Contents

Preface to the second edition

In writing the second edition to this work, I have been initially guided by the old axiom: if it's not broke, don't try to fix it. The response by students and faculty to the first edition has been such, including translation into five foreign languages, that I have left unchanged the basic approach and overall structure of the book. The emphasis remains on the transnational policy making process concerned with internationally recognized human rights. The nine chapters remain the same in subject matter content.

At the same time, the world has not stood still since the first edition was written in the late 1990s. So a number of changes have been made within chapters to account for various developments: the creation of the International Criminal Court, including the selection of its first prosecutor; a renewed debate about international humanitarian law (for human rights in armed conflict) and whether it has become *passé* in an "era of terrorism"; an accelerated debate about "humanitarian intervention" and its possible misuse in places like Iraq; further developments about the mainstreaming of human rights in the United Nations system; an updated evaluation of the multifaceted efforts to link human rights with the behavior of transnational corporations; an on-going debate about the importance of socio-economic rights compared to civil-political rights; shifts in US foreign policy since September 11, 2001, which affect many things in international relations, given the great power of that state; and so on.

Sometimes I have restructured chapters rather boldly in the hopes of making analysis more systematic and clear. This is the case particularly in Chapter Four dealing with international criminal justice and the debate about prosecution of those who have done terrible things, versus other means to the progressive development of a rights-protective society. In the same vein I have added a section to the conclusion to make it more reflective of social science research on human rights.

As was true of the first edition, it is a daunting task to try to provide anything approaching a timely and comprehensive introduction to the subject of internationally recognized human rights. When I was an undergraduate student, I took no classes in human rights – because there weren't any. Now there are many human rights classes in law, political science, philosophy, sociology, anthropology, etc. These reflect the growing attention to the subject, accompanied by a great variety of intriguing perspectives. The law on human rights is further developed, the court cases more numerous, the impact on diplomacy more thorough, the very notion of human rights more pervasive in society, the debates broader. I suppose one should not complain if a certain ideational or normative progress makes even a summary introduction exceedingly difficult. One can legitimately complain, however, about the remaining gap between human rights standards on the one hand, and on the other the human wrongs that are so clearly manifest.

In any event, the second edition seeks to refine the first, without changing drastically what I try to accomplish. I still try to give the reader a reasonably succinct overview of the extent to which the idea of internationally recognized human rights does or does not affect behavior around the world. The target audience is comprised of university students and the general public, not advanced law students. In this quest I have been greatly aided by the students and colleagues at various institutions who have told me what worked and what did not in the first edition, what was clear and what was not, what was omitted and should be added. I am particularly grateful to Barb Rieffer, Mutuma Ruteere, Collin Sullivan, Jordan Milliken, Evian Littrell, Carrie Heaton, Eric Heinze, Peter R. Baehr, Eva Brems, Mark Janis, Rhoda Howard Hassmann, Jack Donnelly, Robert Johansen, Bill Schabas, and James Patrick Flood. Richard Claude gave support to my earliest efforts and pushed me into needed changes. To all of them I am very grateful, as well as to the editors and staff and Cambridge University Press who have expressed confidence not only in this work but also in another book I wrote for them in 2004–2005 on the International Committee of the Red Cross. I am especially appreciative of John Haslam and his guidance and support at CUP.

DAVID P. FORSYTHE
Lincoln, September 2005

Preface to the first edition

This book is intended for students interested in international relations. Rather than do a third edition of an earlier work of similar scope and purpose, I decided to start again from scratch. The changes in international relations have been so momentous, with the end of the Cold War and the collapse of European communism, that mere revisions seemed inadequate.

My emphasis is on political and diplomatic processes. I seek in general to show *how and why* human rights standards come into being, impact the notion of sovereignty, become secondary or tertiary to other values and goals, are manipulated for reasons other than advancing human dignity and social justice, and sometimes change behavior to improve the human condition. I use particular legal cases and material situations mainly to demonstrate the policy-making processes associated with international human rights. I conceive of law and legal cases as derivative from politics and diplomacy, mostly. I make little attempt to summarize the substantive decisions of particular human rights agencies and courts, other than to give an indication of their general importance or irrelevance. My central objective remains that of giving the reader an overview of decision-making processes pertaining to human rights in the context of international relations. I intend to give readers a framework of process, within which, or from which, they can plug in whatever changing particulars seem important.

I seek to show two important trends:
(1) the extent of changes in international relations pertaining to human rights over the second half of the twentieth century, and
(2) how difficult it is to mesh personal human rights, based on the liberal tradition, with the state system dominated as it has been by the realist approach to international relations.

Along the way I repeatedly address the distinction between human rights and humanitarian affairs. Legally and traditionally speaking, human rights pertains to fundamental personal rights in peace, and humanitarian affairs pertains to protecting and assisting victims of war and other victims in exceptional situations. International human rights law and international humanitarian law are different bodies of law, with different histories, and supposedly pertaining to different situations. But in the scrum of international relations, legal categories get blurred. Legal categories sometimes entail distinctions without a difference. Was the situation in Bosnia 1992–1995 an international war, an internal war, both, or neither? Did it matter for practical action on the ground? And Somalia 1992–1995? And Kosovo in 1998–1999? What does the United Nations mean by "complex emergency"? The point I stress is the following: the international community, represented by different actors, is taking an increasing interest in persons in dire straits, whether in peace or war or some mixture of the two. If states cannot maintain a humane order, the international community may take a variety of steps, sometimes referring to human rights, and sometimes to humanitarian law and diplomacy. It is thus important not only to understand the law and diplomacy of human rights, but also – to give a few concrete examples – the Geneva Conventions and Protocols for victims of war, and the International Committee of the Red Cross which is the theoretical and practical guardian of that humanitarian tradition. In other words, I take a broad, practical definition of human rights – including human rights in war and political unrest.

The book is organized according to two concepts that are both useful and imperfect: the idea of levels of analysis; and the idea of organizations that act, or may act, for human rights. As for the first, after an introduction I proceed from the global level (the United Nations), through the regional (in Europe and the Western Hemisphere and Africa), through the national (state foreign policy), to the sub-national (private human rights groups and transnational corporations). This means that I take up global actors like the United Nations and associated international criminal courts; regional organizations such as the Council of Europe, European Union, Organization of Security and Cooperation in Europe, Organization of American States, and Organization of African Unity; state foreign policy in comparative perspective (especially that of the United States); private groups active on human rights (e.g., Amnesty International), relief (e.g., the International Committee of the Red Cross), and development (e.g., Oxfam); and transnational corporations like Nike and Royal Dutch Shell. This structure is useful for organizing an ever-growing body of information into an introductory overview.

The structure is also imperfect. There is nothing magical about four levels of analysis. Other authors have used both more and fewer. Also, one level can intrude into others. The United Nations is made up of state representatives as well as personnel not instructed by states. So in discussing UN action for human rights, one has to deal with state foreign policy. Likewise in analyzing the impact of transnational corporations on human rights, especially on labor rights, one has to talk about both states and traditional human rights advocacy groups like the Lawyers Committee for Human Rights.

There are other actors for human rights besides the ones emphasized in this work. One could just as well have a separate chapter on religious organizations, rather than dealing with them briefly as part of human rights movements entailing traditional advocacy groups like Human Rights Watch. One could well envisage a separate chapter on the communications media and human rights.

Yet given the purpose of this book, viz., to provide an overview of the status of human rights in contemporary international relations, and the limitation on length imposed by the publisher, the combination of levels of analysis and actors allows a reasonably accurate survey. This is, after all, an introductory overview. It does not pretend to be the definitive word on international human rights.

I have also tried to pull together in this work much of my thinking on international human rights from the past thirty years. If the reader finds that I cite my own previous publications, it is not because I am thrilled to see my name in the reference notes. Like some other authors who have worked in a field for some time, I have tried to put in one publication, in an integrated way, my cumulative – and sometimes revised – thoughts on the subject.

A number of persons have helped me refine my thinking along the long, unusually tortuous path to publication of this book. None has been more helpful than Jack Donnelly, although some might think he and I have been competitors in writing for university students of human rights. I published the first classroom book on the subject for political science students, he then came out with a similar book that pretty much pre-empted my second edition, and now I presume this book will at least compete with his recent edition. But he assigned my first work to his students, I praised and assigned his parallel publication to my students, and I am pleased to acknowledge his helpful role in this work. I am glad to say I think of Jack more as a colleague with shared interests than a competitor.

Special thanks should also go to Peter Baehr who invited me to be a Visiting Fellow at the Research School for the Study of Human Rights based at the University of Utrecht in the Netherlands, which allowed me an excellent opportunity to work on this project. Peter also gave me insightful comments on parts of the book. The University of Nebraska-Lincoln, especially my Dean, Brian Foster, was flexible in accommodating my stay in Utrecht. I should also like to thank the Graduate Institute of International Studies of the University of Geneva for inviting me to be a Visiting Professor there, where the final revisions were made. Danny Warner was most helpful in arranging my renewed contacts in a city closely associated with international human rights.

I would like to acknowledge those, in addition to Professors Donnelly and Baehr, who read all or parts of this work in manuscript form and whose comments led to helpful revisions: William P. Avery, David R. Rapkin, Jeffery Spinner-Halev, and Claude Welch.

A special word of thanks goes to Ms. Barbara Ann J. Rieffer, who was my graduate assistant for part of the time this work was in preparation. She helped enormously not only with technical matters but in commenting on substance and thereby helping with the task of revisions.

Ms. Monica Mason was of great assistance in the preparation of final copy.

Mr. John Haslam was a most understanding editor at Cambridge University Press, despite the fact that events beyond my control delayed the publication of the manuscript more than is my custom.

Part I

The foundations

1 Introduction: human rights in international relations

Human rights are widely considered to be those fundamental moral rights of the person that are necessary for a life with human dignity. Human rights are thus means to a greater social end, and it is the legal system that tells us at any given point in time which rights are considered most fundamental in society. Even if human rights are thought to be inalienable, a moral attribute of persons that the state cannot contravene, rights still have to be identified – that is, constructed – by human beings and codified in the legal system.[1] While human rights have a long history in theory and even in spasmodic practice, it was the American and French revolutions of the eighteenth century that sought to create national polities based on broadly shared human rights. Despite the rhetoric of universality, however, human rights remained essentially a national matter, to be accepted or not, until 1945 when they were recognized in global international law.

This book is about the evolution and status of human rights in international relations at the start of the twenty-first century. Thus this extended essay is about the effort to liberalize international relations – to make international relations conform to the liberal prescription for the good society. In the classical liberal view, the good society is based on respect for the equality and autonomy of individuals, which is assured through the recognition and application of the fundamental legal rights of the person. In this book liberalism is a synonym for attention to personal rights. But in international relations it has been widely believed that the state, not the individual, is the basic unit. And the core principle has been said to be state sovereignty and non-interference in the domestic affairs of states. In this book realism is a synonym for attention to state interests – foremost among which is security – and state power. The subject of international human rights thus projects liberalism into a realist world – a

---

[1] Jack Donnelly, "The Social Construction of International Human Rights," in Tim Dunne and Nicholas J. Wheeler, eds., *Human Rights in Global Politics* (Cambridge: Cambridge University Press, 1999), 71–102.

world dominated for several centuries by states and their collective inter-ests.[2] I develop these ideas further in chapter 2.

To paraphrase Charles Dickens, human rights in modern international relations represents both the best of times and the worst of times.[3] During the half-century after the Second World War, truly revolutionary develop-ments occurred in the legal theory and diplomatic practice of internation-ally recognized human rights. Human rights language was written into the United Nations Charter, which was not the case with the Covenant of the League of Nations. Member states of the United Nations negotiated an international bill of rights, which was then supplemented by other treaties and declarations codifying that human beings had certain fun-damental legal rights that were to be respected. By the early twenty-first century more than 140 states (United Nations membership was 191 in 2005) had formally adhered to the International Covenant on Civil and Political Rights and the companion International Covenant on Economic, Social, and Cultural Rights. Some regional developments were even more impressive. The Council of Europe manifested not only a regional con-vention on civil and political rights, widely accepted, but also an interna-tional court to adjudicate disputes arising under that treaty. The Western Hemisphere was also characterized by a regional treaty on human rights and a supranational court to give binding judgments. The 1949 Geneva Conventions were formally accepted by virtually all states; they enshrined the view that certain humanitarian values were to be respected even by parties engaged in armed conflict. In the fall of 1993 the UN General Assembly approved the creation of a High Commissioner for Human Rights. In the mid-1990s the UN Security Council created international criminal courts to try individuals for violations of the laws of war, geno-cide, and crimes against humanity in the former Yugoslavia and Rwanda, thus rejuvenating international criminal responsibility after the Nurem-berg and Tokyo trials of the 1940s. In the summer of 1998 a diplomatic conference in Rome approved the statute for a standing international criminal court with jurisdiction similar to the two *ad hoc* courts.

Other developments also indicated the central point that human rights was no longer a matter necessarily or always within state domestic juris-diction. In principle, states were to answer to the international commu-nity for their treatment of individuals. International relations regularly entailed not only subjects like war and trade, but also human rights. Human rights had been internationalized, and at least some attention to

---

[2] For an excellent discussion of varieties of liberalism and realism, see Michael W. Doyle, *Ways of War and Peace* (New York: Norton, 1997), especially 41–48 and 205–13.

[3] Lynn Miller, *World Order: Power and Values in International Politics*, 3rd edn (Boulder: Westview, 1994), ch. 1.

internationally recognized rights had become routinized. International relations involved aspects of governance in the sense of public management of policy questions.[4] Attention to human rights was part of this international governance. Concerns about the equal value, freedom, and welfare of individuals had long affected many national constitutions and much domestic public policy. From 1945 those same concerns about individual autonomy and respect and welfare also began to affect international relations in important ways – regardless of whether the distribution of power was bi-polar, multi-polar, or uni-polar.[5]

The other side of the coin, however, merits summary attention as well. Perhaps no other situation captures so well the inhumanity that occurs in the world as the famine in China between 1958 and 1962, induced by Mao's regime, that claimed approximately 30 million lives.[6] Not only did the international community not respond, but also many outsiders even denied that a catastrophe of major proportion was occurring or had occurred. If one judges events by number of human lives lost, Mao's famine made him a greater mass murderer than either Hitler or Stalin. The twentieth century, with its record of mass murder and mass misery, was plainly not a good era for the practice of liberal values in many ways. It has been estimated that some 35 million persons were killed in armed conflict during the twentieth century; but perhaps 150–170 million persons were killed by their own governments through political murder or mass misery that could have been ameliorated.[7] The journalist David Rieff was quite perceptive when he wrote that the twentieth century, by comparison to those that came before, had the best norms and the worst realities.[8]

Even after the collapse of European communism and the demise of communist economics in other places like China and Vietnam, a number of persons embraced the traditional view that international relations remained a dangerous game, and that those who wanted decisive international action for human rights were naively optimistic.[9] Thus the end of the Cold War did not mean the demise of "realists" who argued that pursuit of human rights in international relations had to take a back seat to

[4] James N. Rosenau and Ernst-Otto Czempiel, eds., *Governance Without Government: Order and Change in World Politics* (Cambridge: Cambridge University Press, 1992).

[5] Lea Brilmayer, *American Hegemony: Political Morality in a One-Superpower World* (New Haven: Yale University Press, 1994).

[6] Jasper Becker, *Hungary Ghosts: China's Secret Famine* (London: J. Murray, 1996).

[7] R.J. Rummel, *Death by Government* (Somerset, NJ: Transaction Publishers, 1996).

[8] *A Bed for the Night:Humanitarianism In Crisis* (New York: Simon & Schuster, 2002), 70.

[9] E.g., John Mearsheimer, "Disorder Restored," in Graham Allison and Gregory Treverton, eds., *Rethinking America's Security: Beyond Cold War to New World Order* (New York: Norton, 1992), 213–237.

the self-interested pursuits of the territorial state. It was ironic but never-theless true that democratic realists like Henry Kissinger, however much they might be liberals at home in their support for democracy and human rights, were prepared to sacrifice foreign rights and foreign democracy to advance the interests of their state. Democratic societies surely had a collective right to defend themselves. The rub came in whether a demo-cratic society should sacrifice the human rights of others to advance its own security and prosperity. Even commentators sympathetic to univer-sal human rights agreed that anarchical international relations, without central government, meant that it was not easy to interject human rights considerations into the small policy space left over from intense national competition.[10]

This book, focusing on human rights in international relations since the Second World War, will present an analysis of competing liberal and realist perspectives. It will also chart the enormous gap between legal theory and political behavior, as public authorities both endorsed human rights standards and systematically violated – or failed to correct viola-tions of – the newly emergent norms. The following pages will explain why legal and diplomatic progress transpired, analyzing both moral and expediential influences. It will also outline major sources of opposition to the consolidation of the legal-diplomatic revolution. The analysis will hence trace the successes and failures of international action for human rights, with the latter being frequently more visible than the former. Along the way we will pay attention to critiques of liberalism other than realism, such as feminism and Marxism.

The long-term vision that emerges from the pages that follow is guard-edly optimistic, even if the short-term balance sheet is rather pessimistic. We should keep in mind that contemporary international relations is char-acterized by much turbulence, with ample evidence of contradictory find-ings and trends.[11] Nevertheless, for pragmatic liberals such as the author who regard international human rights as good and proper, but whose application must be matched to contextual realities thus leading to dif-ficult policy choices, the twenty-first century should be better than the twentieth. Like other observers, but for different reasons, I am cautiously optimistic about a liberal world order in the long term.[12] I hold to this

[10] Stanley Hoffmann, *Duties Beyond Borders: On the Limits and Possibilities of Ethical Inter-national Politics* (Syracuse: Syracuse University Press, 1981).
[11] James N. Rosenau, *Turbulence in World Politics: A Theory of Change and Continuity* (Prince-ton: Princeton University Press, 1990).
[12] Max Singer and Aaron Wildavsky, *The Real World Order: Zones of Peace, Zones of Turmoil*, 2nd edn (Chatham, NJ: Chatham House Publishers, 1996).

view even after the events of September 11, 2001 that supposedly ushered in an era of terrorism, leading to tough counter-terrorism policies by many states.

In addressing this subject, one has to admit that the topic of human rights in international relations is too big and complex for one macrothesis – aside from an optimistic if long-term interpretation about the evolution of ideas. Four smaller themes, however, permeate the pages that follow. The first is that international concern with human rights is here to stay. The second is that one should appreciate human rights as important and pervasive soft law, not just the occasional hard law of court pronouncements. The third is that private parties merit extensive attention, not just public authorities. The fourth is that the notion of state sovereignty is undergoing fundamental change, the "final" form of which is difficult to discern.

Human rights as end of history?

There is no reasonable prospect of a return to the international relations of, say, the early nineteenth century. As mentioned above, and as will be shown in some detail in chapters 2 and 3, human rights standards and basic diplomatic practices have been institutionalized in international relations.[13] The simple explanation for this is that there are now so many treaties, declarations, and agencies dealing with internationally recognized human rights that especially the last fifty years of international interactions cannot be undone. But there are deeper and more interesting explanations, some accepted, some debated.

Liberal democracies constitute the most important coalition in international relations. The affluent liberal democracies of the Organization for Economic Cooperation and Development (OECD) constitute not only a caucus or interest group. These states also exercise considerable military, economic, and diplomatic power. They constitute the current motor to a process that has been going on for several centuries: the westernization of international relations.[14] In general, these states and the non-governmental actors based within them have been introducing human rights into world affairs especially since 1945. The globalization of liberalism has been going on for some time, especially when one understands that globalization pertains to social as well as economic issues.

[13] David P. Forsythe, "The United Nations and Human Rights at Fifty: An Incremental but Incomplete Revolution," *Global Governance*, 1, 3 (September 1995), 297–318.
[14] Theodore H. Von Laue, *The World Revolution of Westernization: The Twentieth Century in Global Perspective* (New York: Oxford University Press, 1987).

If the Axis powers had won the Second World War, or if the communist alliance had won the Cold War, international relations would be different than it is today – and much less supportive of human rights. In broader retrospective, if conservative Islamic actors had proved dominant over the past four centuries, and not western ones, human rights would not have fared so well. I do not mean that each liberal democracy has been genuinely supportive of every human rights issue that arose in international relations. Clearly that was not the case. France and the United States, the two western states most prone to present themselves to the rest of the world as a universal model for human rights, have compiled a quite mixed record on the practice of human rights in international relations. France actively supported various repressive regimes within its former African colonies, even in the 1990s. During the Algerian war of 1954–1962 it operated a torture bureau as part of its military structure. The United States, to put it kindly, did not always interest itself in various individual freedoms in Central America during much of the Cold War. In places like Guatemala, Nicaragua, and El Salvador Washington was indirectly responsible for many political killings and other forms of repression. It is quite clear that during the Cold War, the democratic West, to protect its own human rights, supported the denial of many human rights in many parts of the world many times. It has proved all too possible for liberal democracies at home to manifest less than liberal foreign policies abroad.

But a larger point remains valid. Dominant international norms and central international organizations reflect to a large extent the values of the most powerful members of the international community. The OECD coalition has been the most powerful, and particularly in terms of basic norms and diplomatic practices, OECD states, along with certain other actors, have made a liberal imprint on international relations. At least in this one sense, and for limited purposes, it is correct to view international relations sometimes as a clash of civilizations.[15] For all their domestic imperfections and imperialistic foreign policies, the liberal democracies have advanced the notion of the equal autonomy of and respect for the individual. History does not move in straight lines, but certain ideas do advance. Should an authoritarian China come to dominate international relations, the place of human rights in world affairs would change. But for the foreseeable future OECD power will be generally dominant and thus generate important pressures in favor of human rights.

There is a more intriguing but debatable explanation for the staying power of human rights in world affairs, beyond these first two and related

---

[15] Samuel P. Huntington, "The Clash of Civilizations," *Foreign Affairs*, 72, 3 (Summer 1993), 22–49; Samuel P. Huntington, *The Clash of Civilizations and the Remaking of World Order* (New York: Simon & Schuster, 1996).

factors: the weight of international institutions (meaning the cumulative weight of international law and organizations), and the political influence of the most powerful states. This third factor pertains to political theory and personal values. Francis Fukuyama argues that all persons have a drive to be respected, and that the ultimate form of personal respect finds satisfaction in the idea of human rights.[16] Stated differently, Fukuyama argues that the process of history drives persons toward acknowledgment of human rights, since the *ideal* of human rights (rather than its imperfect practice) constitutes the most perfect form of contribution to human dignity. In this Hegelian interpretation of purposeful or teleological world history, liberal democracies have been instrumental to the institutionalization of human rights less because of their military and economic power, and more because they have adopted an ideology of human respect that cannot be improved upon. Or, liberal democracies exert influence for human rights because they reflect an appealing way to legitimate power. Liberal democracies stipulate that power must be exercised in conformity with, primarily, individual civil and political rights. Other states, such as Indonesia or Iran, may temporarily achieve popular goals such as economic growth or conformity with fundamentalist religious principles. But in the long run they suffer a crisis of legitimacy, because they have an inferior way of trying to justify their power. In this view, accepting human rights is the best way to legitimate power. Thus human rights becomes a hegemonic idea with staying power because of its theoretical or ideational supremacy. We have the "end of history" and have seen the "last political man" because the formal-legal triumph of human rights cannot be improved upon as legitimating ideal. Never mind for now that human practice fails to fully implement the theoretical ideal.

It is true that a number of authoritarian governments especially in the Islamic world and also in Asia criticize the view that Fukuyama personifies. These governments and more broadly many elites in the non-western world see a smug self-satisfaction in his argument. They are inclined to argue that in particular the US model of human rights is overly individualistic, causing great damage to a sense of community and perhaps even to order. This view is sometimes presented in the form of the superiority of certain Asian values.[17] Several western observers are also critical of the

---

[16] Francis Fukuyama, *The End of History and the Last Man* (New York: The Free Press, 1992). Fukuyama has not changed his views, except to say that if medical psychology could change the nature of man, his theory would have to be revisited. See Fukuyama, "Second Thoughts: The Last Man in a Bottle," *The National Interest*, 56 (Summer 1999).

[17] See further among many sources Joanne R. Bauer and Daniel A. Bell, eds., *The East Asian Challenge for Human Rights* (New York: Cambridge University Press, 1999).

extent of individual rights found especially in the United States.[18] Some critics argue there is too much western emphasis on civil and political rights, and not enough emphasis on the economic, social, and cultural aspects of human dignity, which after all is the commonly agreed end product. Others argue that Fukuyama's view of human rights is too secular as well as too universal, and thus too demeaning to local cultures and religions that give fundamental meaning to many people.[19] Some observers saw socio-economic globalization giving rise to a particularistic and fundamentalist backlash that was the antithesis of the triumph of the idea of universal human rights.[20] Even many pragmatic liberals said that human rights is only one means, and not necessarily always the most significant one, for achieving human dignity.[21]

Fukuyama is correct, however, when he notes that as of the end of the twentieth century, neither the Chinese model of society, nor the Iranian, nor the Sudanese, nor the Libyan, nor the Cuban, nor any other illiberal society has proved broadly appealing. Liberal democratic state capitalism, as practiced by the OECD states, has. One has only to compare the numbers seeking entrance to OECD states with those seeking to enter any of the states mentioned above. This is not to say that the OECD states do not present problems of material consumption, ecological overload, democratic deficits, and a host of other problems. The perfect society has yet to manifest itself. Nevertheless, liberal democratic state capitalism is associated with a broadly appealing series of human rights centering on civil and political rights, including a right to private property. (Left open is the question of whether modern capitalism based on private property causes or reinforces liberal democracy based on human rights beyond property rights.) Most OECD states other than the USA have added the conception of economic and social human rights to their view of the fundamental entitlements of the individual in society. This OECD model has indeed proved broadly attractive even beyond the western world. Many

---

[18] Michael Hunt writes of those critics of the USA who worried about its "aggressive and asocial individualism," in *Ideology and US Foreign Policy* (New Haven: Yale University Press, 1987), 44 and *passim*. Rhoda Howard, *Human Rights and the Search for Community* (Boulder: Westview, 1995), believes that the US version of human rights has undermined a sense of community but suggests that Canada's version has not.

[19] Michael J. Perry in *The Idea of Human Rights: Four Inquiries* (New York: Oxford University Press, 1998) argues that religion is a necessary base for human rights.

[20] Benjamin R. Barber, *Jihad v. McWorld* (New York: Ballantine Publishing Group, 1995).

[21] See further Herbert C. Kelman, "The Conditions, Criteria, and Dialectics of Human Dignity: A Transnational Perspective," *International Studies Quarterly*, 21, 3 (September 1977), 529–552; and Harold K. Jacobson, "The Global System and the Realization of Human Dignity and Justice," *International Studies Quarterly*, 26, 3 (September 1982), 315–332. And see below, especially ch. 4.

"have nots" in places like Asia, the Arab world, Africa, etc. do indeed accept the superiority of the idea of respect for human rights, and they are active in organizing groups to pursue that goal. Some non-western elites, too, have endorsed the human rights model in places like Japan and South Korea. Just as the originally western notion of state sovereignty has been widely accepted, so the once western notion of human rights has found broad acceptance especially during the past fifty years of world history. This stems in part from western military and economic achievements. But it also stems in part from an intellectual or ethical hegemony as outlined by Fukuyama. The *idea* of individual human rights has proved broadly appealing. Even those like Stalin, who denied most human rights in practice, wrote liberal constitutions and organized elections so as to pretend to recognize human rights.

It bears stressing that Fukuyama's argument in support of human rights is mostly about political theory. One of the points emphasized in this book is that western states, including the USA, can greatly benefit from a more serious consideration of how internationally recognized human rights might improve their societies.[22] Ultra-nationalists like former US Senator Jesse Helms resist international review of the racist strains and other imperfections in American society, as shown especially in chapters 4 and 6 of the present volume. A certain intellectual isolationism persists among some US policy makers and voters. They easily accept the notion that because the US constitution is revered, and because the United States manifests an independent and powerful judicial system, American society has no need of international standards or international review of human rights practices. Their intellectual or cultural isolationism causes them to overlook much pertinent evidence.

During the Cold War the Council of Europe was made up of only liberal democracies (excepting Greek and Turkish governments during certain periods). Yet human rights violations by these liberal democracies, under the European Convention on Human Rights, as reviewed by the European Commission on Human Rights and the European Court on Human Rights, were not few. As will be noted in chapter 5, the case load at the European Court on Human Rights was such that procedures had to be changed to accommodate the large and growing number of cases. Against this background, it is difficult to sustain the view that the US constitution and Bill of Rights emphasizing the American version of human rights could not benefit from further international review. It is perfectly clear

---

[22] See further David P. Forsythe, *Global Human Rights and American Exceptionalism* (Lincoln: University of Nebraska, University Professor Distinguished Lecture, 1999); and Forsythe, ed., *The United States and Human Rights: Looking Inward and Outward* (Lincoln: University of Nebraska Press, 1999.)

that even well-intentioned democracies violate some human rights, both at home and through their foreign policies.[23] Fukuyama's argument was not that western democracies are perfect or cannot be improved, only that they institutionalize a superior political theory for legitimating power (that they helped transfer to international relations from 1945). This mode of legitimating power is the theory of protecting human rights.

For the foreseeable future, the primary issue about human rights in international relations is not whether we should acknowledge them as fundamental norms. Rather, the primary issue is when and how to implement human rights in particular situations. A central dilemma has always been, and remains, how to guarantee personal rights when the community itself is threatened. Thus, what is the proper protection of human rights when the order or security of the nation-state is at risk?

Human rights as soft law

Hard law is "black letter law," the exact law as specified in court decisions. Soft law comes in two forms. There are legal rules that are not the subject of court decisions, but which nevertheless influence extra-judicial policy making. For example, some influential treaties are never or rarely adjudicated in court. Additionally there are norms that do not meet the procedural test of being law, but which nevertheless influence policy making as if they were law. For example, some UN resolutions become accepted as authoritative guidelines even while remaining, legally speaking, non-binding recommendations.

One of the official long-term goals of many actors in international relations is to institute the rule of law on behalf of human rights. This means not only that world affairs would be characterized by human rights standards, but also that these general norms would lead regularly to international and national court cases to protect human rights. Court cases would transform international legal principles into specific rules providing concrete protection. This is an admirable goal, already partially realized.

For example, within the Council of Europe, and under the European Convention on Human Rights, we already have hard law. As will be shown primarily in chapter 5, we have not just legal principles on behalf of civil and political rights. We also have hard or black letter law: we have court cases comprising specific judgments about what is legal and illegal in particular situations. The European states party to this legal system, which

---

[23] Donald W. Jackson, *The United Kingdom Confronts the European Convention on Human Rights* (Gainesville: University Press of Florida, 1997).

created, *inter alia*, a supranational court to issue binding judgments in human rights matters under this multilateral treaty, have thus far complied with all judgments of the European Court on Human Rights. There is nothing in the nature of the international law of human rights that prevents it from becoming hard law, even effective hard law.

This book, however, is not a case book for law students. While covering some traditional legal materials, it stresses the importance, perhaps sometimes even the superiority, of soft law on human rights. The primary form of soft law covered is the attention given to international human rights standards through non-judicial means such as state foreign policy, the action of non-profit non-governmental organizations (NGOs) like Amnesty International, the action of for-profit corporations, and the actions of private individuals. When these actors pursue human rights standards through their various actions, sometimes they can have greater impact than through court cases. Apartheid was not ended in South Africa by a court case. Communism was not ended in Europe by a court case. Torture was not terminated in the Shah's Iran by a court case. Death squads were not suppressed in El Salvador by a court case. In all these examples, considerable progress was made on human rights through non-judicial action. This book emphasizes the reality of action on human rights through policy decisions – public policy by governments and inter-governmental organizations, and private policy by NGOs, corporations, and even individuals.

Global international relations would be much improved if it approximated the regional international law of Western Europe with its interlocking human rights standards as specified by the European Court on Human Rights and European Court of Justice – the latter court ruling on certain human rights questions although it is supposedly and primarily a court for economic issues. When US courts have ruled on certain human rights issues affecting foreign relations, at least some symbolic victories have been achieved on such matters as prosecution of alien torturers.[24]

But one can make advances on human rights apart from courts and hard law. Armed conflict is a clear case in point. Since 1864 there have been a number of treaties codifying various legal protections for persons not active in armed conflict. What is now called international humanitarian law, or the law for the protection of victims of war, or the law of human

---

[24] US federal courts have asserted jurisdiction over alien torts that violate the law of nations. Thus certain foreign or alien torturers who enter the United States have been successfully prosecuted for violations of international human rights. Monetary judgments have rarely been collected, but international travel has been restricted for those convicted. See further Henry J. Steiner and Philip Alton, *International Human Rights in Context: Law, Politics, Morals* (New York: Oxford University Press, 1996), 779–810. This subject is updated later in the text.

rights in armed conflict, manifests a rich normative history. Numerous books, and even a few libraries, focus on these legal standards. We do not lack for lawyers in the various national military establishments. However, the number of important or influential national and international court cases adjudicating this international law, and the national laws derived from it, over the past 140 years is minuscule by any means of calculation. The relative paucity of court cases (excepting Germany after World War II) pertaining to the international law of human rights in armed conflict does not mean that the law is irrelevant to armed conflict. Rather, this law is brought to bear (to the extent that it is) mostly by military and political decisions, and by the private efforts of groups like the International Committee of the Red Cross.

In the complicated armed conflicts that characterized much of the territory of the former Yugoslavia between 1992 and 1995, eventually it proved possible to reduce the violations of international humanitarian law. This was achieved primarily by political means, chief of which was the negotiation of the 1995 Dayton accords. Systematic rape as a weapon of war, the killing and mistreatment of prisoners, and attacks on – and evictions of – civilians were all reduced over time, but not through court cases. Indeed, chapter 4 in particular addresses the thorny question of whether attempts at war crimes trials during or immediately after an armed conflict always comprise a preferred course of action. Suffice it to say at this point that the Clinton Administration, with widespread support among European governments, decided not to vigorously pursue certain of those indicted as war criminals during 1995–1998, making the political judgment that pursuit of peace in former Yugoslavia – and with it the reduction of abuses of civilians and prisoners – overruled pursuit of legal justice at least for certain persons for certain times. This book emphasizes those types of policy decisions in relation to international human rights, rather than hard law emerging from courts.

One of the basic functions of all law, international law included, is to educate in an informal sense. To the extent that the international law of human rights informs military training, foreign policy decisions, and the actions of private groups, *inter alia*, it has achieved one of its primary purposes. It is not necessary to have court cases for the law to exert influence – and sometimes broad influence. It is commonplace to have legal obedience or compliance without legal enforcement. Indeed, the optimum situation is for legal standards to be internalized by individuals to such an extent that court cases are unnecessary. Effective law is usually that law which is internalized successfully, with court cases attempting to sanction a few violators. When violations are widespread, they overwhelm the justice system and usually lead to the collapse of the law. The prohibition era in the USA classically demonstrates this point.

A number of lawyers active on human rights issues always argue for more hard law on human rights. From one point of view that is a laudable objective. The OECD states endorse the principle that all individuals are equal before the law. All those who violate the law should be prosecuted without regard to "political" considerations. From another point of view, however, the pursuit of international human rights standards through mostly hard law decisions is not likely to transpire with any regularity in the coming century – nor should it in all situations. The USA tried to arrest one of the more powerful warlords in Somalia during the early 1990s, holding him personally responsible for a number of violations of international law. The result was a firefight in downtown Mogadishu in October of 1993 that killed eighteen US soldiers and many more Somalis, led to the US withdrawal from that failed state, and contributed to the reluctance of the USA to have the UN decisively engage to stop massive genocide in Rwanda during 1994. There is no doubt in retrospect that the pursuit of legal justice in Somalia led to a hell of good intentions, and that it would have been better, for Somalia and for the entire Great Lakes region of Africa, if the USA and other actors had defined their objectives in less criminal terms.

At the end of the Desert Storm campaign in early 1991, the USA and its coalition partners decided not to follow up on all their talk about war crimes committed by the Iraqi leadership. Such a pursuit would have entailed a continuation of the war, as the Allied Coalition would have had to launch a ground attack on Baghdad in order to try to capture Saddam Hussein and his commanders. That attack would have cost many Coalition lives and entailed much "collateral damage" to civilians in Baghdad. It is highly doubtful if American public opinion would have sustained such an operation. To expect the first President Bush and his military staff to ignore such political calculations and look only at human rights violations and other violations of international law is to joust with windmills in the tradition of Don Quixote. Litigation is, after all, only one human rights strategy.[25] After the US invasion of Iraq in 2003, with a prolonged insurgency that cost 2,000 US military deaths by 2005, and tens of thousands of Iraqi deaths, mostly civilian, debate grew about the wisdom of decisions by George W. Bush.

In El Salvador by the early 1990s, the USA, the UN, and others decided that human dignity would be best advanced by avoiding the question

[25] Paul Hunt, *Reclaiming Social Rights: International and Comparative Perspectives* (Aldershot: Dartmouth, 1997), 41.

of legal justice for those on both sides of the civil war who had murdered civilians or engaged in other violations of human rights. Human rights concerns were addressed through various political and administrative steps, but prosecutions of past crimes associated with the political struggle were not attempted. Likewise in the Republic of South Africa after the era of apartheid, the government of Nelson Mandela decided to emphasize a national Truth and Reconciliation Commission that had the authority to pardon those on either side who had violated human rights during the long and brutal conflict over apartheid, provided they were truthful and publicly took full responsibility for their actions. This policy decision was widely debated. Nevertheless, as of the late 1990s the South African government held course, believing that national peace and reconciliation – and with it long-term liberal democracy – would be best served by de-emphasizing criminal justice.

Whether international courts are created, whether they are supported with adequate political and material resources, and whether national courts are to be encouraged to take up human rights issues on sensitive foreign policy questions are all considerations that policy makers face. Whether and how far human rights issues should be pushed at the expense of traditional security and economic concerns is a classic dilemma in soft law decisions. This is the clash of liberalism and realism. Foreign policy is inescapably about the management of contradictions.[26] This fact means that policy makers will frequently find it necessary to strike compromises between the advancement of human rights and that of another perceived public good.

Even after a "third wave" of democratization in the world,[27] many governments remain authoritarian and without serious interest in advancing democratic and other rights. Moreover, public and especially corporate opinion in the liberal democracies does not always or easily endorse national cost in order to advance the rights of foreigners. As one scholar has written, even in the 1990s there were many "structural" constraints faced by those interested in international human rights.[28] Policy makers, including those in the OECD states, operate in this context, in which there can be genuine debate about how best to advance human dignity, and what can be attempted with reasonable prospect of success. This book focuses on those debates and dilemmas in soft law decisions – while not omitting the contributions of hard law to the place of international human rights in the modern world.

---

[26] Stanley Hoffmann, "The Hell of Good Intentions," *Foreign Policy*, 29 (1977–1978), 3–26.

[27] Samuel P. Huntington, *The Third Wave: Democratization in the Late Twentieth Century* (Norman: University of Oklahoma Press, 1991).

[28] Jack Donnelly, *International Human Rights*, 2nd edn (Boulder: Westview, 1997).

This orientation leads to an emphasis on politics in the form of power and policy choice, not just legal judgments. In both national and international societies, it is politics that determines the content of the law. All law is made in a legislative process, and the legislative process always involves policy choice and calculations of power.[29]

With regard to applying the law, even in the OECD states a political decision frequently affects judicial or administrative application of the law. If a federal or state attorney-general in the USA decides to make the prosecution of a certain category of crime – or a particular defendant – a high priority, this is in essence a policy choice; no legal rule tells an attorney-general that he/she must have certain priorities. If the US Environmental Protection Agency or an equivalent agency in one of the states decides to prosecute an entity for violation of environmental laws, as opposed to seeking a negotiated solution outside of court, that decision is in essence a policy one, not controlled by a rule of law. So even in the OECD states characterized by the rule of law in general, the law does not make itself or apply itself. Political decisions based on policy choice and calculations of power are intertwined in various ways with decisions mandated by legal rules. Within states, chief executive officers and their legal staff make political decisions all the time about whether and how to apply the law in particular situations. International relations presents this same basic situation, but with much greater emphasis on political decisions in a soft law process, and relatively less emphasis on hard law emerging from judges in adjudication.

Because my approach does not simply ask, "What is the law, and how can we get courts to adjudicate it?," in chapter 2 I explain the difference between classical liberals (who emphasize hard law for personal rights), pragmatic liberals (who emphasize both hard law and various soft law decisions for personal welfare, not just for rights), and realists (who emphasize national interest and power).

Non-governmental actors

Under the Westphalian system of international relations, in place more or less since the middle of the seventeenth century, it is states that make the basic rules of the game. It is states that are full legal subjects, or have full legal personality, under the international law which is fashioned on the basis of state consent – explicit consent via treaty law, implicit consent via international customary law. As noted above, states can fulfil their duties and exercise their rights through judicial action, but even

---

[29] See further Werner Levi, *Law and Politics in the International Society* (Beverly Hills: Sage Publications, 1976).

more so by their extra-judicial foreign policies. But this traditional and somewhat legalistic view of international relations has great difficulty in accommodating the sometimes important role played by various non-governmental actors. This book seeks to expand the usual state-centric focus by paying considerable attention to non-profit and for-profit private actors. Whether or not the state has actually lost control of many important foreign policy decisions to a variety of non-state actors is a matter of considerable debate.[30] It is reasonably clear that on many issues in international relations, including those pertaining to human rights, the state *shares* decisions with important non-state actors – especially from a political rather than strictly legal perspective.

Chapters 7 and 8 focus on private action and human rights in international relations, and attention to non-governmental actors is woven throughout the other chapters. It should be noted here that some observers view human rights NGOs as the real motor to the process of growing attention to international human rights. In this view, it is the relatively well known transnational human rights organizations (e.g., Amnesty International, Human Rights Watch, the International Commission of Jurists, the International Federation for Human Rights, etc.) and their less well known colleagues (e.g., Africa Rights, Lawyer's Committee for International Human Rights, now renamed Human Rights First, etc.) that push states into giving attention to rights issues. Without the sum total of human rights NGOs, it is said, contemporary international relations would be far less supportive of human rights.

A related view is that it is not human rights NGOs *per se* that account for much transnational influence on behalf of human rights, but rather these groups acting in tandem with others actors, the sum total of which is a human rights network.[31] It is said that various human rights actors, the international communications media, the Catholic Church, the Inter-American Commission on Human Rights, etc. all brought effective pressure to bear on certain countries in the Western Hemisphere leading to an improved human rights situation. In this view, state foreign policy was relatively unimportant in improving the human rights situation in places like Mexico, because it was an essentially non-governmental network that generated most of the effective pressure.

It follows from the above that if important for-profit actors such as multinational corporations join this transnational human rights network,

---

[30] See further Robert H. Jackson and Alan James, eds., *States in a Changing World: A Contemporary Analysis* (New York: Oxford University Press, 1993).

[31] See especially Kathryn Sikkink, "Human Rights, Principled Issue-Networks, and Sovereignty in Latin America," *International Organization*, 47, 3 (Summer 1993), 411–442.

or act parallel to it, even more pressure can be generated for human rights – whatever the position taken by states through their official foreign policies. Some believe it was a series of private decisions by for-profit actors that helped convince white supremacists in the Republic of South Africa that apartheid, and with it, minority rule, had to be abandoned. When western investors judged the future of South Africa too risky and otherwise problematical for safe and productive investments, in this view progressive change was accelerated. In other situations for-profit actors have taken clear human rights decisions in fashioning their various market strategies, as will be noted especially in chapter 8. Pepsico has refused to expand operations into Burma/Myanmar because of military rule there, with related rights violations of various types. Levi Strauss refused to make blue jeans in China between 1993 and 1998 because of certain violations of labor rights.[32] A coalition of sporting goods companies, including Nike and Reebok, will only produce soccer balls in Pakistan and elsewhere if they can certify that child labor is not involved.

At the same time, if important corporations refuse to engage for the advancement of human rights, but rather take the view that profits and not human rights are their proper concern, then that is a factor of considerable importance. In the 1990s there was considerable debate about the role of the Royal Dutch Shell Oil Company in Nigeria, where authoritarian government, human rights violations, and ecological damage led some states to consider various types of sanctions.

The central debate for present purposes concerns the precise role played, and influence generated, by all these non-governmental actors, relative to governments and their inter-governmental organizations. This is a long-standing and complex debate, similar to the debate about national politics and the role and influence of interest groups. Some observers and policy makers are not convinced that governments have been so relatively unimportant in international human rights developments. Two examples suffice to make the point. One author believes that officials in the Truman Administration, not the representatives of private groups (or Latin American states), were primarily responsible for the human rights language that eventually appeared in the UN Charter.[33] Also, Donald Fraser, who organized a series of hearings on human rights and foreign policy when he was a Member of Congress in 1974, and who is generally regarded as having been instrumental in the placing of human rights on the agenda of US foreign policy from that time, indicated that he

[32] Mark Landler, "Levi Strauss Going Back to China Market," *International Herald Tribune*, April 9, 1998, 1.
[33] Cathal Nolan, *Principled Diplomacy: Security and Rights in US Foreign Policy* (Westport: Greenwood, 1993).

was not pushed into that action by any human rights NGO.[34] His account is that the basic idea of renewed attention to human rights in US foreign policy was his, and that he then subsequently invited the rights groups to testify in order to support his objectives. This subject is pursued further in chapter 7.

This latter situation typifies the problems for social science analysis in this regard. Private action for human rights is frequently merged, or dovetails, with public action (governmental and inter-governmental), making it extremely difficult to separate the lines of influence that went into a decision or impacted a situation. Was US foreign policy, bilaterally and through NAFTA, really unimportant for rights in Mexico, relative to an essentially private and transnational network at play? How can we be sure, since we cannot hold one line of influence constant or even remove it, while we replay history with only the other line of influence at play?

Fortunately we do not need to be so precise about who generated what exact influence in what exact situation. For some questions, it is enough to know that the combined weight of public and private actors for human rights led to definite developments. We know, for example, that both representatives of Amnesty International and the Dutch government, *inter alia*, combined to negotiate the UN Convention against Torture.[35] We know that various public and private actors combined to negotiate the UN Convention on the Rights of the Child.[36]

Because of such cumulative effects of non-governmental *and* governmental actors on human rights matters, we know that there have been considerable changes in international relations.

Changing state sovereignty

This book treats the notion of state sovereignty as a social construct.[37] It is an idea devised by social beings. It can change along with changing circumstances. Like the concept of human rights itself, the idea of state sovereignty is a claim relating to proper exercise of public authority, a claim to be evaluated by the rest of the international community. Thus state sovereignty is not some immutable principle decreed in fixed form once and for all time, but rather an argument about state authority

---

[34] David P. Forsythe, *US Foreign Policy and Human Rights: Congress Reconsidered* (Gainesville: University Press of Florida, 1989).

[35] Peter R. Baehr, "Negotiating the Convention on Torture," in David P. Forsythe, ed., *The United Nations in the World Political Economy* (London: Macmillan, 1989), 36–53.

[36] Lawrence J. LeBlanc, *The Convention on the Rights of the Child: United Nations Lawmaking on Human Rights* (Lincoln: University of Nebraska Press, 1995).

[37] Thomas J. Biersteker and Cynthia Weber, eds., *State Sovereignty as Social Construct* (Cambridge: Cambridge University Press, 1996).

whose meaning and scope are constantly subject to re-evaluation. Just as the nature of "states' rights" can change over time in a federal political-legal system, ebbing and flowing with political tides, so the notion of state sovereignty can change in international relations. (The content of the notion of "human rights" ebbs and flows as well. Certain principles may remain immutable and inalienable, such as the right to life. The specific content of the principle changes with time according, sometimes, to medical science – as in the development of the birth control pill, the "morning after" pill, the pill to induce abortions, etc.)

Prior to 1945, the relation between an individual and the state controlling "its" citizens was a matter for that state alone. The state was sovereign in an almost absolute sense, exercising supreme legal authority within its jurisdiction. International law existed primarily to keep states apart, and thus prevent conflicts, by confirming separate national jurisdictions.[38] Prior to 1945 there were four exceptions to the basic rule that individual rights were a matter of national rather than international concern.[39] In war, or international armed conflict, from the 1860s belligerent states were obligated to allow neutral medical assistance to the sick and wounded under their control, and from the 1920s a humanitarian quarantine to prisoners of war. In peace, foreigners residing in a state, called legal aliens, were granted some minimum civil rights. Also in peace, from 1920, laborers might be legally protected under conventions developed and supervised by the International Labor Organization. Finally in what passed for peace in the European interwar years of 1919–1939, certain minorities in some of the defeated states were officially afforded certain international rights as supervised by the League of Nations. Furthermore, certain of the European Great Powers claimed a right to act in foreign states when events shocked public morality. As noted below, these claims to "humanitarian intervention" were never collectively approved, and most European interventions for supposedly humanitarian purposes were heavily affected by political calculations. Otherwise, while European states and private actors might debate human rights, they remained a matter of national rather than international law and policy.[40]

The situation summarized above represents the basic legal view. Rules for organizing international relations and centering on the central notion of state sovereignty (with few restrictions) was always "organized hypocrisy," because states often violated in practice the rules that they

---

[38] Among many sources see C. Wilfred Jenks, *The Common Law of Mankind* (London: Stevens, 1958).

[39] See in general Forsythe, *Human Rights and World Politics*.

[40] Herman Burgers, "The Road to San Francisco: The Revival of the Human Rights Idea in the Twentieth Century," *Human Rights Quarterly*, 14, 4 (November 1992), 447–477.

endorsed in theory.[41] Nevertheless, international relations was indeed affected by the notion derived from state sovereignty, that states should not intervene in the domestic affairs of other states; and while this norm was violated, it also exerted considerable influence.[42]

International human rights trends since 1945, summarized in the first paragraph of this chapter, have, in tandem with certain other developments in international relations, caused some to see a radical reformulation of state sovereignty. Javier Perez de Cuellar, UN Secretary-General 1981–1991, saw "an irresistible shift in public attitudes toward the belief that the defense of the oppressed in the name of morality should prevail over frontiers and legal documents."[43] This statement was made during the high tide of multilateral optimism immediately after the end of the Cold War. His successor during 1992–1996, Boutros Boutros-Ghali, believed that, "The time of absolute and exclusive sovereignty ... has passed."[44] Because of aggression against Kuwait and subsequently renewed abuse of Iraqi citizens, Iraq was placed in a kind of "receivership" by the international community and denied the normal perks of state sovereignty during 1991–2003. Baghdad was not allowed to develop weapons of mass destruction, to engage in full trade with others, or even to have full control of parts of its territory. Because of Milosevic's repression of the Albanian Kosovars in 1999, other western states overrode his claims to state sovereignty and tried to coerce him into a change of policy.

Outside Europe, one should not overstate, however, the importance of various "humanitarian interventions" in international relations after the Cold War.[45] As suggested above, international law had never codified a clear right of humanitarian intervention for the benefit of nationals oppressed by their own government. Particularly developing countries, fearful of the action of the most powerful states, and ever mindful of their colonial experience, remained opposed during the 1990s to any such effort at codification. Even developed countries like the USA and UK resisted international review of national policy in the name of human rights when the issue was something like racial discrimination in the application of the death penalty or UN debate on Northern Ireland.

By comparison especially with the statement of Perez de Cuellar above, a more analytical view was that the nature of state sovereignty had

[41] Stephen D. Krasner, *Sovereignty: Organized Hypocrisy* (Princeton: Princeton University Press, 1999).

[42] R. J. Vincent, *Human Rights and International Relations* (Cambridge: Cambridge University Press, 1986).

[43] Quoted in Thomas G. Weiss, ed., *Collective Security in a Changing World* (Boulder: Lynne Rienner, 1993), 14.

[44] "Agenda for Peace," A/47/277 and S/24111, June 17, 1992, para. 17.

[45] Kelly Kate Pease and David P. Forsythe, "Human Rights, Humanitarian Intervention, and World Politics," *Human Rights Quarterly*, 15, 2 (May 1993), 290–314.

indeed changed, but that the "reality of state power and authority cannot be ignored."[46] State consent was still a bedrock principle of international law. But increasingly states were using their sovereign consent to create international institutions that restricted the subsequent operation of state sovereignty. Almost all of the states of Eastern Europe emerged from the control of the Soviet empire only to stand in line to join the Council of Europe, the European Union, and NATO. Each of these international organizations would reduce the operational independence of the state. Even the USA, the one superpower on the planet, chose to use its sovereign authority to join international institutions like NAFTA and the World Trade Organization that restricted its subsequent freedom of choice. In general, virtually all states felt the necessity to choose to participate in international legal regimes that "enmeshed" the state in international governing arrangements.[47] International arrangements concerning human rights constituted an important part of this trend.

States came to share jurisdiction over human rights issues with various international organizations and even foreign governments. Routinized international diplomacy confirmed the legality and legitimacy of state and IGO discussion of almost all human rights issues. This debate, and resulting forms of diplomatic pressure, constituted an international attempt at *indirect* protection of human rights. IGOs, and also NGOs, tried to get states to meet their responsibilities under international rights standards. Emerging practice suggested that if a state failed to meet its responsibility to protect internationally recognized human rights, then the UN Security Council or some other entity might override traditional notions of state sovereignty and try international *direct* protection of rights. Where political will was adequate, the UN Security Council might declare large-scale human rights violations to constitute a threat to, or breach of, international peace and security, permitting authoritative action under Chapter VII of the UN Charter. The Council, using Cold War precedents stemming from Rhodesia and South Africa, had done so after the Cold War in places like Iraq, Somalia, the former Yugoslavia, and Haiti. The result might be military coercion, economic coercion, or the creation of international courts entailing mandatory cooperation, etc.[48]

---

[46] Oscar Schachter, "Sovereignty and Threats to Peace," in Weiss, ed., *Collective Security*, 20.

[47] Mark Zacher, "The Decaying Pillars of the Westphalian Temple: Implications for International Order and Governance," in Rosenau and Czempiel, eds., *Governance without Government*, 58–101.

[48] See further Oliver Ramsbotham and Tom Woodhouse, *Humanitarian Intervention in Contemporary Conflict* (Cambridge: Polity Press, 1996) on the various forms of international involvement in conflict situations.

While some observers had been predicting the decline of the territorial state for a considerable time,[49] international relations on the eve of the twenty-first century remained a modified state system. The territorial state and its claim to sovereignty remained important features of this international political system. But increasingly the territorial state was obliged to share the international stage with other actors. On some issues the state might retain supreme or ultimate authority. But in Western Europe on migration issues the national executives became intermediate authorities, sandwiched between individual claims on the one hand and the rulings of courts about international law on the other.[50] On still other issues the state might be legally superseded by another organization such as the European Court on Human Rights, the European Court of Justice, the UN Security Council, a dispute resolution panel of the World Trade Organization, etc. It was states themselves that found it desirable to create these processes that some called supranational. Others referred to "pooled sovereignty." States themselves recognized that state independence might need to be restricted for the achievement of other public goods such as prosperity, security, or human rights. Once these international organs that transcended state sovereignty were created, they might in certain cases override the particular wishes of a particular state. This was the price paid for orderly and beneficial international relations, a situation long recognized in most national societies. As President Eisenhower remarked about binding international decisions, "It is better to lose a point now and then in an international tribunal and gain a world in which everyone lives at peace under the rule of law."[51] (Ike's view might be seen as heresy if not treason to later Republican Presidents like Ronald Reagan and George W. Bush.)

The changing nature of state sovereignty, and along with it the changing nature of international norms and organizations, was produced by many causes. Science and technology had produced both terribly destructive wars and globalized markets. Following in the wake of each was a process of social globalization, with human rights as the cutting edge. The Geneva Convention of 1864, mandating neutral medical assistance to the sick and wounded in war, came about in part because improved communications allowed news of the wounded to reach the home front more quickly. European governments realized they had to do more for the wounded, in an era in which armies had more veterinarians to care for horses than

---

[49] John Herz, *The Nation-State and the Crises of World Politics* (New York: D. McKay, 1976).

[50] David Jacobson, *Rights Across Borders: Immigration and the Decline of Citizenship* (Baltimore: Johns Hopkins University Press, 1995).

[51] Quoted in David P. Forsythe, *The Politics of International Law: US Foreign Policy Reconsidered* (Boulder: Lynne Rienner, 1990), 55.

doctors to care for the wounded,[52] in order to preserve support for the war back home.[53] Especially by 1945 there was a widespread moral revulsion against large-scale industrialized warfare,[54] and the idea took hold that internationalizing the concept of human rights might help erect barriers against the destruction so evident in the two world wars.[55] By about 2000, globally integrated markets had also led to increased emphasis on the plight of workers world-wide, such as the estimated 250 million child laborers.

In sum, science and technology had produced changing material and psychological conditions so that state sovereignty was no longer what it once was. Reference to the idea of state sovereignty no longer provided an automatic and impenetrable shield against international action on issues once regarded as essentially domestic. But then, human rights was also not what it had been. Human rights was essentially a western concept, first put into widespread political and legal practice by western states.[56] But over time and for various reasons human rights had become internationalized.[57] Modern war, modern markets, modern repression all presented similar threats to human dignity. Human rights was widely seen as a useful means to help achieve human dignity in contemporary international relations.

Conclusion

As we look at global, regional, national, and sub-national actors for international human rights, we will see time and time again that liberal norms have indeed been injected into international relations, and that:
(1) the notion of human rights is here to stay in international relations,
(2) human rights as soft law is important and pervasive,
(3) private actors – not just public ones – play a very large role, and
(4) state sovereignty is not what it used to be.

---

[52] François Bugnion, *Le Comité International de la Croix-Rouge et la Protection des Victimes de la Guerre* (Geneva: ICRC, 1994). An English edition was published subsequently.

[53] John Hutchinson, *Champions of Charity: War and the Rise of the Red Cross* (Boulder: Westview, 1996).

[54] John Mueller, *Retreat from Doomsday: The Obsolescence of Major War* (New York: Basic Books, 1989).

[55] Nolan, *Principled Diplomacy.*

[56] See especially Burns Weston, "Human Rights," in Richard P. Claude and Burns Weston, eds., *Human Rights in the World Community*, 2nd rev. edn (Philadelphia: University of Pennsylvania Press, 1992), 14–30; and also Jack Donnelly, *Universal Human Rights in Theory and Practice* (Ithaca: Cornell University Press, 1989).

[57] David P. Forsythe, *The Internationalization of Human Rights* (Lexington: Lexington Books, 1991).

Because of these changes, one can be guardedly optimistic about the future of human rights in international relations – of liberalism in a realist world.

Discussion questions

– Is support for international human rights a form of western imperialism? Is Francis Fukuyama correct that history shows no better way to legitimize and limit government's power aside from human rights? Is it not true that those supporting "Asian values" are correct in pointing out excessive individualism and legalism and too much litigation in the West? How can human rights be a good thing when the western liberal democracies, based on human rights, show so many problems?

– Which is more important, hard law or soft law? How do we know when to pursue hard law options, viz., litigation, as opposed to soft law options, viz., extra-judicial policy? Is it sufficient for law to educate over time, as opposed to providing legal rules for litigation? Whatever our conclusions about sufficiency, is soft law a necessity much of the time in international relations?

– How can we separate out, and therefore know, precisely the role and influence of non-governmental organizations in the human rights area, as compared with governments and inter-governmental organizations? Do we know for sure the impact of private actors for human rights in historical situations like Eastern Europe under communism or South Africa under apartheid? What are the advantages and disadvantages of focusing on networks and movements made up of diverse actors, as compared with focusing on distinct NGOs?

– Is state sovereignty a good thing or a bad thing? Should the international community disregard claims to state sovereignty when gross violations of human rights are at issue? Is any subject essentially or totally within the sovereign domestic affairs of states? Is it not true that state power, state authority and citizen loyalty to the nation state are still very strong in modern international relations? Is it not true that the nation-state and state sovereignty will be with us for some time? But in what precise form?

Suggestions for further reading

Barber, Benjamin R., *Jihad v. McWorld* (New York: Ballantine Publishing Group, 1995). Sees the world as a contest between universal secularism (human rights fits here) and romantic particularism such as renewed assertions of virulent nationalism as in the Balkans, Iran, and other places.

Biersteker, Thomas J., and Cynthia Weber, eds., *State Sovereignty as Social Construct* (Cambridge: Cambridge University Press, 1996). A good collection of essays showing that state sovereignty is not an immutable principle but changes according to history and human desires.

Burgers, Jan Herman, "The Road to San Francisco: The Revival of the Human Rights Idea in the Twentieth Century," *Human Rights Quarterly*, 14, 4 (November 1992), 447–477. The best short treatment of the origins of human rights as practical politics and diplomacy in the twentieth century.

Claude, Richard P., and Burns Weston, eds., *Human Rights in the World Community*, 2nd rev. edn (Philadelphia: University of Pennsylvania Press, 1992). A standard reader covering many important aspects.

Donnelly, Jack, *International Human Rights*, 2nd edn (Boulder: Westview, 1997). A sound introduction by a leading social scientist on the subject. Strong on theory.

  Universal Human Rights in Theory and Practice (Ithaca: Cornell University Press, 1989). One of the best advanced treatments of human rights in international context. The second edition is now available.

Doyle, Michael, *Ways of War and Peace* (New York: Norton, 1997). An outstanding synthesis of liberalism, realism, and socialism in international context.

Freeman, Michael, *Human Rights* (Cambridge: Polity, 2002). A very good introductory overview, strong on political theory.

Fukuyama, Francis, *The End of History and the Last Man* (New York: The Free Press, 1992). A former US foreign service officer and leading conservative intellectual argues that the highest stage of history reflects recognition of human rights as the superior way to legitimize the exercise of power.

Hoffmann, Stanley, *Duties Beyond Borders: On the Limits and Possibilities of Ethical International Politics* (Syracuse: Syracuse University Press, 1981). A leading Harvard professor of United States foreign policy and international relations examines international ethics from a liberal perspective.

Howard, Rhoda E., *Human Rights in Commonwealth Africa* (Totowa, NJ: Rowman & Littlefield, 1986). A thorough look at human rights in British Africa, arguing among other things that the quality of life in pre-human rights British Africa, especially for women, has been overly romanticized.

Ignatieff, Michael, *Human Rights as Politics and Idolatry* (Princeton: Princeton University Press, 1999). A short, provocative treatment, stressing the social construction of human rights and emphasizing the value of the individual.

Ishay, Micheline R., ed., *The Human Rights Reader: Major Political Essays, Speeches, and Documents From the Bible to the Present* (London: Routledge, 1997). A good selection of documents along the lines suggested by the sub-title.

  The History of Human Rights: From Ancient Times to the Globalization Era (Berkeley: University of California Press, 2004). A thematic, conceptually interesting, and provocative history of human rights.

Jacobson, David, *Rights Across Borders: Immigration and the Decline of Citizenship* (Baltimore: Johns Hopkins University Press, 1995). An advanced study showing that especially in Europe the state is becoming sandwiched between the international law of human rights and citizens claiming those rights, thus making national citizenship, nationalism, and the nation-state less important.

Krasner, Stephen D., *Sovereignty: Organized Hypocrisy* (Princeton: Princeton University Press, 1999). A critical look at the theory and practice of this central concept.

Mullerson, Rein, *Human Rights Diplomacy* (London: Routledge, 1997). A solid introduction, strong on concrete diplomacy.

Ramsbotham, Oliver, and Tom Woodhouse, *Humanitarian Intervention in Contemporary Conflict* (Cambridge: Polity Press, 1996). A very broad-ranging discussion of international action for human rights and humanitarian affairs.

Rosenau, James N., and Ernst-Otto Czempiel, eds., *Governance Without Government: Order and Change in World Politics* (Cambridge: Cambridge University Press, 1992). An excellent collection showing the extensive efforts to collectively manage problems in international relations, with a good chapter pertaining to human rights by Marc Zacher.

Singer, Max, and Aaron Wildavsky, *The Real World Order: Zones of Peace, Zones of Turmoil*, 2nd edn (Chatham, NJ: Chatham House Publishers, 1996). Two conservatives indicate why they are optimistic about the future of international relations, believing that current authoritarian and failed states will learn the proper lessons about the benefits of democratic capitalism.

Vincent, R.J., *Human Rights and International Relations* (Cambridge: Cambridge University Press, 1986). A somewhat dated introduction, but still good on basic philosophical and legal points.

2 Establishing human rights standards

It is quite remarkable that the notion of human rights has played such a large role in western history, and now in international relations since 1945, and yet no one has been able to definitively settle questions about the origins and "true" nature of these rights. Despite continuing debate over such philosophical matters, the international community – mostly through the United Nations – has agreed on a modern version of human rights. States, the most important actors in that community, who supposedly follow "realist" principles of harsh self-interest, have used international law and organization to adopt "liberal" standards requiring attention to individual and collective human rights.[1] Internationally recognized human rights, as social construct, are a fact of international relations.

A philosophy of rights?

We do not lack for differing theories about human rights.[2] Even among western philosophers there is great variation. For Edmund Burke, the concept of human rights was a monstrous fiction.[3] For Jeremy Bentham, it was absurd to base human rights on natural rights, because *Natural rights* is simple nonsense ... nonsense upon stilts."[4] The contemporary philosopher Alasdair MacIntyre tells us there are no such things as human rights; they are similar to witches and unicorns and other figments of the

[1] David P. Forsythe, "Human Rights and US Foreign Policy: Two Levels, Two Worlds," in David Beetham, ed., *Politics and Human Rights* (Oxford: Blackwell, 1996), 111–130.
[2] In a voluminous literature see further David P. Forsythe, *Human Rights and World Politics*, 2nd rev. edn (Lincoln: University of Nebraska Press, 1989), ch. 7; Morton E. Winston, ed., *The Philosophy of Human Rights* (Belmont: Wadsworth, 1989), and Part I of Tim Dunne and Nicholas J. Wheeler, eds., *Human Rights in Global Politics* (Cambridge: Cambridge University Press, 1999).
[3] Jeremy Waldron, ed., *Nonsense upon Stilts: Bentham, Burke and Marx on the Rights of Man* (London: Methuen, 1987).
[4] Quoted in ibid., 53.

imagination.[5] Karl Marx, for that matter, was not born in Beijing. He too was western, both by birth and by principal area of concern. At the risk of over-simplifying his many and not always consistent writings, one can say that he regarded many civil rights as inherently good and tactically helpful in achieving socialism, while regarding property rights as contributing to the social ills of the modern world.[6]

John Locke has been subjected to many interpretations. In a dominant strain of western political philosophy, he seems to say natural law provides human rights as property rights – owned by each individual. Human rights are moral rights that no public authority can transgress. Individuals, in his liberal view, are equal and autonomous beings whose natural rights predate national and international laws. A primary purpose of public authority is to secure these rights in legal practice. Attracta Ingram tells us, on the other hand, that human rights are not property rights that derive from natural law.[7] They are constructed in a political process featuring self-government, not discovery of metaphysical principles. There are other constructivist or analytical theories of human rights.[8]

Ingram goes on to argue for the legitimacy of economic and social rights in addition to civil and political rights. She emphasizes the importance of the positive rights featuring entitlements to minimal standards of food, clothing, shelter, and health care. On the other hand, Maurice Cranston argues that human rights can only be civil-political, not economic-social.[9] He ends his list of fundamental personal rights with the negative rights that block governmental interference into the private domain. Morris Abrams agrees,[10] but Donnelly disagrees – supporting Ingram on the validity of economic and social rights.[11] Henry Shue and John Vincent argue for the primacy of subsistence rights (mostly but not entirely socio-economic) over procedural rights (which are civil and

---

[5] Alasdair MacIntyre, *After Virtue* (Notre Dame: University of Notre Dame Press, 1981), 61–69. See also Susan Mendus, "Human Rights in Political Theory," in Beetham, ed., *Politics and Human Rights*, 10–24.

[6] I am indebted to Professor Donnelly for much of this formulation.

[7] Attracta Ingram, *A Political Theory of Rights* (New York: Oxford University Press, 1994).

[8] See, e.g., Stephen Shute and Susan Hurley, eds., *On Human Rights: The Oxford Amnesty Lectures* 1993 (New York: Basic Books, 1993).

[9] Maurice Cranston, "Human Rights, Real and Supposed," in D.D. Raphael, ed., *Political Theory and the Rights of Man* (Bloomington: Indiana University Press, 1967), 43–53; also Cranston, *What Are Human Rights?* (New York: Basic Books, 1964).

[10] Morris Abrams, "The United Nations, the United States, and International Human Rights," in Roger A. Coate, ed., *US Policy and the Future of the United Nations* (New York: Twentieth Century Fund Press, 1994), 113–138.

[11] Jack Donnelly, *Universal Human Rights in Theory and Practice* (Ithaca: Cornell University Press, 1989).

political).[12] Donnelly in turn says that human rights can only be individual, not collective. William Felice disagrees, arguing for the legitimacy of group rights.[13] Some go beyond the first generation of negative rights (said to be of the first generation because they were recognized first), and the second generation of positive rights, to a third generation of synthetic rights: the rights to peace, a healthy environment, development, and perhaps humanitarian assistance.[14]

One could continue with arguments and citations, but almost every notion put forward in regard to human rights has become what political scientists like to call a "contested concept." Ingram notes that "propositions of rights are a pervasive and contested feature of our political practice."[15] Chris Brown writes that "Virtually everything encompassed by the notion of 'human rights' is the subject of controversy."[16] Belden Fields, in an excellent review of differing theoretical justifications for human rights, notes that none are perfect and that all have strong and weak points; he then puts forward his own grounding and justification, centering on development of the human personality.[17] Especially given the lack of intellectual agreement on the sources and nature of fundamental personal rights, one might well agree with Vincent "that the list of objections to the idea of human rights seems formidable."[18]

In so far as the notion of human rights is associated with the West (and it is only western scholars that have been cited above), the unity and coherence of western civilization on the rights question have been greatly overstated. It remains true, however, that the dominant western view of rights comprises some version of liberalism. Individuals, at least, are said to have rights that public authority must respect. They are to be written into law and defended via independent courts. Debate then ensues over which individuals should have recognized rights (women, racial minorities, gays, members of certain political groups?), who besides individuals have rights (animals, human groups, which groups?), whether rights

[12] Henry Shue, *Basic Rights: Subsistence, Affluence, and US Foreign Policy*, 2nd edn (Princeton: Princeton University Press, 1997); John Vincent, *Human Rights and International Relations* (Cambridge: Cambridge University Press, 1986).

[13] William Felice, *Taking Suffering Seriously: The Importance of Collective Human Rights* (Albany: SUNY Press, 1996). In addition to Belden Fields (see note 17 below), see also Gene M. Lyons and James Mayall, eds., *International Human Rights in the 21st Century: Protecting the Rights of Groups* (London: Rowman and Littlefield, 2003).

[14] For a review see Forsythe, *Human Rights and World Politics*.

[15] Ingram, *Political Theory of Rights*.

[16] Chris Brown, "Universal Human Rights: A Critique," in Dunne and Wheeler, eds., *Human Rights in Global Politics*, 103.

[17] A. Belden Fields, *Rethinking Human Rights For The New Millennium* (New York: Palgrave Macmillan, 2003). See also Michael Freeman, *Human Rights* (Cambridge: Polity, 2002) for a good introduction with much attention to political theory.

[18] Vincent, *Human Rights and International Relations*, 35.

should go beyond traditional civil and political rights (socio-economic rights, cultural rights, solidarity rights to peace, or economic development, or a healthy environment?), where rights originate (god, natural law, human construction?), and what is the best way to implement them (courts, extra-judicial policy, private action, education?).[19]

Despite these disagreements, human rights as intellectual construct and as widespread political-legal practice was indeed first associated with the West. Other regions or cultures displayed moral principles and movements in favor of some version of human dignity, but they were not grounded in a rights discourse.[20] It was in the West that individuals were first said to be entitled to fundamental personal rights, giving rise to institutionalized claims that public authority had to respect them. Britain pioneered the development of constitutionalism, in this case monarchical government limited by the rights of other elites. France and the USA began to practice a type of democratic politics based on individual rights from the 1780s – at least for white males. In most non-western cultures individuals were still dependent on rulers to recognize abstract principles of good governance; individuals were not seen as having personal rights and the means (such as access to independent courts) to compel rulers to respect them.

Thus western states, some earlier and some later, became associated with a set of liberal principles: personal rights matter, the vulnerable and marginalized should be accorded special attention, public authority should respect personal autonomy and preferences, reason should prevail over emotionalism, violence should give way to negotiated arrangements, progress is possible.[21]

For present purposes, as stated in the previous chapter, and consistent with John Locke, I consider liberalism to connote above all attention to the essential moral and legal rights of the person. These fundamental rights, these human rights, are supposed to be trumps in that public policies must respect them.

---

[19] See further Rhoda E. Howard-Hassmann, *Compassionate Canadians: Civic Leaders Discuss Human Rights* (Toronto: University of Toronto Press, 2003). This work, based on interviews with civic leaders in Hamilton, Ontario, Canada, shows, among other things, that it is possible to have a conception of human rights and a sense of community at the same time.

[20] Donnelly, "Human Rights and Human Dignity: An Analytic Critique of Non-Western Human Rights Conceptions," *American Political Science Review*, 76, 2 (June 1982), 433–449. For a different view see Paul Gordon Lauren, *The Evolution of International Human Rights: Visions Seen* (Philadelphia: University of Pennsylvania Press, 1998); and Micheline Ishay, ed., *The Human Rights Reader: Major Political Essays, Speeches, and Documents from the Bible to the Present* (London: Routledge, 1997).

[21] In addition to the fine synthesis of liberalism by Michael Doyle cited in ch. 1, see further Andrew Moravcsik, "Taking Preferences Seriously: A Liberal Theory of International Politics," *International Organization*, 51, 4 (Winter 1997), 513–554.

Also for present purposes, I want to distinguish a modern version of classical political liberals from pragmatic liberals. The former emphasize peaceful and rational discussion to the point that sometimes they become judicial romantics and opposed to forceful action to stop human rights violations. They over-emphasize the role of adjudication by courts, either national or international, and they over-emphasize as well what diplomacy can achieve when divorced from considerations of coercion.

A pragmatic liberal, by comparison, while starting from the same assumption that human rights in general are a good thing, recognizes that there is morality or ethics beyond the human rights discourse. Thus a pragmatic liberal believes there are forms of justice apart from criminal justice, and is therefore sometimes prepared to suspend court action on behalf of personal rights for other values such as peace or reconciliation. A pragmatic liberal also believes that while one of the important goals of international relations should remain peaceful and rational diplomacy, at times the only realistic way to end some calculated human rights violations by evil persons is through coercion.

In sum, this work employs a set of simple or "thin" conceptions to aid in the organization of analysis. They are basically consistent with original thinkers like Locke and later synthesizers like Doyle. While there are many varieties of liberalism and liberals, the core idea of liberalism centers on respect for personal moral rights, based above all on the equal worth of the individual, whose preferences should be followed in the public domain. Classical liberals emphasize above all legal rights, independent court judgments, and peaceful policy making.[22] Pragmatic liberals emphasize the importance of other values *in addition to human rights*, other modes of conduct *in addition to rational discourse*, and wind up recognizing the necessity of difficult choices in the context of how to better human dignity and social justice. In the face of human rights violations the classical liberal almost always looks to the rule of law and court decisions, whereas the pragmatic liberal may well favor diplomatic compromises and other extra-judicial action. For both the classical and the pragmatic liberal, the good or welfare of the person remains their touchstone for policy making.[23] Realists remain focused on the power of the state.

---

[22] It is true that Locke argued for a right of rebellion as a last resort in the face of tyranny, but short of persistent and systematic gross violations of human rights, Locke emphasizes the role of independent courts to protect human rights.

[23] My concern is with liberalism as a political (and legal) philosophy. Liberalism applied to economics is mostly a separate subject, except that political liberalism suggests the right to personal property, which may have some role in also producing limited (constitutional) government. Liberalism and economics is an important subject, but it is not necessary for my primary purposes to go into it in great detail here.

Bringing some closure to this brief synopsis about especially a liberal philosophy of rights, Susan Mendus correctly observes that the more philosophers find theories of rights to be wanting, the more public authorities proceed to codify human rights in public law.[24] There is a remarkable lack of connection between philosophical or theoretical debate on the one hand, and, on the other, considerable agreement on behalf of internationally recognized human rights – "one of the twentieth century's most powerful ideas."[25] According to Zbigniew Brzezinski, national security advisor to President Jimmy Carter, "Human rights is the single most magnetic political idea of the contemporary time."[26]

The American lawyer Cass R. Sunstein, when noting agreement on the 1948 Universal Declaration of Human Rights, quotes Jacques Maritain's explanation: "Yes, we agree about the rights but on condition that no one asks us why."[27] Sunstein then notes that "A nation's constitutional rights are often respected without anything like agreement about what best justifies them."[28] The Canadian Michael Ignatieff provides a good reason why: historical awareness. "Our grounds for believing that the spread of human rights represent moral progress . . . are pragmatic and historical. We know from historical experience that when human beings have defensible rights . . . they are less likely to be abused and oppressed."[29]

So we have, in the notion of human rights, perhaps a matter of secular religion, something which is metaphysical and cannot be proved, but often taken on faith, or different versions of faith. But by reading history, we can see and study the results of that belief, that human beings are usually more secure, free, and prosperous when they exist in a society that takes human rights seriously. After all, other ideas, like Locke's social contract, cannot be proven to exist independently of belief. But when believed, such ideas have affected behavioural reality and have bettered lives.

An international politics of rights

Western power has been dominant in international relations for about two centuries, which means for present purposes that powerful western states

---

[24] Mendus, "Human Rights in Political Theory."

[25] Tony Evans, *US Hegemony and the Project of Universal Human Rights* (New York: St. Martin's Press, 1996), 41.

[26] Zbigniew Brzezinski, *The Grand Failure: The Birth and Death of Communism in the Twentieth Century* (New York: Collier Books, 1990), 256.

[27] Cass R. Sunstein, *The Second Billl of Rights: FDR's Unfinished Revolution and Why We Need It More Than Ever* (New York: Basic Books, 2004).

[28] Ibid., 177.

[29] Michael Ignatieff, *Human Rights as Politics and Idolatry* (Princeton: Princeton University Press, 2001), 4.

have been in a central position to advance or retard ideas about the human being in world affairs.[30] From more or less the middle of the nineteenth century, western transnational moralism made itself felt in international public policy. Nineteenth- and early twentieth-century action occurred against slavery and the slave trade, on behalf of war wounded, for the protection of industrialized labor, and in behalf of legal aliens. Most of this western-based moralism was of a liberal nature, focusing on down-trodden individuals and seeking to legally require changes in public policy.

Even Marxism can be seen as part of this western-based international moralism.[31] Marx's concern for the industrialized laborer under crude capitalism occurred at more or less the same time as Henry Dunant's concern for victims of war and the start of the Red Cross, as well as widespread western concern about slavery and the African slave trade.

Within western states, it was accepted that the legitimate purposes of public authority extended beyond defense against external threat and maintenance of minimal public order. Such a libertarian or "night watch-man" view was superseded everywhere, to varying degrees, by the view that the state should advance the health and welfare, defined rather broadly, of its citizens. This same expansive view about public authority, which led to the welfare state everywhere in the West, but again to vary-ing degrees, has produced similar developments in international relations. For example, the magnitude of refugee and disaster problems outstripped private charitable efforts, leading to expanding public policies.[32] Other regions of the world also displayed moral principles and movements,[33] but they were not in a position to influence the western states that dom-inated world affairs.

Curiously enough, the discourse of human rights was largely absent from western-inspired transnational moral developments during roughly 1845–1945.[34] Private groups such as the Anti-Slavery Society in London or what became the International Committee of the Red Cross in Geneva pushed western states to adopt treaties obligating governments to correct injustices (stop the slave trade from Africa, provide neutral med-ical assistance to the sick and wounded in war). The International Labor

[30] See further Eivind Hovden and Edward Keene, eds., *The Globalization of Liberalism* (New York: Palgrave, 2002).

[31] See especially John Hutchinson, "Rethinking the Origins of the Red Cross," *Bulletin of the History of Medicine*, 63 (1989), 557–578.

[32] David P. Forsythe, "Humanitarian Assistance in US Foreign Policy, 1947–1987," in Bruce Nichols and Gil Loescher, eds., *The Moral Nation: Humanitarianism and US Foreign Policy Today* (Notre Dame: University of Notre Dame Press, 1989), 63–90.

[33] Donnelly, "Human Rights and Human Dignity," at note 20.

[34] Jan Herman Burgers, "The Road to San Francisco: The Revival of the Human Rights Idea in the Twentieth Century," *Human Rights Quarterly*, 14, 4 (November 1992), 447–477.

Organization was created. But for the most part personal human rights were bypassed. Human rights as such remained largely a national rather than international matter. The most notable exception pertained to the minority treaties and declarations in Central and Eastern Europe after World War I, in which individuals from minority groups were afforded certain rights of petition to international bodies in order to hopefully off-set any prospect of discrimination by a tyranny of the national majority.[35] The League of Nations did guarantee, with deployment of military force, a democratic election in the Saar in 1934, and did allow individual peti-tions to the Mandates Commission which "supervised" certain territories not deemed ready for legal independence or statehood.[36] Some efforts would have transformed moral concern for individuals into internation-ally recognized human rights. A few European non-governmental orga-nizations were active in this regard, as were a few states, during the 1920s and 1930s. Poland and even Haiti were advocates of universal human rights during the League era. Britain and the United States had tried to write the principle of individual religious freedom into the Versailles Peace Treaty and League of Nations Covenant, but withdrew the pro-posal in order to block Japan from advancing the principle of racial equal-ity.[37] Thus the League was silent about human rights, although it later developed social agencies and programs dealing with refugees, slave-like practices, etc.

Key developments that were to lead to the international recognition of human rights occurred when Franklin D. Roosevelt and others drew the conclusion that human rights were connected to international peace and security. It cannot be stressed too strongly, because the point has not been sufficiently emphasized, that human rights as such became a formal part of international relations when important states believed that universal human rights affected their own self-interests. The human rights language that was written into the United Nations Charter had less to do with a western moral crusade to do good for others, than with the expediential concerns of particularly the United States. It is not by accident that the UN Charter's Article 55 reads: "*With a view to the creation of conditions of stability and well-being which are necessary for peaceful and friendly relations among nations,* based on respect for the principle of equal rights and self-determination of peoples, the United Nations shall promote . . . universal respect for, and observance of, human rights and fundamental freedoms

---

[35] See especially Inis L. Claude, Jr., *National Minorities* (Cambridge, MA: Harvard University Press, 1955).
[36] See Neta Crawford, *Argument and Change in World Politics: Ethics, Decolonization, and Humanitarian Intervention* (Cambridge: Cambridge University Press, 2002).
[37] Burgers, "The Road to San Francisco," 449.

for all without distinction as to race, sex, language, or religion" (emphasis added).

President Roosevelt was familiar with the British intellectual H.G. Wells and his proposals for an international code of human rights.[38] In late 1941 FDR made his famous "four freedoms" speech in which he tried to give both an ideological framework for US participation in World War II, and a blueprint for the post-war peace. The four freedoms (freedom of speech, of religion, from want, and from fear) were to presage much of the International Bill of Rights. In the early 1940s US planning moved ahead with regard to a post-war international organization, with continuing attention to human rights. Roosevelt, along with Truman after him, was convinced that attention to a broad range of human rights in international relations was needed in order to forestall a repeat of the kind of aggression witnessed in the 1930s from Japan, Germany, and Italy. In this view the United Nations was needed not just to coordinate traditional interstate diplomacy, but to adopt social and economic programs in order to deal with the national conditions that led to dictators and military governments – and eventually to world wars. Roosevelt believed strongly that aggression grew out of deprivation and persecution.[39] International attention to universal human rights was in the security interests of the USA, western states, and everyone else. So much the better if self-interest dovetailed with political morality.

The US Executive, aware of racists and ultra-nationalists at home, a sceptical United Kingdom still interested in maintaining colonialism, and a brutally repressive Soviet Union, abandoned plans for writing into international law immediately binding human rights language of a specific nature. Human rights proposals were extremely modest at Dumbarton Oaks and other allied conferences during the war. Eventually the USA led a coalition at the San Francisco conference, which created the United Nations, that was in favor of general human rights language in the Charter.[40] This general language was slightly expanded by several western

---

[38] Ibid., *passim*.

[39] In the context of American politics in the 1990s, and in particular in the context of attacks from the American right wing stating that the UN was somehow injurious to US security, two authors present FDR as a classic power politician who saw the UN as part of his realist plans to keep the peace after 1945. There are realist elements to FDR's thinking, but he and Truman saw the UN as also advancing peace by attacking human rights violations and poverty. See further Townsend Hoopes and Douglas Brinkley, *FDR and the Creation of the UN* (New Haven: Yale University Press, 1997). Compare Ruth B. Russell, *A History of the UN Charter: The Role of the US 1940–1945* (Washington, DC: Brookings, 1958).

[40] Antonio Cassese, "The General Assembly: Historical Perspective 1945–1989," in Philip Alston, ed., *The United Nations and Human Rights: A Critical Appraisal* (New York: Oxford University Press, 1992), 25–54. See also Cathal Nolan, *Principled Diplomacy: Security and Rights in US Foreign Policy* (Westport: Greenwood Press, 1993), 181–206.

NGOs and Latin American states, that were, nevertheless, unable to get the USA to agree to specific commitments to protect rights in the here and now.

Here we see a basic and still incompletely unresolved contradiction about international human rights. Violations of human rights domestically may lead to aggression abroad. But if you establish a global rule of law to deal with the human rights violations of others, you will restrict your own freedom of maneuver and highlight your own defects. Roosevelt and Truman were convinced that the origins of World War II lay in Germany's internal policies of the 1930s. But if they created precise international law with strong enforcement mechanisms, these arrangements would reduce US freedom of choice in the making of public policy. A strong international legal regime for human rights costs something in national discretion.

Despite contradictions, the UN Charter came to be the first treaty in world history to recognize universal human rights. Yet no Great Power proposed a radical restructuring of international relations to benefit individuals after the two immensely destructive world wars of the twentieth century. Human rights were vaguely endorsed, but they were to be pursued by traditional state diplomacy. The theory of rights was revolutionary: all individuals manifested them, and even sovereign states had to respect them. But neither the United Nations nor any other international organization in 1945 was given clear supranational authority to ensure their respect. The UN Charter allowed the Security Council to take binding decisions on security questions, but not on social questions. The Charter also contained a prohibition on UN interference in national domestic affairs. Much of world politics in subsequent years was to deal with this contradiction between the affirmation of universal human rights and the reaffirmation of state sovereignty over domestic social issues.

At about the same time as the UN Charter was adopted, the victorious states in World War II organized the Nuremberg and Tokyo international criminal tribunals for the prosecution of German and Japanese leaders. International prosecutions for war crimes and crimes against peace solidified the notion that individuals could be held legally responsible for violating the laws of war and for waging aggressive war. But the idea of a "crime against humanity," while somewhat new and thus raising questions about due process, implied that individual leaders could be held responsible for violating certain human rights of their own citizens.[41] Certain gross

---

[41] The notion of a crime against humanity was articulated by the British after World War I with regard to the Ottoman Empire and its atrocities against the Armenian community of that Empire. But since the defeated Ottomans, or Turks, still held some British prisoners of war, Britain dropped the subject of crimes against humanity by the Turks, in

violations of human rights, such as murder, enslavement, deportation, pseudo-medical experiments, when practiced on a mass scale, could lead to prosecution, conviction, and even the death penalty. These two international criminal proceedings were not free from well-founded charges of bias and "victor's justice," but they did further the idea that all individuals had fundamental rights in both peace and war.[42]

An international bill of rights

Because the Charter made references to universal human rights but did not specify them, early UN diplomacy sought to fill that void. On December 10, 1948, the General Assembly adopted the Universal Declaration of Human Rights, which was, according to Eleanor Roosevelt, then chair of the UN Human Rights Commission, a statement of aspirations.[43] Its thirty principles covered the same range of rights long endorsed by many western leaders and private parties: rights of political participation and of civic freedom; rights to freedom from want in the form of entitlements to adequate food, clothing, shelter, and health care; and rights to freedom from fear in the form of a pursuit of an international order in which all other rights could be realized. Even this Declaration, which in international law was not immediately binding, proved too much for Saudi Arabia, South Africa, and the Soviet Union and five of its allies – all of which abstained. (All successor governments excepting Saudi Arabia publicly disavowed their abstentions by the mid-1990s.)

For the remaining forty-six members of the UN in 1948, the Declaration could be negotiated rather rapidly by international standards, although there were many specific points of controversy.[44] Most of the General Assembly members were represented by governments comfortable with the notion of individual fundamental rights in the abstract, who did not object to their elaboration in this general way. During 1946–1948 there was relatively little acrimonious debate about universalism versus

order to secure the release of its POWs. During World War II, no treaty covered crimes against humanity, nor was this latter legal notion part of international customary law. Yet German leaders were prosecuted for violating this "rule" nevertheless. See further Gary Jonathan Bass, *Stay The Hand of Vengeance: The Politics of War Crimes Tribunals* (Princeton: Princeton University Press, 2000), 114–146.

[42] Christian Tomuschat, "International Criminal Prosecution: The Precedent of Nuremberg Confirmed," *Criminal Law Forum*, 5, 2–3 (1994), 237–248. Debate continues over whether crimes against humanity exist only during armed conflict or also during peace time.

[43] Mary Ann Glendon, *A World Made New: Eleanor Roosevelt and the Universal Declaration of Human Rights* (New York: Random House, 2001).

[44] See further Johannes Morsink, *The Universal Declaration of Human Rights: Origins, Drafting, and Intent* (Philadelphia: University of Pennsylvania Press, 1998).

relativism, or about various generations of rights. Especially the West European democracies were comfortable with the values found in the Universal Declaration, as it closely paralleled the domestic policies they wanted to pursue. Moreover, it cannot be stressed too much that in the mid-1940s the US Executive was in favor of socio-economic as well as civil-political rights. The Democratic Party, through its long control of the White House, had coped with economic depression after 1932 with broad governmental programming that responded to the failures of capitalist markets to provide for the people (and, it must be noted, with participation in the Second World War which finally conquered high unemployment). Roosevelt had proposed an economic bill of rights in 1944.[45] Truman strongly advocated a right to national health care, although he was never able to get his proposals approved by Congress. (Members of the Democratic Party from the states of the former Confederacy, however, were mostly opposed to internationally recognized human rights.)

Women's organizations were highly active in negotiating the Declaration and achieved a number of semantical changes to their liking.[46] Feminist critiques of mainstream UN human rights developments were largely absent. With a female as chair of the Human Rights Commission, and with the creation of the UN Commission on the Status of Women, dominant opinion within the UN believed that sufficient attention was being paid to gender issues – especially since the UN Charter spoke of equality without regard to sex.

The negotiating process entailed a broad range of views, not just Western ones, although Africa and Asia were under-represented.[47] Beyond Western Europe and North America, Latin American political elites were essentially western. Their governments reflected Iberian, and hence western, values in the abstract, rather than indigenous Indian values.[48] The Latin American social democrats, working with the Canadian social democrat John Humphrey, who was a UN international civil servant, were largely responsible for the wording on socio-economic rights; this language was not the product of the communist states.[49] Lebanon was also strongly in favor of international human rights, being greatly affected

---

[45] Bertram Gross, "The Human Rights Paradox," in Peter Juviler and Bertram Gross, *Human Rights for the 21st Century: Foundations for Responsible Hope* (Armonk: M.E. Sharpe, 1993), 128.

[46] Morsink, *Universal Declaration*, ch. 3 and *passim*.

[47] Ibid., *passim*.

[48] On the compatibility of abstract Latin American Iberian values with international human rights standards, the many violations of these rights notwithstanding, see David P. Forsythe, "Human Rights, the United States and the Organization of American States," *Human Rights Quarterly*, 13, 1 (February 1991), 66–98. And see below, ch. 5.

[49] Morsink, *Universal Declaration*, chs. 5, 6, and *passim*.

by French influence. The same was true for the Philippines, being affected by American influence. The relatively easy adoption of the 1948 Universal Declaration, a "mere" General Assembly non-binding recommendation, was to prove a major step in the evolving attention to internationally recognized human rights. According to one source, it is "the essential document, the touchstone, the creed of humanity that surely sums up all other creeds directing human behaviour."[50] This most basic statement of international ethics is liberal in tone and content. In late 1948 the Cold War had not fully emerged, and so the Universal Declaration was approved. Had it been delayed for any reason beyond December 1948, it might never have passed the General Assembly. The Cold War soon deeply divided that body.

It proved much more time-consuming and controversial to translate the Universal Declaration into supposedly enforceable treaties. The Great Powers were preoccupied by the Cold War. It was to take from 1948 to 1966 to accomplish the task of producing the International Covenant on Civil and Political Rights, and also the International Covenant on Economic, Social, and Cultural Rights. These two treaties, discussed in chapter 3, together with the Universal Declaration, against the background of the UN Charter, make up the International Bill of Rights. Despite the fact that substantive negotiations for the two treaties were completed by 1966, it took another decade for the required number of legal adherences to be obtained in order to bring the treaties into legal force for full parties. This indicated a certain caution by states in moving from general principles to specific treaty provisions that might prove to limit their freedom of choice in foreign and domestic policy – or what had been domestic policy prior to international legislation.

The negotiations after 1948 were complicated by several factors.[51] The USA was in no hurry to move things forward, since the Executive Branch was under attack by certain powerful domestic groups fearful of international pressures to change the existing American way of life. The Executive was sometimes seen as in favor of a domineering federal government that would introduce foreign and excessively permissive principles and thus destroy the existing *status quo* as protected by the US Constitution and state/provincial governments. The Soviet bloc and the developing countries seized the opportunity to push for economic and social rights in ways, and to an extent, that troubled the western bloc. The western group finally accepted socio-economic rights

---

[50] Nadine Gordimer, "Reflections by Nobel Laureates," in Yeal Danieli, Elsa Stamatopoulou, and Clarence J. Dias, eds., *The Universal Declaration of Human Rights: Fifty Years and Beyond* (Amityville, NY: Baywood, 1998).

[51] See further Evans, *US Hegemony*.

in treaty form only as realized gradually over time, and when two separate Covenants were drafted – with different supervisory mechanisms. The developing countries, supported by the communist coalition, pressed hard for rewriting the principle of national self-determination as a collective human right. The western states finally accepted political reality and agreed to a common Article 1 in the two Covenants focusing on a highly ambiguous right to collective self-determination. It has never been clear in international law as to what exactly comprises a people entitled to self-determination, what form self-determination should take, or who can pronounce authoritatively on these controversies.[52] There was also controversy about whether ratification of the Covenants obligated a colonial state to apply human rights provisions in dependent territories. Thus many of the disputes between the East and West, between the North and South, played themselves out in UN debates about human rights.

It bears emphasizing that the General Assembly changed in composition, especially from the mid-1950s. Many non-western states were added to UN membership. This complicated negotiations concerning human rights compared with 1948. Most of these newer states were not only non-western, but also non-affluent and non-democratic. They were therefore not hesitant in expressing concern about an emphasis on democratic rights and a civic society replete with many civil rights, or in emphasizing economic rights to an extent that troubled particularly the USA.[53] These developments were welcomed by the Soviet Union and its allies. Moreover, as noted above, a number of states were hesitant to place themselves under specific international legal obligation in the field of human rights, even though they had voted for the Universal Declaration – and even though a UN human rights court had not been created. The Covenants always entailed weak supervisory or enforcement mechanisms, as we will see. Many states sought to preserve considerable independence in policy making, even as they found it prudent to be associated with the notion of human rights.

[52] From a vast literature see especially Hurst Hannum, *Autonomy, Sovereignty, and Self-Determination: The Accommodation of Conflicting Rights* (Philadelphia: University of Pennsylvania Press, 1992); and Morton H. Halperin and David J. Scheffer, with Patricia L. Small, *Self-Determination in the New World Order* (Washington: Carnegie Endowment, 1992). The UN Charter endorses human rights in the name of promotion of international peace and security. But in writing the national self-determination of peoples into subsequent human rights legal instruments, the international community endorsed a principle of collective human rights that has caused much mischief and no little instability in both national and international politics.

[53] See further David P. Forsythe, "The United Nations, Human Rights, and Development," *Human Rights Quarterly*, 19, 2 (May, 1997), 334–349, especially where relying on publications by Theo van Boven, former Director of the UN Human Rights Center.

Be all that as it may, by 2005 many states had become parties to the International Covenants on Civil and Political Rights (153), and also to the International Covenant on Economic, Social, and Cultural Rights (150). With UN membership at 191 states in 2005, it is apparent that most states found it desirable to at least give formal endorsement to the liberal notion of universal human rights. There is something about the idea of human rights that has proved widely attractive, as Francis Fukuyama predicted, even as endorsement has not always been followed by compliance. As we will see, many states including liberal ones like the USA wish to have it both ways. They wish to identify with support for human rights, but they wish to maintain national independence in policy making both at home and abroad.

Legal regimes without hegemonic leadership

One of the central problems in the development of international human rights law at the United Nations was that the USA was compelled by domestic politics to abandon a position of clear leadership in the setting of international human rights standards.[54] FDR had led on human rights, up to a point. But Truman, Eisenhower, and other presidents were severely constrained by American domestic politics. The start of the Cold War between the USA and the USSR caused some members of Congress to view socio-economic rights as a form of creeping socialism on the road to communism. The conservative and fanatical movement known as McCarthyism made rational congressional discourse about international rights difficult if not impossible; that movement only allowed in Washington's policy debates a mindless defense of a chauvinistic version of American moral superiority and security. Racists took courage from the overall situation and demanded an end to international developments in support of racial equality and freedom from racial discrimination. Nationalists championed the supremacy of the US Constitution compared with treaty law. The American Bar Association acted irresponsibly, manufacturing and exaggerating problems supposedly entailed in US adherence to the International Bill of Rights. When the Bricker movement in Congress sought to undermine the Executive's authority to negotiate and ratify self-implementing treaties, the Eisenhower Administration agreed to back away from open support for human rights treaties. In this way the Executive preserved its overall position in tugs of war with Congress, but at the sacrifice of leadership on international human rights matters. UN human rights developments were left without the full support of the most

[54] Evans, *US Hegemony.*

powerful state in the world, despite the US penchant for seeing itself as a human rights model for others.[55]

In other parts or issue-areas of international relations, a hegemonic power had taken the lead in the construction of norms and organizations to manage important issues.[56] For example, the USA had taken the lead in both Western Europe and the Western Hemisphere to construct security arrangements for the defense of multilateral interests. NATO and the workings of the Inter-American system reflected broad deference to, or cooperation with, US views on security. The USA did not have to coerce other states into compliance with its views (Cuba excepted after 1959) but rather exercised hegemonic leadership through a series of initiatives, burdens, payments, etc.

But with regard to global human rights, the USA was not able to play this role of hegemon, not so much because of clear Executive disagreement with the course of UN human rights developments. Rather, congressional and public views relegated the Executive Branch, under both Republicans and Democrats, to a background and low-profile role regarding international rights. From Dwight Eisenhower through Gerald Ford, the USA did not emphasize international human rights in its foreign policy, and this orientation certainly was evident in UN proceedings. It was only when Congress shifted position in the mid-1970s, and began to stress what it had rejected in the 1940s, namely an emphasis on human rights in foreign policy, that presidents like Jimmy Carter felt free to make human rights a more salient issue in world politics.[57] Even after 1976 the USA did not ratify the International Covenant on Economic, Social, and Cultural Rights or the Convention on the Rights of the Child or the Convention on the Elimination of Discrimination Against Women; it ratified other human rights treaties only with restrictive conditions; still manifested evident and widespread problems of racism; and utilized the death penalty for common, non-political crime far more than any other industrialized democracy. Thus the USA still found it difficult to play the role of hegemonic leader at the UN on human rights issues, although it tried to a greater extent than during the classic Cold War years.

---

[55] In addition to Evans, *US Hegemony*, and Forsythe, "Human Rights and US Foreign Policy," see Natalie Hevener Kaufman, *Human Rights Treaties and The Senate: A History of Opposition* (Chapel Hill: The University of North Carolina Press, 1990); and Lawrence J. LeBlanc, *The United States and the Genocide Convention* (Durham: Duke University Press, 1991).

[56] See especially Stephen D. Krasner, ed., *International Regimes* (Ithaca: Cornell University Press, 1983); Volker Rittberger and Peter Mayer, eds., *Regime Theory and International Relations* (New York: Oxford University Press, 1993).

[57] See further David P. Forsythe, *Human Rights and US Foreign Policy: Congress Reconsidered* (Gainesville: University Press of Florida, 1988).

After the terroristic attacks of September 11, 2001, however, and given especially its policies and events related to prisoners in its "war" on terrorism, the USA found it again difficult to play the role of hegemonic leader on human rights. High US officials authorized the secret holding of some prisoners, the coercive interrogation of these and some others, and in general failed to maintain a careful watch over many other prisoners in Iraq and Afghanistan and at the Guantanamo Bay detention facility. In Iraq in particular, but also in Afghanistan, many prisoners were badly abused, some fatally. This situation undercut the US claim to be a model for others regarding human rights and made it virtually impossible for the USA to approach other countries about torture and mistreatment of prisoners in particular. Over time the USA did begin to reform at least somewhat its detention policies associated with military action abroad.[58]

Beyond the International Bill of Rights

Despite the absence of hegemonic leadership from the USA, other states, international civil servants, and non-governmental organizations combined their efforts to provide at the UN a relatively large body of treaties and declarations about universal human rights. Through the UN General Assembly, in 1948 states adopted the Convention on the Prevention and Punishment of the Crime of Genocide, making individuals responsible for prosecution if they intend to destroy a national, ethnic, religious, or racial, group, in whole or in part. Only four groups fall under this treaty, and the very notion of genocide is vaguely defined. Nevertheless, the convention represents some progress in humane matters. The Assembly adopted a treaty regulating prostitution in 1949, and in 1951 it adopted the Convention Relating to the Status of Refugees, adding a Protocol in 1967. The central rule in international refugee law obliges states to give temporary asylum to those who have fled their homeland because of a well-founded fear of persecution. In 1953 the Assembly amended the 1926 Slavery Convention. In the same year it adopted the Convention on the Political Rights of Women, and the following year the Convention Relating to the Status of Stateless Persons. In 1956 the Assembly approved the Convention on the Abolition of Slavery, the Slave Trade, and Institutions and Practices Similar to Slavery, thus supplementing earlier treaties and protocols on this subject. The treaty on the Reduction of Statelessness was adopted in 1961. Reflecting the impact of many new non-western member states, the General Assembly in 1965 adopted the Convention on Racial Discrimination. This was followed in 1973 by the Convention

---

[58] David P. Forsythe, *The Humanitarians: The International Committee of the Red Cross* (Cambridge: Cambridge University Press, 2005), chapter 4; Seymour Hersch, *Chain of Command* (New York: Harper Collins, 2004).

against Apartheid, referring to legal racial segregation primarily as then practiced by the Republic of South Africa. In 1979 the Assembly adopted the Convention on General Discrimination against Women and the UN Convention against Torture was approved in 1984. In a highly popular move, the Assembly in 1989 adopted the Convention on the Rights of the Child.

During this same era, the International Labor Organization, a carry-over from the League of Nations period but after 1945 technically part of the UN system, adopted a series of treaties dealing with such subjects as freedom of association (1948), the right of labor movements to engage in collective bargaining (1949), freedom from forced labor (1957), freedom from social discrimination (1958), and the protection of indigenous peoples (1989). The United Nations Educational, Scientific, and Cultural Organization adopted a Convention in 1960 dealing with Discrimination in Education.

Outside of the United Nations, but still concerning universal standards, states agreed to further develop international humanitarian law – sometimes also referred to as international law for human rights in armed conflict. In 1949 they adopted the interlocking four Geneva Conventions of 12 August for Protection of Victims of War. In a subsequent diplomatic conference during 1974–1977, also called by the Swiss government, the depository state for humanitarian law since 1864, two Protocols were added to the 1949 law. The first Protocol increased humanitarian regulation of international armed conflict. The second provided a mini-convention, the first ever, on internal armed conflict, sometimes called civil war. In 1980 many states agreed to a framework convention on conventional weapons that might cause indiscriminate or unnecessary suffering. The sum total of this Geneva law or Red Cross law, so named because of the supporting role played by the Geneva-based International Committee of the Red Cross (ICRC), an independent component of the International Red Cross and Red Crescent Movement, focused on inactive or non-combatant victims of war.

The thrust of international humanitarian law was nothing less than to humanize war, in the sense of trying to protect and assist those fighters held as prisoners or otherwise inactive through sickness or wounds; civilians; those in occupied territory; those separated from and without information about family members; those in a war zone and in need of food, clothing, shelter, and medical care; and those victimized by certain weaponry – among other subject matter.[59] A fundamental point is that even in war, international or civil, fighting parties are not legally free to

---

[59] From a vast literature which frequently focuses on legal aspects, see especially the following policy-oriented sources: Geoffrey Best, *War and Law Since 1945* (Oxford: Clarendon Press, 1994); Caroline Morehead, *Dunant's Dream: War, Switzerland, and the History of*

engage in wanton destruction, but rather must direct military action only to permissible targets in an effort to minimize human misery. This general principle is formally accepted by all professional military establishments, even as many civilians still wonder how there can be a humane law of war in the midst of intentional killing.

Much has been written about the relationship between the international law for human rights in peace time, and international humanitarian law for situations of international and non-international armed conflict. The essential and non-legalistic point is that these two bodies of international law share the objective of creating minimal standards of human dignity by establishing humane standards that states are legally obligated to meet in different situations.[60] The United Nations, which historically dealt with human rights in peace, has increasingly developed policies and programs for humanitarian action in war. The ICRC, the theoretical coordinator for the private Red Cross Movement in wartime, increasingly interacts with UN bodies (and other actors) about its humanitarian action. Legal distinctions should not be allowed to obscure common objectives and cooperation in programs.[61]

If one adds together the human rights and humanitarian treaties negotiated through the UN General Assembly, the ILO, UNESCO, and the Diplomatic Conferences called by Switzerland in consultation with the ICRC, it is clear we do not lack global or universal humane standards in both peace and war. One could add to the list certain declarations and other forms of soft law adopted by various international organizations on these same subjects. States clearly wish to picture themselves as standing for something besides harsh realist principles of narrow

the Red Cross (New York: St. Martin's Press, 1998); Francois Bugnion, *The International Committee of the Red Cross and the Protection of War Victims* (Geneva: ICRC, 2003) ; John Hutchinson, *Champions of Charity: War and the Rise of the Red Cross* (Boulder: Westview, 1996); David P. Forsythe, *Humanitarian Politics: The International Committee of the Red Cross* (Baltimore: Johns Hopkins University Press, 1977); Forsythe, *The Internationalization of Human Rights* (Lexington: Lexington Books for D.C. Heath, 1991), ch. 6; and Forsythe, *The Humanitarians*.

60 It has never been clear how international law can obligate non-state parties in a non-international armed conflict. International law is state centric. The rebel side in a civil war did not participate in the drafting of the laws of war, and cannot deposit a signature of adherence with the depository agent giving its consent to be bound. Nevertheless, a number of rebel movements have promised to abide by humanitarian law, whatever their subsequent behavior. It is not legal technicalities but political calculation that is important. If a rebel side seeks recognition as a responsible party, it frequently is an asset to have a reputation for humane conduct.

61 See further David P. Forsythe, "The International Committee of the Red Cross and Humanitarian Assistance: A Policy Analysis," *International Review of the Red Cross*, 314 (September–October, 1996), 512–531; Larry Minear and Thomas G. Weiss, *Mercy Under Fire: War and the Global Humanitarian Community* (Boulder: Westview, 1995); and Thomas G. Weiss, David P. Forsythe, and Roger Coate, *The United Nations and Changing World Politics*, 2nd edn (Boulder: Westview, 1997), ch. 5.

self-interest. Even many non-western and non-democratic states have become legal parties to human rights treaties. Actual behavior in concrete situations will be examined later. Enough was said at the start of chapter 1 to suggest a yawning chasm between statements of noble principle and the reality of political action under the pressures of winning and losing power struggles – or perhaps under the weight of sheer indifference to human suffering. Still, human rights standards are indeed a liberal fact of international relations, and the possibility of their actually generating some beneficial influence on behalf of human dignity cannot be discounted out of hand. As has been said of the United Nations, so it can be said of international human rights standards: their purpose is not to get us to heaven, but to save us from hell.[62]

Continuing debates

It was clear at the 1993 UN Vienna Conference on Human Rights that a number of states harbored serious reservations about internationally recognized human rights as codified and interpreted up to that time. In the view of the USA, which took the lead in an effort to reaffirm universal human rights, a number of states tried to say at Vienna that international human rights were essentially western and therefore inappropriate to other societies. In this group of states at that time were China, Cuba, Syria, Iran, Vietnam, Pakistan, Malaysia, Singapore, Yemen, and Indonesia.[63] From Singapore's view,[64] it was legitimate to note that certain Asian countries were so crowded as to call into question the wisdom of pursuing a highly individualistic human rights orientation that might jeopardize the welfare of the community as a whole. Moreover, Asian societies had long emphasized precisely that emphasis on collective welfare that seems notably lacking in the West. Some western observers found it hypocritical that the USA should push for universal human rights in international relations while itself refusing to fully endorse socio-economic rights as approved by the international community, continuing to employ the death penalty for common crime despite considerable opposition from the rest of the democratic community, and violating refugee rights when

---

[62] Weiss, et al., *The United Nations*, 282.

[63] *New York Times*, June 14, 1993, A3.

[64] See further Mark Hong, "Convergence and Divergence in Human Rights," in David P. Forsythe, ed., *The United States and Human Rights: Looking Inward and Outward* (Lincoln: University of Nebraska Press, 1999); Fareed Zakaria, "A Conversation with Lee Kuan Yew," *Foreign Affairs*, 73, 2 (March/April 1994), 109–127; Bilahari Kausikan, "Asia's Different Standard," *Foreign Policy*, 92 (Fall 1993), 24–41. In general see Joanne R. Bauer and Daniel A. Bell, eds., *The East Asian Challenge For Human Rights* (Cambridge: Cambridge University Press, 1999).

convenient – as in dealing with Haitians in the late 1980s and early 1990s.[65] As noted above, the USA intentionally abused some detainees in its "war on terrorism" after September 11, 2001.

As so often happens in international conferences, basic differences were not fully resolved. The Vienna Final Declaration reaffirmed "universal respect for and observance of, human rights and fundamental freedoms for all ... The universal nature of these rights and freedoms is beyond question." But the Declaration also stated, "While the significance of national and regional particularities and various historical, cultural, and religious backgrounds must be borne in mind, it is the duty of states, regardless of their political, economic and cultural systems, to promote and protect all human rights and fundamental freedoms." This latter language gave some "wiggle room" to the Singapores of the world who claimed they were not in fact authoritarian but had devised a successful and regionally particular Asian-style democracy.

It cannot be denied, however, that those in favor of universal human rights, with only a weak form of particularism allowed, constituted a majority at the end of the Vienna meeting, even if that position did not fully convert those on the other side of the question.[66] The dominant view was that universal human rights responded to universal problems such as governmental repression and harsh capitalistic markets. This was recognized by any number of non-western observers.[67] Persons need protection from these problems regardless of civilization, region, or nation. States might well differ, for example, on whether presidential or parliamentary models best implemented the right to political participation in policy making, but they were obligated to provide a genuine and not bogus right to democratic governance. It was a historical fact that the human rights discourse arose in the West, but so did the discourse about state sovereignty. Just as the idea of state sovereignty had found broad acceptance in the non-western world, it was argued, so should the notion of human rights. Like state sovereignty, there was nothing in the history of human rights that made it *ipso facto* inappropriate to non-western societies.

There were other critiques of the International Bill of Rights towards the close of the twentieth century. In the final chapter I discuss a number of these further – especially feminist perspectives. For the moment it

---

[65] Beth Stephens, "Hypocrisy on Rights," *New York Times*, June 24, 1993, A13.

[66] On combining universal principles with weak cultural relativism, or some particular/local variation in how the principles are implemented, see especially Jack Donnelly, *Universal Human Rights in Theory and Practice* (Ithaca: Cornell University Press, 1989), Part III.

[67] See the clear exposition by Onuma Yasuaki, *In Quest of Intercivilizational Human Rights: "Universal" vs. "Relative" Human Rights Viewed from an Asian Perspective*, Occasional Paper No. 2, Center for Asian Pacific Affairs, the Asia Foundation (March 1996), 15.

suffices to note that the most important critique of liberalism has come from the realists.

Contemporary realists like former National Security Advisor and Secretary of State Henry Kissinger regard international human rights as mostly an unfortunate and sentimental intrusion into the real stuff of international relations – interstate power calculations. Realists barely tolerate diplomacy for human rights because they know states like the USA or the Netherlands will insist sometimes on attention to democracy and hence civil and political rights, but they still think an emphasis on such things is unwise. Rational states in anarchic international relations concentrate on the power relations that can protect their existence and domestic values. Unique and sentimental states, above all the USA, unwisely try to project their domestic values and conditions into international relations, where the situation of anarchy and lack of moral and political consensus means a very different context.[68]

A widely cited version of this realist position regarded international action to stop gross violations of internationally recognized human rights as more properly in the domain of the late Mother Teresa, known for her charitable works with the poor in India.[69] In this view, United States' and others' actions to stop mass misery in Somalia or misrule in Haiti and Kosovo were not things that rational states did. Such action was supposedly best left to private social agencies, not rational Great Powers. States needed to keep their powder dry, and their military forces prepared, for traditional wars involving traditional vital national interests, and not dissipate their power in what the Pentagon called "operations other than war." If this realist approach meant ineffective policies to cope with human suffering abroad, this might be unfortunate. But the wise policy maker or diplomat was not moved by sentiment, only by hard-headed calculations of power and security. The touchstone for realist policy was narrow and expedient national interest, not personal welfare and certainly not universal human rights. Condoleezza Rice, National Security Advisor to President George W. Bush, reflected this realist tradition when she wrote that the USA should focus on transcendent national interests; by implication she was suggesting that the Clinton Administration had wrongly used the US military for nation-building in the Balkans and other diversions from true national interests.[70]

---

[68] See especially Henry Kissinger, *Diplomacy* (New York: Simon and Schuster, 1994).

[69] Michael Mandelbaum, "Foreign Policy as Social Work," *Foreign Affairs*, 75, 1 (January/February 1996), 16–32. See the rejoinder by Stanley Hoffmann in the same journal, "In Defense of Mother Teresa," 75, 2 (March/April 1996), 172–176.

[70] Condoleezza Rice, "Promoting the National Interest," *Foreign Affairs*, 79, 1 (January/February 2000), pp. 45-62.

It does not go too far to say that a central problem of contemporary international relations is how to reconcile the liberal framework of international human rights law with the widespread practice of realist foreign policy based on the fact that in anarchic international relations each state must provide for its own security. International law and organization demand liberalism, but traditional international relations has coughed up realism.

In the dialectical clash of liberalism and realism, questions of human rights remain central. The liberal concept of human rights is a malleable and evolving notion. Without doubt new human rights norms would be adopted and new meanings read into existing documents, as new threats to human dignity emerged. When science made the cloning of animals possible, it gave rise to a new debate on the ethics of cloning, with laws sure to follow. When science made possible the freezing of sperm and delayed *in vitro* fertilization of the human egg, it produced both ethical debate and new legislation. Threats to human dignity change with time and place. International human rights standards, as means to ensure minimal standards of human dignity, change as well. It is a normal, even necessary, process to debate universal human rights in an effort to retain what is still sound and valid, and to make changes as moral and political judgment dictate. But how to protect human rights in international relations remains a perplexing question.

Discussion questions

- Do human rights derive from basic humane principles that are found in various societies around the world, as Professor Lauren argues, or do human rights derive from western liberal principles as Professor Donnelly argues? Should we expect non-western societies, without a long history of exposure to liberalism, to accept and protect human rights on a par with industrialized western democracies? Is it philosophical tradition that matters for the protection of human rights, or economic development? Where does India fit in this debate? South Korea? Botswana?
- Given the lack of connection between philosophical argument on the one hand, and on the other the widespread acceptance of human rights treaties, is the philosophy of human rights irrelevant to the practice of human rights? Or do we have great problems in applying human rights standards because we do not sufficiently understand the difference between liberalism and other "isms" like conservatism, communitarianism, and realism?
- What is the significance of widespread formal acceptance by states of the international law of human rights? When states consent to human

rights treaties and diplomatic practice, is this realist hypocrisy? Is it sincere commitment to liberalism that they are sometimes unable to implement in specific situations? Why do states that practice liberalism and human rights at home sometimes find it difficult to advance human rights in international relations?

- Do international organizations always reflect the policies of their most powerful members? Can international civil servants, less powerful states, and private organizations advance human rights through these IOs, even if the major states are not always in favor?

- Do we have human rights in the UN Charter because of a concern for the human dignity of persons, that is because of some sort of liberal crusade; or because of a concern for the security of states, that is because of realist concerns? Is it possible that human rights contribute to security? Is liberalism sometimes compatible with realism? And sometimes not?

- Do human rights properly encompass only civil and political rights, as Professor Cranston (and the USA) argues, or also economic and social rights as Professor Shue (and most of the rest of the world) argues? Should we recognize a third generation of solidarity rights including rights to development, peace, and a healthy or safe environment? Should we have a moratorium on further internationally recognized human rights until we can better implement the ones already recognized?

Suggestions for further reading

Best, Geoffrey, *War and Law Since 1945* (Oxford: Clarendon Press, 1994). A readable account of the modern development of international humanitarian law, its content, and efforts to apply it.

Brownlie, Ian, ed., *Basic Documents on Human Rights*, 3rd edn (New York: Oxford University Press, 1992). An extensive and useful collection.

Claude, Inis L., Jr., *National Minorities* (Cambridge, MA: Harvard University Press, 1955). A classic study of the effort to use international law to protect minority rights in Europe in the interwar years, and of the causes of failure.

Cook, Rebecca J., *Human Rights of Women: National and International Perspectives* (Philadelphia: University of Pennsylvania Press, 1994). An excellent overview of a subject of growing importance.

Cranston, Maurice, "Human Rights, Real and Supposed," in D.D. Raphael, ed., *Political Theory and the Rights of Man* (Bloomington: Indiana University Press, 1967). A classic defense of civil and political rights, especially as utilitarian to state stability and security, and an attack on economic and social rights. Other chapters in this book are useful as well.

Crawford, Neta, *Argument and Change in World Politics: Ethics, Decolonization, and Humanitarian Intervention* (Cambridge: Cambridge University Press, 2002).

A good study of the impact of ideas and arguments over time to delegitimize colonialism and other violations of human rights. In the last analysis, she is somewhat vague about the exact interaction of ideas, military power, and economic resources.

Donnelly, Jack, "Human Rights and Human Dignity: An Analytic Critique of Non-Western Human Rights Conceptions,"*American Political Science Review*, 76, 2 (June 1982), 433–449. A seminal article noting the distinction between human rights and other means to advance human dignity. Argues that human rights in history was an essentially western construct.

Dunne, Tim, and Nicholas J. Wheeler, eds., *Human Rights in Global Politics* (Cambridge: Cambridge University Press, 1999). Advanced discussions of the conceptual bases of human rights and their relations to different cultures and societies. Addresses the question of whether human rights are violated because there is something fundamentally wrong with the concept of human rights in international relations.

Evans, Tony, *US Hegemony and the Project of Universal Human Rights* (New York: St. Martin's Press, 1996). A European academic takes a critical look at the US role in the evolution of international human rights standards, stressing the nefarious impact of American domestic politics on international developments.

Evans, Tony, ed., *Human Rights Fifty Years On: A Reappraisal* (Manchester: University of Manchester Press, 1998). A critical, even hyper-critical, evaluation of international human rights fifty years after the adoption of the 1948 Universal Declaration of Human Rights.

Fields, A. Belden, *Rethinking Human Rights For The New Millennium* (New York: Palgrave Macmillan, 2003). A good introduction to the theory of human rights. A review of major thinkers is followed by Belden's own attempt at justification, centering on what is needed for proper development of the human personality.

Glendon, Mary Ann, *A World Made New: Eleanor Roosevelt and the Universal Declaration of Human Rights* (New York: Random House, 2001). A readable history showing how Ms. Roosevelt made her contributions through social diplomacy rather than engaging on the substantive wording of different articles in the Declaration.

Hannum, Hurst, *Autonomy, Sovereignty, and Self-Determination: The Accommodation of Conflicting Rights* (Philadelphia: University of Pennsylvania Press, 1992). A lawyer provides a sound review, with case studies, of how various claims to the collective human right of national self-determination have been handled in different parts of the world. A good blend of general legal principles with knowledge of specific problems.

Hunt, Paul, *Reclaiming Social Rights: International and Comparative Perspectives* (Aldershot: Dartmouth, 1996). One of the few books to give serious and in-depth treatment to economic and social rights, arguing that they are important, and some of them can be adjudicated.

Hutchinson, John F., *Champions of Charity: War and the Rise of the Red Cross* (Boulder: Westview, 1996). Takes a critical look at the International Red Cross and Red Crescent Movement from its origins in about 1859 to just after World War I. Stresses the strength of nationalism and militarism in the face of private efforts for victims of war.

Ignatieff, Michael, *Human Rights as Politics and Idolatry* (Princeton: Princeton University Press, 2001). Two short but provocative essays by a prolific Canadian thinker, now at Harvard University. He defends civil and political rights on the basis of historical pragmatism. He also sees human rights as individuals "worshipping" their own worth and agency.

Klotz, Audie, *Norms in International Relations: The Struggle against Apartheid* (Ithaca: Cornell University Press, 1995). An advanced and complex discussion of the role of human rights ideas in international relations. She argues that human rights ideas and action, not just economic and security considerations, helped transform South Africa.

Krasner, Stephen D., ed., *International Regimes* (Ithaca: Cornell University Press, 1983). Reprint of a special issue of the journal *International Organization* dealing with the concept of international regimes. Useful background for discussion of one or more international human rights regimes, a popular concept among social scientists.

Lauren, Paul Gordon, *The Evolution of International Human Rights: Visions Seen* (Philadelphia: University of Pennsylvania Press, 1998). Emphasizes the role of private organizations and individuals, including non-western ones, in advancing human rights over time in international relations. Argues that the human rights idea is not a strictly western one.

Morsink, Johannes, *The Universal Declaration of Human Rights: Origins, Drafting, and Intent* (Philadelphia: University of Pennsylvania Press, 1998). The definitive treatment, fifteen years in the making, about this legislative process.

Sen, Amartya, *Development as Freedom* (New York: Anchor, 1999). A Nobel laureate in economics argues, like FDR, that persons in socio-economic need are not free persons. Thus for him a certain socio-economic development, especially in education and health care, is necessary for real freedom.

Shestack, Jerome, "The Philosophic Foundations of Human Rights," *Human Rights Quarterly*, 20, 2 (May 1998), 201–234. An activist reflects on the differing philosophical bases for human rights; a good survey but without resolution of conceptual debates.

Shue, Henry, *Basic Rights: Subsistence, Affluence, and US Foreign Policy*, 2nd edn (Princeton: Princeton University Press, 1997). An influential book arguing that the most important human rights cut across traditional categories, thus including some civil rights such as the right to life in the form of freedom from summary execution, and the right to life in the form of adequate food, clothing, and shelter. In his view, some economic and social rights are fundamental, being necessary for the enjoyment of certain other rights.

Sunstein, Cass R., *The Second Bill of Rights: FDR's Unfinished Revolution And Why We Need It More Than Ever* (New York: Basic Books, 2004). An argument, grounded in American history, for socio-economic rights, at least as "constitutive principles" if not as full fledged constitutional or international law.

Winston, Morton, ed., *The Philosophy of Human Rights* (Belmont: Wadsworth, 1989). A sound overview.

Part II

Implementing human rights standards

3   Global application of human rights norms

In the previous chapter we noted a fundamental contradiction between new norms of human rights in the United Nations Charter, and the lack of a UN human rights court to enforce them. As we saw, new human rights goals were proclaimed in 1945, and many human rights treaties were subsequently adopted. But apparently one was to rely mostly on traditional diplomacy, grounded in state sovereignty, to realize them. This meant that realist principles of state interest loomed large. In this chapter we examine more closely the evolving process for applying universal human rights standards on a global basis. We inquire whether there is now more commitment to liberalism, as shown through institutionalized procedures to protect human rights.

International law has traditionally been clearer about "What?" than "Who?"[1] The law has emphasized what legal rules apply in different situations. It has frequently not explicitly addressed who is authorized to make authoritative judgments about legal compliance. By default this means that states remain judge and jury in conflicts involving themselves – a principle accepted by no well-ordered society. Certainly the global law on human rights and humanitarian affairs has been characterized by decentralized decision making leading to much ambiguity about compliance. As this author concluded some time ago, "Most states, in negotiating human rights agreements, do not want authoritative international means of protection."[2] Many states have asserted an apparently liberal commitment to internationally recognized human rights. But most states have elevated national independence, particularly the supremacy of national policy making, over the realization of universal human rights.

Is this conventional wisdom still valid? This chapter will show that, first, global enforcement of human rights, in the form of international court judgments and other forms of direct international responsibility for

---

[1] David P. Forsythe, "Who Guards the Guardians: Third Parties and the Law of Armed Conflict," *American Journal of International Law*, 70, 2 (January 1976), 41–61.

[2] David P. Forsythe, *Human Rights and World Politics*, 2nd rev. edn (Lincoln: University of Nebraska Press, 1989), 46.

the application of human rights standards, is still a relatively rare event. Direct protection by international agencies exists, but not often. Neither the International Court of Justice, nor other international courts, nor the UN Security Council, frequently assumes direct responsibility in seeing that universal human rights norms prevail over competing values. This is so especially outside of Europe. There may be some change under-way on this point as the twentieth century draws to a close, suggested by NATO's use of force in Kosovo in 1999 in the name of protecting ethnic Albanians, and by the creation of the International Criminal Court dur-ing the period 1998–2002. But the generalization still holds. The global international community does not often frontally and flagrantly override state sovereignty in the name of human rights.

At the same time, states generally find themselves enmeshed in global governance.[3] By their own consent, they find themselves part of inter-national legal regimes that generate diplomatic pressure to conform to human rights standards. While direct international protection or enforce-ment of human rights is mostly absent, attempts at indirect international implementation of human rights are frequently present. There still is no world government to systematically override state sovereignty. But there are arrangements for global governance to restrict and redefine state sovereignty. The last quarter of the twentieth century has seen a proliferation of these international, indirect means of applying universal human rights. The effectiveness of these many implementation efforts, which still fall short of direct enforcement, is a matter requiring careful analysis.[4]

State sovereignty is not likely to disappear from world affairs any time soon, but it is being restricted and revised in a continuing and complex process.[5] Human rights norms are at the core of this historical evolution. States may use their sovereignty to restrict their sovereignty in the name of human rights. In general, the importance of internationally recognized human rights is increasing, and the value placed on full national indepen-dence decreasing. This pattern is more evident, with some exceptions, in the global north than the global south. Again in general, but again with

---

[3] Mark W. Zacher, "The Decaying Pillars of the Westphalian Temple: Implications for International Order and Governance," in James N. Rosenau and Ernst-Otto Czempiel, eds., *Governance Without Government: Order and Change in World Politics* (Cambridge: Cambridge University Press, 1992), 58–101.

[4] See further B. G. Ramcharan, *The Concept and Present Status of the International Protection of Human Rights* (Dordrecht: Martinus Nijhoff, 1989), 37 and *passim*.

[5] The realist Stephan Krasner, in *Sovereignty: Organized Hypocrisy* (Princeton: Princeton University Press, 1999), reminds us states have long endorsed state sovereignty and vio-lated that norm when power allowed. See also his *Problematic Sovereignty* (New York: Columbia University Press, 2001).

some exceptions, moral interdependence accompanies material interdependence – albeit with a time lag. As will become even clearer after chapter 5 on regional developments, for some states, especially in Europe, achieving human rights through international action is more important than maintaining full freedom of strictly national policy making. Liberalism is relatively more important in international relations than it used to be. But realism, especially in times of insecurity, is still a potent force.

Principal UN organs

The Security Council

A fair reading of the UN Charter, as it was drawn up in 1945, indicates that the Security Council was given primary responsibility for the maintenance of international peace and security, which meant issues of peace and war. On security issues the Council could take legally binding decisions under Chapter VII of the Charter pertaining to enforcement action. In addition, there were economic, social, cultural, and humanitarian issues. On these issues the Council, like the General Assembly, could make recommendations under Chapter VI. Presumably human rights fell into one of the categories other than security – such as social or humanitarian. But the Council was authorized by the Charter to take action to remove threats to the peace. Logically, threats to the peace could arise from violations of human rights. In political fact, early in the life of the Security Council some states did attempt to bring human rights issues before it, precisely on grounds of a relationship to security. The early Council responded to these human rights issues in an inconsistent fashion,[6] being greatly affected by the Cold War. From about 1960 to the end of the Cold War, the Council began to deal more systematically with human rights issues as linked to four subjects: racism giving rise to violence – especially in southern Africa; human rights in armed conflict; armed intervention across international boundaries; and armed supervision of elections and plebiscites.[7] During this era the Council sometimes asserted a link between human rights issues and transnational violence.

After the Cold War the Security Council, building on some of these earlier decisions, especially those pertaining to Southern Rhodesia and the Republic of South Africa, expanded the notion of international peace

---

[6] Sydney D. Bailey, "The Security Council," in Philip Alston, ed., *The United Nations and Human Rights: A Critical Appraisal* (Oxford: Clarendon Press, 1995), 304–336.
[7] Ibid.

and security.[8] The line dividing security issues from human rights issues was often blurred. The Council thus expanded the range of Chapter VII enforcement action and stated, much more often compared with the past, that human rights violations were linked to international peace and security, thus permitting invocation of Chapter VII and even leading to an occasional enforcement action. In the process the Council shrank the scope of domestic jurisdiction protected by state sovereignty. In so doing, the Council implied more than once that security could refer to the security of persons within states, based on their human rights, and not just to traditional military violence across international frontiers. All these developments, mostly during the 1990s, held out the potential of increasing the UN Security Council's systematic action for human rights, based on pooled or collective sovereignty, relative to autonomous state sovereignty.

Five summary points deserve emphasis. Firstly, there were numerous situations of violence in world affairs around the close of the Cold War; the UN Security Council did not address all of them. Vicious wars in places like Chechnya, Sri Lanka and Algeria never drew systematic Council attention, much less bold assertions of international authority. Realist principles still mattered; if major states, especially the United States, did not see their narrow interests threatened, or believed a conflict resided in another's sphere of influence, the Council might not be activated. Secondly, on occasion the Council has continued to say that human rights violations inside states can threaten international peace and security, at least implying the possibility of enforcement action under Chapter VII to correct the violations. In early 1992 a Council summit meeting of heads of state issued a very expansive statement indicating that threats to security could arise from economic, ecological, and social causes, not just traditional military ones. Thirdly, the Council sometimes made bold pronouncements on behalf of Council authority, but then proceeded to seek extensive consent from the parties to a conflict. Sometimes, as in dealing with Iraq in the spring of 1991, there were enough votes in the Council to declare the consequences of repression a matter that

---

[8] The Council invoked Chapter VII in the mid-1960s in dealing with the situation in Southern Rhodesia (now Zimbabwe) without making clear whether the central issue was illegal secession from the United Kingdom, racism and other violations of human rights including denial of national self-determination and majority rule, or fighting between the Patriotic Front and the Ian Smith government. The Council invoked Chapter VII in the late 1970s in dealing with the situation in the Republic of South Africa without making clear whether the issue was denial of majority rule or political violence and instability. For political reasons, the Council sometimes acts in ways that make life difficult for professors of international law.

[9] S/23500, January 31, 1992, "Note by the President of the Security Council."

threatened international peace and security, but not enough votes to proceed to an explicit authorization to take collective action. Sometimes, as in dealing with Somalia during 1992–1994, or Cambodia 1993–1996, or Bosnia in 1992–1995, the Council would adopt a bold stand in New York, asserting broad international authority, but in the field UN officials made every effort to obtain local consent for what the Council had mandated. (4) Fourthly, the Council has frequently deployed lightly armed forces in "peacekeeping operations" under Chapter VI, with the consent of the parties, to help ensure not just simple peace based on the constellation of military forces, but a more complex liberal democratic peace based on civil and political rights. (5) Fifthly, the Council has asserted the authority under Chapter VII to create *ad hoc* criminal courts, to prosecute and try those engaging in war crimes, crimes against humanity, and genocide. In this last regard the Council has asserted that all member states of the UN are legally obligated to cooperate with the *ad hoc* courts in order to pursue those who have committed certain gross violations of internationally recognized human rights. These courts are reviewed in chapter 4. Other uses of Chapter VII are discussed below.

Other sources provide detailed information on the Security Council's invocation of Chapters VI and VII to deal with putative security issues since the end of the Cold War.[12] Aside from Iraq's invasion of Kuwait in 1990, and South Africa's involvement in Namibia, most of these situations drew international attention because of the death and debilitation of civilians inside states. (The breakup of communist Yugoslavia in the early 1990s raised complex questions about how to view the situation. From one point of view, Serbian and Croatian aggression against Bosnia was part of the problem.) The Security Council, no longer

---

[10] On Somalia see Mohamed Sahnoun, *Somalia: The Missed Opportunities* (Washington: US Institute for Peace Press, 1994). On Cambodia, see Steven J. Ratner, *The New UN Peacekeeping* (New York: St. Martin's Press, 1995).

[11] In addition to Ratner, *The New UN Peacekeeping*, see: Ramesh Thakur and Carlyle A. Thayer, eds., *A Crisis of Expectations: UN Peacekeeping in the 1990s* (Boulder: Westview, 1995); Paul F. Diehl, *International Peacekeeping* (Baltimore: Johns Hopkins University Press, 1993); William J. Durch, *The Evolution of UN Peacekeeping: Case Studies and Comparative Analysis* (New York: St. Martin's Press, 1993).

[12] Lori Fisler Damrosch, ed., *Enforcing Restraint: Collective Intervention in Internal Conflicts* (New York: Council on Foreign Relations Press, 1993); James Mayall, ed., *The New Interventionism: United Nations Experience in Cambodia, Former Yugoslavia, and Somalia* (Cambridge: Cambridge University Press, 1996). For a good overview of more recent developments involving the UN Security Council and its focus on individuals inside states, see Edward Newman and Oliver P. Richmond, *The United Nations and Human Security* (New York: Palgrave, 2001). See also Richard M. Price and Mark W. Zacher, eds., *The United Nations and Global Security* (New York: Palgrave, 2005).

Steps in several cases of death or ill-treatment

paralyzed by Cold War divisions, responded in various ways to: repression, oppression, and civil war in El Salvador from 1990; attacks by the Iraqi government on Iraqi Kurds and Shi'ites in the spring of 1991; systematic rape, ethnic cleansing, and other gross violations of human rights in the former Yugoslavia from 1992 to 1995; widespread malnutrition and starvation in Somalia during 1992–1994; the absence of liberal democracy and political stability in Cambodia during 1991–1997; the absence of liberal democracy and economic well-being in Haiti during 1993–1996; ethnic violence constituting genocide in Rwanda from 1994; and a long-running low-intensity conflict in Guatemala from 1996. The Council also paid considerable attention to murderous wars in places like Angola and Mozambique during this same era. At the time of writing the Council was dealing both with the Democratic Republic of the Congo (DRC), where more persons had been killed in political conflict than any other place on the planet during a five year period since 1945, and the Sudan, where millions were affected by displacement, rape, disease and malnutrition, and political killing. The latter amounted to, in the official view of the USA, genocide.

National (worry) not Int'n'l. "Who runs?" "Humane?"

With due respect to the continuing importance of interstate conflict in places like Afghanistan and Iraq, nevertheless the most striking feature about Security Council action in the past fifteen years was its willingness to deal with conflicts whose origins and most fundamental issues were essentially national rather than international. In El Salvador, Iraq, Somalia, Cambodia, Haiti, Rwanda, Guatemala, Liberia, Angola, Mozambique, the DRC, and the Sudan, central issues of conflict revolved around "who governs" and "how humanely."

In a few of these situations there were indeed international dimensions to the conflict that pushed the Council into action. Iraqi flight into Iran and Turkey, Haitian flight to the United States, Rwandan flight into Tanzania and eastern Zaire, for example, did call for an international response. The protracted political instability of the DRC invited unauthorized military intervention by a handful of neighboring states, interested either in natural resources or eliminating sanctuaries for enemies. In places like El Salvador and Bosnia, among others, there was real concern that the violence might expand to engulf nearby states. Yet in places like Somalia, Cambodia, and Guatemala, the international dimensions were not so pressing. The really core issues remained those pertaining to effective and democratic and humane governance – which inherently raised questions about human rights. The bright aspect of this picture was the willingness of the Council to expand the notions of both security and Chapter VII to try to improve the personal security of citizens inside various states by improving attention to their human rights.

"Human security" became a new buzzword at the United Nations.[13] The not-so-bright aspect of this picture was the gap between the blizzard of Council resolutions endorsing human rights and even making reference to Chapter VII enforcement actions, and the paucity of political will to take the costly steps necessary to make Council resolutions effective on the ground. In Somalia, the Council declared that to interfere with the delivery of humanitarian assistance was a war crime. But when certain Somalis not only continued to interfere with relief, but killed eighteen US Rangers in one incident, the US removed most of its military personnel from the country. Extensive starvation was eventually checked in Somalia, but national reconciliation and humane governance were not quickly established. US casualties in Somalia caused Washington to block deployment of a significant UN force in Rwanda, despite clear and massive genocide.[14]

In Cambodia the first national election was successfully organized by the UN, but the Khmer Rouge were not brought to heel at that time, and the UN mission was terminated prematurely – setting the stage for a coup in 1997 and the return of controversial and contested rule by Hun Sen and his supporters. In former Yugoslavia 1992–1995, the Council focused in large part on human rights and humanitarian issues in order to avoid tough decisions about self-determination of peoples and later collective security for Bosnia. When the Council did authorize strong measures particularly against Bosnian Serbs and their supporters, and when the Serbs responded in tough ways, such as by taking UN personnel hostage, the Council generally backed down. The Council was willing to declare "safe areas" within Bosnia, but then it refused to provide the military forces necessary to effectively defend them, which again set the stage for massacres at Srebrenica and elsewhere.[15] The key states on the Council, meaning the USA, France, and Britain, had no stomach for decisive but costly action in places like Bosnia and Cambodia, Somalia and Rwanda.[16]

Likewise in the DRC, the UN Security Council only put a small contingent of blue helmets on the ground, policing just a small area of that very large state. A later expansion of this force was much less than what

[handwritten margin note: Council did not defend itself. Allowed murders/hostages to take place.]

[handwritten margin note: Police only small area. Not many troops]

[13] Lloyd Axworthy, "Human Security: An Opening for UN Reform," in Richard M. Price and Mark W. Zacher, eds., The United Nations and Global Security (New York: Palgrave, 2004), 245–260.

[14] The ethics of non-intervention in Rwanda are well discussed in Michael A. Barnett, Eyewitness to a Genocide: The United Nations and Rwanda (Ithaca: Cornell University Press, 2002).

[15] Srebrenica represented the worst massacre in Europe since World War II. See David Rohde, End Game: the Betrayal and Fall of Srebrenica (Boulder: Westview, 1997).

[16] Edward Luttwak, "Where Are the Great Powers?," Foreign Affairs, 73, 4 (July/August, 1994), 23–29.

the Secretary-General recommended. In the Sudan, to cope with massive misery in the area of Western Darfur, the Council tried to mobilize troops through the African Union (formerly the Organization of African States). But the process proceeded slowly, with much foot dragging by the government in Khartoum and various other parties not tremendously concerned about death and destruction in the African part of that tormented country.

Truly horrific situations in places like Sierra Leone and Liberia were only improved when Britain took special interest in the former and committed some effective troops, and when the USA exercised its special relationship with the latter to mediate the departure of the rapacious Charles Taylor to neighboring Nigeria.

This trend of limited and indecisive action by the international community to guarantee human security made NATO's intervention in Kosovo in 1999 all the more remarkable. With the western states bypassing the Security Council because of Chinese and Russian opposition to what the West wanted to do, NATO and particularly the United States expended considerable treasure and prestige to try to stop and then reverse the repression, ethnic cleansing, and other violations of human rights being visited upon ethnic Albanians by the Serbian-dominated government of Yugoslavia.[17] In a portentous development, members of NATO declared that liberal democracy in Yugoslavia constituted a vital interest, justifying the use of military force despite the absence of explicit Security Council authorization. Yet the main problem for most situations of human insecurity remained lack of humanitarian intervention, not too much of it. NATO's intervention in Kosovo remained the exception that proved the general rule. The international community normally did not intervene decisively and quickly in response to gross violations of human rights. Transnational morality remained thin or weak. Often, third parties with the military muscle to make a difference perceived no self interest at risk in the situation.

Despite the inconsistency of US and other state policies, some improvements were achieved. El Salvador and Namibia were clearly more humane places after extensive UN involvement, especially when compared with the preceding decade. Mozambique and Guatemala eventually stumbled toward improved respect for many human rights. If the Council could help conflicting parties move toward accommodation and humane governance through Chapter VI peacekeeping, which did not entail large-scale combat or other costly enforcement measures, then its record was

---

[17] A good inside look at the details of the process can be found in Wesley Clark, *Waging Modern War* (New York: Perseus, 2002).

commendable in many respects. The UN spent more than $2 billion in trying to advance liberal democracy in Cambodia, and some improvements – however incomplete – were made. A study by the Rand Corporation showed that when the UN undertook moderately challenging field operations directed to establishing humane governance after violent conflict, the organization used its experience and soft power to manage matters reasonably well, although some problems were evident – such as delay in the arrival of resources and inconsistency in quality of personnel loaned by states.[18] This study concluded that the UN record in this regard was not inferior to that of the USA, although the latter took on tougher situations in places like Afghanistan and Iraq from about 2002–2003.

The overall record of the Council on human rights issues after the Cold War was complex, defying simple summation. Clearly the Council was more extensively involved in trying to help apply human rights standards than ever before. It had demonstrated on a number of occasions that human rights protections could be intertwined with considerations of peace and security. It had certainly blurred the outer boundaries of state sovereignty and its corollary, domestic jurisdiction. If it lacked the collective political will to make effective on the ground some of its bolder pronouncements from New York, it had nevertheless expanded second-generation peacekeeping to encompass more attention to a rather broad range of human rights.[19]

A continuing problem was the inconsistent record of the Permanent Five (P-5) members of the Security Council when dealing with human security. This was certainly true of the USA, which took much more interest in Kosovo than in almost all problems in Africa (even before it became preoccupied with Afghanistan and Iraq after September 11, 2001). Russia and China had not been eager to take decisive action to protect the Albanian Kosovars. Britain and France had not been on the front lines of those pressing for action in Rwanda and the Sudan. If a regional power did not step forward as Australia did in regard to East Timor and Indonesia, and as the Nigerians attempted to do less successfully in West Africa (Liberia and Sierra Leone), the UN Security Council was often less than impressive in its response to human insecurity.

---

[18] James Dobbins, et al., *The UN's Role in Nation-Building: From the Congo to Iraq* (Santa Monica, CA: Rand, 2005).

[19] For an overview of UN second generation peacekeeping and human rights, see David P. Forsythe, "Human Rights and International Security: United Nations Field Operations Redux," in Monique Castermans-Holleman, et al., eds., *The Role of the Nation-State in the 21st Century* (The Hague: Kluwer, 1998), pp. 265–276.

Office of the Secretary-General

Although relatively little has been published about the office of the UN Secretary-General and human rights, it appears that two factors explain a great deal about the evolution of events in this area. On the one hand, as human rights have become more institutionalized in UN affairs, Secretaries-General have spoken out more frequently and been generally more active in this domain.[20] There is almost a straight line progression on increasing action by Secretaries-General on human rights over time. Secondly, while all Secretaries-General have given priority to trying to resolve issues of international peace and security, increasingly they have found human rights intertwined with security. In so far as security issues can be separated from human rights, rights issues tended to be either down-graded or dealt with by quiet diplomacy.[21] If U Thant had been outspoken in condemning communist violations of human rights, it is doubtful he would have been acceptable to the Soviet Union for sensitive mediation in the 1962 Cuban missile crisis. In contemporary times, with human rights increasingly institutionalized within the UN and meshed with many security concerns, a Secretary-General like Kofi Annan appeared to be more willing to take firm stands for the protection of human rights. The fate of his nomination of Mary Robinson, former President of Ireland, to be the second High Commissioner for Human Rights, however, indicates that all executive authority in the UN, as an intergovernmental system, remains fragile – as explained below.

From the earliest days of the UN there were Secretariat officials active in the promotion of human rights through setting of standards, even if they were not able to achieve a great deal in specific protection efforts.[22] At the highest level, however, neither Trygve Lie nor Dag Hammarskjöld showed much direct and clear interest in internationally recognized human rights. Lie became ineffective and eventually resigned because of his clear opposition to the communist invasion of South Korea, and there is no reason to think the result would have been any different had he strongly opposed communist violations of human rights. During the Cold War, forthright and public stands on any major issue were likely to make any Secretary-General *persona non grata* to one coalition or the other.

---

[20] David P. Forsythe, "The UN Secretary-General and Human Rights: The Question of Leadership in a Changing Context," in Benjamin Rivlin and Leon Gordenker, eds., *The Challenging Role of the UN Secretary-General: Making "The Most Impossible Job in the World" Possible* (Westport: Praeger, 1993), 211–232.

[21] In addition to ibid., see Theo van Boven, "The Role of the United Nations Secretariat," in Alston, ed., *United Nations and Human Rights*, 549–579.

[22] John P. Humphrey, *Human Rights and the United Nations: A Great Adventure* (Dobbs Ferry: Transnational, 1984).

Hammarskjöld was, surprisingly enough given his Swedish nationality and overall dynamism and creativity, not much interested in human rights at the UN. While he was willing to take a strong stand on security issues in the Belgian Congo (now Zaire), even to the point of serious friction with both the Soviet Union and France, he never devoted much effort to more than a handful of rights issues via quiet diplomacy.

After U Thant, a transitional figure for present purposes, both Kurt Waldheim and Perez de Cuellar showed relatively more interest in the protection of human rights. Given the personal histories of the two men, this trend is partly explained by the institutionalization factor. The Austrian Waldheim had been in the Nazi army and had consistently misrepresented that part of his past. De Cuellar had been a traditional Peruvian diplomat well versed in diplomacy based on state sovereignty, whose first major act as Secretary-General was to decide not to renew the contract of the then activist UN Director of Human Rights – the Dutch-man Theo van Boven.[23] Van Boven had proved an irritant to both the military junta in Argentina and the Reagan Administration in Washington, then aligned with Buenos Aires. Yet both Waldheim and de Cuellar turned out to be more active in the protection of human rights than their predecessors, clearly so in de Cuellar's case.[24] Particularly in dealing with Central America, de Cuellar came to realize that peace and security in places like Nicaragua and El Salvador depended on progress in human rights. He therefore helped arrange deeply intrusive rights agreements, especially in El Salvador, and persistently acted to rein in death squads and other gross violators of human rights through his mediation and other diplomatic actions.[25] By the end of his second term, de Cuellar held quite different views on the importance of human rights, compared with when he entered office and got rid of van Boven.[26]

Boutros Boutros-Ghali was the most outspoken Secretary-General on human rights up to that time, making a strong case in particular for democracy. His *Agenda for Development* strongly advocated democratic development, based on civil and political rights, at a time when the General Assembly and the World Bank were, to put it kindly, less than clear

[23] See further Theo van Boven, *People Matter: Views on International Human Rights Policy* (Amsterdam: Beulenhoff Netherlands, 1982).
[24] De Cuellar listed human rights second in importance only to disarmament among pressing issues. See his "The Role of the UN Secretary-General," in Adam Roberts and Benedict Kingsbury, eds., *United Nations, Divided World: The UN's Roles in International Relations*, 2nd edn (Oxford: Clarendon, 1993), 125 and *passim*.
[25] See the details in David P. Forsythe, "The United Nations, Democracy, and the Americas," in Tom J. Farer, ed., *Beyond Sovereignty: Collectively Defending Democracy in the Americas* (Baltimore: Johns Hopkins University Press, 1996), 107–131.
[26] This argument, already expressed in print, I recently reconfirmed via interviews with some of those close to de Cuellar during his time in New York.

in their support for civil and political rights.[27] He thus sought to correct what had been a major deficiency in human rights programming at the UN, the lack of integration between human rights and development activities.[28]

Boutros-Ghali had appointed the Ecuadoran, José Ayala Lasso, as the first UN High Commissioner for Human Rights, probably hoping to assuage the fears of developing countries that the new post would be used only to hammer them on issues of civil and political rights. Thus the Secretary-General probably hoped to encourage acceptance by developing countries over time of this new and controversial post. The new High Commissioner had been a foreign minister in a previous military government in Quito.[29] Upon Ayala Lasso's resignation to return to Ecuadoran politics, Secretary-General Annan turned to Ms. Robinson, a westerner with the promise of more dynamism on rights issues. The Cold War was over, human rights had been integrated with many security concerns, and much of the powerful West was demanding more vigorous UN diplomacy for human rights. The USA was very happy with the nomination of Ms. Robinson, and her subsequent approval by the General Assembly.

One of the reasons for having a UN High Commissioner for Human Rights was to free the Secretary-General in public diplomacy to concentrate on security issues. A dynamic High Commissioner might play the role that van Boven tried to play as Director of the UN Human Rights Program. But since the Director was nominated by the Secretary-General, and without an independent power base, disaffected countries like Argentina under military rule could bring pressure on him through having a patron–in this case the Reagan Administration – lobby the Secretary-General to reign in or get rid of a human rights official causing a state embarrassment.[30]

In theory, an independent High Commissioner, once appointed in a higher-profile position created by the General Assembly, had slightly more protection from such pressures. But the fate of Ms. Robinson, the second High Commissioner for Human Rights, suggested that things had not progressed much beyond the era of de Cuellar and van Boven.

[27] A/48/935 (1994). See further David P. Forsythe, "The United Nations, Human Rights, and Development," *Human Rights Quarterly*, 19, 2 (May 1997), 334–349.

[28] Theo van Boven, "Human Rights and Development: The UN Experience," in David P. Forsythe, ed., *Human Rights and Development: International Views* (London: Macmillian, 1989), 121–136. Compare James Gustave Speth, "Poverty: A Denial of Human Rights," *Journal of International Affairs*, 52, 1 (Fall 1998), 277–292.

[29] Ayala Lasso did originate the operation of UN field offices for human rights, generating grass-roots activities for human rights within consenting countries.

[30] See further Iain Guest, *Behind the Disappearances: Argentina's Dirty War Against Human Rights and the United Nations* (Philadelphia: University of Pennsylvania Press, 1990).

Robinson was so outspoken about rights violations in places like China and Israel and Russia that she raised questions about whether her activism was matched by enough diplomatic acumen. Especially after a UN Conference at Durban, South Africa on the subject of racism and xenophobia, in which the USA and Israel walked out after repeated speeches denouncing Israel, Washington became deeply dissatisfied with Ms. Robinson. The George W. Bush Administration leaned on the Secretary-General, Kofi Annan, not to renew her contract. He finally did as Washington desired, although Ms. Robinson wanted to continue. The critique of Ms. Robinson for being too outspoken in defense of human rights was somewhat ironic, given that the first High Commissioner, Mr. Ayala Lasso of Ecuador, had been criticized by a number of human rights advocacy groups for being too diplomatic and not assertive enough.

After Ms. Robinson, the Secretary-General then nominated, and the General Assembly approved, Sergio de Mello of Brazil, who was an experienced diplomat with a career in the UN refugee office. But he was killed by an insurgent bombing in Iraq, and so Louise Arbour of Canada became the UN High Commissioner for Human Rights. She was a jurist, formerly the prosecutor for the UN ad hoc criminal court for Yugoslavia (covered in chapter four). She was widely respected and had more of a "judicial temperament" than Ms. Robinson. Seeing what had happened to Robinson, in general she relied more on quiet diplomacy than public criticism.

In sum, the office of the Secretary-General represented the purposes of the organization as found in the Charter. Among these purposes was international cooperation on human rights. Yet most decisions taken in the name of the UN were taken by states, and the Secretary-General, while independent, was also given instructions by states acting collectively through UN organs. Moreover, he (or she in the future) could only be effective when he retained the confidence of the more important states. Thus there was room for action on human rights, which Secretaries-General had progressively exercised as human rights became more and more a regular part of international and UN affairs. The Secretary-General's protective action, beyond promotional activities, consisted mostly of reasoning in quiet diplomacy.

But there were also major constraints imposed by states – such as lack of real commitment to international human rights, lack of consensus on priorities, and lack of adequate funding. Even as states endorsed human rights norms, they still did not like being criticized in public on human rights issues, as Theo van Boven and Mary Robinson discovered when they were eased out of office. It was certainly ironic that the USA, which often presented itself to the world as a model on human rights, undercut both van Boven and Ms. Robinson when an ally – military government in Argentina or Israel as occupying power – were publicly criticized by the UN High Commissioner for Human Rights.

The General Assembly, ECOSOC, and the ICJ

The UN General Assembly has been instrumental in the promotion of human rights, approving some two dozen treaties and adopting a number of "motherhood" resolutions endorsing various human rights in general. The Assembly has played a much less important role in the protection of specific human rights in specific situations, although much ambiguity inheres in this subject.

One can take a minimalist approach and note that the General Assembly did not try to reverse certain decisions taken in the Economic and Social Council (ECOSOC) and the UN Human Rights Commission that were directed to specific protection attempts (see below).[31] Furthermore, since many of the treaty monitoring mechanisms report to the Assembly, the same can be said for the Assembly's review of those bodies (see below). More optimistically, after the Cold War as before, the Assembly adopted a number of specific resolutions condemning human rights violations in various countries.[32] During the Cold War, it is likely that repeated Assembly condemnation of Israeli and South African policies had little immediate remedial effect on those two target states, as they viewed the Assembly as inherently biased against them. This was certainly the case when the Assembly declared Zionism to be a form of racism, a resolution eventually rescinded. It is possible that repeated Assembly attacks on apartheid policies in South Africa contributed to an international normative climate in which powerful states eventually brought pressure to bear on racist South Africa.[33] How ideas as expressed in Assembly resolutions affect states' definitions of their national interests remains a murky matter.[34] In any event the Assembly shrank the realm of state sovereignty by demonstrating clearly that diplomatic discussion of specific human rights situations in specific countries was indeed part of routinized

---

[31] John Quinn, "The General Assembly into the 1990s," in Alston, ed., *United Nations and Human Rights*, 55–106.

[32] Soo Yeon Kim and Bruce Russett, "The New Politics of Voting Alignments in the United Nations General Assembly," *International Organization*, 50, 4 (Autumn 1996), 629–652.

[33] See further Audie Klotz, "Norms Reconstituting Interests: Global Racial Equality and US Sanctions Against South Africa," *International Organization*, 49, 3 (Summer 1995), 451–478.

[34] See further Judith Goldstein and Robert O. Keohane, eds., *Ideas and Foreign Policy: Beliefs, Institutions and Political Change* (Ithaca: Cornell University Press, 1993); and Albert S. Yee, "The Causal Effects of Ideas on Politics," *International Organization*, 50, 1 (Winter 1996), 69–108.

international relations, even if the Assembly displayed a tendency to adopt paper solutions to complex and controversial subjects.[35]

ECOSOC, officially one of the UN's principal organs, very rapidly became little more than a mailbox between the Assembly and various bodies subsidiary to ECOSOC, transmitting or reaffirming instructions from the Assembly to a proliferation of social and economic agencies. ECOSOC is not, and has never been, a major actor for human rights.[36] The states elected to ECOSOC have taken three decisions of importance since 1945 regarding human rights, one essentially negative and two positive. Firstly, ECOSOC decided that the members of the UN Human Rights Commission should be state representatives and not independent experts. This decision put the foxes inside the hen house. Later ECOSOC adopted its resolution 1235, permitting the Commission to take up specific complaints about specific countries. Resolution 1503 was also eventually adopted, permitting the Commission to deal with private petitions indicating a systematic pattern of gross violations of internationally recognized human rights. While ECOSOC resolutions 1235 and 1503 affected considerable diplomacy, they did not lead to sure protection of human rights on the ground.

In addition, ECOSOC maintains a committee that decides which non-governmental organizations (NGOs) will be given which category of consultative status with the UN system. The highest status allows NGOs to attend UN meetings and submit documents. Both before and after the Cold War, this committee was the scene of various struggles over human rights NGOs. Certain states that were defensive about human rights matters tried, with periodic success, to deny full status, or sometimes any status, to legitimate human rights NGOs. These problems diminished by the end of the twentieth century. Still, in the late 1990s, a western-based NGO that had antagonized the Sudanese government and engaged in a controversial policy of buying back hostages taken in Sudan's long-running civil war (such a policy provided money to the fighting parties and led to the retaking of sometimes the same hostages) was denied consultative status.

The International Court of Justice (ICJ), technically a principal UN organ but highly independent once its judges are elected by the Security Council and General Assembly, has not made a major imprint on the protection of international human rights. This is primarily because only states have standing before the Court, and states have demonstrated for

---

[35] Antonio Cassese, "The General Assembly: Historical Perspective 1945–1989," in Alston, ed., *United Nations and Human Rights*, 25–54.

[36] Declan O'Donovan, "The Economic and Social Council," in Alston, ed., *United Nations and Human Rights*, 107–125.

a long time a reluctance to either sue or be sued – especially on human rights – in international tribunals.[37] Without allowing individuals legal standing, the ICJ's case load on human rights is highly likely to remain light.

From time to time the Court is presented with the opportunity to rule on issues of international human rights and humanitarian law. In 1986 in *Nicaragua v. the United States* it reaffirmed some points about both human rights and international humanitarian law. In 1995 it issued some interim injunctions about genocide in the former Yugoslavia. In 2004 it gave an advisory opinion on the legality of Israel's new security wall, part of which was built on territory beyond "the green line" or Israel's de facto borders in 1949. In this case the ICJ showed evident concern for the fate of Palestinians adversely affected by the wall, with the Court paying much attention to the Fourth Geneva Convention of 1949 dealing with occupied territory. But in general, while the ICJ's case load has increased on average from two to three cases per year to ten to eleven after the Cold War, it is still rare for the Court to make a major pronouncement on human rights. States still generally regard human rights as too important a subject to entrust to some fifteen independent judges of various nationalities who make their judgments with reference to rules of law rather than national interest or public opinion. Thus, for example, while the 1948 Genocide Convention contains an article providing for compulsory jurisdiction for the ICJ in resolving disputes under this treaty, states like the USA reserved against this article when ratifying the treaty. Under the Court's Statute, states can give a blanket jurisdiction to the ICJ to rule on all or some legal issues, but few states have done so in unambiguous fashion. In this respect the end of the Cold War has made no difference. State defense of sovereignty still trumps interest in orderly and humane international relations, at least in so far as the ICJ is concerned. The ICJ shows that realism is alive and well, even if other parts of international relations show an advance for liberalism.

Major subsidiary bodies

In addition to the principal UN organs, there are several subsidiary bodies that concern themselves with the application of human rights standards. The focus here is on the Human Rights Commission, the International Labor Organization, and the Office of the UN High Commissioner for Refugees. The Sub-Commission on Prevention of Discrimination and

---

[37] A.S. Muller, D. Raic, and J. M. Thuranszky, eds., *The International Court of Justice: Its Future Role after Fifty Years* (The Hague: Martinus Nijhoff, 1997), especially the chapter by Mark Janis.

Protection of Minorities, now renamed the UN Sub-Commission on Human Rights has been active but reports to the Commission. Space constraints oblige its omission. The Commission on the Status of Women has been primarily engaged in promotional and assistance activities rather than protection efforts. The two *ad hoc* criminal courts are addressed in chapter 4. UNESCO can be mentioned in passing.[38]

The Human Rights Commission

It used to be said of the UN Human Rights Commission that it was the organization's premier body, or diplomatic hub, for human rights issues. After the Cold War this is no longer completely the case. If the Security Council establishes a connection between human rights and international peace and security, then the Council becomes the most important UN forum for human rights – as demonstrated above. What can be said is that until 2005 the Commission remained the center for traditional or routine human rights diplomacy, in addition to the Secretary-General's office, and in loose tandem with the UN High Commissioner for Human Rights. The UN system has never been known for tight organization and streamlined, clear chains of command.

The Commission for Human Rights was anticipated from the very beginning of the UN and first served as a technical drafting body for the International Bill of Rights and other international instruments on human rights.[39] As noted above, it is composed of representatives of states, elected by ECOSOC, itself composed of states. Because of its composition as well as its focus on drafting legal standards, for its first twenty years the Commission avoided specific inquiries about specific rights in specific countries. In one wonderful phrase, it demonstrated a "fierce commitment to inoffensiveness."[40] Contributing to this situation was the fact that both the East and West during the Cold War knew that if they raised specific human rights issues, such inquiries could be turned against them. The West controlled the Commission in its early days, but its own record on racism and discrimination suggested prudence in the face of any desire to hammer the communists on their evident violations of civil and political rights. In any event, Cold War debates about human rights violations occurred in the UN General Assembly,

---

[38] David Weissbrodt and Rose Farley, "The UNESCO Human Rights Procedure: An Evaluation," *Human Rights Quarterly*, 16, 2 (May 1994), 391–414.

[39] This and many other points about the Commission are drawn from Alston, ed., *United Nations and Human Rights*, 126–210.

[40] Tom J. Farer, "The UN and Human Rights: More than a Whimper, Less than a Roar," in Roberts and Kingsbury, *United Nations, Divided World*, 23.

without any notable effects on improving the actual practice of human rights on either side.

Beginning in about 1967 the Commission began to stumble toward more protection activities rather than just promotional ones. This change was made possible primarily by the greater number of developing countries in the organization. They were determined to do something about racism in southern Africa and what they saw as neo-imperialism and racism via the Zionist movement in the Middle East. They did not apparently anticipate how a focus on specific rights in specific places could also be turned against them in the future. Some western governments, pushed by western-based non-governmental organizations, then struck a deal with the developing countries in the newly expanded ECOSOC and Commission, agreeing to debates about Israel and South Africa in return for similar attention to countries like Haiti and Greece, both then under authoritarian government. The door was opened for attempts under the Charter to monitor and supervise all state behavior relative to international rights standards.

ECOSOC's Resolutions 1235 and 1503, mentioned above, authorized specific review of state behavior on rights, and a Commission response to private petitions alleging a pattern of gross violations of rights, respectively. In theory, both procedures represented a constriction of absolute and expansive state sovereignty. In practice, neither procedure resulted in systematic, sure, and impressive protections of specific rights for specific persons in specific countries. Lawyers sometimes got excited about the new procedures, but victims of rights violations were much less impressed. Mostly because of the 1235 procedure, allowing a debate and resolutions on particular states, the Commission sometimes appointed country investigators, by whatever name, to continue investigations and keep the diplomatic spotlight on certain states, thus continuing the politics of embarrassment. This step, too, while sometimes bringing some limited improvement to a rights situation, failed to provide systematic and sure protection. The 1503 procedure, triggered by NGOs as well as by individuals, took too long to transpire and was mostly shielded from publicity by its confidential nature. Somewhat more effective was the Commission's use of *thematic* investigators or working groups, such as on forced disappearances. These developed the techniques of "urgent action" and "prompt intervention." The Commission also started the practice of emergency sessions. Yet if at the end of emergency sessions and reports by the country, thematic, or emergency investigators, member states were not prepared to take further action, Commission proceedings still failed to generate the necessary impact on violative states.

Summarizing the protective role of the Commission has never been easy.[41] If one looks at what transpires inside Commission meetings, there has been clear progress since 1947, and particularly since 1967, in attempts by this UN agency to pressure states into complying with internationally recognized human rights. States mostly take Commission proceedings seriously. They do not like to have the Commission focus on their deficiencies. Many go to great efforts to block, delay, or weaken criticism by the Commission and its agents. This was true, for example, of Argentina in the 1980s and China in the 1990s. Despite these obstructionist efforts, at first a fairly balanced list of states was publicly put in the diplomatic dock via the Commission.

Over time, however, the Commission suffered a decline of reputation. The main reason for this was state foreign policy, since the Commission is made up of states. The intermediate reason was that in the geographical caucuses of the UN, where many real decisions about the UN are made, member states elevated certain concerns like equitable geographical representation over concern for serious and impartial protection of human rights. Thus the Latin American caucus elected Cuba to the UN Human Rights Commission, despite its poor record on civil and political rights. Thus the African and Arab caucuses combined to ensure the election of repressive Libya as President of the Commission at one point. Also debilitating in the Commission were persistent double standards in rights debates, especially by the major countries. The P-5 countries were always elected to the Commission by tradition (with the USA denied a seat only one time in a controversial vote in its caucuses group). China, for example, was certainly not committed to systematic protection of human rights, going to great lengths, including use of foreign assistance, to try to ensure that its rights record was not the target of a critical resolution. The USA, for example, spent much time in focusing on the rights record of adversaries like Cuba, while remaining silent on egregious human rights violations in allies like Saudi Arabia. African and other developing countries were reluctant to address the rights violations of their compatriots in places like Zimbabwe, preferring to focus on Israeli policies in the occupied territories. So the Commission lost legitimacy in the eyes of many who were seriously interested in the impartial and effective protection of human rights.

If one looks at the Commission in broad context, it is clear that many states are prepared to continue with rights violations, even if this brings various forms of criticism and condemnation. In places like the former

---

[41] See further Howard Tolley, Jr., *The UN Commission on Human Rights* (Boulder: Westview, 1987).

Yugoslavia or the Great Lakes region of Africa, numerous parties were prepared to go on killing and maiming in the name of ethnic group or political power, regardless of words spoken or written in Geneva where the Commission is based. Russia was the only P-5 country to be the target of a resolution of criticism in the Commission, but this did not change to any appreciable extent its brutal policies in the secessionist region of Chechnya. In the last analysis the Commission was divorced from control of military, economic, and the more important diplomatic sanctions. If the Commission's thematic measures (such as special reporters and special working groups) on forced disappearances can provide some protection to 25 per cent of its targets, this is considered a very good relative figure of success. Diplomatic pressure conducted on such a basis stood little chance of cracking the hard nut of intentional and systematic, rather than accidental and episodic, violations of human rights.

Such was the dissatisfaction with the UN Human Rights Commission that during 2005 Secretary-General Kofi Annan proposed the dissolution of the Commission and its replacement by a Human Rights Council as a major organ of the UN. In his view, state members of the new Council would be elected by a super-majority of UN member states, which supposedly would guarantee a membership more genuinely committed to human rights. Why such an election would lead to such a result was not clear, especially if states continued with traditional policies. Moreover, as long as the new Council consisted of states rather than independent experts like human rights lawyers, it was not at all clear that the new Council would act any differently from the UN Security Council, already characterized by inconsistent action for human rights.

International Labor Organization

The ILO has long been concerned with labor rights, first as a parallel organization to the League of Nations, then as a specialized agency of the UN system. It has developed several complicated procedures for monitoring state behavior in the area of labor rights. In general, certain differences aside, its record on helping apply international labor rights is similar to that of the UN Human Rights Commission in two respects: it proceeds according to indirect implementation efforts falling short of direct enforcement; and its exact influence is difficult to specify.[42]

---

[42] For a positive overview see Virginia A. Leary, "Lessons from the Experience of the International Labor Organization," in Alston, ed., *United Nations and Human Rights*, 580–619. Compare Hector G. Bartolomei de la Cruz, Geraldo von Potobsky, and Lee Swepston, *The International Labor Organization: The International Standards System and Basic Human Rights* (Boulder: Westview, 1996); and Nicolas Valticos, "The

Of the more than 170 treaties developed through and supervised by the ILO, a handful are considered oriented toward basic human rights such as the freedom to associate in trade unions, the freedom to bargain collectively, and the right to be free from forced labor. States consenting to these treaties are obligated to submit reports to the ILO, indicating steps they have taken to apply treaty provisions. These reports are reviewed first by a committee of experts, then by a larger and more political body. Specialized ILO secretariat personnel assist the review committees. At both stages, workers' organizations participate actively. Other participants come from owners' organizations, and states. This tripartite membership of the ILO at least reduces or delays some of the problems inherent in the UN Human Rights Commission, such as states' political obstruction that makes serious review difficult. Nevertheless, at the end of the day the ILO regular review process centers on polite if persistent diplomacy devoid of more stringent sanctions beyond public criticism. Some issues remain under review for years. States may not enjoy multilateral criticism, but they learn to live with it as the price of continued political power or economic transactions.

All member states of the ILO are subject to a special review procedure on the key subject of freedom of association, regardless of their consent to various ILO treaties. Despite procedural differences, the outcome of these special procedures is not very different from the regular review. Workers' organizations are more active than owner and state representatives, and public criticism of state malfeasance must be repeated because amelioration comes slowly. Indeed, a study of freedom of association and the ILO during the Cold War concluded that those states most violative of freedom of association were also most resistant to ILO pressures for change.[43] There are procedures for "urgent cases," but these sometimes take months to unfold. If a Chile under Pinochet or a Poland under Jaruzelski was determined to suppress independent labor movements, the ILO was unable to protect them – at least in the short term.

There are still further actions the ILO can take in defense of labor rights, such as sending special representatives of the Director-General for contact with offending governments. Moreover, the ILO is not the only UN agency concerned with labor rights. UNICEF, for example, is

International Labor Organization," in Karel Vasak, ed., *The International Dimensions of Human Rights*, edited for the English edition by Philip Alston (Westport: Greenwood, for UNESCO, 1982).

[43] Ernst B. Haas, *Human Rights and International Action: The Case of Freedom of Association* (Stanford: Stanford University Press, 1970).

much concerned with child labor, arguing in early 1997 that some 250 million child laborers were being harshly exploited.[44]

All this diplomacy, public and private, for labor rights no doubt has an educational effect over time and constitutes a certain nuisance factor for states interested in their reputations in international circles. It remains true, however, that some states regard cheap and disorganized labor as part of their "comparative advantage" in international markets, and therefore useful in pursuit of economic growth for the nation as a whole. Suppressed labor organizations may also prove convenient to ruling elites. While some see labor rights as an essential part of human rights, others see labor rights as disguised claims to privileges or special benefits.[45] There are those who see the western emphasis on labor rights as part of neo-imperialism, designed to hamstring developing countries' drive for economic growth by saddling them with labor standards that the more developed countries never met in their "takeoff" stage of "crude capitalism" in the earlier years of the industrial revolution. The contrary view was that international labor rights were necessary to protect labor even in the developed countries, by mandating equal competition and a level playing field in global economic matters. As the twentieth century moved to a close, with more global markets than ever before, labor issues remained one of the more controversial features of global efforts to apply human rights standards. We return to this subject in chapter 8, dealing with transnational corporations.

The High Commissioner for Refugees

After World War II, such was the naïvety of the international community that it was thought the problem of refugees was a small residue of that war and would be cleared up rather quickly.[46] Over half a century later, refugees as defined in international law numbered about 13–15 million each year, perhaps another 25 million persons found themselves in a refugee-like situation, and the UN Office of the High Commissioner for Refugees (UNHCR) had become a permanent organization with an annual budget of around $1 billion. Some 2 million persons fled genocide

---

[44] UNICEF helped develop the Convention on the Rights of the Child, which contains provisions relevant to child labor. See Lawrence J. LeBlanc, *The Convention on the Rights of the Child: United Nations Lawmaking on Human Rights* (Lincoln: University of Nebraska Press, 1995).

[45] See further Lance A. Compa and Stephen F. Diamond, *Human Rights, Labor Rights, and International Trade* (Philadelphia: University of Pennsylvania Press, 1996).

[46] On this and subsequent points see in particular Gil Loescher, *Beyond Charity: International Cooperation and the Global Refugee Crisis* (New York: Oxford University Press, 1993, for the Twentieth Century Fund).

in the Great Lakes region of Africa in 1994–1995. Some 800,000 ethnic Albanians were forced out of Yugoslavia's Kosovo area in 1999.

International law provided for legal refugees – those individuals crossing an international boundary on the basis of a well-founded fear of persecution (also called social, political or convention refugees). Such persons had the legal right not to be returned to a threatening situation, and thus were to be granted at least temporary asylum in states of first sanctuary. But in addition, many persons fled disorder without being individually singled out for persecution, and others found themselves displaced but still within their country of habitual residence. Others needed international protection after returning to their original state. After the Cold War, virtually all of the traditional states of asylum, historically speaking, adopted more restrictive policies regarding refugees and asylum. Being protective of traditional national values and numbers, these western states feared being overwhelmed with outsiders in an era of easier transportation.

The UNHCR started out primarily as a protective agency that sought to represent legal refugees diplomatically and legally. States retained final authority as to who was recognized as a legal refugee, and who was to be granted temporary or permanent entrance to the country. Thus the early role of the UNHCR was primarily to contact states' legal authorities and/or foreign ministries on behalf of those exiles with a well-founded fear of persecution. Increasingly the UNHCR was drawn into the relief business, to the extent that some observers believed it was no longer able to adequately protect refugees because its time, personnel, and budgets were consumed by relief operations. In its relief, the UNHCR felt compelled by moral concerns to disregard most distinctions among legal refugees, war refugees, and internally displaced persons. They were all in humanitarian need. This approach was approved by the General Assembly. Given that repatriation rather than resettlement became increasingly the only hope for a durable solution to refugee problems, the UNHCR increasingly addressed itself to the human rights problems causing flight in the first place. Thus the UNHCR became less and less a strictly humanitarian actor, and more and more a human rights actor dealing with the root causes of refugee problems.[47] In 1999, for example, High Commissioner Sadako Ogata testified to the UN Security Council that the primary cause of flight from Kosovo was not NATO bombing but mass persecution and terror by the Serbian authorities in Yugoslavia.

[47] See further Gil Loescher, "Refugees: A Global Human Rights and Security Crisis," in Tim Dunne and Nicholas J. Wheeler, eds., *Human Rights in Global Politics* (Cambridge: Cambridge University Press, 1999), 233–258.

The UNHCR faced numerous and complex issues while trying to provide protection and relief to those who had broken normal relations with their governments. In Bosnia in the early 1990s the UNHCR found itself contributing to ethnic cleansing by moving persons out of harm's way in accordance with the desires of certain fighting parties, but it was morally preferable to do so rather than see the persons killed. In the Great Lakes region of Africa, armed militia were mixed with civilian refugees. UNHCR had no authority or power to police refugee areas, and thus faced the dilemma of whether to provide relief to all or to withdraw in protest against the presence of armed groups interested in continuing the violence. While some private relief agencies pulled out, UNHCR stayed – and tried to arrange the proper policing of refugee camps by certain local states.[48]

Despite some evidence of accounting and other mismanagement, the UNHCR remained one of the more respected UN agencies. It became one of the more important UN relief agencies, it was trying to re-establish a sound record of protection, and it had been a pioneer in addressing the special problems of women refugees.[49]

Treaty-specific bodies

The United Nations is a decentralized and poorly coordinated system. Since states are unwilling thus far to create a human rights court to coordinate the protection of internationally recognized human rights, each human rights treaty provides its own monitoring mechanism. (The 1948 Genocide Convention, with 136 parties as of 2005, refers disputes to the International Court of Justice.) Since obviously the UN Human Rights Commission, the ILO, and the UNHCR have not resolved all or even most human rights problems, the tendency is to respond to pressing problems via a specialized treaty with an additional supervisory system. States keep adopting human rights standards, but avoiding the hard issue of effective enforcement. The result is a proliferation of weak implementation agencies and a further lack of coordination. The heads of the treaty monitoring mechanisms, however, have started meeting together to exchange views. Sometimes they try concerted or pooled diplomacy, as when in 2004–2005 they asked to visit the US detention center at

---

[48] See Sadako Ogata, *The Turbulent Decade: Confronting the Refugee Crises of the 1990s* (New York: Norton, 2005).

[49] Unfortunately some of its local personnel in East Africa were implicated in the sexual harassment of women and girls, in that special attention was offered in return for sexual favors. The problem also sometimes occurred in UN peacekeeping operations. A principal problem was that the UN Secretariat lacked the authority to properly train, and in some cases ensure the punishment of, personnel loaned by states.

Guantanamo Bay. The existence of the post of UN High Commissioner for Human Rights since 1993 may eventually improve coordination in relative terms. (There is also the embryonic international criminal court analyzed in chapter 4.) Here we cover the two monitoring mechanisms under the two basic Covenants, then make quick reference to other treaty-based bodies.

The Human Rights Committee

The International Covenant on Civil and Political Rights, with 154 parties as of 2005, provides for a Human Rights Committee with two basic protective functions. Composed of individual experts nominated and elected by states that are party to the Covenant, the Committee reviews and comments on obligatory state reports. The Committee also processes individual petitions alleging violations of rights under the Covenant, from those states consenting to an optional protocol. As of 2005, 104 states had provided that specialized consent. There is also a procedure for state-to-state complaints, but it has never been activated. A second protocol forbidding the death penalty has many fewer ratifications, and has had no discernible influence on states like the USA, Japan, China, and Iran, inter alia that widely use the death penalty for common crime (as compared to political crime like treason).

States report on measures they have taken to make national law and practice compatible with their obligations under the Covenant. The Committee, however, was divided during the Cold War on its proper role. A minimalist view, articulated mostly by individuals from the European socialist states, maintained that the Committee was only to facilitate dialogue among sovereign states. A maximalist view was that the Committee was to pronounce both on whether a state had reported correctly, and on whether that state was in compliance with its legal obligations. Since the end of the Cold War the Committee has been more free to adopt the maximalist view.[50] But once again we see that the Committee could not proceed beyond some public criticism of the states that were found to be wanting in one respect or another via their reports. The volume of Committee proceedings and comments appeared to be in inverse proportion to the actual protection of civil and political rights in violative states.[51] Some states, mostly western democracies, did make changes in their national

---

[50] An optimistic account is found in Ineke Boerfijn, "Towards a Strong System of Supervision," *Human Rights Quarterly*, 17, 4 (November 1995), 766–793.
[51] Dominic McGoldrick, *The Human Rights Committee* (Oxford: Clarendon, 1991); Manfred Nowak, *UN Covenant on Civil and Political Rights: CCPR Comments* (Arlington: Engel, 1993).

law and practice in the wake of Committee questions. The USA, however, proved more recalcitrant. The US Senate Foreign Relations Committee, ironically identifying with the old European communist position, challenged the right of the Committee to pass judgment on US reservations, understandings, and comments concerning the Covenant.[52]

When individuals bring complaints under the Optional Protocol, having exhausted national remedies, the situation is not so very different. The Committee, when justified, will make public its views, frequently holding states to be in violation of their obligations. The range of countries found to be in violation is rather broad, ranging from one case of technical deficiencies (Canada) to numerous cases of gross violations (Uruguay). It remains uncertain in how many of these cases ameliorative steps were taken by offending governments, and whether such steps, if taken, were due strictly to the Committee. Uruguay eventually moved away from massive repression, because of which at one time it had more political prisoners per capita than any other country in the world. Whether progressive change was due to the Committee, to any great extent, is dubious.

The Committee on Economic, Social, and Cultural Rights

The International Covenant on Economic, Social, and Cultural Rights, despite 151 adherences by 2005, has always been the step-child of the international human rights movement. Certain states, when speaking in the General Assembly or another political forum, may give it some prominence in order to deflect attention away from violations of civil and political rights. But few states have paid serious and sustained attention to this convention. The same is true for the question of its application.

After the E/S/C Covenant came into legal force in 1976, it took a full two years for any monitoring mechanism to be put in place. This first body, a working group of states derived from ECOSOC, compiled a truly miserable record of incompetence and was replaced in 1986 by an independent Committee of Experts. This Committee has shown considerable dynamism in confronting some daunting tasks: imprecision of the Covenant's terms; lack of jurisprudence to clarify obligations; lack of broad and sustained governmental interest in the subject matter; paucity of national and transnational private organizations interested in socio-economic and cultural rights as rights and not as aspects of

---

[52] William A. Schabas, "Spare the RUD or Spoil the Treaty: The United States Challenges the Human Rights Committee on the Subject of Reservations," in David P. Forsythe, ed., *The United States and Human Rights: Looking Inward and Outward* (Lincoln: University of Nebraska Press, 2000).

development; and lack of, *inter alia*, relevant information for arriving at judgments.[53]

The Committee has struggled first with the problem of states' failing to submit even an initial report on compliance, although legally required. This problem is widespread across the UN system of human rights reporting, but it is a pronounced problem under this Covenant. It has also faced the usual problem that many states' reports, even when submitted, are more designed to meet formal obligations than to give a full and frank picture of the true situation of E/S/C rights in the country. The Committee has persisted in trying to serve as an effective catalyst for serious national policy making in this domain, and has tried mostly to establish minimum base lines for national requirements – rather than universal rules – regarding economic, social, and cultural rights.[54] Some argue that socioeconomic rights are receiving more attention now than in the past, and that a new monitoring mechanism is in order.[55]

Other treaty based mechanisms

Control committees exist under conventions on the Rights of the Child (192 state parties, 2005), Racial Discrimination (170 parties), Torture (139 parties), Discrimination Against Women (180 parties), and Apartheid (102 parties). State endorsement of international human rights in these areas is generally not matched by timely and fulsome reporting by the state, nor by a willingness to respond affirmatively and quickly to critical comments by the control committees – which are composed of individual experts. As with other human rights treaties discussed above, UN secretariat assistance is meager owing to budgetary problems. Some NGOs do give special attention to one or more of these treaties. For example, Amnesty International gives considerable support to the Committee Against Torture. But the Committee Against Racial Discrimination has adopted restrictive decisions about the use of NGO information, as has the Committee on Discrimination Against Women. This latter Committee operates under a treaty that does not allow individual petitions, in part because the UN Commission on the Status of Women does. The Committee dealing with apartheid has faced few private petitions, because most state parties from outside Europe have not given their consent for

---

[53] Philip Alston, "The Committee on Economic, Social, and Cultural Rights," in Alston, ed., *United Nations and Human Rights*, 473–508.

[54] See further Robert E. Robertson, "Measuring State Compliance with the Obligation to Devote the 'Maximum Available Resources' to Realizing Economic, Social, and Cultural Rights," *Human Rights Quarterly*, 16, 4 (November 1994), 693–714.

[55] Mario Gomez, "Social Economic Rights and Human Rights Commissions," *Human Rights Quarterly*, 17, 1 (February 1995), 155–169.

them to be lodged. Most of these treaties contain a provision on interstate complaints, but these provisions have remained dormant. States do not like to petition other states about human rights, because of the boomerang effect on themselves. The Committee Against Torture exercises a right of automatic investigation unless a state expressly reserves against that article; relatively few parties have. But as of 2005 UN prison inspections had yet to become systematic, because of the lack of large numbers of ratifications of this legal instrument. The Committee on the Rights of the Child has functioned for such a short time that its influence cannot be judged. There has been some effort to improve the coordination of all of these treaty-based monitoring mechanisms, but one cannot yet discern any greater influence in the short term generated by the sum of the parts, or the separate parts themselves.

In general, the regimes that center on these human rights treaties and their monitoring mechanisms constitute weak regimes that have not been able to make a significant dent thus far in violations of various human rights on a global scale.[56] The control committees do make their contribution to long-term promotion via socialization or informal and practical education for human rights.[57] States have to report and subject themselves to various forms of review. Their sovereignty is not absolute but restricted. At the end of the day, however, it is not these regimes, but the Security Council and the Secretary-General – and perhaps the High Commissioner for Human Rights – that are best positioned among UN actors to effectively press states to improve their human rights records in the short term.

International humanitarian law

If states are reluctant to enforce global human rights norms in peace, or what passes for peace in modern international relations, it is not surprising to find that they are even more reluctant to engage in prosecution and other forms of direct enforcement of violations of international humanitarian law.[58] In all states, including liberal democracies, it is politically difficult to put the national military in harm's way and then prosecute its members for violating the laws of war pertaining to humane values.

---

[56] Jack Donnelly, *Universal Human Rights in Theory and Practice* (Ithaca: Cornell University Press, 1989), ch. 11.

[57] David P. Forsythe, "The United Nations and Human Rights 1945–1985," *Political Science Quarterly*, 100 (Summer 1985), 249–269; and Forsythe, "The UN and Human Rights at Fifty: An Incremental but Incomplete Revolution," *Global Governance*, 1, 3 (September–December 1995), 297–318.

[58] Among many sources see Hazel Fox and Michael A. Meyer, eds., *Effecting Compliance* (London: British Institute of International and Comparative Law, 1993).

Internationally, prosecuting the enemy for war crimes can also prove difficult. Often one has control of neither the guilty person nor the documentary evidence that would stand judicial scrutiny. Obtaining such persons or evidence may require combat, with more death and destruction. Given difficulties of enforcement via prosecution, or various forms of collectively organized sanctions, once again interested parties must look primarily to diplomacy or other means of political application of human rights norms.

Under the Geneva Conventions of 1949 and Additional Protocol I of 1977 pertaining to international armed conflict, fighting states are supposed to appoint a neutral state as a Protecting Power to oversee application of appropriate international rules. Few Protecting Powers have been appointed since the Second World War. This situation leaves the International Committee of the Red Cross, a private Swiss agency, to do what it can to see that captured, wounded, and sick military personnel benefit from international legal provisions as written, and that civilians in occupied territory and other war zones likewise benefit from protective norms. The overall record is not an altogether happy one, especially in internal armed conflicts where the rules are more lenient and the fighting parties sometimes woefully uninformed about humanitarian standards.[59] Occasionally, as in the Falklands/Malvinas war of 1982, states like Argentina and the United Kingdom engage in combat more or less according to humanitarian law. Even in places like the former Yugoslavia during 1992–1995, perhaps more civilians benefited from humanitarian protection and assistance than were intentionally shot, raped, tortured, maimed, or otherwise attacked and persecuted. It is a difficult comparison and judgment to make. Never before in world history have civilians constituted such a high percentage of the casualties in armed conflicts. But never have there been so many rules and actors trying to humanize war.[60] We will continue this subject in chapter 4, when we address criminal prosecution in more detail.

If one compares the United Nations and the League of Nations with regard to setting human rights standards and trying to apply them, one can clearly see the increased commitment to liberal values centering on personal human rights in international relations. But one can also see that much of this commitment is pro forma, which is to say, insincere. The members of the United Nations are states, and they still express considerable interest in their independence and freedom from

---

[59] A useful overview is Larry Minear and Thomas G. Weiss, *Mercy Under Fire: War and the Global Humanitarian Community* (Boulder: Westview, 1995).

[60] David P. Forsythe, "The International Committee of the Red Cross and Humanitarian Assistance: A Policy Analysis," *International Review of the Red Cross*, 314 (September–October 1996), 512–531.

authoritative international supervision on rights issues. Yet gradually, as subsequent chapters will also demonstrate, they are beginning to redefine their national interests to include more attention to human rights, even if realist concerns with independent power have not vanished.

Discussion questions

– Can a decentralized or Westphalian system of international law and diplomacy, in which equal sovereign states apply human rights norms, be fully effective? To what extent have contemporary states moved away from this Westphalian system for the purpose of using the United Nations to protect internationally recognized human rights?
– Can one always draw a clear distinction between security issues and human rights issues? Can a putative human rights issue also be a genuine security issue? Is it ever proper for the UN Security Council to invoke Charter Chapter VII, thus permitting legally binding enforcement decisions, when dealing with violations of human rights?
– Is it ever proper for a state, or a collection of states, to use coercion in another state to protect human rights, without the explicit and advance approval of the UN Security Council? What lessons should be drawn from NATO's action in Kosovo? Is this a form of humanitarian intervention that should be approved and repeated by the international community?
– What is the difference between international and internal (civil) armed conflicts, from the standpoint of law, and from the standpoint of practical action, when it comes to protecting human rights in such conflicts?
– Beyond the Security Council, which parts of the UN system, if any, have compiled a noteworthy record in applying human rights standards? Is this because of direct protection, indirect protection, or long-term education? Is it possible to generalize about the UN and protecting human rights under Charter Chapter VI and peaceful or quasi-peaceful diplomacy? What is the relationship between human rights and UN complex peacekeeping?
– What is the relationship between the international law of human rights and international humanitarian law concerning practical action to advance human dignity in "failed states" and "complex emergencies"?

Suggestions for further reading

Alston, Philip, ed., *The United Nations and Human Rights: A Critical Appraisal* (Oxford: Clarendon Press, 1995; 2nd ed., 2006). A broad and excellent survey by experts on the subject; indispensable.

Cohen, Roberta, and Francis M. Deng, eds., *The Forsaken People: Case Studies of the Internally Displaced* (Washington: Brookings, 1998). An authoritative look at a growing human rights problem, as displaced persons do not always benefit from the protection and assistance given to official refugees.

Bartolomei de la Cruz, Hector G., Geraldo von Potobsky, and Lee Swepston, *The International Labor Organization: The International Standards System and Basic Human Rights* (Boulder: Westview, 1996). A balanced overview.

Dobbins, James, et.al., *The UN's Role In Nation-Building: From the Congo to Iraq* (Santa Monica, CA: Rand, 2005). A good analytical overview, noting several positive contributions.

Farer, Tom, ed., *Beyond Sovereignty: Collectively Defending Democracy in the Americas* (Baltimore: Johns Hopkins University Press, 1996). A good analysis of the Western Hemisphere, showing the advancement and limits of collective action for liberal democracy.

Goldstein, Judith, and Robert O. Keohane, eds., *Ideas and Foreign Policy: Beliefs, Institutions and Political Change* (Ithaca: Cornell University Press, 1993). Ideas, not just material power, matter in international relations, but specifying exactly how ideas affect politics remains elusive. The chapter on human rights by Kathryn Sikkink is particularly good.

Guest, Iain, *Behind the Disappearances: Argentina's Dirty War Against Human Rights and the United Nations* (Philadelphia: University of Pennsylvania Press, 1990). A journalist uncovers Argentina's extensive efforts, supported by the Reagan Administration in Washington, to block UN investigation into its brutal policies during military rule in the 1980s.

Humphrey, John P., *Human Rights and the United Nations: A Great Adventure* (Dobbs Ferry: Transnational, 1984). The first Director of the Human Rights Division in the UN Secretariat reflects on his experiences. Humphrey, a Canadian social democrat, was influential behind the scenes in the drafting of the Universal Declaration of Human Rights, although others like the Frenchman René Casin were often given more credit in public.

Loescher, Gil, *The UNHCR and World Politics: A Perilous Path* (New York and Oxford: Oxford University Press, 2001). The best comprehensive treatment of the UN Refugee Office (UNHCR) . His proposals for change in the future are well considered but stand little chance of being adopted by states.

Luttwak, Edward, "Where Are the Great Powers?," *Foreign Affairs*, 73, 4 (July/August, 1994), 23–29. A conservative Washington insider notes the reluctance of major states to incur significant costs for almost any foreign policy objective, and certainly including human rights. Written five years before NATO's intervention in Kosovo.

McGoldrick, Dominic, *The Human Rights Committee* (Oxford: Clarendon, 1991). An exhaustive compilation of decisions by the monitoring mechanism under the International Covenant on Civil and Political Rights, with a legal orientation.

Mertus, Julie, *The United Nations and Human Rights* (New York: Routledge, 2005). A basic survey of the different agents in the UN system, intended for students.

Minear, Larry, and Thomas G. Weiss, *Mercy Under Fire: War and the Global Humanitarian Community* (Boulder: Westview, 1995). An insightful analysis of how the international community deals with human rights and humanitarian assistance in complex emergencies and wars.

Nowak, Manfred, *UN Covenant on Civil and Political Rights: CCPR Comments* (Arlington: Engel, 1993). A distinguished European lawyer looks in detail at the general comments made by the UN Human Rights Committee. Explains the process well, though now dated.

Ogata, Sadako, *Turbulent Decade: Confronting the Refugee Crises of the 1990s* (New York: Norton, 2005). Account by the former head of the UNHCR about the problems she faced in places like Bosnia and the Great Lakes region of Africa.

Ratner, Steven J., *The New UN Peacekeeping* (New York: St. Martin's Press, 1995). An analytical look at second-generation or complex peacekeeping, designed not just to stop violence but to create a liberal democratic peace, with much attention to especially Cambodia.

Rivlin, Benjamin, and Leon Gordenker, eds., *The Challenging Role of the UN Secretary-General: Making "The Most Impossible Job in the World" Possible* (Westport: Praeger, 1993). A good collection, with some attention to human rights.

Roberts, Adam, and Benedict Kingsbury, eds., *United Nations, Divided World: The UN's Roles in International Relations*, 2nd edn (Oxford: Clarendon, 1993). A good collection of essays, mostly by legal experts, with considerable attention to human rights. The chapter centering on human rights by Tom Farer and Felice Gaer was one of the best short analyses that existed at that time.

Thakur, Ramesh, and Carlyle A. Thayer, eds., *A Crisis of Expectations: UN Peace-keeping in the 1990s* (Boulder: Westview, 1995). A good analysis of how expectations outstrip resources given to the United Nations for complex peacekeeping.

Tolley, Howard, Jr., *The UN Commission on Human Rights* (Boulder: Westview, 1987). While this book is now dated, it remains the definitive treatment for its time. No one has written a comparable sequel.

Weiss, Thomas G., David P. Forsythe, and Roger A. Coate, *The United Nations and Changing World Politics*, 2nd edn (Boulder: Westview, 1997). A widely used text devotes Part II to human rights and humanitarian affairs.

4 Transitional justice: criminal courts and alternatives

After gross violations of human rights, what is one to do? This is the subject of transitional justice, a growth industry for intellectuals and policy makers after the Cold War. Should one prosecute individuals in international courts, or in hybrid or special courts, or in national courts? Should one avoid courts and rely on truth commissions, or bar violators from public office, or just move on to concentrate on building a rights protective state in the future rather than looking back via criminal prosecution? There are many complexities facing those interested in international criminal justice – meaning those interested in whether to prosecute against the background of international human rights and humanitarian norms. Beyond punishment of evil doers, one needs to keep in mind other possible goals of transitional justice: deterring future atrocities, bringing psychological closure to victims and/or relatives, producing reconciliation among divided communities, building a rights protective polity in the future, adjusting to the lingering power of elements of the old regime.

In the last decade of the twentieth century the United Nations created two international criminal courts, the first in almost fifty years. Moreover a new International Criminal Court (ICC) came into legal existence in July, 2002. Furthermore, special courts were created in the aftermath of atrocities in Sierra Leone, East Timor, Kosovo, and Cambodia, while a new court was created by the interim government of Iraq after the US invasion and occupation of 2003 to try Saddam Hussein and his lieutenants. The United Kingdom agreed that the former dictator of Chile, Augusto Pinochet, could be extradicted to Spain to stand trial there at least for torture.

In the abstract it is hard to disagree with the proposition that those who commit gross violations of internationally recognized standards pertaining to genocide, war crimes, and crimes against humanity should face criminal justice. If we had reliable criminal justice on a global scale we could punish individual criminals with more certainty, bring some catharsis to victims and/or their relatives, try to break the vicious circle of group violence, and hope to deter similar future acts.

In international relations as it continues to exist on the eve of the twenty-first century, however, while there may be an embryonic trend toward "legalization" and more use of adjudication,[1] many policy makers are obviously reluctant to pursue criminal justice – especially through international tribunals. Sometimes this hesitancy is the product of realist attitudes and/or chauvinistic nationalism. But sometimes these policies of hesitation are characterized by careful reasoning and serious liberal argument.

Hesitancy about international criminal justice is thus not always a reaction by those who wish to elevate repressive privilege over protection of international human rights. Caution is also sometimes evidenced by persons of relatively liberal persuasion who by definition are motivated by considerable concern for human dignity. In general they are in favor of human rights, but on occasion they find it both politically prudent and morally defensible to bypass the enforcement of human rights through criminal justice. I term this position pragmatic liberalism. This view can be contrasted with judicial romanticism, which brushes aside such political and diplomatic concerns in the belief that criminal justice is a panacea for violations of human rights, and that "impunity" for those violations ought never be allowed. Judicial romantics overestimate what courts can achieve and underestimate the role of soft law and essentially political approaches to advancing human rights and humanitarian norms.

Like Martha Minow, this chapter suggests that in the wake of atrocities there is no single response that is always appropriate everywhere, but rather a menu of choice in which the proper selection depends upon context.[2] Like Richard J. Goldstone, the first ICTY prosecutor, this chapter argues that considerations of peace and justice have to be carefully calculated, and that pursuit of justice does not always require criminal justice as compared to social and political forms of justice.[3]

---

[1] See the special issue of the journal *International Organization* on "Legalization and World Politics," March, 2001. See also Mary L. Volcansek, *Law Above Nations: Supranational Courts and the Legalization of Politics* (Gainesville: University Press of Florida, 1997).

[2] Martha Minow, in *Between Vengeance and Forgiveness: Facing History After Genocide and Mass Violence* (Boston: Beacon Press, 1998), argues that neither trials nor truth commissions are always most appropriate option. Compare Andrew Rigby, *Justice and Reconciliation: After the Violence* (Boulder: Lynne Rienner, 2001). And Ruti G. Teitel, *Transitional Justice* (New York: Oxford University Press, 2002).

[3] "Bringing War Criminals to Justice during an Ongoing War," in Jonathan Moore, ed., *Hard Choices: Moral Dilemmas in Humanitarian Intervention* (Lanham, MD: Rowman & Littlefield, 1998), 195–210.

Historical background to 1991: few trials, small impact

The history of criminal prosecution – both international and national – related to international events is reasonably well known, at least to some legal scholars.[4] Since books have been written on the subject, here I seek merely to highlight several important points. Even a cursory retrospective shows that many policy makers have found ample reason to avoid international trials, with a few exceptions. As is usually the case, political calculation precedes reference to legal rules. As Werner Levi has written, "[P]olitics decides who the lawmaker and what the formulation of the law shall be; law formalizes these decisions and makes them binding. This distribution of functions makes law dependent upon politics."[5]

While there was some discussion of criminal prosecution of German leaders after World War I, movement in that direction was aborted.[6] It was only after World War II that the first international criminal proceedings transpired, with well-known defects.[7] For a time allied leaders leaned toward summary execution of high German policy makers, but eventually concluded a treaty creating the Nuremberg tribunal. The stated objectives were lofty enough, but the taint of victor's justice was pervasive. At Nuremberg (and Tokyo) only the losing leaders were tried, even though allied leaders had engaged in such acts as attacking cities through conventional, incendiary, and atomic bombings, thus failing to distinguish between combatants and civilians – a cardinal principle of international humanitarian law (viz., that part of the law of war oriented to the protection of victims of war, especially the 1949 Geneva Conventions). Soviet military personnel committed perhaps 100,000 rapes in Berlin after the defeat of the Nazis. Rapes were systematic practice, yet no commanding officers, much less lower ranking soldiers, were ever held accountable. The Soviet Union then sat in judgment of Germans at Nuremberg.[8]

There was also some prosecution and conviction via *ex post facto* laws (laws created after the act in question). The concept of individual responsibility for war crimes was reasonably well established through national laws by 1939. But crimes against peace and crimes against humanity were

---

[4] Steven R. Ratner and Jason S. Abrams, *Accountability for Human Rights Atrocities in International Law: Beyond the Nuremberg Legacy* (Oxford: Clarendon Press, 1997; 2nd ed., 2001).

[5] Werner Levi, *Law and Politics in the International Society* (Beverly Hills: Sage, 1976), 31.

[6] James F. Willis, *Prologue to Nuremberg: The Politics and Diplomacy of Punishing War Criminals of the First World War* (Westport: Greenwood, 1982).

[7] A vast bibliography is recorded in Telford Taylor, *The Anatomy of the Nuremberg Tribunal: A Personal Memoir* (New York: Knopf, 1992).

[8] Anonymous, *A Woman in Berlin* (Boston: Henry Holt, 2005).

concepts that had never been the subject of precise legislation or prosecution until 1946. Also, procedural guarantees of a fair trial could have been improved.[9]

Twenty-two German leaders were prosecuted at Nuremberg in the first round of trials, nineteen of whom were convicted, with twelve of these being executed. Other individual German cases occurred, in both international and national courts. Similar proceedings were held at Tokyo for Japanese leaders, through fiat of the US military command.[10] A pronounced defect of especially the Tokyo tribunal was the total ignoring of gender crimes, despite a broad policy of sexual slavery carried out by Japanese officials.[11]

The effect of these trials on subsequent thinking in Germany and Japan remains a matter of conjecture. Did the Nuremberg and Tokyo trials, through emphasis on individual criminal responsibility, force those nations to confront the past and face up to the individual moral choices that existed? There is widespread agreement that Germany more than Japan has tried to come to terms with the atrocities of the past – although Japan made increased gestures in that direction toward the end of the twentieth century. Yet both nations experienced similar international criminal tribunals. A researcher for the *Congressional Quarterly* wrote that "The tribunals were viewed as illegitimate by the defendants and by much, perhaps most, of the German and Japanese publics."[12]

Regarding Germany at least, much debate continues about mass versus elite responsibility for the Holocaust. Daniel J. Goldhagen argues that many if not most typical Germans willingly embraced the Holocaust and were not compelled to support it by a totalitarian state.[13] But other scholars vociferously disagree, arguing that Goldhagen has misread the historical record. Thus even with regard to Germany and Japan there is much we still do not know about the effect of international criminal

---

[9] Michael P. Scharf, *Balkan Justice: The Story Behind the First International War Crimes Trial Since Nuremberg* (Durham: Carolina Academic Press, 1997).

[10] Arnold Brackman, *The Other Nuremberg: The Untold Story of the Tokyo War Crimes Trials* (New York: Morrow, 1987). Compare Richard Minear, *Victor's Justice: The Tokyo War Crimes Trial* (Princeton: Princeton University Press, 1971).

[11] For a concise review see Kelly D. Askin, "A Decade of the Development of Gender Crimes in International Courts and Tribunals: 1993 to 2003," in *Human Rights Brief*, American University, Center for Human Rights and Humanitarian Law, 11, 3 (Spring 2004), 16–19.

[12] "War Crimes," *CQ Researcher*, 5, 25 (July 5, 1995), 589. See further Wilbourn E. Benton and Georg Grimm, eds., *Nuremberg: German Views of the War Trials* (Dallas: Southern Methodist University Press, 1955).

[13] Daniel J. Goldhagen, *Hitler's Willing Executioners: Germany and the Holocaust* (New York: Knopf, 1996).

justice on responsibility for atrocities.[14] Since Nuremberg and Tokyo were not followed by other international tribunals for almost fifty years, it is clear that the international trials of the 1940s did little to deter other atrocities through credible threat of sure prosecution. The two tribunals certainly did clarify relevant facts, thus providing some catharsis and relief. Most clearly, the trials provided punishment for some national leaders. In Germany but not in Japan, other trials followed concerning war time atrocities. It is possible, but not certain, that these German trials had an impact on German society.

Particularly in Germany but also in Japan, the USA shielded certain officials, especially scientists, from criminal prosecution and brought them to the USA for work in weapons development – given the start of the Cold War with the Soviet Union. In Japan, the USA shielded the Emperor from prosecution, judging him useful in democratic state building after the war.[15]

In numerous situations between the end of World War II and the end of the Cold War international criminal proceedings were not practical. As in the Korean War, most international armed conflicts ended inconclusively, and certainly without unconditional surrender, thus preventing the trial of those not in custody who were suspected of violations of international law. Those wars like the 1991 Persian Gulf War that ended in decisive military defeat still did not result in unconditional surrender and the victors gaining control over the losers. The George H. W. Bush Administration made the judgment, among other considerations, that pursuit of prosecution for Iraqi war crimes was not worth the continued death, injury, and destruction that would have been involved in the attempted capture of the Iraqi leadership. This was a reasoned policy, not devoid of moral considerations. It was almost universally accepted at that time as the proper policy. Later the US House of Representatives voted overwhelmingly in

---

[14] My personal impression is that the Nuremberg tribunal, combined with other reminders of the German past such as a massive and persistent socialization project about the Holocaust, has caused Germany to be highly sensitive to most human rights issues today. Similar western pressure on Japan has been less, providing one major reason why Japan has been more reluctant to come to terms with its past. The Tokyo trial was less well known in the West, Japanese atrocities such as the rape of Nanking were less well known, and there has been no western-based project like that remembering the Holocaust that is comparable in the Japanese case. But Nuremberg is part of a much broader campaign to remind Germans of their history during 1933–1945, making it difficult to factor out the singular impact of international criminal justice.

[15] See further Dapo Akande, "International law Immunities and the International Criminal Court," *American Journal of International Law*, 98, 3 (July 2004), 417. And Timothy Brook, "The Tokyo Judgment and the Rape of Nanking," *Journal of Asian Studies*, 60, 3 (August 2001), 673–700.

favor of Iraqi trials for war crimes. But based on congressional reactions to American casualties in both Lebanon in the 1980s and Somalia in the 1990s, that body would have been among the first to heatedly criticize a costly ground war designed to apprehend the Iraqi leadership had such been launched by the senior Bush or his successor. By 2005, a majority of the American public gave the George W. Bush Administration very low marks for its Iraqi policy. Even though that Administration could point to the capture and forthcoming trial of Saddam Hussein (and others), the public was primarily concerned with American casualties and lack of a clear exit strategy.

In other situations international tribunals could have been organized but for the strength of nationalism. Decisive outcomes produced by such as the Soviet intervention in Hungary or the US intervention in Grenada did not result in international trials since the victors did not want an international tribunal to closely examine embarrassing aspects of the use of force. Clearly the preferred value was not impartial application of human rights, humanitarian law, or criminal justice but rather protection of the national record and safeguarding unfettered decision making in the future.

Some war crimes usually occur during any use of force. This was made clear, *inter alia*, by eventual disclosure that Israelis had massacred a number of Egyptian prisoners of war during the 1956 Middle East War.[16] Either by design, in the context of what is judged to be pressing military necessity, or by loss of control, even personnel of democracies commit war crimes.

As for crimes against humanity, before the 1990s only the French and Israelis held national trials involving this concept. Britain, France, the Soviet Union, and the United States were willing enough to apply this concept *ex post facto* to Nazi Germany and Imperial Japan, but of these only France developed the concept (slightly) in its own national law. French and Israeli cases were exceedingly few in number, and, with the exception of the Eichmann trial in Jerusalem, pursued with considerable domestic political difficulties. This was especially so in France, as charges against French citizens for aiding in the Holocaust through crimes against humanity resurrected a painful episode in French history. Officials of the Vichy government administered half of France during World War II. Some of its French officials displayed a vicious anti-Semitism.

---

[16] Barton Gellman, "Confronting History," *Washington Post*, National Weekly Edition, August 28–September 3, 1995, 12; Serge Schmemann, "After a General Tells of Killing POWs in 1956, Israelis Argue Over Ethics of War," *New York Times*, August 21, 1995, A1.

As for genocide, until the mid-1990s and events in Bosnia and Rwanda, no procedurally correct national trials were held entailing this concept, only procedurally suspect trials in places like Equatorial Guinea. Germany, being the temporary home of a number of refugees from the fighting in the former Yugoslavia, found itself the site of at least one national trial pertaining to both war crimes and genocide in the 1990s.[17] Rwandan national courts were to pursue this subject in numerous cases.

By far the most numerous national trials for gross violations of human rights connected to international events concern war crimes, although they are not always technically called that when prosecuted under national military law. For the most part these trials involve western liberal democracies applying the laws of war to their own military personnel. Very rarely, a country such as Denmark, Switzerland or Germany will hold a war crimes trial concerning a foreigner, usually pertaining to events in the former Yugoslavia. National war crimes trials have not been without problems. As noted above, the military personnel even of democracies do commit war crimes, for those democracies that have used force abroad have not lacked for courts martial for violations of the laws of war. This, for example, the Americans discovered at My Lai and other places in Vietnam, the Israelis discovered in Arab territory occupied since 1967, and the Canadians and Italians discovered in Somalia during the 1990s.

Even when such national trials are held in liberal democracies, it has not always proved easy to apply the full force of national military law (which is derived from international law). No US senior officers were ever held responsible for the massacre at My Lai. Moreover, President Nixon felt compelled by public opinion to reduce the punishment for Lt. Calley who was held responsible for the deaths of between twenty and seventy "Oriental" civilians at My Lai. At the time of writing US officials have moved only against low ranking soldiers for prisoner abuse connected to Washington's "war on terrorism." The Israeli authorities have been quite lenient in punishing their military personnel for violations of various human rights and humanitarian norms in disputed territory. The Canadians have found it difficult to come to full terms with the actions of some of their troops in Somalia. Only the Italians moved rapidly and vigorously against some of their soldiers who had abused Somalis. Rome concluded that the incidents in question were the result of a few "bad apples" and not part of a systematic or structural problem.

---

[17] In re Jorgic (http://www.domovina.net/calenddar.html), regarding the Bosnian Serb convicted in Germany for atrocities committed in Bosnia during 1992–1993.

More than anything else this national record suggests the continuing power of nationalism, rather than any carefully reasoned and morally compelling argument about national criminal justice associated with war. That is to say that no compelling political or moral argument explains why the US military justice system mostly failed in its handling of the My Lai massacre.[18] (First the military attempted to suppress the facts. Then the military establishment focused the spotlight of inquiry at platoon level, mostly ignoring the training and orders given to foot soldiers by superior commanders. There was never punishment that fitted the extent of the crime.) A defensive and emotional nationalism has frequently overwhelmed aspects of proper criminal justice. If this is true in national trials, it indicates much difficulty for the prospects of international criminal justice. If national governments have trouble prosecuting their own, particularly those who authorized or allowed the wrong doing, how much more difficult it will be for them to turn over their own for trial by others. Serbia and America are not so different in this regard.

In sum, international criminal proceedings have been very rare, and thus we do not know very much about their effects. Rare also have been national proceedings for crimes against humanity and genocide. Only national trials for war crimes have occurred with any regularity, and these – mostly in democracies – have been frequently undermined by the continuing strength of nationalism.

International criminal justice since 1991

After the Cold War and the demise of European communism, international relations saw the creation of two UN ad hoc criminal courts, several special hybrid criminal courts, and for the first time in history a standing – which is to say permanent – International Criminal Court. There were also important national developments in criminal justice, linked to international human rights and humanitarian law. Paradoxically, this movement toward increased international criminal justice only intensified the debate about other forms of transitional justice – and whether some forms of justice might be preferred that downplayed criminal justice in favour of social or political justice.

The ICTY

At first glance, the creation of the International Criminal Tribunal for the former Yugoslavia (ICTY) in 1993 by the UN Security Council

---

[18] Joseph Goldstein, Burke Marshall, and Jack Schwartz, eds., *The My Lai Massacre and Its Cover-Up: Beyond the Reach of Law?* (New York: The Free Press, 1976).

seemed to usher in a new age in international criminal justice.[19] The Security Council voted to create a balanced and mostly procedurally correct international tribunal while the fighting and atrocities still raged, and legally required all UN member states to cooperate with the tribunal by invoking Chapter VII of the Charter. Those who committed war crimes, crimes against humanity, and genocide in that particular situation were to be prosecuted. The emphasis was on commanders who authorized or allowed the crimes.

Several commentators tried to create the impression that pursuit of criminal justice in the former Yugoslavia was a clear and simple matter. David Scheffer, soon to become head of a new office in the State Department for war crimes, wrote of the creation of the ICTY: "The Council recognized the enforcement of international law as an immediate priority, subordinate to neither political nor military imperatives."[20] A United Nations lawyer, Payam Akhavan, wrote: "there was a political consensus on the complementary interrelationship between the establishment of the Tribunal and the restoration of peace and security in the former Yugoslavia."[21] With due respect, these quotes reflect some of the most evident legalistic-moralistic reasoning since many western publications on the virtues of arbitration treaties in the 1920s.[22] This was judicial romanticism *par excellence*. Public documents (and public posturing) notwithstanding, the tribunal was created in large part because of realist reasoning, not because of moral or legal commitment to human rights standards.[23] States like the USA were under pressure to act to stop the

---

[19] A useful compilation of documents about the creation of the ICTY can be found in Virginia Morris and Michael Scharf, *An Insider's Guide to the International Criminal Tribunal for the Former Yugoslavia* (Irvington-on-Hudson: Transnational Publishers, 1995).

[20] David Scheffer, "International Judicial Intervention," *Foreign Policy*, 102 (Spring 1996), 38.

[21] Payam Akhavan, "The Yugoslav Tribunal at a Crossroads: The Dayton Peace Agreement and Beyond," *Human Rights Quarterly*, 18, 2 (May 1996), 267. See also his views in "Justice in the Hague, Peace in the Former Yugoslavia?," *Human Rights Quarterly*, 20, 4 (November 1998), 737–816. In this latter article he refers to me as a "realist," and acknowledges "judicial romanticism" while saying the latter concept does not apply to him. I am not a realist of either the classical (Hans Morgenthau) or structural (Kenneth Walz) variety, but a pragmatic liberal. I am in favor of attention to human dignity, frequently via human rights, but recognize the pervasive power and interests of the territorial state. See further Forsythe, "International Criminal Courts: A Political View," *Netherlands Quarterly of Human Rights*, 15, 1 (March 1997), 5–19.

[22] See further George Kennan, *American Diplomacy 1900–1950* (Chicago: University of Chicago, 1951).

[23] I lay out the evidence in "Politics and the International Tribunal for the Former Yugoslavia," *Criminal Law Forum*, 5, 2–3 (Spring 1994), 401–422; also in Robert S. Clark and Madeleine Sann, eds., *The Prosecution of International Crimes* (New Brunswick: Transaction Publishers, 1996), 185–206.

atrocities being reported by the communications media. The USA and some other Security Council members did not want to engage in a decisive intervention that could prove costly in terms of blood and treasure. They saw no self-interest in a complicated intervention. But they felt the need to do something. So they created the tribunal in a short-term, public relations maneuver, leaving various contradictions to sort themselves out later.

From the creation of the tribunal in 1993 to the conclusion of the Dayton agreement in 1995, many policy makers and observers found fault with the very existence of the ICTY for possibly impeding diplomatic peacemaking.[24] The logic was clear enough. Would one prolong the fighting, with accompanying atrocities, by requiring that the principal fighting parties make a just peace – after which their responsible officials would be subjected to criminal justice? Would they not prefer to fight on, rather than cooperate in a peace agreement that would make their arrest and trial more likely?

This classic dilemma between peace and justice, between stability and punishment, became pronounced with the creation of the new court. Thus particularly the British during the John Major government played a hypocritical double game, voting for the tribunal but operating behind the scenes to hamper its work. London preferred the diplomatic to the juridical track, arguing in private that diplomacy was a better path to peace and human security. Public posturing aside, this was a pragmatic liberal strategy, hopeful of ending atrocities via diplomacy, but not one that gave more than cosmetic support to adjudication. Even Scheffer, before he entered the State Department, perhaps with El Salvador or South Africa in mind where criminal justice had been bypassed or minimized, wrote that "Despite the hard hits human rights standards take in these [unspecified] cases and the risk of never breaking the cycle of retribution and violence, the choice of 'peace over justice' is sometimes the most effective means of reconciliation."[25] It can be a serious matter to question the wisdom of international criminal justice, and whether its pursuit reflects judicial romanticism.

Even Judge Goldstone, the first prosecutor for the ICTY, noted that truth commissions had certain advantages over criminal trials as far as establishing facts in a form broadly understandable and thus in providing

---

[24] See further Anthony D'Amato, "Peace v. Accountability in Bosnia," *American Journal of International Law*, 88, 3 (July 1994), 500–506. And Anonymous, "Human Rights in Peace Negotiations," *Human Rights Quarterly*, 18, 2 (May 1966), 249–258.
[25] Scheffer, "International Judicial Intervention," 37.

education and catharsis. He advocated both trials and truth commissions.[26]

The Dayton agreement showed that at least superficially or on paper one could have both relative peace and some criminal justice – one could end most of the combat and reduce much of the multifaceted victimization of individuals while at least promising criminal justice for those who had engaged in war crimes, crimes against humanity, and genocide.[27] However, one could secure the cooperation of Slobodan Milosevic, and the Serb-dominated Yugoslavian army that he controlled, only by an evident deal at Dayton exempting him from prosecution – at least for a time. At that time there was no public indictment against Milosevic who, more than any other single individual, was responsible for the break up of former Yugoslavia and no doubt the Serbian strategy of ethnic cleansing. As far as we know from the public record and the logic of the situation, in Milosevic's case one had to trade away in 1995 criminal justice for diplomatic peacemaking, although lawyers for the ICTY argued that they simply did not have a good legal case against him. It seemed to be a fact that Western states did not make a serious effort to go after certain individuals like Milosevic, Radko Mladic, and Radovan Karadic until later – when the Dayton agreement was more secure.

The same dilemma resurfaced regarding Kosovo. Milosevic was both the arsonist and the fire fighter in that situation, as in Bosnia earlier. He undertook repressive policies and forced expulsions in Kosovo, a province in new Yugoslavia, that inflamed discontent among the ethnic Albanians who made up 90 per cent of the local population. But the West had to deal with him, since he possessed the authority and power to restrain the Yugoslav forces (of Serbian ethnicity) who were engaged in hostilities in the province. How could one solicit his cooperation in reducing human rights and humanitarian violations if one threatened him with criminal justice? The US Congress, on record earlier as in favor of prosecuting Iraqi war criminals, voted to urge the Clinton Administration to offer Milosevic a deal – sanctuary in a friendly country in return for his abdication of power within new Yugoslavia. The prosecutor's office

---

[26] "Ethnic Reconciliation Needs the Help of a Truth Commission," *International Herald Tribune*, October 24, 1998, 6. See also Goldstone, "Bringing War Criminls to Justice during an Ongoing War," in Jonathan Moore, ed., *Hard Choices: Moral Dilemmas in Humanitarian Intervention*, (Lanham, MD: Rowman and Littlefield, 1998), 195–210. Given the difficulty of educating the public via technical trials, Mark Osiel proposes liberal show trials in *Mass Atrocity, Collective Memory, and the Law* (New Brunswick: Transaction Publishers, 1997). But liberal show trials are inherently contradictory, as Samantha Power notes in the *New Republic*, March 2, 1998, 32–38.

[27] See further Richard Holbrooke, *To End A War* (New York: Random House, 1998). Holbrooke was the key mediator at Dayton.

of the ICTY finally indicted Milosevic and several of his high-ranking colleagues in Belgrade for ordering criminal acts in Kosovo, but this was after hope was lost for a negotiated deal with Milosevic, à la Bosnia, to end the atrocities in Kosovo.

Immediately after Dayton, the fear of doing more harm than good via criminal justice resurfaced in still other forms. One fear was that pursuit of indicted suspects would cause the fragile commitment to the Dayton accord to collapse. In early 1996 certain Bosnian Serb military officers wandered into areas controlled by the Bosnian Muslims by error and were arrested on suspicion of war crimes. Bosnian Serb parties then refused to cooperate with talks on continued military disengagement called for under the peace agreements and supervised by IFOR (the NATO implementation force). A political crisis resulted, entailing high-level mediation by US diplomats. The Serbian officers were eventually returned to Serbia rather than transferred to The Hague for trial. It was a vivid if small demonstration of how pursuit of legal justice could endanger the broader political agreements that had ended both the combat and related human rights violations.

A similar fear was that pursuit of criminal justice in Bosnia would produce another Somalia. In that East African country in 1993, the attempt to arrest one of the warlords, General Aideed, leading as it did to the deaths of eighteen US soldiers and the wounding of many more, produced an early US withdrawal from that country and more generally a US reluctance to support other UN-approved deployments of force in places like Rwanda the following year. The goal of national reconciliation with liberal democracy was never achieved by the international community in Somalia, arguably at least in part because of the defection of the USA from the international effort in 1994. The companion fear in Bosnia was that similar US casualties would force a premature withdrawal of NATO forces (via IFOR and SFOR – the latter being the stabilization force) and a collapse of the effort to make the Dayton agreement work. European contributors to NATO deployments made it clear that if the USA pulled out, they would also.

After a passive policy of non-arrests by NATO forces during 1993–1995, some arrests were made after 1995. But for considerable time NATO did not seek to arrest the Serbian leaders who had devised and commanded the policies of ethnic cleansing of Muslims in Bosnia. They were well connected and well protected. In Washington especially, it was feared that a costly shoot-out would undermine the shaky congressional tolerance of American military personnel on the ground in the Balkans. It was only later, when the Dayton agreement seemed more secure, as enforced by a sizable contingent of first NATO and then EU troops on the ground, that a more vigorous pursuit of Milosevic, Mladic, and Karadic took place. Eventually, particularly because of US financial pressure, a newly elected Serbian government detained Milosevic in spring of 2001 and transferred him to The Hague for trial in the ICTY. Thus in 1995 the USA negotiated with Milosevic at Dayton, but by 2001 the USA was demanding his arrest and trial. Either policy could be justified, taking into account the broader political context of the Balkans.

What we see with regard to the ICTY is an early tension between pragmatic liberalism and international criminal justice, a tension that was resolved only with the negotiated Dayton peace agreement for Bosnia, plus NATO intervention regarding Kosovo. It was only after these political events that there was serious pursuit of various Serbian leaders in order to hold them personally accountable for certain crimes. What we also see in the example of the ICTY is the creation of the court for essentially realist reasons, but then the transformation of the Court into a serious enterprise of criminal justice largely through the office of its Prosecutor, supported by many non-governmental organizations and a few states.

The USA, which had led in the creation of the Court for cosmetic and self-serving reasons, then became the key backer of the Court. Having authored the Court, Washington felt it had to make it a success. Until 1999 and the NATO bombing of Serbia because of Kosovo, Washington could support the ICTY as criminal justice for others, the Court's jurisdiction being limited to behaviour within the boundaries of the former Yugoslavia. But with the 1999 NATO bombing, NATO personnel became subject to the jurisdiction of the Court. The ICTY prosecutor declined, on the basis of a staff investigation, to pursue charges of war crimes articulated against certain NATO personnel. Some observers thought this was a political decision, it being difficult to carry out military actions over several months without serious war crimes. (Serbia also pursued a legal complaint in the International Court of Justice against certain NATO states for violations of international law in the bombing campaign, but this legal action also came to naught. There was also a case filed with the European Court of Human Rights against certain European states that were members of NATO, but this litigation also failed.)

Out of these complicated origins, the ICTY compiled a complicated record. Without question the Court was able to punish a number a persons, including some high officials; it also helped develop international law in important ways.

As of the fall of 2004 the ICTY had issued final judgments pertaining to 30 persons. The Court in various cases held that: the 1995 massacre at Srebrenica constituted genocide, in that there was an intentional attempt to destroy a substantial part of the Bosnian Muslim people through the killing of over 7,000 men and boys; that individuals could be held respon-sible for crimes committed in internal war, not just international war; that a detention camp commander was responsible for crimes, including sex crimes, that occurred under his command, whether committed against men or women; that rape crimes could constitute war crimes or crimes against humanity, not just individual illegal acts; that someone who did not participate directly in rapes could be convicted of rape for allowing or encouraging it to happen, and that rape was also a form of torture and discrimination. It can be seen that the ICTY was especially attentive to various gender issues.

The most important case, that of Milosevic, was continuing at the time of writing. The Serb leader insisted on defending himself. This fact pro-longed the trial, both because of health-related delays and time he devoted to histrionics. There were also disputes between the defendant and his court appointed lawyers. It took some two years for the prosecution to present its case, with the defence phase promising to last longer. Much of the trial centered on proof of Milosevic's role in various war crimes, crimes against humanity, and genocide. The latter seemed the most dif-ficult to prove, given that any commands reflecting an intent to destroy a national, ethnic, religious, or racial people were not likely to be found in written documents or clear and uncontested statements.

It was difficult to say whether the Court contributed much beyond punishment and legal development, since it was hard to gauge its effect on regional reconciliation and stability, and closure for affected individ-uals.[28] The Court did not have a good outreach program, explaining its actions to parties in the Balkans. Certainly in much of Serbia and the Serb part of Bosnia, the ICTY was widely seen as anti-Serb. This was partially because of the large number of Serbs indicted, arrested, and made defendants. Also, the third prosecutor, Carla del Ponte of Switzer-land, often had pointed things to say about the lack of Serb and Bosnian Serb cooperation with the Court.[29] Mladic, Bosnian Serb military com-mander, and Karadic, Bosnian Serb political leader, remained at large as of the summer of 2005, the former having been seen on occasion in Serbia and the latter presumed to be hiding in the Serbian part of Bosnia. Whether the 2005 indictment of Ramush Haradinaj, the ethnic Albanian prime minister of Kosovo, would change the dominant Serb view of the

---

[28] Daid Tolbert, "The Criminal Tribunal for the Former Yugoslavia: Unforeseen Successes and Unforeseeable Shortcomings," *The Fletcher Forum of World Affairs*, 26, 2 (Sum-mer/Fall, 2002).

[29] Misha Glenny, "The Prosecutor Muddies Serbian Waters," *International Her-ald Tribune*, February 17, 2004, www.iht.com/cgi-bin/ generic.cgi? template= articleprint.tmplh@ArticleId=129800.

ICTY remained to be seen. Also in 2005, the widespread showing in Serbia of video clips of Serb involvement in the massacre at Srebrenica might also change Serb views of the court.

It was certainly difficult for the ICTY to promote reconciliation among Bosnian Muslims, Serbs of various sorts, and Croats, when the Dayton agreement itself had recognized largely autonomous Serb, Croat, and Muslim sectors within Bosnia. As of 2005 there was clearly substantial antagonism among the various communities in the Balkans, with a rather fragile peace being mainly the result of interposition and enforcement by NATO and EU states, under UN aegis, rather than because of genuine inter-communal reconciliation. Despite various Court judgments, Muslim refugees and displaced persons had trouble returning to their homes in Serb portions of Bosnia. Tensions also remained high in Kosovo between the Serbs and Albanians.

The ICTY, costing slightly less than $275 million per year, had been asked to finish its trials (but not appeals) by 2008. The existence of the court did contribute to the move to create a permanent international criminal court, as noted below.

The Rwandan court

The reasons for the creation of a second *ad hoc* UN criminal court were similar to the first. States on the Security Council, principally the United States, did not want to incur the costs of a decisive intervention in Rwanda in 1994 to stop the long standing conflict between Hutu and Tutsi communities which resulted in a genocide with perhaps 500,000–800,000 deaths.[30] They saw no vital self interests in such action. Somalia in 1993 had shown that international intervention in a situation where persons of ill will engaged in brutal and inhumane power struggles could be a dangerous venture. The USA and others were eventually willing to pay billions of dollars for the care of those fleeing genocide in Rwanda.

---

[30] The difference between Hutus and Tutsis had been codified by Belgium when colonial power and was originally more a class than biological or blood distinction. By the time of Rwandan independence the distinction had been solidified, and it had great political significance – as those identifying as Hutu made up a large majority of the country, controlling the outcome of elections. By 1994 the Hutu community was divided between militants advocating Hutu power to the detriment of Tutsi, and moderates interested in power sharing. By contrast to the perhaps 800,000 killed in Rwanda in 1994, eighteen US soldiers were killed in one day in Mogadishu, among a total of some thirty-five US military deaths in Somalia in the early 1990s overall. This is a modest cost for a "great power" or superpower in relative terms. The USA suffered nine deaths in one military air crash off South Africa in September 1997, but the media did not emphasize it and commentators did not call for a change of policy there. See further Edward N. Luttwak, "Where Are the Great Powers?" *Foreign Affairs*, 73, 4 (July/August 1994), 23–29.

But loss of western life, even in a professional and volunteer military establishment, was another matter. This was certainly true of Belgium, a former colonial power in Rwanda, which, when faced with ten deaths in its peacekeeping unit there, was in favour of the withdrawal, not the expansion, of those forces. Feeling nevertheless the impulse to do something, states on the Council created a second criminal court with similar jurisdiction and authority. Thus, as in former Yugoslavia, it was not consistent attention to moral norms and legal rules that drove the Security Council to action. Rather, it was a search for a tolerable expedient that resulted in attention to criminal justice. The best that can be said for the USA and the Security Council was that evident unease at the absence of moral and legal consistency across roughly similar cases produced at least some action on the question of prosecution for atrocities via ethnic/tribal slaughter in Rwanda.

As was true for the ICTY, so for the ICTR, it fell to the prosecutor's office, supporting NGOs, and a few concerned states to turn a venture based on guilt and public relations into something more substantive. The prosecutor's position proved problematic. The initial shared prosecutor showed more interest in former Yugoslavia than in Rwanda, and a later prosecutor, del Ponte, developed major frictions with the Rwanda government (Tutsi controlled) that had triumphed in the fighting of 1994. So eventually a separate prosecutor was established for the ICTR in 2003.

The court has been hamstrung by petty corruption, mismanagement, lack of adequate support, and not so veiled hostility on the part of more than one Rwandan.[31] Despite all this, by fall of 2004 the Court had rendered 17 final judgments involving 23 persons.[32] Several high officials had been convicted, including a prime minister and a mayor. The ICTR produced the first conviction for genocide ever recorded in a proper court of law. This was the Akayesu case, in which, in the view of the trial chamber, the major of the Taba Commune "had reason to know and in fact knew that sexual violence was taking place ... and that women were being taken away ... and sexually violated."[33] In this same judgment, rape of women was seen as part of genocide and crimes against humanity.

Ironically, high Hutu officials convicted of genocide and/or crimes against humanity in the ICTR received only a maximum sentence of life imprisonment, whereas lower Hutu officials or citizens convicted in

---

[31] For a brief summary see Paul Lewis, "UN Report Comes Down Hard on Rwandan Genocide Tribunal," *New York Times*, February 13, 1997, A9.

[32] Even early on, those so inclined had made a positive assessment of the ICTR. See Payam Akhavan, "Justice and Reconciliation in the Great Lakes Region of Africa: The Contribution of the International Criminal Tribunal for Rwanda," *Duke Journal of Comparative & International Law*, 7 (1997), 325–348.

[33] Prosecutor v. Akayesu, Judgment, Case No. 96-4-T (September 2, 1998).

Rwanda national courts– mostly staffed by Tutsi – could receive the death penalty (after being held in squalid conditions, and convicted in a proceeding lacking full due process).

Beyond punishment of individuals and development of legal concepts, the ICTR merits further discussion. First, it was highly unlikely that an international tribunal prosecuting Hutus during a time of Tutsi control of Rwanda could interject a decisive break in the cycle of ethnic violence that had long characterized that country. True, Hutus had planned, organized, and executed the wave of killing in 1994. But consider the parallels with former Yugoslavia. By most accounts, Serbs had committed the greatest number of atrocities during 1992–1995, even though Croats and Bosnian Muslims did not have clean hands. And Serbs had certainly persecuted ethnic Albanians in Kosovo. But when the prosecutor brought indictments mostly against Serbs, many in this latter ethnic group claimed bias by the ICTY.[34] Thus the pattern of indictments and convictions did little to break down group allegiance and group hostility. In similar fashion, it was unlikely that many Rwandan Hutus would be led to re-evaluate their prejudices by trials focusing only on Hutus, especially when earlier waves of Tutsi violence had not been met with international prosecution.[35] So one might punish leading Hutu criminals, but using the tribunal to break the cycle of ethnic violence was a tougher nut to crack. It was fairly clear, unfortunately, that the ICTR had not contributed to regional stability.

Second, during the life of the ICTR, ethnic violence continued on a large scale in the Great Lakes region of Africa with only relative decline compared with 1994. There was mounting evidence that Tutsis had massacred Hutus in eastern Zaire during the struggle for control of that country. That is precisely why the late President Kabila in the new Congo, who owed his position to Tutsi support, among other factors, consistently tried to block a United Nations investigation into the reported massacre. Tutsi and Hutu continued to fight in both the Democratic Republic of the Congo and Burundi, as well as in Rwanda. Murder and torture continued to be practiced by both sides. Could one realistically expect one international court, with a lack of respect and support from either ethnic group, to make any great difference in the evolution of events?

So for both the ICTY and the ICTR, punishment and legal development were one thing; personal closure and reconciliation were something else. By late 2004, the ICTR, operating on an annual budget of about

---

[34] For a critique of the pattern of indictments by the office of the independent prosecutor, see Cedric Thornberry, "Saving the War Crimes Tribunal," *Foreign Policy*, 104 (Fall 1996), 72–86.

[35] See further Leo J. DeSouza, "Assigning Blame in Rwanda," *Washington Monthly*, 29, 9 (September 1997), 40–43.

$235 million, has been asked to close up shop by 2008, excepting appeals. Like the ICTY, the ICTR made some contribution to the new ICC.

The International Criminal Court

On July 17 1998 a Diplomatic Conference meeting in Rome, relying heavily on the experience of the ICTY and ICTR, approved the statute of a permanent criminal court to be loosely associated with the United Nations. The statute consists of 128 articles and is longer than the UN Charter.[36] Subject matter jurisdiction covers genocide, crimes against humanity, war crimes – and aggression (crimes against peace) when international law presents a sufficiently precise definition, which was not the case in July 1998. Judges are elected by the states that are parties to the statute; these judges sit in their individual capacity and not as state representatives. An independent prosecutor is attached to the court. The final vote was 120 in favor, 7 opposed (the USA, Israel, China, Iraq, Sudan, Yemen, Libya), and the rest abstaining.

The court operates, as of July 1, 2002, sixty ratifications being obtained, on the basis of complementarity. This means that the court does not function unless a state in question is unable or unwilling to investigate and, if warranted, prosecute for one of the covered crimes. Thus, whereas the ICTY and ICTR had primary jurisdiction and could supersede state action, the ICC only has complementary jurisdiction. It is a backup system, designed to encourage states to exercise their primary jurisdiction and authority in responsible ways. The prosecutor can go forward with a case if the state where the crime has been committed is a party to the statute, or is the state of the defendant. But the prosecutor must obtain approval of a pre-trial chamber of the court, whose decision to approve prosecution is subject to appeal to another chamber. This is designed to prevent political or other improper action by the prosecutor, who is also elected by state parties to the statute. The UN Security Council can also refer cases to the court, or can delay proceedings for up to a year, renewable. This latter provision is to allow for diplomacy to trump prosecution – to allow pragmatic liberalism to trump criminal justice.

In the final analysis the ICC court was the product of a group of "like-minded" states, led periodically by Canada, and a swarm of NGOs. They, as in Ottawa a year earlier with regard to a treaty banning anti-personnel landmines, decided to move ahead despite belated but clear opposition from the USA. Ironically, part of the momentum for a standing criminal court had come from the latter. But in Rome the USA made very clear

[36] This section draws on my editorial comment in *The Netherlands Quarterly of Human Rights*, 16, 3 (September 1998), 259–260.

that it did not intend to have its nationals appear before the tribunal. According to Scheffer, Ambassador at Large for War Crimes Issues:

"There is a reality, and the reality is that the United States is a global military power and presence. Other countries are not. We are. Our military forces are often called upon to engage overseas in conflict situations, for purposes of humanitarian intervention, to rescue hostages, to bring out American citizens from threatening environments, to deal with terrorists. We have to be extremely careful that this proposal [for a standing court] does not limit the capacity of our armed forces to legitimately operate internationally. We have to be careful that it does not open up opportunities for endless frivolous complaints to be lodged against the United States as a global military power."[37]

This was largely a smokescreen argument. The rule of complementarity meant that if US personnel should be charged with international crime, a proper investigation by the USA and, if warranted, prosecution would keep the new court from functioning. A prosecutor who wanted to bring charges against the USA would need to secure approval from the pre-trial chamber, whose approval could be appealed to a different chamber. By simple majority vote, the UN Security Council could delay proceedings, renewable, against the USA. Yet the Clinton Administration was unyielding in opposition. This was largely in deference to the Pentagon, and to the ultra-nationalists in the Congress. Senator Jesse Helms, the Chair of the Senate Foreign Relations Committee, declared the treaty dead on arrival should it ever be submitted to the Senate.

For a country that saw itself as a leader for human rights, and that had led the effort to create two *ad hoc* criminal tribunals with jurisdiction over others, its posture at Rome was not a policy designed to appeal to the rest of the world. The double standards were too evident. (The French did successfully insist on a seven-year grace period for war crimes proceedings against adhering states, apparently to give it some wiggle room in the event of investigations into its African policies.)[38]

The George W. Bush Administration "unsigned" the Clinton signature on the Rome statute, sought through bilateral diplomacy to persuade or coerce other states into exempting US personnel from the coverage of the ICC, delayed UN peacekeeping deployments until the Security Council exempted any participating US personnel from any review by the

---

[37] *New York Times*, August 13, 1997, A8.
[38] The British, in breaking with the USA over this issue, issued the following statement: "we and other major NATO allies are satisfied that the safeguards that are built in to the International Criminal Court will protect our servicemen against malicious or politically motivated prosecution." British Information Services, Press Release 214/98, July 20, 1998.

ICC, and in almost every way imaginable tried to undermine the ICC. In 2005, however, the USA abstained on a UN Security Council resolution that authorized the ICC prosecutor to open investigations about possibly indicting certain Sudanese leaders for atrocities in the Darfur region of that country.

For its part the Congress passed the so-called American Service Members Protection Act, which among other provisions authorized in advance US military action to free any US national detained abroad in connection to ICC proceedings. President George W. Bush signed it, despite considerable foreign criticism.

The real reasons for such a US assault on the ICC were not hard to discern. After the September 11, 2001 attacks on New York and Washington by Al-Qaeda, high US officials authorized the abuse of certain enemy detainees held under US authority at various places.[39] Some of this coercive interrogation violated not only international humanitarian law but also the UN Convention against Torture. Hence behind the rhetoric about rogue prosecutors and politicized trials lay the reality that Washington officials might choose realist policies resulting in torture and/or degrading treatment of prisoners and other violations of human rights and humanitarian norms. Some of these actions would almost assuredly result in serious violations of these international norms and so constitute war crimes if not crimes against humanity. (Systematic torture of civilians might qualify as a crime against humanity.) It was also reasonably clear that during time of war, real or metaphorical, the US Congress would not exercise close oversight of Presidential claims to be acting properly in the name of national security. US courts would likely prove slow to get involved. Thus it might well be the case that the USA would prove unwilling or unable to seriously investigate charges of wrong doing and if necessary prosecute under the Rome statute. This was indeed the factual situation between early 2002 and late 2005 with regard to high level authorization of abuse of enemy prisoners in the "war on terrorism." Such a situation could logically lead a responsible prosecutor for the ICC to consider serious war crimes proceedings against a US official under the principle of complementarity.

It was for this same reason that Israel voted against the Rome Statute and refused to ratify or accede to it. It had used coercive interrogation against Palestinian and other detainees, which violated international

---

[39] See further David P. Forsythe, *The Humanitarians: The International Committee of the Red Cross* (Cambridge: Cambridge University Press, 2005); Mark Danner, *Torture and Truth: American, Abu Ghraib, and the War on Terror* (New York: New York Review of Books, Inc., 2003); Seymour Hersh, *Chain of Command: The Road from 9/11 to Abu Ghraib* (New York: Harper Collins, 2004).

humanitarian and human rights law.[40] Interestingly, other democracies like Britain and France, which had used coercive interrogation in the past in places like Algeria, Cyprus, Aden, and Northern Ireland,[41] voted for the Rome Statute and ratified it. So did Canada and Italy, whose troops had misbehaved in Somalia in the early 1990s.

Stripped of misleading rhetoric, Washington's position toward the ICC was that international relations was still a dangerous game meriting realist rather than liberal policies. To protect the security of the USA, Washington might have to authorize torture, degrading treatment, and other policies that violated international human rights and humanitarian law. Rather than being brutally truthful about its perception of the need to play dirty in a dangerous world, Washington preferred to talk about rogue prosecutors and politicized trials. What it really wanted was international criminal justice for Slobodan Milosevic but not for Donald Rumsfeld.[42] In Washington's eyes, Milosevic had engaged in ethnic cleansing and worse, while Rumsfeld was defending US security and advancing freedom in the world.[43]

The USA being firmly opposed to international juridical review of its policies, the election of the first ICC prosecutor, the respected Argentine lawyer Luis Moreno-Ocampo, who had taught in the law schools at Harvard and Stanford, and who had been active in the restoration of liberal democracy in his native country, did not mollify US opposition to the ICC. His careful selection of initial ICC cases dealing with the Democratic Republic of the Congo and Uganda also did not change Washington's view of the ICC. As long as ICC cases were not referred to that Court solely through the UN Security Council, where the US veto applied, the USA was adamantly opposed to international criminal justice that might apply to the USA. Washington insisted on a double standard

---

[40] Forsythe, ibid.

[41] See Kirsten Sellars, *The Rise and Rise of Human Rights* (Phoenix Mill, UK: Sutton Publishing, 2002).

[42] Secretary of Defense Rumsfeld had authorized abusive treatment of certain prisoners at Guantanamo and perhaps in Afghanistan and Iraq. There are two schools of thought about all this in the US security community. The first is that coercive interrogation, principally based on sensory deprivation, can produce useful information. The second is that abuse is only guaranteed to produce pain, not reliable information, since a person under duress will say anything to stop the pain. It is not clear which school of thought is correct. Parts of the US security community are opposed to torture, and parts are not. See Forsythe, *The Humanitarians*.

[43] Mixed in with Washington's realist calculations was American exceptionalism, a version of romantic or chauvinistic nationalism, that saw the USA as a shining city on a hill. American exceptionalism also rejected muscular multilateralism in which US independence would be restricted by an international court. See further David P. Forsythe, "The US and International Criminal Justice," *Human Rights Quarterly*, 24, 4 (Fall, 2002), 974–991.

that exempted itself from such review. Of course what the USA wanted would also exempt any other permanent member of the Security Council, such as Russia and China, from ICC review as well. Washington was prepared to pay this price for restricted criminal justice, as were some others,[44] as the compromise appropriate to Great Power politics in international relations. But other states continued to support the ICC and especially its prosecutor.

The future of the ICC was very much in question, principally because of active and intense opposition by the USA, but also opposition from China, Russia, India, and certain other important states. In 2005 it was not at all clear why the USA indirectly approved of some role for the ICC in relation to the Sudan, or whether this one situation meant that the USA, even under ultra-nationalist leadership, might tolerate a general and growing role of the ICC as long as US nationals were exempted from the court's purview.

Hybrid courts

After atrocities in Kosovo, East Timor, Sierra Leone, and Cambodia, courts were created that might be called special, hybrid, or transnational.[45] In Kosovo in 1999, the UN field mission (UNMIK), operating under Security Council resolutions, created a hybrid court with local and international judges, applying a mixture of local and international law. The focus was mostly war crimes. Particularly the Serb population preferred this court to any court that would be dominated by the local majority of ethnic Albanians. The respect earned by this court was impressive in the context of continuing Serb–Albanian frictions. But the jurisprudence of this hybrid court did not mesh well with the ICTY, since the former did not use the cases of the latter as precedent.

In East Timor in 2000, the UN field mission there (UNTAET), again under UN Security Council mandate, created another hybrid court since the local legal infrastructure was non-existent. Panels of three judges contained two international and one local judge. The focus was on serious violations of international humanitarian law. A rather large number of indictments by the special prosecutor did not lead to rapid trials, as both neighboring Indonesia and the new authorities in East Timor showed considerable hesitance about cooperating on criminal justice

---

[44] Eric Posner, law professor at the University of Chicago, argued that double standards and exemptions for the USA were appropriate in International Relations. "All Justice, Too, Is Local," *New York Times*, December 30, 2004, A23.

[45] For futher information, with the exception of Cambodia, see Laura A. Dickinson, "The Promise of Hybrid Courts," *American Journal of International Law*, 97, 2 (April 2003), 295–310.

matters. Indonesian authorities had much to hide about their brutal attempt to hang on to East Timor, while the new authorities in the latter were wary of antagonizing their powerful neighbour. From the latter's view, criminal justice might interfere with building a stable, rights protective state respected by Indonesia. When an Indonesian commander (General Wiranto) was indicted, East Timor said it would not cooperate in the case.

In Sierra Leone in 2002, the government that emerged from a brutal internal armed conflict signed an agreement with the United Nations to create a special criminal court. Local authorities wanted some hand in trials, but not total responsibility. This court operates outside of, and has legal primacy over, local courts. Again, there are two international judges and one local judge in each case, and they use a mixture of local and international law. Indictments have been issued against pro-government individuals as well as against rebel commanders. Among those indicted was Charles Taylor, the former President of neighboring Liberia, but at the time of writing he had been given asylum and immunity in Nigeria. From Nigeria's view, this was the price for getting him out of Liberia and reducing the fighting and atrocities there. Among rulings of this special court was a judgment that the recruitment of child soldiers constituted a war crime. In Sierra Leone there was also a truth commission to establish past facts, completely apart from considerations of criminal justice.[46]

Finally in this brief review, long and tortuous negotiations finally in 2004 produced a special criminal court in Cambodia, long after the agrarian communists known as the Khmers Rouges had killed about two million persons during 1975–1979. The government of Hun Sen, who himself had been a low level member of the Khmers Rouges, was ambivalent about criminal justice, but finally agreed to panels entailing two local and one international judge. This arrangement, against the background of a very weak local judicial system, prompted criticism by international human rights advocacy groups, as well as from the UN Secretary General. But certain circles of opinion thought that imperfect legal justice was better than no legal justice, particularly since the senior Khmers Rouges leadership was rapidly dying off.

One reason for having the ICC is to reduce the "transaction costs" so evident in the creation of the two UN ad hoc courts and these hybrid courts. It takes much time to negotiate the composition, jurisdiction, authority, and rules of the court – and sometimes the details of the additional prosecutor's office. Moreover, these hybrid courts do not produce

[46] See further William A Schabas, "The Relationship Between Truth Commissions and International Courts: The Case of Sierra Leone," *Human Rights Quarterly*, 25, 4 (November 2003), 1035–1066.

a uniform jurisprudence, as their rules of procedure and substantive judgments do not always follow similar tracks.

National courts

It should not be forgotten that most international law, to the extent that it is adjudicated at all, is treated in national courts. That being so, it is impossible here to review over 190 national legal systems and their treatment of major violations of international human rights and humanitarian law. Two points began to deal with the tip of this large iceberg.

First, after atrocities, particularly during and after war, real or metaphorical, it is often difficult for national courts to provide independent and impartial due process, leading to substantive judgments widely regarded as legitimate forms of criminal justice. After the fall of communism in Poland, for example, the subsequent trial of General Jaruzelski turned into a comical show trial, with numerous irregularities. At one point in his trial the presiding official said that "The hearings will continue, and the accusations will be formulated later."[47] Victor's justice is often easy to identify.

Against this background, the new criminal court created by the Interim Government in Iraq after the fall of the Saddam Hussein regime raised questions about proper criminal justice. Given the political instability of that situation after the US-led invasion and occupation, the newness and transitory nature of the ruling authorities, the weakness of the embryonic Iraqi judicial system – if there was a real system, the lack of due process already evident in the interrogation of defendants, and so on, it was hardly surprising that the UN Secretary-General and many international human rights advocacy groups were critical of the process. Even the 2004 announcement of the planned start of trials for leading Hussein lieutenants seemed more like a pre-election ploy designed to secure Iraqi Shia support for the Interim Government (but much Iraqi

---

[47] Tina Rosenberg, *The Haunted Land: Facing Europe's Ghosts After Communism* (New York: Vintage Books, 1996), 254. She argues that criminal trials were inappropriate for the violations of human rights committed under European communism. In passing she suggests that trials were more appropriate in Latin America for human rights violations under military regimes. But it was precisely in Latin America that the military remained strong, and a threat to democracy, after the end of formal military rule. See also David Pion-Berlin, "To Prosecute or Pardon: Human Rights Decisions in the Latin American Southern Cone," *Human Rights Quarterly*, 15, 1 (Winter 1993), 105–130, who tries to explain different policies in Argentina, Chile, and Uruguay regarding investigations and trials for human rights violations. See further the special issue "Accountability for International Crime and Serious Violations of Fundamental Human Rights," *Law and Contemporary Problems*, 59, 4 (Autumn 1996). Most of the authors are lawyers who predictably endorse legal proceedings and oppose impunity. But see the articles by Stephan Landsman, Naomi Roht-Arriaza, and Neil J. Kritz.

Sunni disaffection) than a non-partisan and independent legal step. Yet the USA, highly influential in such matters, was so opposed to the ICC and many international forms of criminal justice that it and its Iraqi allies pushed ahead with national legal measures that were sure to remain controversial. In Iraq it might have been better to proceed with a hybrid court, with some international judges and international standards of due process, in order to enhance independence, impartiality, and ultimately legitimacy.

Moreover, often remnants of the previous regime remain powerful for a time, as in Chile or Argentina, blocking serious national criminal justice based on due process.

Second, the principle of universal jurisdiction has had something of a renaissance, stimulated by the Pinochet case. But states like Britain and Belgium found the subject perplexing.

The concept of universal jurisdiction attaches to certain crimes like torture, genocide, and crimes against humanity – and also to serious violations of the Geneva Conventions of August 12, 1949 pertaining to victims of war.[48] Thus the principle of universal jurisdiction permits national authorities to pursue foreign as well as domestic suspects. Certain crimes are seen as so heinous that prosecution is allowed regardless of the place of the crime or the nationality of the defendant. In general, however, states remain reluctant to exercise extensive universal jurisdiction. They remain reluctant to open Pandora's box by establishing themselves as a global judge that would complicate relations with other states by legally judging their citizens.

In 1998, Spanish legal authorities presented British authorities with a request to extradite the visiting former Chilean dictator to Spain, to stand trial for genocide, terrorism, and torture. Britain arrested Pinochet, and in complicated and confusing rulings finally decided that the former head of state was indeed extradictable, since Britain had ratified, and incorporated into British law, the UN Torture Convention. This treaty recognized that universal jurisdiction was appropriate in the case of charges of torture.

While the British ruling technically was a matter of interpreting British law, it held among other things that Pinochet's status as former head of state offered him no immunity from Spanish charges. Indeed, Slobodan Milosevic had been indicted by the prosecutor of the ICTY while he was a sitting high Serbian official. And Charles Taylor had been indicted by

---

[48] Darren Hawkins, "Universal Jurisdiction for Human Rights: From Legal Principle to Limited Reality," *Global Governance*, 9, 3 (July–Sept., 2003), 347–366. And Stephen Macedo, ed., *Universal Jurisdiction: National Courts and the Prosecution of Serious Crimes under International Law* (Philadelphia: University of Pennsylvania Press, 2004).

the special court in Sierra Leone despite his being a high former official of Liberia. Moreover, the British ruling made clear that it made no difference that the victims of Pinochet's alleged abuses were Spanish or otherwise. For heinous crimes like torture, the nationality of the victims or the defendant is not a relevant factor.

It is true that under intense pressure from former Prime Minister Margaret Thatcher and other British arch conservatives, who were admirers of the staunch anti-communist Pinochet, British executive authorities released Pinochet to Chile on grounds of alleged poor health. Thus he was in fact not extradicted to Spain to face charges. But the importance of the Pinochet ruling was that he legally could have been extradicted to Spain, that as a legal matter claims to sovereign immunity did not trump valid attention to gross violations of human rights, and that other high officials in other situations might indeed have to face accountability for deeds done in office. There were other ripple effects from the British ruling in Chile, Argentina, and other places.[49]

As for Belgium, in 1993 its parliament passed a broad law opening the door to many suits in Belgian courts based on universal jurisdiction.[50] While the legislative history of this Belgian statute showed an intent to allow cases in Belgium stemming originally from Rwanda, very quickly enterprising lawyers filed cases against a variety of public officials including Ariel Sharon of Israel, Yasir Arafat of the Palestinian authority, George H. W. Bush of the USA, and so on. The Belgian executive was certainly not happy about that country being involved in so many controversial matters, and so successfully worked for a much narrower statute requiring some Belgian connection to charges. The USA brought heavy pressure on Belgium, including discussing the relocation of NATO headquarters from Brussels, to alter the broad assertion of Belgian judicial authority.

In both the British and Belgian examples above, it is clear that many executive branch officials are highly reluctant to see criminal justice proceedings interfere with good relations with other states. And the activation of the principle of universal jurisdiction, by an investigative judge like Baltasar Garzon of Spain, can certainly generate frictions that many national authorities, especially in Foreign Offices, would prefer to avoid. Noting this situation is not an argument for amnesty, immunity, or tolerance for

[49] Stacie Jonas, "The Ripple Effect of the Pinochet Case," *Human Rights Brief*, 36–38. See also Richard Falk, "Assessing the Pinochet Litigation," in Macedo, *Universal Jurisdiction*, 97–120. At the time of writing, Spanish courts were trying an Argentine for acts in the Dirty War carried out by the Argentine Junta against a variety of victims in that country. Finding the defendant within Spain, Spanish legal authorities moved against him in an exercise of universal jurisdiction.

[50] Richard Bernstein, "Belgium Rethinks Its Prosecutorial Zeal," *New York Times*, April 1, 2003, A8.

heinous crimes like torture, genocide, crimes against humanity, or major breaches of international humanitarian law. It is only to note that political difficulties often arise in exercising universal jurisdiction in contemporary international relations.

Other aspects of national proceedings in the wake of atrocities certainly exist, and the matter of US treatment of enemy prisoners taken in its "war on terrorism" is addressed in the chapter below on foreign policy.

Alternatives to criminal justice

A large number of human rights activists, like Aryeh Neier, argue for consistent implementation of criminal justice and decry any amnesty or immunity offered to those who have committed atrocities.[51] But our discussion above of criminal justice in places like Bosnia, Somalia, Rwanda, Sierra Leone, Poland, Iraq, etc. has already suggested that criminal justice might interfere with, or fail to make a contribution to, other desirable goals such as peace, stability, reconciliation, consolidation of liberal democracy, or full closure for affected individuals.

Criminal justice is not the only way to advance human rights, and the human rights discourse is not the only way to advance human dignity in international relations. Well considered diplomatic/political steps also have their role to play in advancing a liberal international order beneficial to individuals.[52]

No less than Nelson Mandela, supported by others with impeccable liberal and human rights credentials like Bishop Desmond Tutu, thought that in the Republic of South Africa after the apartheid era, the best way to build a multi-racial rights-protective society there was to avoid criminal justice as much as possible. They opted for a truth and reconciliation commission with apologies and reparations as the preferred course of action. If those responsible for political violence, on both the government and rebel sides, would acknowledge what they had done and express remorse, trials would be avoided and reparations paid to victims or their families. After all, trials focus on the past and often stir up animosities. Complicated rules of evidence can sometimes make it difficult to get the truth out in a clear and simple way. Truth commissions may be better than courts at getting to the "macro-truth" – the big social and political

---

51 Aryeh Neier, "The New Double Standard," *Foreign Policy*, 105 (Winter 1996–1997), 91–101. See further Aryeh Neier's book extolling the virtues of criminal justice: *War Crimes: Brutality, Genocide, Terror, and the Struggle for Justice* (New York: Times Books, 1998).

52 See further Jeffrey E. Garten, "Comment: The Need for Pragmatism," *Foreign Policy*, 105 (Winter 1996–1997), 103–106. This is a rebuttal to the Neier argument for consistent implementation of criminal justice.

picture of why atrocities took place.[53] Since criminal courts focus on individual responsibility for particular acts, the larger context with its group responsibility may escape examination in judicial proceedings and remain in place to impede "social repair."[54]

Certainly the relatives of some victims of white minority rule in South Africa are not happy that the perpetrators of foul deeds have gone unpunished. A full accounting of the pluses and minuses of the South African T&R Commission is still in progress. But the South African model for dealing with transitional justice, which downplays criminal justice, is an interesting one – especially since the new South Africa features all-race elections and the protection of many human rights.[55]

In other places like El Salvador after protracted civil war, again trials were avoided. Leading suspects in criminal behaviour were eased out of public office and sometimes eased out of the country altogether. Two commissions made their reports. In this case, as in some other cases like Chile and Argentina, the continuing power of the supporters of the old regime made full and fair criminal justice exceedingly difficult in the short run. El Salvador is another country that has made progress toward stable liberal democracy without a prominent role for criminal justice after atrocities.[56] Still other countries like Spain and Portugal moved from dictatorships to stable liberal democracy without either criminal trials for past political behaviour or even truth commissions. But not all countries can be like Spain and Portugal and join regional organizations like the Council of Europe and the European Union that strongly insist on liberal democracy in member states.

---

[53] See Audrey R. Chapman and Patrick Ball, "The Truth of Truth Commissions: Comparative Lessons from Haiti, South Africa, and Guatemala," *Human Rights Quarterly*, 23, 1 (February 2001), 1–43.

[54] Laurel E. Fletcher and Harvey M. Weinstein, "Violence and Social Repair: Rethinking the Contribution of Justice to Reconciliation," *Human Rights Quarterly*, 24, 3 (August 2002), 573–639.

[55] Priscilla B. Hayner, *Unspeakable Truths: Facing the Challenge of Truth Commissions* (New York: Routledge, 2002). She places the South African experience in the context of some 20 other truth commissions dealing with human rights, concluding that there is no one way to create a model truth commission. She also deals with the relationship between such commissions and criminal justice. See further the substantive book review of the Hayner volume by Juan E. Mendez and Javier Mariezcurrena in *Human Rights Quarterly*, 25, 1 (February 2003), 237–256.

[56] We note in passing that not all relatives of victims were satisfied with the absence of criminal justice related to the past civil war. Some Salvadorans have pursued legal action in US courts under provisions allowing civil suits for aliens claiming violation of international law. Under the US 1879 Alien Tort Statute, these Salvadorans sought monetary compensation from former Salvadoran security officials now residing in the USA. So while avoidance of public criminal justice was part of the political deal to end fighting and atrocities in El Salvador, some civil litigation went forward in US courts. For a journalistic summary, see David Gonzalez, "Victim Links Retired General to Torture in El Salvador War," *New York Times*, June 25, 2002.

What is now the Czech Republic implemented a policy of barring former high communist officials from public office after the fall of communism in that country. Yet controversy and hard feelings were still evident in 2005. A former judge in the communist era, not a party member but one who had supported the old regime with repressive rulings, was elevated to the Constitutional Court, as confirmed by the democratic Senate. This provoked outrage on the part of some, but not on the part of others who felt the democratic state needed experienced judges.[57]

Through an act of Congress, the USA apologized for, and paid reparations for, the internment of Japanese-Americans during World War II. Since that time there has been considerable debate in the USA over an apology and reparations to African-Americans for slavery and racial discrimination in that country.[58]

Democracy was at least encouraged in Haiti by offering the high officials of the Cedras regime a pleasant amnesty abroad, a diplomatic move by the USA and others that managed to restore an elected President Aristide there without major bloodshed. Likewise, George W. Bush offered Saddam Hussein safe passage out of Iraq in 2003. In this latter case, more than 2,000 American lives, and no doubt tens of thousands of Iraqi lives, along with much injury and destruction, would have been saved had Saddam accepted the offer of asylum. True, criminal trials would not have been held for him and his equally despicable colleagues. But what price to human life and dignity will those trials eventually entail? Avoiding war is also a liberal value.

In Uganda, the government sought the aid of the International Criminal Court in order to prosecute leaders of the vicious rebel movement known as The Lord's Resistance Army. Yet a number of traditional Ugandans preferred traditional rituals emphasizing forgiveness, rather than criminal prosecution.[59]

Conclusion

Suffice it to say that transitional justice can take, and has taken, many forms. None are perfect. All are controversial in that they entail pluses and minuses.

---

[57] Matt Reynolds, "A Top Judicial Posting Stirs Anger in Prague," *International Herald Tribune*, August 22, 2005.

[58] See further Mark Gibney and Erik Roxstrom, "The Status of State Apologies," *Human Rights Quarterly*, 23, 4 (November 2001), 911–939. And Max du Plessis, "Historical Injustice and International Law: An Exploratory Discussion of Reparation for Slavery," *Human Rights Quarterly*, 25, 3 (August 2003), 624–659.

[59] Mark Lacey, "Victims of Uganda Atrocities Follow a Path of Forgiveness," *New York Times*, April 18, 2005, A1.

Pursuit of an effective rule of law in international relations is a noble quest. But criminal justice in relation to international events is no simple matter. A morally pure and consistent approach to the subject advocated by the distinguished human rights activist Aryeh Neier is inadequate for both policy making and general understanding. Judicial romanticism is not an adequate policy; it is a moral posture. As such, it is widely endorsed by many private lawyers and human rights activists, but evaluated more carefully by most diplomats.

There are ways of doing good for individuals, and maybe even advancing certain human rights over time, through delaying or bypassing criminal justice. As noted in chapter 1, litigation is only one human rights strategy. The liberal West did not try to shun or isolate Stalin for his various crimes, but actively supported him during World War II in order to defeat fascism. The liberal West brought a great reduction in violence to the former Yugoslavia by giving a temporary *de facto* immunity from prosecution to Slobodan Milosevic.[60] The liberal West supported legal impunity in South Africa, El Salvador and the Czech Republic and many other places with adequate if not perfect results. One does not always advance human welfare and human rights by criminalizing behavior, as the attempted arrest of General Aideed in Somalia shows. There is much to be said for pragmatic liberalism at times as one approach to international human rights, however morally mixed the outcome.[61]

The process of making complicated contextual analyses leads to competing judgments because of the inability of the legal and policy sciences, or of policy makers, to accurately predict the future. Will provisions on criminal justice impede peacemaking? Can suspects be arrested without undermining the limited peace already achieved? Will court judgments against gross violators of human rights really have any major impact concerning ongoing patterns of violence or future atrocities? Would more good be achieved, with less bad, via truth commissions rather than criminal proceedings? These are important questions, to which no one's crystal ball has adequate answers.

Discussion questions

– Did the Nuremberg and Tokyo trials make a positive contribution to the evolution of human rights in international relations, despite their

---

[60] The question can fairly be raised, however, of whether NATO would have bombed Yugoslavia in 1999 over Kosovo, had Milosevic been indicted and arrested for his role in Bosnia. Then again, would NATO have had to fight in Bosnia, if Milosevic had not cooperated in producing the Dayton peace agreement?

[61] See further Mahmood Monshipouri and Claude E. Welch, "The Search for International Human Rights and Justice: Coming to Terms with the New Global Realities," *Human Rights Quarterly*, 23, 2 (May 2001), 370–401.

procedural and substantive errors, not to mention their use of the death penalty?
- Was the indictment and perhaps arrest of certain persons in the Balkans during 1992–1999 an impediment to peace, or compatible with peace? Would the indictment and perhaps arrest of Saddam Hussein in Iraq after his invasion of Kuwait have been an impediment to peace, or compatible with peace?
- What explains the US opposition to the 1998 statute of the projected International Criminal Court, when US democratic allies like Britain, Italy, Canada, France, etc. all voted to approve the statute?
- What impact, if any, has the International Criminal Tribunal for Rwanda made on the politics of the Great Lakes region of Africa?
- In South Africa after apartheid and El Salvador after civil war, among other places, there was considerable national reconciliation, and more liberal democracy, at least relatively speaking, while avoiding criminal prosecution for most political acts of the past. Is this a useful model for the future?
- What are the advantages and disadvantages of truth commissions as compared with judicial proceedings, concerning past gross violations of human rights?

Suggestions for further reading

Bass, Gary Jonathan, *Stay The Hand of Vengeance: The Politics of War Crimes Tribunals* (Princeton: Princeton University Press, 2000). An excellent historical overview of the political decisions preceding the establishment of, or in some cases the failure to establish, international criminal courts.

Garten, Jeffrey, "Comment: The Need for Pragmatism," *Foreign Policy*, 105 (Winter 1996–1997), 103–106. Criticizes consistent emphasis on legal punishment in international relations; emphasizes other ways of doing good for persons and improving the environment for human rights besides judicial action.

Goldhagen, Daniel J., *Hitler's Willing Executioners: Germany and the Holocaust* (New York: Knopf, 1996). Controversial bestseller about responsibility for the Holocaust in Nazi Germany. Chastises dominant strains in the German nation, not just the Nazi leadership. Implies that holding the Nazi leadership criminally responsible at the Nuremberg trial did not address properly the responsibility of the German people.

Goldstein, Joseph, et al., eds., *The My Lai Massacre and Its Cover-Up: Beyond the Reach of Law?* (New York: The Free Press, 1976). Excellent collection about an American military unit that committed a massacre in Vietnam, but whose members never were subjected to appropriate punishment because of the Pentagon's maneuvering and nationalist American public opinion.

Holbrooke, Richard, *To End A War* (New York: Random House, 1998). By the principal mediator at Dayton on dealing with Milosevic to end the war in

Bosnia. Holbrooke was also influential in the West's dealing with Kosovo four years later. Upon his nomination to be US Ambassador at the United Nations, at his Senate confirmation hearings Holbrooke said his job in 1995 was to end the war, not pass judgment on various leaders.

Minow, Martha, *Between Vengeance and Forgiveness: Facing History After Genocide and Mass Violence* (Boston: Beacon Press, 1998). Careful reflection about whether there is any particular policy response that is always appropriate after atrocities, suggesting that debates over peace v. justice and reconciliation v. punishment have to be resolved case by case.

Neier, Aryeh, *War Crimes: Brutality, Genocide, Terror, and the Struggle for Justice* (New York: Times Books, 1998). Passionate but one-sided advocacy for criminal justice in all situations.

"The New Double Standard," *Foreign Policy*, 105 (Winter 1996–1997), 91–101. A short form of the preceding book.

Ratner, Steven R., and Jason S. Abrams, *Accountability for Human Rights Atrocities in International Law: Beyond the Nuremberg Legacy* (Oxford: Clarendon Press, 1997; 2nd ed. 2001). An overview of legal developments about international criminal justice in contemporary times.

Rosenberg, Tina, *The Haunted Land: Facing Europe's Ghosts After Communism* (New York: Vintage Books, 1996). A journalist gives a fascinating account of her travels and interviews on the subject of how to respond to communist violations of human rights in Europe after 1991, but her conclusions based on quick comparisons with Latin America are not fully persuasive.

Scheffer, David, "International Judicial Intervention," *Foreign Policy*, 102 (Spring 1996). Later a State Department official, Scheffer argues for criminal justice, but suggests in passing that there are some situations in which national peace and reconciliation may hinge on bypassing it.

Visscher, Charles de, *Theory and Reality in Public International Law* (Princeton: Princeton University Press, 1957). Classic treatment of, among other subjects, peace v. justice in international relations.

5   Regional application of human rights norms

The world may be a smaller place in the light of improving communication and travel technology, but it is still a large planet when it comes to effective international governance. Given the approximately 6 billion persons and the 190 states or so that existed at the turn of the twenty-first century, and given the weakness of global organizations like the United Nations, it was both logical and sometimes politically feasible to look to regional organizations for the advancement of human rights. This chapter will show that regional developments for human rights have been truly remarkable in Europe, decidedly ambiguous in the Western Hemisphere, embryonic in Africa, and otherwise weak. The key to the effective regional protection of human rights is not legal drafting, but underlying political culture, political will, and political acumen. In Europe where there are considerable cases and other regional human rights decisions to analyze, I provide a summary analysis. In the Western Hemisphere in the absence of substantial case law and other important regional decisions, I provide mostly political analysis of underlying conditions. I treat Africa briefly because of lack of impact through regional arrangements.

Europe

After World War II, significant US foreign aid to Europe in the form of the Marshall Plan encouraged regional cooperation, especially of an economic nature. Most West European elites endorsed this approach at least to some degree, both in pursuit of economic recovery and to defend traditional western values in the face of Soviet-led communism. The result was the creation of the Council of Europe (CE), followed by the European Communities, which more or less evolved into the European Union (EU). For complicated reasons having to do at least partially with differing state views about the extent of international integration, these two separate organizations, the CE and EU, came into existence. That is to say, while originally the CE was to promote the economic and political integration of Europe, British opposition produced weaker forms of regional cooperation such as the European Coal and Steel Community and then the Common Market. By the start of the twenty-first century it was evident that this bifurcation, while it had "worked" to a considerable degree, was not a completely happy situation. As European international integration proceeded, the contradictions of bifurcation were becoming evident. In addition to the EU (and lingering EC) and the CE, there was also the Organization for Security and Cooperation in Europe (OSCE), not to mention the North Atlantic Treaty Organization (NATO).[1]

Council of Europe

European Convention on Human Rights

From the very beginning of European regionalism in the 1940s, West European governments made it clear that promotion and protection of civil and political rights lay at the core of these regional developments.[2] They created the Council of Europe in the late 1940s to coordinate social policies; the centerpiece of the CE's efforts was the European Convention on Human Rights and Fundamental Freedoms (hereafter the Convention). This legal instrument was approved in 1950 and took legal effect in 1953. It covered only fundamental civil and political rights. (The Convention covers property rights and rights to education, both of which are sometimes viewed as civil rights.) Slightly later these same governments negotiated the European Social Charter to deal with social and economic rights. Attention to labor rights lay at the center of this development. The CE, whose governing organs are entirely separate from the EU's, eventually produced still other human rights documents including a 1986 convention for the prevention of torture, and a 1995 framework convention for the protection of national minorities. The 1950 Human Rights Convention remains the principal achievement of the CE. It does not go too far to say that it comprises a quasi-constitutional regional bill of rights for Europe. The Convention is the foundation for the "most successful system of international law for the protection of human rights . . . "[3] The influence of the Convention in European public law is "immense."[4]

---

[1] For the sake of completeness one can also mention other European regional organizations, such as the Western European Union (WEU), a strictly European military arrangement, and the European Free Trade Agreement (EFTA). They had little impact on human rights.

[2] Mark Janis, Richard Kay, and Anthony Bradly, *European Human Rights Law* (New York: Oxford University Press, 1995), 3.

[3] Ibid., 3.

[4] R. Beddard, *Human Rights and Europe*, 3rd edn (Cambridge: Grotius Publications, 1993), 6–7.

The Convention specifies a series of mostly negative or blocking rights familiar to western liberals. These rights are designed to block public interference with the citizen's private domain; to block the government from overstepping its rightful authority when the citizen encounters public authority through arrest, detention, and trial; and to guarantee citizen participation in public affairs. Of course governmental positive steps are required to make these negative rights effective. Public monies have to be spent to supervise and sometimes correct governmental policies; to run police departments, prisons, and courts; and to hold free and fair elections. The state may need to take positive action to ensure the dignity of children born outside marriage and to prevent discrimination against them. None of this is very new to liberalism, except that in Europe these norms are articulated on a regional basis in addition to national norms.

The really interesting aspect to the CE's work on human rights concerns methods to ensure compliance with the norms. In this regard under the Convention, the CE proceeded cautiously. Despite general agreement on the desirability of international norms on civil and political rights, the original ratifying states differed over how much state sovereignty should be restricted by regional international organizations. Under the Convention and additional protocols, therefore, early ratifying states had the option of accepting or not the jurisdiction and supranational authority of the European Court of Human Rights. States also had the option of allowing private petitions to the separate European Commission of Human Rights. This latter body was a screening commission of first recourse, as well as a fact-finding and conciliation commission. Thus complaints about violations could be brought by one ratifying state against another, with the Commission taking its findings to the Committee of Ministers if a state involved had not yet accepted the jurisdiction of the Court. Pending the consent of ratifying states, complaints could also be brought by private parties whether individuals, non-governmental organizations, or associations of persons. Again the Commission had the option of taking its conclusions to the Committee of Ministers or to the Court (the state involved also could pursue several avenues). Originally private parties had no legal standing before the Court, being dependent on representation by the Commission. But under Protocol 9, additional to the Convention, if the Commission rules in favor of a private petition, the private party then appears before a special chamber of the larger Court for a further hearing.

Lest one become lost in legal technicalities, it is important to stay focused on summary developments. First, over time the number of states adhering to the Convention increased. This was particularly evident after the Cold War, when Central and East European states, having recovered their operational sovereignty from the Soviet empire, sought membership in the CE and legal adherence to the Convention. Such adherence was a sign of being European, as well as a stepping stone to possible membership in the EU. CE membership reached forty-six states by early 2005, with all of these (except Monaco) ratifying the Convention.

Second, over time all forty-five of these states accepted the right of private petition, as well as the jurisdiction in all complaints of the supranational Court of Human Rights. Thus particularly the former communist states of Eastern Europe recovered their sovereignty only to immediately trade aspects of it away for enhanced international protection of human rights. It was also noteworthy that highly nationalistic states like France, with a long history of national discourse about human rights, finally also accepted the need for individual petitions and supranational adjudication at the regional level. Equally noteworthy was the decision by Turkey to accept the right of private petitions and the supranational role of the Court, despite evident human rights problems – particularly associated with the Kurdish question in that state. Again, some state motivation can be attributed as much to the desire to be considered for membership in the EU, with its projected economic benefits, as to a simpler or purer commitment to civil and political rights *per se*. Politically speaking, the Council of Europe, with the Human Rights Convention required for membership, became an ante-chamber leading to the doorway of the EU.[5] By 1998 the CE had decided that individual petitions and acceptance of the Court were no longer options, but had to be part of a state's adherence to the Convention. From a cautious beginning the CE had developed rigorous standards for protection. The newly independent states of Eastern Europe were immediately held to standards that the West European states were allowed to accept over time. As we will see, judicial enforcement existed on a regular basis.

Third, the Commission has traditionally thrown out around 90 per cent of the private petitions filed in support of an alleged violation of the Convention as being ill-founded. From 1955 to 1994, the Commission accepted only 8 per cent of the petitions submitted. But in 1994 it accepted 25 per cent of petitions, suggesting a new trend of better prepared petitions and a more sympathetic Commission.[6]

Fourth, despite the rejection rate, the overall number of such private petitions has been growing consistently. In 1955, the Commission had received a total of 138 private petitions. In 1997, it received 4,750. In

---

[5] Hugo Storey, "Human Rights and the New Europe: Experience and Experiment," in David Beetham, ed., *Politics and Human Rights* (Oxford: Blackwell, 1995), 131–151.

[6] C.A. Gearty, ed., *European Civil Liberties and the European Convention on Human Rights* (The Hague: Martinus Nijhoff, 1997), 14–16.

1979 the Commission had declared that 25 petitions were admissible for further review. In 1991, it admitted 217 for further consideration.[7] Or, in a different summary indicating the same trend, as of 1991 the Commission had dealt with 19,000 petitions, all but 8 of which (13 if you count the same case presented in different forms) were triggered by private petitions. Of the 19,000 petitions, 3,000 were discussed seriously further, and 1,000 pursued by either the Commission, the Court, and/or the Committee of Ministers. This, despite the fact that ratifying states were all either liberal democracies or aspired to be. But the evident fact was that liberal democracy at the national level did not guarantee that there would be no further violations of human rights. Indeed, the history of the CE and Convention indicated just the opposite: that even with liberal democracy at the national level, there was still a need for regional monitoring of human rights – there being evident violations by national authorities.

Fifth, public confidence in the system was high. Some further statistics are revealing.[8] (One should keep in mind that petitions against a given government do not come only from the citizens of that one state.) Concerning petitions against the Polish government during the years 1995–1997, private petitions increased from 242, already a relatively high number, to 461, for Romania, from 107 to 160, and Bulgaria, from 29 to 48. The Finnish government, having thrown off sensitivity to Soviet concerns, saw petitions jump from 78 to 102. But even among original members of the CE and early ratifiers of the Convention, the numbers proved eye-catching. The French government faced 392 petitions in 1995, and 448 in 1997. For Germany, the numbers increased from 180 to 298. In Italy from 567 to 825. In the United Kingdom, from 372 to 400. Even in the small and progressive Netherlands, the relevant numbers were 103 and 114. It was clear that many persons within the jurisdiction of the CE thought their international rights were being violated, that they increasingly looked to the regional "machinery" of the CE for relief, and that they were not deterred by the evident "conservatism" of the Commission in screening out the overwhelming number of petitions at the very first stage of review.

Sixth, one could not rely on state action to consistently protect human rights in another state. If one moves from private to interstate complaints, the numbers change dramatically. Without doubt, private petitions, and within these, individual complaints, drive the work of the Commission and Court. Even in Europe, states do not like to petition each other

---

[7] Beddard, *Human Rights and Europe*, 6–7.
[8] Drawn from links connected to the Council of Europe home page on the Internet: http://194.250.50.201/eng/97TABLES.BIL.html.

about human rights. Under the principle of reciprocity, my complaint about you today may lead you to complain about me tomorrow. States normally put a premium on good relations, especially among trading partners and security allies. There have been only eight state-to-state complaints up to the time of writing, not counting second and third phases of the same dispute. Several of these occurred in the context of already strained relations: Greece v. the UK over Cyprus (twice), Ireland v. the UK (twice), Cyprus v. Turkey (four times). Military government in Greece in 1967–1974 produced two complaints by a group made up of Denmark, Norway, Sweden, and the Netherlands. The same group plus France brought a complaint against Turkey. Denmark alone also brought a case against Turkey.[9] But these are small numbers over a 35–40-year period. Between 1959 and 1985 the Court handled 100 cases; 98 of these started with private petitions.[10] This pattern has profound relevance for other efforts to apply human rights standards relying on state complaints.

Seventh, if one can get a private petition cleared for admissibility in the first stage of technical review, one stands a rather good chance of prevailing on substance. One of the reasons that private petitions continue to mount is that if one's petition is declared admissible, if a friendly settlement cannot be achieved between petitioner and state, and if the matter goes to the Court of Human Rights, the petitioner stands a very good chance of winning the case. For many states, the success rate of complaints against it is over 50 percent. As of 2004, the Court had found at least one violation in 11 of 15 cases against Belgium; for France, 59 out of 75; for Greece, 32 out of 40; for Italy, 36 out of 47; for the Netherlands, 6 out of 10; for the UK, 19 out of 23. The total was 589 violations (at a minimum) out of 719 admitted petitions. When one includes multiple violations, it appears that petitioners usually win about two-thirds of their claims.[11]

These are good odds for the petitioner across all types of European states, including some of those with the best general reputations for serious attention to civil and political rights. The judges of the European

---

[9] Turkey might be considered a special case by European standards. The military was highly influential, taking over the government on several occasions and conducting, by almost all accounts, a brutal suppression of the Kurdish separatist movement. NGOs were reporting torture and other gross violations of human rights, especially in connection with the Kurdish question. But many in the Turkish elite believed that some Christian European political circles were using the human rights issue as an effort to block Muslim Turkey's entrance into the EU. It was said that these Christian circles feared the free movement of Muslim Turks as labor within the EU.

[10] Janis, et al., *European Human Rights Law*, 70.

[11] Council of Europe, Survey of Activities 2004 at: http://www.echr.coe.int/ NR/rdonlyres/461D3893-D3B7-4ED9-AC59-8BD9CA328E14/0/SurveyofActivities 2004.pdf.

Court of Human Rights, sitting in their personal capacity through election by the CE's European Parliamentary Assembly, were not hesitant to find fault with governmental policy. They had once been cautious about ruling against states, in order to build state support for the CE system. It took the Court ten years to make its first ruling against a state.[12] But things have changed.

Eighth, the Court was over-burdened with cases. It took thirty years to decide its first 200 cases; it only took three years to decide the next 200.[13] During its lifetime, the European Court on Human Rights has decided twenty times the cases handled by the World Court – the International Court of Justice at The Hague, to which only states have access for legally binding cases.[14] The case load for the Court, and delays in reaching it, had become of such concern that a protocol (number 11) to the Convention that would expedite proceedings went into legal force during the fall of 1998. All details of that change need not concern us here, but Protocol 11 eliminated the Commission, created a chamber of the Court made up of several judges to take over the screening functions, and utilized other chambers of several judges in order to process more cases at once. The full Court still sat to hear certain cases, including all state-to-state complaints. Thus, far from withering away because of national commitment to civil and political rights, the European Court of Human Rights was trying to figure out how to accommodate increased demand for its services.

To further improve the efficiency of the Court, Protocol 14 to the Convention was drafted and opened on May 13, 2004. The Protocol, with complicated wording, seeks to provide the Court with the procedural flexibility and means to expeditiously process cases. Where a state has failed to comply with the decision of the Court, the Committee of Ministers will be able to bring the state to the Court for non-compliance.

It should be noted, however, that most breaches of the Convention did not concern what are sometimes called gross and systematic violations. (The question of torture is covered below.) Most CE states were genuinely sympathetic to civil and political rights. But where the CE faced a government that was non-cooperative and determined to engage in gross and systematic violations, the CE functioned in a way not dissimilar to the United Nations or the Organization of American States. This is shown by the Greek case of 1967–1974, and also by Turkish policy in Cyprus and perhaps in Turkey itself. The CE system for protecting civil and political rights did not prevent or easily correct violations in those situations,

[12] Janis, et al., *European Human Rights Law*, 71.
[13] D. J. Harris, M. O'Boyle and C. Warbrick, *The Law of the European Convention on Human Rights* (London: Butterworths, 1995), 35–6.
[14] Janis, et.al., *European Human Rights Law*, 71.

because the target government was basically non-cooperative. Liberal democracies might sometimes violate civil and political rights here and there, perhaps inadvertently, or due to delay or personal malfeasance, and therefore be in need of regional monitoring. But the presence of genuine liberal democracy at the national level was a *sine qua non* for an effective regional protective system.[15]

As for the Court's jurisprudence, it covered, among other subjects, treatment while detained, freedom of expression, respect for private and family life, the right to liberty and security of person, the right to fair and public hearing, and the effect of the Convention in national law.[16]

A special consideration was the "margin of appreciation" afforded to states in applying the Convention. For example, Article 15 allowed states to derogate from many provisions of the Convention in "public emergencies threatening the life of the nation." A democratic state did have the right to defend itself. (Whether or not this is an example of a collective human right is an interesting question.) On the other hand certain articles could never be legally abridged, such as those prohibiting torture. States had to formally declare such emergencies and subject them to authoritative review. In the matter of the seizure of the government by the Greek military in 1967, the Commission held that such action was not justified under Article 15. The Committee of Ministers, however, was not able to take corrective action. (The junta collapsed of its own ineffectiveness in 1974.) But in general, under Article 15 and others, the review organs tend to give some leeway to states – a margin of appreciation – in highly controversial interpretations of the Convention. The Court did so in upholding invocation of Article 15 by the UK regarding Northern Ireland. "Margin of appreciation," perhaps like "executive privilege" in US constitutional law, was a matter of great complexity and continuing case law.[17]

The Court can order that compensation be paid because of breach of the Convention. It can challenge national court decisions. It is up to the Committee of Ministers to supervise the implementation of Court judgments. In general, this has not been a great problem, as most states have complied with most judgments most of the time. By 2000, before the expansion of State Parties to the Court, Britain and Italy had been found in violation of the Convention more times than any other of the

---

[15] Menno T. Kamminga, "Is the European Convention on Human Rights Sufficiently Equipped to Cope with Gross and Systematic Violations?," *Netherlands Human Rights Quarterly*, 12, 2 (1994), 153–164.

[16] Ibid. More traditional legal analysis covers the details of actual cases. That is not my intent here, and space does not allow it.

[17] Yutaka Arat, "The Margin of Appreciation Doctrine in the Jurisprudence of Article 8 of the European Convention on Human Rights," *Netherlands Human Rights Quarterly*, 16, 1 (1998), 41–56.

thirty-eight states then subject to its terms. In Britain it is said that this is because of its unwritten constitution and lack of judicial review.[18] But these factors, if true, do not explain Italy's record. The slowness of Italian judicial procedures seems to account for a considerable number of Italian violations of the Convention. By 2005, however, the bulk of the findings of violations were against Turkey, rising from 18 in 1999 to 154 in 2004.[19] Another potential target of massive cases is the Russian Federation, against which about 7,500 applications had been registered by the end of 2003.[20]

In the past, the role of the Committee of Ministers has been generally under-appreciated in human rights matters. When the Commission reached a decision on a petition, and could not advance the matter to the Court because of lack of state consent, its decision was only intermediate – with the final decision up to the Committee of Ministers. At least one observer holds that the Committee, made up of state representatives, was overly "statist" in its orientation by comparison with the Commission made up of independent experts.[21] All states have now accepted the Court's jurisdiction, and all new ratifiers of the Convention must do the same. Under Protocol 11, the Commission is eliminated, the Court will judge all well-founded petitions, and the role of the Committee will remain solely that of supervising the execution of Court judgments.

In all CE states the guarantees of the Convention can be invoked before the domestic courts, once the petitioner has exhausted local remedies (meaning, has tried national and sub-national norms and procedures first.) There was a cottage industry for lawyers and law professors deciding on the exact legal effects of the Convention at the national level, either via direct effects or via domestic legislation. Yet forty-five European states remained bound by the Convention and subject to the rulings by the Court, however the legal specifics might play out in national courts and other national public bodies.

Clearly, the European Convention had evolved in impressive ways, fueled by the underlying political agreement among national policy makers that protection of civil and political rights was central to their self-identification and self-image. This commitment was so strong that significant elements of state sovereignty were to be yielded in order to achieve

[18] Donald W. Jackson, *The United Kingdom Confronts the European Convention on Human Rights* (Gainesville: University Press of Florida, 1997).
[19] See further Arthur Bonner, "Turkey, the European Union and Paradigm Shifts," *Middle East Policy*, 7, 1 (2005), 44–71.
[20] Netherlands School of Human Rights Research , *Newsletter*, Volume 7, Issue 3, September (2003).
[21] Adam Tomkins, "Civil Liberties in the Council of Europe: A Critical Survey," in C. Gearty, ed., *European Civil Liberties and the European Convention on Human Rights* (The Hague: Martinus Nijhoff, 1977), 1–52.

it. To be sure there was some grumbling, especially in Britain, about the intrusiveness of regional norms and the assertiveness of the Court. Yet overall, trends were clear. National decisions about human rights would be authoritatively reviewed by the European Court of Human Rights. The real question for the future, discussed below in the section on the EU, was how these decisions could be coordinated with other human rights judgments handed down by the EU's supranational court, the European Court of Justice. As of the time of writing, twenty-five European states were subject to a potential double human rights review by supranational courts – once in the CE and once in the EU.

CE Social Charter

This 1961 legal instrument covers social and economic rights, originally workers' rights in and out of the work environment.[22] As of 1996 it had been comprehensively revised into a new document, and there was talk in the advisory European Assembly of converting some of its ideas into a new protocol that would be added to the European Convention on Human Rights, and thus made subject to the authoritative review of the European Court of Human Rights.[23] Thus there was increased attention to social (and economic) rights in Europe, and some effort was being made to deal with their secondary or inferior status.

The revised European Social Charter had been formally accepted by nineteen states as of 2005, less than half the number that had adhered to the European Convention on civil and political rights. (States that accepted the original Social Charter remained bound by it, if they did not accept the revised version.) There was no court dealing with economic and social rights, but a European Committee of Social Rights, composed of independent experts, made recommendations to superior inter-governmental bodies about application of the Charter. This Committee was advised by the International Labor Organization. It frequently found states to be in violation of their reporting obligations under the Charter, doing so, for example, in forty-seven cases in early 1999. It lacked the authority, however, to compel a change in policy by the states in violation. Its superior bodies also pursued the path of persuasion over time, rather than punitive enforcement.

A 1995 protocol adding a right of collective private petition, by trade unions and certain human rights groups, for alleged Charter violations had been accepted by over half of the states ratifying the original Charter.

---

[22] http.//www:oneworld.org/oxfam/policy.html.
[23] This and other specific information about the status of the Charter is drawn from links to the home page of the Council of Europe: www.coe.fr.

Hence there was some effort to profit from the lessons drawn from the experience with civil and political rights. As noted above, private petitions drive the work of the European Court of Human Rights. Since 1999, 26 collective complaints lodged under this Protocol have been declared admissible. Of these, 23 have been heard on the merits and 16 held to be violations of rights by states. The Committee has found states in violation in a diversity of areas: child labor in Portugal, forced labor in Greece, right to organize in Sweden, discrimination on basis of disability in France, and protection of children against corporal punishment in Ireland and Belgium among others.

The 1996 revised Social Charter put into one new text a number of amendments and protocols that had been added to the 1961 Charter over the years. As of mid-2005, the new document was in force for nineteen states with more expected to give their consent, since many of the added provisions had been widely accepted previously in incremental steps. The revised Charter specified a number of new rights in addition to existing labor rights: the right to protection against poverty and social exclusion, to housing, to protection in case of termination of employment, to protection against sexual harassment and victimization, etc. Certain existing economic and social rights were revised: reinforcement of the principle of non-discrimination, increased equality between genders, better maternity protection and social protection for mothers, increased protection for children and disabled persons.

Still, even under the 1996 revisions of the Social Charter, the control mechanisms remained unchanged. That caused the Parliamentary Assembly of the CE in 1999 to call for a new protocol to the European Convention on Human Rights covering certain economic and social rights. Outside experts had agreed that some economic and social rights could be adjudicated, being not very different in some substantive respects from civil rights.[24] Should such a protocol to the European Convention be adopted, the question of subject matter jurisdiction between the European Court of Human Rights and the European Court of Justice would be brought into bold relief. Both would be dealing more with labor rights and economic matters. But a number of experts thought such a protocol was unlikely to be accepted by very many member states.

As of 2005 one could not say what the effect of the revised Social Charter might be. In general it was still true to say that European states were not prepared to subject themselves to the same type of authoritative third-party review concerning economic and social rights as they had accepted

---

[24] Paul Hunt, *Reclaiming Social Rights: International and Comparative Perspectives* (Aldershot: Dartmouth, 1996).

for civil and political rights. On the other hand, they were experimenting with procedures of application that might direct more attention to labor rights, the right to housing, and various forms of social security. Unlike the USA, most European states, including those in Central and Eastern Europe, were social democracies that believed in extensive economic and social rights, as well as civil and political ones.

CE Prevention of Torture

All forty-five of the states that ratified the European Convention also ratified the European Convention for the Prevention of Torture. Under this treaty a committee of uninstructed persons had the right to regularly visit ratifying states to inquire into measures and conditions pertaining to torture. The committee could also make *ad hoc* visits with minimal advance notification. The committee operated on the basis of confidentiality. Similar to the detention visits of the International Committee of the Red Cross, if a state did not show adequate progress over time in meeting the norms of the Convention, the committee might publicize its conclusions. Over time the committee interpreted its mandate broadly, so that general prison conditions, and not just torture, were reviewed. The committee also developed the tradition of making very specific recommendations to governments.

Some might assume that this treaty was made possible by the absence of torture in Europe. Such an assumption might be mistaken for several reasons. First, older CE member states like Britain, when dealing with perceived public emergencies like Northern Ireland, had been known to engage in controversial interrogation techniques. Whether these techniques should be properly labeled torture, mistreatment, or something else was for review bodies to determine.[25] In the summer of 1999 France, having abused a suspected drug dealer while detained, was found guilty of torture by the European Court of Human Rights. Second, some of the newer members of the CE, especially the former communist states, displayed a history that was not free of a pattern of controversial interrogation techniques. Third, Turkey, and also Russia, which ratified the European torture convention, were regularly charged with using torture as public policy by various human rights groups, as well as the media.

---

[25] At one point the European Commission on Human Rights held that the UK had employed torture in dealing with Northern Ireland, whereas the European Court of Human Rights held only that the UK had engaged in mistreatment. In any event, because of domestic as well as international criticism, the British government presumably altered the interrogation techniques in question – at least officially in that particular controversy.

CE Protection of Minorities

The European Convention on Human Rights and Fundamental Freedoms deals explicitly only with individual civil and political rights. Likewise, the European Social Charter does not mention national minorities. Given the changing membership of the CE, and the importance of national minorities not only in Central and Eastern Europe, but also in Western European states such as Spain, the CE in 1995 concluded a Framework Convention for the Protection of National Minorities.

The Convention entered into force in 1998 and had been ratified by thirty-six states as of 2005. It contains no special monitoring mechanisms aside from an unspecified role for the CE's Committee of Ministers. The Committee of Ministers has however created an Advisory Committee of eighteen independent experts to assist in the monitoring of state compliance. The Advisory Committee examines state reports and gives an Opinion on the measures taken by the reporting state. It is the Committee of Ministers however that adopts Conclusions and issues Recommendations to states. As of 2005, the Advisory Committee had received thirty-five state reports and adopted thirty-four Opinions with the Committee of Ministers adopting Conclusions and Recommendations to twenty-nine states. The Advisory Committee had also introduced country-visits as part of its monitoring mandate.

The treaty, rather than endorsing assimilation of all groups into one homogeneous society, endorses the preservation of national minorities. It urges governments to accommodate national minorities, although they are not defined in the treaty, through public policies on language, state services, etc. Some observers found great fault with this approach to minority protection.[26]

European Union

In the treaties during the 1950s that lay at the origin of the present EU, there was no mention of human rights. This anomaly was formally corrected in the 1992 Maastricht Treaty transforming the Communities into the EU, whereby it was stipulated (in Article F.2) that "the Union shall respect fundamental rights, as guaranteed by the European Convention for the Protection of Human Rights and Fundamental Freedoms . . . and as they result from the constitutional traditions common to the Member States, as general principles of Community law." This treaty provision

---

[26] Geof Gilbert, "The Council of Europe and Minority Rights," *Human Rights Quarterly*, 18, 1 (Winter 1996), 160–189.

codified important human rights developments that had already been occurring in the EU.

The European Court of Justice (ECJ), the supranational court of the EU, had been encouraging European integration by, among other things, declaring the supremacy of Community law compared with national law. German and Italian courts, against the background of their countries' experience with fascism, balked at supranational economic integration without explicit protections of human rights.[27] These and eventually other national bodies feared that national bills of rights and other national protections of human rights – primarily civil and political rights – would be washed away by Community law geared to purely economic considerations. The ECJ, therefore, began to address human rights issues as they related to economic decisions by Community institutions – the Commission (the collective executive), the Council of Ministers (officially a meeting of cabinet ministers of the member states), and the Parliament (a mostly advisory body).

All of these other EU organs, and also a periodic meeting of heads of state, eventually took up human rights subjects. EU bodies addressed human rights issues from the late 1960s, and in 1977 the European Commission, Council, and Parliament issued a joint declaration saying what Article F.2 was to say in 1992 – namely that human rights were to be protected as found in the European Convention on Human Rights and in the constitutional traditions of member states. In 1989 the European Parliament proposed a European declaration of human rights. This was never acted upon by the Commission and Council.

Indeed, by 1992 the EU aspired not only to protecting human rights within its jurisdiction but also in a "common foreign and security policy" (Article J.1{2}).[28] The EU pledged to "develop and consolidate democracy and the rule of law, and respect for human rights and fundamental freedoms" in its dealings with other states. EU resources are devoted to this objective, and the EU is one of the major donors to international humanitarian assistance designed to secure rights to adequate food, clothing, shelter, and health care in emergency situations. References to human rights are included in treaties with other countries, although some object and resist. No economic transactions have been interrupted by the EU on the grounds that these human rights clauses have been violated. Many EU statements on human rights abroad are just that: statements devoid of further action. But sometimes the EU votes sanctions for human rights

---

[27] See especially Nanette A. Neuwahl, "The Treaty on European Union: A Step Forward in the Protection of Human Rights?," in Nanette A. Neuwahl and Allan Rosas, eds., *The European Union and Human Rights* (The Hague: Martinus Nijhoff, 1995), 1–22.

[28] Daniela Napoli, "The European Union's Foreign Policy and Human Rights," in ibid., 297–312.

reasons, usually in responding to UN Security Council decisions – as on Haiti and former Yugoslavia. The EU has helped supervise elections in numerous countries. The EU Council sometimes tries to coordinate the foreign policies of its member states at the United Nations Human Rights Commission and General Assembly, but without total success. For example, EU member states split badly on how to deal with China at the UN Commission in 1997.[29]

It was the ECJ that had led the way in interjecting human rights into EU proceedings, and some observers – but certainly not all – thought the court might rule on foreign policy decisions in the future. Recent case law by the ECJ suggests that human rights values must be respected not only by EU organs but also by member states when taking decisions within the EU framework.[30] A 1997 summary seems quite accurate regarding the introduction of civil and political rights into the EU: "The concern with human rights is recognized in [the EU], and the case law of the ECJ is flourishing, even though there is no bill of rights nor any general guarantee of fundamental rights in the [EU] Treaties."[31] This situation is explained by the widespread support for civil and political rights in the traditional liberal democracies of Western Europe, so that particularly regional courts but also other regional bodies can advance effective judicial activism and creativity in interpreting the law.

In Europe at the beginning of the twenty-first century there were two supranational courts making judgments on regional human rights law – the EU's ECJ and the CE's Court of Human Rights. There was no explicit coordination between the two. The latter worked from an explicit human rights treaty containing specified human rights. The former did not, but rather worked from "principles" vaguely derived from other sources, including the CE treaty. The potential for conflict and confusion was considerable between the CE's Strasburg court and the EU's Luxemburg court. The Strasburg court was staffed by human rights specialists. The Luxemburg court was staffed by judges primarily interested in economic law, but they had shown remarkable flexibility and creativity in adapting EU law to broad concerns – including human rights.[32]

For some time there has been discussion about whether the EC, as it then was, and which has some legal personality in international law,

---

[29] See further Marine Fouwels, "The European Union's Common Foreign and Security Policy and Human Rights," *Netherlands Quarterly of Human Rights*, 15, 3 (September 1997), 291–324.

[30] Ibid., 9.   [31] Ibid., 11.9

[32] G. Federico Manchini, "The Making of a Constitution for Europe," in Robert O. Keohane and Stanley Hoffmann, eds., *The New European Community: Decisionmaking and Institutional Change* (Boulder: Westview Press, 1991), 177–194.

should try to formally adhere to the European Convention on Human Rights. The CE/EU Commission was in favor, but the ECJ held that under current law this was not possible, as the European Convention was open only to states and the CE did not have comparable legal personality. The state members of the CE/EU declined to change the appropriate law to make such an adherence possible, perhaps fearing the further loss of influence for national constitutions as the cost of Community law. The continued bifurcation in Europe between economic and social institutions no doubt would demand sorting out in the future, especially if there is ever to be a "United States of Europe."

By 2005 events had progressed to the point that an EU Charter of Fundamental Rights was negotiated by the leaders of the 25 EU member nations as part of the projected EU Constitution. This Charter represented a further integration among the 25, as well as providing the most detailed legal obligations yet in the area of human rights. In effect, the Charter moved the 25 further toward what was in reality a regional bill of rights.[33] As it turned out, some of the nations of Europe were not completely sold on the Constitutional project, and at the time of writing voters in both France and the Netherlands had refused to accept the Charter in referenda. Since approval by all 25 states was required, the movement for a more tightly unified Europe was thrown into turmoil. It was not clear what the outcome of the situation might portend. As for the Charter of Fundamental Rights, it has already been separately accepted as a stand-alone document in 2000 and had been applied from time to time by the European Court of Justice as part of "the general principles of Community law."

After the no vote in France and the Netherlands, the status quo ante prevailed. This meant that the EU was still an actor for human rights both within its own jurisdiction and through its emerging but mostly disjointed foreign policy.[34] On the latter subject, European states were badly divided over the issue of the US invasion of Iraq in 2003. In 1998 an EU committee of eminent persons had issued a detailed statement on EU human rights policy.[35] A companion report in the same publication urged numerous changes to make human rights a more serious commitment both within the EU and in its emerging foreign and security policy. Whether "Europe" could move beyond this situation was not clear.

---

[33] See further Victor Bojkov, "National Identity, Political Interest and Human Rights in Europe: the Charter of Fundamental Rights of the European Union," *Nationalities Papers* 32, no. 2 (2004), 323–353.

[34] See further Andrew Williams, *EU Human Rights Policies: A Study in Irony* (Oxford: Oxford University Press, 2004).

[35] *Leading by Example: A Human Rights Agenda for the European Union for the Year 2000; Agenda of the Comité des Sages and Final Project Report* (Florence: European University Institute, 1998).

Organization for Security and Cooperation in Europe

The diplomatic process known during the Cold War as the CSCE – the Conference on Security and Cooperation in Europe – became an organization, and hence OSCE, after the Cold War.[36] From 1973 to 1974, the communist East sought security and economic objectives *vis-à-vis* the democratic West. The West responded with an insistence that certain principles of human rights and humanitarian affairs be respected by all. The Helsinki Accord of 1975, plus various follow-up conferences, generated considerable pressure on European communist regimes to respect the principles they had formally endorsed. Individuals and private groups in the East, backed by western governments and private human rights groups, became more assertive in demanding respect for rights. The short-term response by communist party-state regimes was more repression, but the long-term outcome was to further undermine an increasingly discredited communist framework in Europe.

It is impossible to scientifically prove the exact role of the CSCE in the decline of European communism and the disintegration of the Soviet Union. As John J. Maresca, a high US diplomat, remarked, "It is a puzzle to analyze Helsinki's accomplishments, because it is impossible to establish what resulted from Helsinki and what was simply the result of history moving on."[37] Stefan Lehne, a high Austrian diplomat, argued that the primary factors leading to dramatic change in European communism were the internal contradictions of the system of political economy, combined with Mikail Gorbachev's refusal to defend the *status quo* with force. But he goes on to argue that the CSCE process played a significant if secondary role.[38] This view was seconded by a number of other observers.[39]

After the Cold War the new OSCE increased its membership from thirty-five to about fifty-five states, which broadened its jurisdiction but weakened its capability. A number of the new states emerging from the old Soviet Union lacked real commitment to human rights as well as the

---

[36] See further David P. Forsythe, "Human Rights and Multilateral Institutions in the New Europe," in Forsythe, ed., *Human Rights in the New Europe: Problems and Progress* (Lincoln: University of Nebraska Press, 1994), 174–204.

[37] Quoted in ibid., p. 176.

[38] Stefan Lehne, *The Vienna Meetings of the Conference on Security and Cooperation in Europe, 1986–1989: A Turning Point in East–West Relations* (Boulder: Westview, 1991).

[39] See, eg., William Korey, *The Promises We Keep: Human Rights, the Helsinki Process, and American Foreign Policy* (New York: St. Martin's Press, 1993). Korey gives pride of place to the US Congress and private interest groups, especially Jewish ones, in generating influence on European communists. See further Sandra L. Gubin, "Between Regimes and Realism – Transnational Agenda Setting: Soviet Compliance with CSCE Human Rights Norms," *Human Rights Quarterly*, 17, 2 (May 1995), 278–302, who argues it was a combination of international and domestic politics in the West that brought effective pressure on the USSR with regard to Jewish emigration.

real capability to resolve human rights problems. Some states such as the former Yugoslavia descended into murderous armed conflict, about which the OSCE could do little since it had no enforcement authority and no military power, aside from suspending Belgrade from the organization. The OSCE operated as a diplomatic framework to try to advance internationally recognized human rights, especially the civil and political rights associated with liberal democracy. To the extent that it manifested a strong point or area of expertise, it lay in the area of minority rights, about which the Council of Europe had been mostly silent.[40] The first OSCE High Commissioner for National Minorities, the Dutchman Max van der Stoel, was widely respected. He operated through quiet diplomacy to try to prevent and resolve conflicts over national minorities. It was difficult to document his success, in part because successful prevention of disputes left very little to document, and in part because not all minority problems could be resolved. He concentrated mostly on Central and Eastern European affairs, there being political opposition to his taking on minority problems in certain Western European states.[41] His office became a focal point for diplomacy on minority issues in Europe, effectively if informally coordinating other IGO and NGO efforts so as to try to make a concentrated impact regarding minority rights.

NATO

While historically NATO had been a traditional military alliance, increasingly after the Cold War it took on human rights duties – such as trying to lay the groundwork for liberal democracy in the former Yugoslavia, including the roles of arresting indicted war crimes suspects and ensuring the safe return of refugees and the internally displaced. Indeed, one of the reasons advanced for the 1998 expansion of NATO to include the Czech Republic, Hungary, and Poland was to provide an additional, military framework for reinforcing liberal democracy in those three formerly communist states. As already noted, in 1999 NATO undertook military force "out of area" in order to try to coerce the Milosevic government in modern Yugoslavia to stop its persecution and expulsion of ethnic Albanians in Kosovo. In fact, regardless of legal argument, NATO became an agent of humanitarian intervention and enforcer of liberal democracy in Europe.

[40] Jane Wright, "The OSCE and the Protection of Minority Rights," *Human Rights Quarterly*, 18, 1 (Winter 1996), 190–205.

[41] Rob Zagman and Joanne Thorburn, *The Role of the High Commission on National Minorities in OSCE Conflict Prevention* (The Hague: Foundation for Inter-Ethnic Relations, 1997). See further Nigel Rodley, "Conception Problems in the Protection of Minorities: International Legal Developments," *Human Rights Quarterly*, 17, 1 (February 1995), 48–71.

A number of realists objected to this orientation, arguing that situations like Bosnia and Kosovo in the 1990s did not engage the vital interests of the West and should not lead to tying down NATO through air campaigns and a presence on the ground. They argued that NATO military action should remain focused on traditional state security issues involving Russia, China, state-supported terrorism, and oil in the Middle East. They objected to military commitment to "minor" problems linked to self-determination and humanitarian assistance, as pushed by the communications media and private human rights groups.[42] For realists, priorities remained centered on collective national interests traditionally defined in geo-political terms, not on alleviating human misery and distress.

The different versions of realism have never been very precise about how states define their vital interests. Realist authors basically *assume* that states define their interests in terms of independent power, and then move on to emphasize competition that supposedly affects the "balance of power." In the third volume of his memoirs, Henry Kissinger refers repeatedly to the US "national interest."[43] He argues that his congressional critics (precisely because they were sentimental McGovernites) were not always interested in US national interests, rather than acknowledging that they had a *different* conception of the national interest. For Kissinger national interest centered on a geo-political power struggle with the old Soviet Union. But it is not self-evident that the USA should have expended blood and treasure in a place like Angola or the Horn of Africa during the Cold War, or that the Congress was in error in trying to block national involvement in such places. After all, if the Soviets wanted to collect a handful of "basket cases" as allies, it is not self-evident that such expansion threatened US security. Thus there is room for reasonable persons to differ over what constitutes national interest, and within that, vital interests. Most realists like Kissinger do not acknowledge the subjective construction of national interests.

In Kosovo in particular, NATO member states defined their vital interests to include a liberal democratic "neighborhood" in Europe. Just as European states had considered human rights important enough to merit two supranational regional courts that restricted state sovereignty in the name of human rights, so they, plus Canada and the USA, considered repression of ethnic Albanians in Kosovo important enough to merit military intervention – having come to feel highly uncomfortable with *not* undertaking military intervention in Bosnia during 1992–1994. Even Kissinger should have understood this, since he tried to justify his

---

[42] See, for example, the special section on NATO at fifty, in *Foreign Affairs*, 78, 3 (May/June 1999), 163–210, especially the articles by Robert E. Hunter and Michael E. Brown.

[43] Henry Kissinger, *Years of Renewal* (New York: Simon & Schuster, 1999).

continued support of South Vietnam in 1975 and thereafter in terms of American honor – the moral obligation to help those who had relied on the United States – and not in terms of directly affecting the balance of power or US security.[44]

Realists warned that western military power was stretched dangerously thin at the end of the twentieth century, with ground commitments in Bosnia and Kosovo, ongoing deployments of sizable numbers of troops on the ground in Afghanistan and Iraq, and long-standing military commitments particularly in East Asia. Should China flex its military muscles about Taiwan, or Russia revert to a more truculent foreign policy, for example, most realists argued that NATO would have to reduce its involvement in places like the Balkans – because traditional vital interests were not involved. It is for this reason that NATO yielded command of pacifying forces in Bosnia and Kosovo to the EU. I pursue this subject further in chapter 6 on comparative foreign policy.

Against the background of there having been no war among the great powers during half a century, and particularly after a Republican administration used military force in Somalia from late 1992 in the context of a failed state and a complex humanitarian emergency, it was no longer clear in contemporary international relations what situation merited the use of force and how states defined their most important interests. Within NATO (and within the Pentagon) debates raged about the wisdom of "operations other than war" and "low-level war" to protect human rights. As of 1999, a relaxation of tensions among the great powers had allowed more liberalism in the form of human rights to be interjected into foreign policy through such instruments as NATO. Realist thinking was not *passé*, but it did share the agenda more with liberalism in relative terms. The Al Qaeda attacks on the USA in 2001 supposedly brought a tough realism back to the fore, with a diminished interest in human rights. But once entangled in Afghanistan and Iraq, the USA talked much about democracy and human rights, and had to answer tough questions about its treatment of enemy prisoners. NATO increasingly played a larger role in efforts to "secure" or "pacify" Afghanistan. So even in "an age of terrorism" or "an age of insecurity," the subject of human rights displayed considerable staying power. In post-combat situations, NATO was often expected to contribute to democratic nation-building and protection of human rights.

The Western Hemisphere

By comparison with Europe, a major paradox exists with regard to regional organization and human rights in the Western Hemisphere.

[44] Ibid.

There we find, similar to Europe, an international organization, the Organization of American States, with human rights programs, a regional convention for the protection of human rights, and a commission and court to move beyond passive standards to active implementation. Yet we also find in that Hemisphere during much of the past fifty years an abundance of gross and systematic violations of human rights by numerous states. How can it be that the states which are members of the Organization of American States engaged both in the repeated endorsement of well-known human rights standards, and at the same time, for much of the time since 1945, in their repeated violation? The answer is to be found most fundamentally in a regional conflicted political culture.[45]

Three hemispheric political values largely account for the creation and continued functioning of this regional regime for the promotion and protection of human rights. The first of these is widespread but abstract agreement that the legitimate state is the liberal democratic state. This is not a newly articulated value; most hemispheric states professed political liberalism from the time of their independence. More recent developments since 1945 mostly reaffirmed what had been preached if not practiced consistently since the early nineteenth century – namely that hemispheric republics aspired to be liberal democracies along the lines of the models in North America. The American Declaration on the Rights and Duties of Man, from 1948, and the InterAmerican Convention on Human Rights, from 1969, were but modern manifestations of this long-standing tradition of lip service to political liberalism.

A second widespread political value that undergirds regional developments in favor of human rights has been moral leadership for rights by OAS agencies and a shifting coalition of hemispheric states. A key player in this regard since the mid-1950s has been the InterAmerican Commission on Human Rights, now a principal organ of the OAS, and a persistent leader for human rights. This uninstructed body, charged with an active program of reporting, investigating, and diplomacy for human rights, also has duties under the InterAmerican Convention. The dynamism of this body has been supported by a variety of states with active and progressive human rights policies – although the composition of this group of states changes according to the government in power. Costa Rica, Venezuela, Uruguay, and other states have been part of this pro-human rights coalition from time to time.

A third supporting factor has been erratic influence for human rights by the United States. Very little happens in the OAS that is strongly opposed by the USA. More positively, the USA on occasion has used the OAS to

---

[45] This section is drawn from a revision of David P. Forsythe, "Human Rights, the United States, and the Organization of American States," *Human Rights Quarterly*, 13, 2 (Spring 1991), 66–98.

push for such things as the American Declaration, diplomatic pressure against particular rights-violating governments at particular times, and OAS supervision of elections in places like Central America. US support for regional human rights standards and action has been highly selective, which is to say inconsistent, as we will note below. Nevertheless, periodic support by the USA for certain human rights developments via the OAS has been important – whether one speaks of efforts to rid Nicaragua of the Somoza dynasty, or efforts on behalf of a diplomacy generally supportive of liberal democracy in the 1990s.

On the other side of the fence, however, three factors have largely constrained regional human rights developments in the Western Hemisphere. The first of these has been the historical trend on the part of Latin and Caribbean states to emphasize the principle of state sovereignty in the wake of repeated US interventions into their domestic affairs. This widespread endorsement of broad and traditional notions of state sovereignty was articulated to block OAS authority as well as US power, since the former (viz., OAS authority) was seen by many in the region to reflect the latter (viz., US power). By the turn of the twenty-first century there had been some movement away from historical patterns in this regard. In 1991 the OAS declared unanimously, apart from Cuba, through its Santiago Declaration, that the question of democratic government within any state was an international and not strictly a domestic matter. But at approximately the same time the OAS continued to resist authorizing the use of force to create, recreate, or protect democratic government, as in Haiti, since such an authorization meant authorizing predominantly US use of force. In the latter situation, the USA had to turn to the United Nations Security Council for authorization of deployment of force to restore the elected government of Father Aristide in Haiti in the face of military usurpation. Thus the OAS remained unreliable for the direct protection of human rights in the Hemisphere, due to lingering widespread fears about US power. This tension resurfaced over Venezuela in 2005, when the OAS refused to lend its name to a US plan to monitor democracy in the Hemisphere. Important OAS member states feared the plan was nothing more than a scheme to undermine the government of Hugo Chavez, whose left of center elected government in Caracas had incurred considerable criticism from Washington.[46]

A second limiting factor on regional action for human rights in the Western Hemisphere stems from the fact that many national elites, while identifying with political liberalism in the abstract, have not really been

---

[46] Joel Brinkley, "Latin Nations Resist Plan For Monitor of Democracy," *New York Times*, June 6, 2005, A9.

able to bring themselves to practice liberal democracy when it meant recognizing human rights for indigenous peoples, the lower classes (the two are not mutually exclusive), those on the political left (the three are not mutually exclusive), etc. Military and other governments in the Hemisphere have often found it "desirable" to emphasize a "national security state" and other departures from liberal democracy in order to save the nation from itself – viz., to save the state from control by some element deemed undesirable by the traditional elites made up of the military, the aristocracy, and conservative elements in the Catholic Church. Thus the abstract endorsement of liberal democracy has been frequently joined by the practice of authoritarian government, and even authoritarian government with a very brutal face, as a "necessary and exceptional" measure when the traditional elites have feared "subversive" movements. This was particularly the case in the Southern Cone of South America during the Cold War years of the 1970s and 1980s.[47]

A third and last limiting factor was the preoccupation of the USA with containing if not rolling back Soviet-led communism during the Cold War. This orientation, a modern version of the Monroe Doctrine designed to keep the Hemisphere free from the influence of any external power, caused the USA to repeatedly emphasize national and regional freedom from communism as compared with individual freedom from non-communist repression. Until the Carter Administration of 1977–1981, the USA repeatedly aligned with repressive but non-communist governments in the Hemisphere. The goal may have been to protect human rights in the USA (along with the power of the USA in international relations), but the means entailed opposition to human rights developments in places like Guatemala in 1954 where the USA organized the overthrow of the genuinely elected and basically progressive Arbenz government. The murderous military governments that followed were propped up by Washington. After the Cold War this type of situation has obviously changed, and the USA has become less opposed to OAS actions for human rights in the Hemisphere. Cuba aside, there are few authoritarian governments and none consistently aligned with an external hostile power.

The interplay of these three supporting factors (abstract commitment to liberal democracy, moral leadership for human rights by various actors, inconsistent leadership for human rights by the USA) and three limiting factors (fondness for traditional notions of state sovereignty, widespread if periodic practice of authoritarianism particularly of a brutal sort, US

---

[47] See further Jack Donnelly, *International Human Rights*, 2nd edn (Boulder: Westview, 1998), ch. 3.

security concerns during the Cold War), meant that one found an ambitious regional human rights program that was mostly ineffective in the actual protection of human rights in most places most of the time. Human rights activities constituted the bright spot of the OAS, compared with security, economic and environmental matters. At the same time regional action for human rights did not prevent or correct gross violations of human rights in many places between the 1940s and the 1990s.

The American Declaration was voted into being (even before the UN Universal Declaration of Human Rights, and before the European regional instruments), and the InterAmerican Convention was formally adhered to by twenty-four of the OAS thirty-five member states (Cuba being the thirty-sixth but suspended). Twenty-one of these accepted the supranational jurisdiction of the InterAmerican Court.

The InterAmerican Commission basically tried to "referee the game of politics" in the Hemisphere by "blowing the whistle" on violations of human rights. But, to continue the analogy, the game continued in brutal fashion in many places as if that referee did not exist. To change the analogy, the InterAmerican Commission generated modest influence as a liberal ombudsman in the region.[48] Until the end of the Cold War, however, only sixteen of thirty-five states consented to supranational adjudication by the InterAmerican Court on Human Rights, which had come into being in 1979. Its case load remains less than those of the two European courts, as by 2004 the Court had handed down only forty-five binding and seventeen advisory opinions. Part of the reason for this low case load for the Court is the fact that only the InterAmerican Commission and states can present cases to the InterAmerican Court. In a sense therefore the Commission operates almost as a court of first instance handling over 12,500 cases since its creation.[49] No state so far has lodged a case at the Court. The USA continued to object to the Court's authority and jurisdiction, and to argue that the American Declaration had not passed into international customary law in whole or in part. In Europe, by contrast, all major states were supportive of most CE and EU human rights developments.

It is a measure of the positive evolution of the InterAmerican system however, that in 1998 regionally important states like Brazil and Mexico accepted the Court's jurisdiction. Moreover, the countries that have accepted the jurisdiction of the InterAmerican Court have demonstrated

---

[48] See, for example, Cecilia Medina, "The Role of Country Reports in the Inter-American System of Human Rights," *Netherlands Quarterly of Human Rights*, 15, 4 (December 1997), 457–473.

[49] Christina M. Cerna, "The Inter-American System for the Protection of Human Rights," *Florida Journal of International Law*, 16, 195 (2004), 195–212.

a surprising willingness to comply with its decisions, when in the past they have ignored the decisions of the Commission. However, while states have been more prepared to pay monetary damages to plaintiffs, they have been less willing to make further investigations and punish perpetrators.[50]

Resistance to the Court still remains, as attested by the withdrawal of Trinidad and Tobago from the InterAmerican Convention in 1999 to shield its death penalty regime from the Court's scrutiny– and Peru's short-lived intended withdrawal in the same year. Further, it is correct to generalize that while Latin American states have accepted the authority of the Court and the Commission (with the exception of Cuba), the English-speaking states of the hemisphere have only partially embraced the system.[51]

Overall, one found in the Western Hemisphere a regional system for the promotion and protection of human rights that resembled the European system on paper, but did not resemble it very much in reality.[52] For example, in both systems one found a right of private petition about human rights violations. But the results of such petitions in Europe provided consistent and real restraints on state policy through binding court judgments, whereas the results in the Americas did not. One could hope that with the end of the Cold War both US policy and other factors would change toward more support for regional human rights values and processes. But more than ten years after the end of the Cold War, the regional system for protecting human rights associated with the OAS remained much weaker than its European counterpart. And the United States remains as strongly opposed to OAS review of its human rights record as during earlier times.

Africa

African states, seared by the experience of colonialism and plagued by numerous problems of political instability, used the Organization of African Unity, created in 1961, primarily to reinforce traditional notions of state sovereignty and domestic jurisdiction. The OAU Charter mentioned human rights. But for the OAU, concern with human rights was restricted to questions of racial discrimination by Whites against Blacks as in Rhodesia, South Africa, and the then remaining Portuguese colonies of Angola, Guinea Bissau, and Mozambique. Even the most egregious violations of human rights in Idi Amin's Uganda or "Emperor" Jean-Bedel

---

[50] Ibid, 203. [51] Ibid, 203.

[52] See further Tom J. Farer, "The Rise of the Inter-American Human Rights Regime: No Longer a Unicorn, Not Yet an Ox," *Human Rights Quarterly*, 19, 3 (August 1997), 510–546.

Bokassa's Central African "Empire" were met with a deafening silence from the OAU.

This embarrassing double standard contributed eventually to adoption of the African Charter on Human and Peoples' Rights – the so-called Banjul Charter – in 1981.[53] It received a sufficient number of ratifications to enter into legal force in 1986, at which time perhaps three states in Africa might be considered something relatively close to a liberal democracy and thus showing national commitment to civil and political rights. In brief summary, the Banjul Charter encompassed: an absolute endorsement of certain civil and political rights familiar to the liberal West; a conditional endorsement of other civil and political rights that were limited by "claw back" clauses permitting deviation from international standards on the basis of national laws; mention of fundamental economic and social rights requiring considerable material resources for their application; a list of individual duties; and a list of "people's" rights such as to existence, self-determination, and disposal of natural resources.

It was said by some that especially individual duties and people's rights reflected uniquely African approaches to internationally recognized human rights.[54] Perhaps more importantly, it was also said that since the Banjul Charter eschewed an African human rights court and established only an advisory African Human Rights Commission to oversee application of the Charter, this approach reflected African preferences for discussion and conciliation rather than adversarial adjudication. The fact remains that during the Cold War, which overlaps partly with the early stages of post-colonial Africa, political liberalism was in short supply on that continent. It would have been inconceivable for the OAU in the 1980s to adopt a human rights convention that was normatively strong and clear on behalf of individual rights, and subject to enforcement by a supranational regional court. Whether this was because of "African culture" or the political self-interests of those who ruled African states I leave to the historians and anthropologists.

What is undeniable, and entirely predictable, was that the Banjul Charter had only slight impact on anyone's behavior in the fifty-three states making up the OAU during the first ten years of its existence. As was true in general in other regions, African states did not avail themselves

---

[53] U. Oji Umozurike, *The African Charter on Human and Peoples' Rights* (The Hague: Martinus Nijhoff, 1997).

[54] In addition to ibid., ch. 8, see Rhoda Howard, *Human Rights in Commonwealth Africa* (Totowa, NJ: Rowman & Littlefield, 1986), ch. 2; Timothy Fernyhough, "Human Rights and Precolonial Africa," in Ronald Cohen, Goran Hyden, and Winston P. Nagan, eds., *Human Rights and Governance in Africa* (Gainesville: University Press of Florida, 1993), ch. 2; and Abdullah Ahmed An-Na'im and Francis M. Deng, eds., *Human Rights in Africa: Cross-Cultural Perspectives* (Washington: Brookings, 1990).

of the opportunity to petition other states about human rights violations. The only state petition lodged was a bogus one: Libya petitioned against the United States. Since the latter was not a member of the OAU, the petition was properly dismissed. Moreover, African states were tardy at best, and frequently negligent, in submitting reports to the Commission about how they were applying the Charter. The Commission had neither the authority nor the power to correct the situation. When the Commission raised questions about the reports that were submitted, states tended toward silence. Likewise, when private communications were submitted to the Commission claiming a violation of the Charter, as best we can tell during the early days (the Commission at that time interpreted its mandate as requiring full confidentiality), states tended to disregard the entire process of inquiry and friendly settlement that the Commission was trying to conduct.[55] It was well known that during the period of 1987–2005 there were many gross and systematic violations of internationally recognized human rights throughout Africa, not to mention more mundane or quotidian violations, and that both types went uncorrected by regional (and other) arrangements.

The Commission was poorly funded, its support staff or secretariat was weak, human rights non-governmental organizations in Africa were neither numerous nor well prepared for interaction with the Commission, and the imposition of confidentiality made the Commission's promotion and protection work exceedingly difficult.[56] Yet by the late 1990s the Commission, with the help of a number of European public and private parties, had managed to escape from some of the confidentiality restrictions, had improved both its staff and the quality of its decisions, had carried out several in-country investigations with the consent of the appropriate state, had taken some initiatives without waiting for petitions, and was in relative terms drawing slightly more support and praise.[57]

In June 1998 the OAU adopted a protocol to the Banjul Charter approving the creation of an African human rights court.[58] The Protocol creating the Court entered into force in 2004, but the court was not

[55] Evelyn A. Ankumah, *The African Commission on Human and Peoples' Rights: Practice and Procedures* (The Hague: Martinus Nijhoff, 1996).

[56] Claude E. Welch, "The African Commission on Human and Peoples' Rights: A Five-Year Report and Assessment," *Human Rights Quarterly*, 14, 1 (February 1992), 43–61.

[57] Chidi Anselm Odinkalu and Camilla Christensen, "The African Commission on Human and Peoples' Rights: The Development of its Non-State Communication Procedures," *Human Rights Quarterly*, 20, 2 (May 1998), 235–280. See also Claude E. Welch, *Protecting Human Rights in Africa* (Philadelphia: University of Pennsylvania Press, 1995), especially ch. 5, on the interaction between the International Commission of Jurists, the NGO based in Geneva, and the African Commission.

[58] Makau Mutua, "The African Human Rights Court: A Two-Legged Stool?," *Human Rights Quarterly*, 21, 2 (May 1999), 342–363.

yet functional as of mid-2005. It was true that Africa, like other regions, had been part of a "third wave" of democratization after the Cold War, and that in relative terms political liberalism had made some advances in Africa by the late 1990s. Large and important countries like South Africa and Nigeria were not the only ones in Africa to move from repression and authoritarianism toward more liberal democracy. In 2001 the African Union succeeded the old OAU. Its Constitutive Act gave a central place to human rights, including a right of humanitarian intervention in cases of genocide, war crime and crimes against humanity.[59] Yet authoritarianism, persistent political instability, violation of many basic civil rights, and even genocidal massacres remained a feature of much of Africa, especially in the Great Lakes Region, parts of West Africa (Liberia, Sierra Leone), plus Somalia, the Sudan, Angola, etc. In this context, not to mention ongoing under-development of the most dire economic sort, it would take a great deal of optimism to believe that a regional human rights court could make a major difference. It is still too early to judge whether the political initiative, the African Peer Review Mechanism, established as part of the African Union's development programme, the New Partnership for Africa's Development (NEPAD), will improve or add confusion to Africa's nascent judicial institutions. Some analysts fear the latter.[60]

Regarding both Europe and the Western Hemisphere, we have already noted that when regional human rights arrangements confront governments unsympathetic to human rights, the regional machinery is not very effective in its protection efforts. Regarding international criminal courts, we have already noted the phenomenon of "judicial romanticism." If the International Criminal Tribunal for Rwanda has not made much of an impact on the Great Lakes Region of Africa, as we saw in chapter 4, surely there is not much reason to believe the impact of an African human rights court would be different – unless there were profoundly progressive changes in its context.

Conclusions

The Arab League's Human Rights Commission has mostly contented itself with ineffectual attention to Israel's policies in territories controlled since 1967, while ignoring gross and systematic violations in many Arab countries. Its impact having been negligible, it does not merit analysis here. Asia, being large and extremely diverse, not to mention being

[59] Article 4 (h) and (j), Constitutive Act of the African Union.
[60] Christof Heyns, "The African Regional Human Rights System: The African Charter," *Penn State Law Review*, 108 (2004), 679–702.

the locus of much criticism of western models of political liberalism, manifests no inter-governmental organizations for human rights.

Regional developments especially in Europe, the Western Hemisphere, and Africa make clear the paradox that in the absence of national commitment to political liberalism including human rights, it is impossible to build a regional system for protecting human rights that is genuinely effective. Where you have illiberal governments of various types, you lack the building blocks for effective regional inter-governmental action for rights. Conversely, however, the experience of Europe shows that just because you have liberal democracy at the national level, that does not mean that you do not need regional systems for review of state policies. Liberal democracy, meaning a commitment to civil and political rights, is a necessary but not entirely sufficient condition for achieving a truly rights protective society. One needs regional review – and perhaps global action as well.

Discussion questions

- What explains the quality of regional protection of human rights in Europe, compared with the Western Hemisphere and Africa? Is it likely that the latter two regions will evolve so as to duplicate the European record?
- Is any one of these three regions seriously interested in the protection of economic and social rights? Can economic and social rights be adjudicated? Is there always a clear distinction between civil rights and economic or social rights?
- With regard to human rights, what is the relationship between the Council of Europe and the European Union? Have the OSCE and NATO carved out a special role for themselves regarding the protection of human rights in Europe?
- Does the United States have a reasonable and coherent policy toward the regional mechanisms for the protection of human rights in the Western Hemisphere? Is the Hemisphere evolving the political context in which the OAS can improve the regional protection of human rights?
- Is it likely that the projected African Court of Human Rights could function so as to make a major difference in the regional protection of human rights on that continent?

Suggestions for further reading

Ankumah, Evelyn A., *The African Commission on Human and Peoples' Rights: Practice and Procedures* (The Hague: Martinus Nijhoff, 1996). A generally sympathetic overview, but with appropriate criticism. Some sections are mainly of use to practicing lawyers who want to use OAU regional procedures.

An-Na'im, Ahmed, and Francis M. Deng, eds., *Human Rights in Africa: Cross-Cultural Perspectives* (Washington: Brookings, 1990). A stimulating collection about universalism and cultural relativism with regard to Africa. Deals broadly and intelligently with the cultural context within which the OAU human rights initiatives occur.

Aziz, Miriam, *The Impact of European Rights on National Legal Cultures* (Oxford: Hart Publishing Ltd., 2004). A study of the interplay of regional and national standards on human rights in Europe.

Bartels, Lorand, *Human Rights Conditionality and EU External Relations* (Oxford: Oxford University Press, 2005). A timely update on a subject of growing importance.

Beddard R., *Human Rights and Europe*, 3rd edn (Cambridge: Grotius Publications, 1993). A good overview, widely used in specialized classes.

Cleary, Edward L., *The Struggle for Human Rights in Latin America* (Westport: Praeger, 1997). An optimistic account of changes in the Western Hemisphere, but very little on regional organizations.

Davidson, Scott, *The Inter-American Human Rights System* (Aldershot: Dartmouth, 1997). A traditional legal overview.

Farer, Tom, "The Rise of the Inter-American Human Rights Regime: No Longer a Unicorn, Not Yet an Ox," *Human Rights Quarterly*, 19, 3 (August 1997), 510–546. One of the best short overviews.

Jackson, Donald W., *The United Kingdom Confronts the European Convention on Human Rights* (Gainesville: University Press of Florida, 1997). A thorough look at why Britain has encountered so much difficulty after becoming a party to the European Convention on Civil and Political Rights. A good reminder that even those Anglo-Saxon states with a long commitment to liberal democracy still violate international human rights and are in need of international (in this case, regional) review.

Janis, Mark, Richard Kay, and Anthony Bradly, *European Human Rights Law* (New York: Oxford University Press, 1995). A broad and analytical introduction.

Kissinger, Henry, *Years of Renewal* (New York: Simon & Schuster, 1999). The former National Security Advisor and Secretary of State warmly endorses human rights in the CSCE process (for which he was not responsible) since it helped to generate problems for the Soviet empire, but generally, and explicitly in his African and Latin American diplomacy, he regarded human rights as frequently an unwelcome addition to his realist orientation. What caused him to work actively for majority rule in southern Africa was the appearance of Soviet and Cuban military personnel in Angola.

Korey, William, *The Promises We Keep: Human Rights, the Helsinki Process, and American Foreign Policy* (New York: St. Martin's, 1993). A favorable overview of the CSCE process that helped to de-legitimize European communism. Emphasizes the roles of the US Congress and private human rights groups, especially Jewish ones.

Leading by Example: A Human Rights Agenda for the European Union for the Year 2000: Agenda of the Comité des Sages and Final Project (Florence: European University Institute, 1998). A stock-taking of the European Union and human rights, with recommendations for the future.

Neuwahl, Nanette A., and Allan Rosas, eds., *The European Union and Human Rights* (The Hague: Martinus Nijhoff, 1995). A solid reminder that the EU has a human rights dimension in addition to its economic activities.

Umozurike, U. Oji, *The African Charter on Human and Peoples' Rights* (The Hague: Martinus Nijhoff, 1997). A direct and to-the-point overview, with sensible interpretations.

Williams, Andrew, *EU Human Rights Policies: A study in Irony* (Oxford: Oxford University Press, 2004). A study of the discrepancy between internal and external EU standards on human rights.

Waltz, Susan E., *Human Rights and Reform: Changing the Face of North African Politics* (Berkeley: University of California Press, 1995). By focusing on North Africa, the author shows the weakness of international human rights in the Arab world, and thus the underlying reasons why the Arab League has such a weak record on human rights. But she also shows emerging changes in favor of human rights.

6   Human rights and foreign policy
in comparative perspective[1]

We saw in earlier chapters that the United Nations Charter in its Articles 55 and 56 required states to cooperate on human rights matters, and the 1948 Universal Declaration of Human Rights was the first inter-governmental statement in world history to approve a set of basic principles on universal human rights. We also saw that since the 1940s, almost all states – not just western ones – have regularly reaffirmed the existence of universal human rights without negative discrimination based on nationality, ethnicity, gender, race, creed, or color. As noted, this reaffirmation occurred most saliently at the 1993 UN conference on human rights at Vienna. We also saw in chapter 5 that regional developments have supplemented this global trend, most notably in Europe and the Western Hemisphere. The international or transnational law of human rights is now a well-developed corpus of law, far more concentrated and specified than other fields such as international environmental law.

We also noted in chapter 1 that the twentieth century, however, was not only a time of increasing professions of international morality and human rights, but also the bloodiest century in human history. At the start of the twenty-first century, a fundamental challenge is how to reduce the enormous gap between the liberal legal framework on human rights that most states have formally endorsed, and the realist principles that they often follow in their foreign policies. Partly as a result of those realist policies, little has been done about the illiberal reality of the human condition that is so evident from Algeria to Angola, from Belarus to Burma, from China to the Central African Republic. The most

[1] The views in this chapter are my own, but I gratefully acknowledge the contributions of others who worked on a research project on this subject funded by the United Nations University: Peter Baehr (the Netherlands), Sally Morphet (the United Kingdom), Chiyuki Aoi and Yozo Yokota (Japan), Gabor Kardos (Central Europe), Sergei Chugrov (Russia), Sanjoy Banerjee (India), Cristina Eguizabal (Latin America), Tiyanjana Maluwa (South Africa), Zachary Karabell (Iran). Jack Donnelly also participated in this project and wrote the final chapter in D. Forsythe, ed., *Human Rights and Comparative Foreign Policy* (Tokyo: United Nations University Press, 2000). An earlier version of this chapter was published in the *International Journal* (Canada), 53, 1 (Winter 1997–1998), 113–132. I am grateful to the editors for their helpful suggestions.

important problem is not that, as noted, certain Asian states at the 1993 Vienna Conference tried to elevate cultural relativism and national particularism over universal (or regional) human rights. The more important problem is that after the Cold War we are now faced with glaring genocide and other crimes against humanity on a massive scale. Treaties to protect the rights of women and children are juxtaposed with a global industry in the sex trade. Treaties to outlaw slavery, the slave trade, and slavery-like practices are combined with daily press accounts of persons held in *de facto* bondage – whether sugar-cane cutters in the Dominican Republic, shirt-makers in Guatemala, or child laborers in India and Pakistan. Two 1977 protocols to the 1949 Geneva Conventions for victims of war meant nothing to those who killed Red Cross workers in Chechnya, UN civilian officials in Iraq, or those working for MSF (Doctors Without Borders) in Afghanistan. The growth of liberal principles has not consistently been matched by a diminishment of brutal power struggles and murderous hatreds.

While inter-governmental agencies and private transnational groups dealing with human rights proliferate, one key to progressive developments remains states and their foreign policies. As we have already seen, IGOs, from the UN through the OAS to the Organization for Security and Cooperation in Europe, have extensive human rights programs. Independent international officials for these organizations generate some influence. But it is state-members of these IGOs that take the most important decisions, and it is states, along with non-state parties, that are the targets of reform efforts. Likewise, as we will see in chapter 7, NGOs such as Amnesty International, Human Rights Watch, and Physicians for Human Rights, among others, are highly active in human rights matters and generate some influence. But again, it is states that approve treaties and their monitoring mechanisms, states that sometimes manipulate foreign assistance in relation to rights, states that (may or may not) arrest war criminals – either singly or via international organizations such as NATO. NGOs mainly pressure *states* to do the right thing.

This chapter looks at human rights and state foreign policy in comparative perspective. It begins with a short discussion of three prominent mechanisms states can and do – at least sometimes – employ to influence another government's human rights policies: diplomatic, economic, and military means. Different approaches may be taken in different situations, as states usually calculate the instruments available, the expected effect of the action taken, and anticipated reactions.[2] This is followed by a focus on the United States, the most important actor in international relations

[2] Peter R. Baehr and Monique Castermans-Holleman, *The Role of Human Rights in Foreign Policy* (New York: Palgrave Macmillan, 2004, 3rd ed.), 69.

at the birth of the twenty-first century. I show that the USA has a particular slant to its foreign policy on rights, and that Washington is more prone to preach to others than to take international rights standards very seriously in its own policies. The chapter then provides a comparative analysis of human rights in the foreign policies of some other states that either are liberal democracies or aspire to be so. I show that most differ from the US approach in one way or another, due to a varying combination of history and political culture, geo-political position, and perceived national interests. This is followed by a brief commentary on the human rights policies of some illiberal states such as Iran.

Finally, the chapter offers some concluding thoughts about human rights and foreign policy.[3] The accent is on the positive, despite ample reason for reserve about the immediate future. Despite the rise of Al Qaeda and other manifestations of radical Islamic groups prone to total war, with their attacks on civilians and abuse of prisoners, and despite a US tendency to respond in kind, with especially abuse of detainees, the historical trend remains in favour of a broad range of human rights. While predicting the future is a notoriously risky business, the one-hundredth anniversary of the Universal Declaration of Human Rights is likely to be more joyous than the fiftieth. As long as states must provide for their own security in the absence of effective international arrangements, realist principles will never be totally absent from foreign policy. But there is good reason to think that certain long-term trends are favorable to more influence for liberal principles in relative terms.

Policy instruments

In the past, states have often proven reluctant to speak out on human rights violations by others, fearing interruption of "business as usual"– not only on business but also on other important matters like security cooperation. It is very clear that states do not like to sue each other about human rights in the International Court of Justice, the number of cases on human rights being very small. Even within the Council of Europe, neighboring states with lots of common concerns do not often sue each other in the European Court of Human Rights, the overwhelming number of cases being triggered by individual rather than state complaint. The same pattern is evident with regard to the InterAmerican Court of Human Rights. Nevertheless, many states do address human rights

---

[3] Compare Jan Egeland, "Focus on Human Rights: Ineffective Big States, Potent Small States," *Journal of Peace Research*, 21, 3 (1984), and his *Impotent Superpower – Potent Small State: Potentialities and Limitations of Human Rights Objectives in the Foreign Policies of the United States and Norway* (Oslo: Norwegian University Press, 1988).

issues in other states, short of judicial proceedings. Sometimes this public diplomacy on human rights is to embarrass enemies, as was true of East-West debates in the UN General Assembly during the Cold War. And sometimes taking a public position on human rights abroad is designed for domestic consumption, as was true of Henry Kissinger's public comments about the importance of human rights in South America – even as he was committing the USA to quiet support for repressive regimes. But sometimes states are genuinely interested in advancing rights abroad; and then they seriously think about ends and means.

Diplomatic means

There are a number of ways a state may utilize diplomacy to try to influence the policies of states violating human rights. The traditional, classical method has been that of "quiet" diplomacy, that is, to hold a confidential discussion behind closed doors and away from public view. Emissaries may meet with foreign officials to discuss a particular human rights situation or to request a halt to certain actions. This is sometimes a useful way to bring objections and matters of concern to the offending party without risk of widespread controversy or public outcry. Sometimes a target government will prove flexible if it can avoid the public appearance of caving in to foreign pressure. Quiet diplomacy is of course hard to track and evaluate, precisely because it may be some years before outsiders know what has transpired.

From time to time private diplomacy for human rights is then followed by public statements, as when President George W. Bush met with Russian President Vladimir Putin in early 2005. President Bush, having devoted his second inaugural address to the theme of freedom, could hardly not raise the subject of Russian policies at home and abroad that touched on human rights. And by all accounts there was some private attention to human rights in places like Chechnya and the Ukraine during this presidential summit.

But when the dialogue moves to the public arena, states undertaking a human rights discourse frequently meet "blowback" or negative reactions. State leaders who are subjected to public criticism often become defensive and inflexible in the name of national pride, state sovereignty, or because they have domestic elements who are "hard liners" about resisting foreign pressure. When in the 1970s the US Congress passed the Jackson–Vanik Amendment publicly requiring greater emigration (freedom of movement) from Romania, the Soviet Union, and other European communist countries, the numbers of those allowed out actually dropped in the short term, as the target governments did not want to be seen caving in to US public pressure.

On the other hand, sometimes some public pressure can be productive, and the human rights NGOs that engage in the "naming and shaming" game can cite a number of situations in which public pressure brought some progressive gains over time. European state pressure on Turkey to improve its human rights record, in the context of the debate over Turkey's admission to the European Union, clearly had some beneficial effect.

Other essentially diplomatic steps can be undertaken, such as cancellation or postponement of ministerial visits or recall of ambassadors. This is likely to draw attention to the issue at hand, particularly when done by prominent states. In early February 2005, in the wake of the assassination of a former Lebanese prime minister, the United States recalled its ambassador to Syria, believing that state bore at least some measure of responsibility. The USA used the opportunity to criticize Syria for its lax border-control policies, its anti-democratic domestic practices, and what it felt was an unnecessary Syrian military presence in Lebanon. While Syria condemned the assassination and denied involvement, greater international attention was being paid to its policies, including human rights policies.[4]

The large number of intergovernmental agencies dealing with human rights means that member states are confronted almost daily about taking a diplomatic position on some human rights question. This is certainly true in the sprawling UN system, but also true in more limited IGOs like the OSCE, Council of Europe, and OAS. Even in the Commonwealth, formerly the British Commonwealth, there are occasions for voting on human rights issues pertaining, for example, to governmental violation of rights in Zimbabwe.

Often less influential, though undeniably symbolic, are various cultural or sports-related embargos enacted by states. For example, many states refused to participate in sporting events with South Africa under white minority rule to protest the country's policy of apartheid . . . These actions were generally supported by apartheid's victims and often found favor with public opinion in criticizing states – in part because one could take a stand for human rights without paying much price in national blood or treasure. While these sports and cultural boycotts did not by themselves lead to the end of apartheid, such policies made their contribution to the broader effort to delegitimize repressive minority rule.

[4] See Steve R. Weissman, "Bush Considers Syria 'Out of Step' with Democracy," *International Herald Tribune*, February 19, 2005, http://www.iht.com/articles/2005/02/18/news/syria.html.

The diplomatic methods discussed above are used to protest or draw attention to particular human rights violations. It can be noted, too, that not all diplomatic techniques are negative in nature. States may offer ministerial visits or invite foreign diplomats or heads of state to visit in an effort to support a country's human rights policies. Governments may be invited to participate in international conferences or to join international organizations, such as the Council of Europe or the European Union, in order to influence human rights policy. Oganizations like the EU do note the domestic human rights policies of member states. One of the reasons for expanding NATO membership was to integrate militarily certain former authoritarian states into an alliance for constitutional democracies.

While diplomatic means may or may not be effective by themselves, they can be linked to other steps.

Economic means

Governments are often reluctant to undertake economic sanctions against another state – whether for human rights or other reasons – as they may hurt themselves. One of the reasons Switzerland did not join the United Nations until 2004 was that the economic sanctions it had imposed on Mussolini's Italy as voted by the League of Nations damaged the Swiss economy as well as proving highly unpopular in Italian-speaking Switzerland. One of the reasons that the USA violated mandatory trade sanctions on the breakaway white minority government of Ian Smith in Rhodesia, now Zimbabwe, was the damage otherwise done to American businesses, particularly Union Carbide. Economic sanctions mostly cut both ways.

States, however, do sometimes suspend full trade, and also development aid or other types of foreign assistance. This may be done for lack of other appealing options – eg., diplomacy alone has proven ineffective but military action is not desired. But this type of sanctioning can have unintended or unwanted effects.[5] Former UN Secretary General Boutros Boutros-Ghali expressed this concern succinctly: "[Economic sanctions] raise the ethical question of whether suffering inflicted on vulnerable groups in the target country is a legitimate means of exerting pressure on political leaders whose behaviour is unlikely to be affected by the plight of their subjects."[6] Indeed, virulent debate ensued during the 1990s regarding sanctions imposed on the people of Iraq, as authorized by the UN Security Council. Supporters of the sanctions pointed to their efficacy in making life difficult for Saddam Hussein's abusive regime, while critics stressed their destructive effects on the people of Iraq, notably

[5] Boutros Boutros Ghali, quoted in Peter Baehr, *The Role of Human Rights*, 74.
[6] Ibid.

children.[7] Eventually the UNSC voted to allow Iraq to sell some oil, using the proceeds supposedly to purchase goods necessary for the civilian population. But the Council failed to supervise the program effectively. Money was siphoned off to the Hussein regime, and other problems manifested themselves.[8]

Most general economic sanctions undoubtedly do not seriously affect the elite, because the rulers and associated social circles are well positioned to avoid inconvenience. Most general economic sanctions fail to drastically change policy by the target state in the short term. On the other hand, "smart sanctions" have been tried on occasion in an effort to affect target governments while avoiding harm to civilian populations. In Haiti, for example, after general sanctions had been tried with predictable results, smart sanctions were applied to the military elite associated with Cedras, that group then blocking the return of the elected President, Father Aristide. These smart sanctions, closing off elite bank accounts and freedom to travel, contributed to the departure of Cedras and his entourage – along with promises of safe passage and comfortable life in exile. Smart sanctions have been either debated or adopted regarding other situations, for example with regard to the Sudanese government because of its policies pertaining to the Darfur region in 2005.

As with diplomatic means, economic steps do not have to be negative in nature. States may often provide loans or credits to governments who are willing to adopt measures conducive to human rights protection. Most liberal democracies, as well as the IGOs that they influence, manifest democracy promotion programs in order to provide economic and technical assistance to certain authoritarian or transitional states. The funding is used to sponsor and supervise free and fair elections, state-building – for example the construction of vigorous parliaments and independent courts, and nation-building – for example encouraging an active and rights-supportive civil society. At the time of writing western states were undertaking unilateral and multilateral democracy promotion and other rights-protective policies costing hundreds of millions of dollars in foreign assistance.

Military means

Finally, there is a range of military steps available at least to those states with effective military establishments. The most dramatic measure is that

---

[7] David P. Forsythe, *The Humanitarians: The International Committee of the Red Cross* (Cambridge: Cambridge University Press, 2005). The private ICRC was the first to raise the alarm, followed by UN agencies like UNICEF and WHO.

[8] While much commentary in the USA focused on "UN" failures and corruption, the main difficulty was that western states turned a blind eye to such things as black market profiteering, since western allies Jordan and Turkey were the main beneficiaries.

of coercive military action. Such action, as a matter of fact and not necessarily of law, may be taken to stop gross human rights violations such
as major war crimes, crimes against humanity, or genocide. When undertaken without UN Security Council approval, such action is highly controversial, as seen by NATO's bombing of Serbia in 1999 to try to stop
violent persecution and forced displacement of the ethnic Albanians constituting a majority of the Kosovars.

There is the long-standing problem that states may claim to be engaged
in "humanitarian intervention" whereas in reality they have other primary motives. The US–UK war in Iraq, though it may produce some
positive long-term consequences for human rights, could not be defined
as a humanitarian intervention. By 2005 the George W. Bush Administration's main justification for the war was advancing democracy. But the
foundations for the war were steeped in the rhetoric of national security.
At the time of the US invasion Washington argued that Iraq had ties to
terrorist groups such as al Qaeda, that it possessed illegal weapons of mass
destruction, and that the Hussein regime needed to be removed because
of future security problems. As Peter Baehr and Monique Castermans-
Holleman note, "This regime had for a number of years been guilty of
human rights violations, but to put an end to these violations was not
mentioned as a main objective of military action."[9]

There have not been many clear cut cases of "humanitarian war" for
obvious reasons: most states have been reluctant to spill national blood
for the protection of the rights of "others," and it is hard to justify such
uses of force when the projected human and other costs may exceed
the humanitarian good accomplished. Humanitarian intervention almost
always makes the situation worse in terms of human costs in the short
run. NATO's bombing of Serbia in 1999 was initially met with expanded
persecution and displacement.

Less controversial than unauthorized state military action is state military support for a UN Security Council resolution designed to alleviate
human rights problems. As discussed in earlier chapters, this may take the
form of an enforcement or peacekeeping field operation. As noted, after
the cold war these multilateral security missions almost always entailed a
human rights dimension. Whether these field operations were designed
to be coercive, evolved into coercion, or remained mostly a matter of
armed diplomacy, states were at the center of action. It was states in the
UN Security Council that authorized the deployment, states that contributed the troops, and often states that pressed for termination of mission when difficulties occurred. It was states that were responsible to see
that "UN" troops were trained – or not – in international humanitarian

---

[9] Baehr and Castermans-Holleman, *The Role of Human Rights*, p. 80.

law, and states that prosecuted troops that engaged in sex trafficking or other abuses – or failed to do so.

As with diplomatic and economic means, there was a positive side to military options. We have already mentioned one reason for expansion of NATO membership, namely to shore up transitional democracies by linking them to more established democracies. Bilaterally, states may choose to expand military assistance to reward another state for democratic and rights reform. In 2005 the USA expanded military assistance to Guatemala, partly in response to some rights-protective reforms in that state. At the same time the USA reduced military assistance to some states supportive of the ICC, thus using military assistance to undercut human rights developments.

US foreign policy and human rights

To a great extent a state's foreign policy on human rights is bound up with its version of nationalism, which is to say with a nation's collective self-image, which is to say with its informal ideology. Since most nations think well of themselves, most states' policies on human rights reflect the conviction that the state has some virtuous point to teach others. In the case of the United States, to understand the interpretation of human rights in foreign policy it is crucial to understand that some in the elite and most in the mass public view the USA as a beacon of freedom to the world. Human rights is equated with personal freedom as found in the US Bill of Rights appended to its constitution, and not with the broader and more complex conception found in the International Bill of Rights (as indicated, this means the UN Charter, the Universal Declaration, and the 1966 International Covenants on Civil-Political and Socio-Economic-Cultural Rights). Human rights in foreign policy is thus primarily a matter of Washington pressing others to improve personal freedom. International human rights is not primarily a matter of the United States applying global or regional standards to itself. Particularly the Ronald Reagan and George W. Bush Administrations – whether one calls them romantic nationalists, chauvinist nationalists, militant American Exceptionalists, crusading neo-conservatives, or some other label – certainly did not try to use internationally recognized human rights to improve American society. They often preferred a strictly American conception of human rights in order to bypass many international rights standards and implementing agencies.

From the early settlers in New England to the powerful Goldwater–Reagan–George W. Bush wing of the Republic Party in contemporary times, important political circles have seen the USA not as an ordinary nation but as a great experiment in personal liberty that has implications for the planet.[10] Well-known defects in American society such as a history of slavery, segregation, racist immigration laws, anti-Semitism, religious and other bigotry, gender discrimination, and grinding poverty have failed to alter this dominant self-image. American exceptionalism, the belief in the exceptional freedom and goodness of the American people, is the core of the dominant American political culture.[11]

The continuing strength of American exceptionalism should not necessarily be equated with an automatic crusade for human rights in US foreign policy. The belief in American greatness, as linked to personal freedom, can lead to involvement or isolationism. Two schools of thought have long competed for control of US foreign policy. The first, associated with Washington, Jefferson, and Patrick Buchanan, would perfect American society at home and thus provide international leadership only by indirect example. This school was clearly dominant in the Congress in the 1930s. The second, associated with Hamilton and most presidents since Woodrow Wilson, would have the USA actively involved in world affairs – on the assumption that US impact would be for the better.[12] As Henry Kissinger has noted,[13] Ronald Reagan was the classic American liberal, albeit tending toward the unilateralist rather than multilateralist pole, believing that an active foreign policy, featuring at least a rhetorical commitment to democracy, would make the world a better place.

American exceptionalism does not so much guarantee specific foreign policy initiatives as it predisposes Washington to talk about freedom and democracy and to assume it can make a difference for the better when and if it gets involved. The American public and Congress were deferential if not supportive in 1992 when President Bush deployed military force to guarantee the secure delivery of humanitarian assistance in Somalia. But after difficulties there, especially in 1993, the American public and Congress were content to avoid military intervention in Rwanda during 1994. The Vietnam syndrome, now supplemented by Somalia, occasionally or inconsistently puts a brake on direct US military intervention in complicated situations. Military operations in places like Haiti, Bosnia, and Kosovo could only be sustained because combat casualties were avoided. But the more fundamental faith in American greatness as

---

[10] T. Davis and S. Lynn-Jones, "City upon a hill," *Foreign Policy*, 66 (1987), 20–38.

[11] See further David P. Forsythe, *American Exceptionalism and Global Human Rights* (Lincoln: University of Nebraska Distinguished Lecture Series, 1999). And Forsythe, "Human Rights and US Foreign Policy: Two Levels, Two Worlds," in David Beetham, ed., *Politics and Human Rights* (Oxford: Blackwell, 1995), 111–130.

[12] See Michael H. Hunt, *Ideology and US Foreign Policy* (New Haven: Yale University Press, 1987).

[13] Henry Kissinger, *Diplomacy* (New York: Simon & Schuster, 1994).

a symbol of freedom is alive and reasonably well, buttressed by success in removing the evil dictator Saddam Hussein from power in 2003.

Events in Kosovo and Yugoslavia can be understood against this background. The United States felt the moral obligation to oppose repression and expulsion of ethnic Albanians, but fear of casualties caused the Clinton Administration and NATO to adopt the military strategy of air strikes without ground troops. This approach failed to protect the Albanian Kosovars in the short term, contributed to destabilizing pressures on neighboring states, and solidified Yugoslav opinion behind the Milosevic government. But in the long term, as noted in chapter 5, the United States and NATO weakened Milosevic's ability to persecute the Albanian Kosovars, and weakened his power in Belgrade. In a quite remarkable if controversial military operation, Washington led NATO in using military force to protect human rights but without suffering more casualties (and civilian damage abroad) than domestic opinion would tolerate. It was a delicate balancing act.

Current public opinion on rights in US foreign policy is a blend of liberalism and realism – of universal concern and narrow self-interest. Polls showed that the general public as well as opinion leaders did indeed list "promoting and defending human rights in other countries," as well as "helping to bring a democratic form of government to other nations" as "very important" goals of US foreign policy. But in 1995 these goals were in thirteenth and fourteenth place, respectively with only 34 per cent and 25 per cent of the general public listing them as very important. Eighty per cent or more of the general public listed "stopping the flow of illegal drugs into the USA," "protecting the jobs of American workers" and "preventing the spread of nuclear weapons" as much more important. Analysts concluded that there was considerable American popular support for pragmatic internationalism, but not a great deal of support for moral internationalism.[14] If human rights could be linked to self-interest, or if human rights do not interfere with self-interest, one could build a political coalition for action. But if one made only moral and altruistic arguments, it was difficult to sustain a principled foreign policy centering on rights. With regard to Kosovo, American public opinion was permissive as long as significant numbers of American casualties were avoided. But in the spring of 1999 polls showed that almost two-thirds of the public were in favor of early negotiations to end the NATO air strikes.

Public opinion polls in 2005 showed that in general or in the abstract, American public support for military means to advance democracy

[14] Ole Holsti, "Public Opinion on Human Rights in American Foreign Policy," in David P. Forsythe, ed., *The United States and Human Rights: Looking Inward and Outward* (Lincoln: University of Nebraska Press, 2000).

abroad was relatively low. It seemed very clear that had the George W. Bush administration gone to the public and Congress in 2003 and asked for a mandate to use force to advance democracy in Iraq, that would have been a hard sell for the President. The actual rationale for that war was national security – links to terrorism, weapons of mass destruction, and general security fears for the future. It was only after clarification of facts – no substantive Hussein links to Al Qaeda, no weapons of mass destruction, and hence no clear and present security danger – that the Bush Administration stressed the role of advancing democracy in Iraq. As noted elsewhere in this text, support for democracy in Iraq and the prospect of Saddam Hussein on trial did not save George W. Bush from very low public approval at home regarding his Iraq policy in 2005.

Because of American exceptionalism, as well as a legal culture, Washington is full of private groups that lobby for some version of human rights abroad. This subject is treated in detail in chapter 7. The national communications media also report on international human rights issues with some regularity. But many of the human rights NGOs in the 1990s bemoaned their inability to stimulate more action, and more consistent action, for rights in US foreign policy.[15] The polls cited above indicate why. There is no grassroots movement supportive of a costly crusade for human rights. Public opinion is reflected in a Republican-controlled Congress that is openly suspicious of multilateral standards and action, although it may (or may not) support particular ventures such as the enlargement of NATO or air strikes on Yugoslavia or Iraq. While "the CNN factor" was given some credit for pushing the USA into action in both northern Iraq (the flight of Kurds) and Somalia (domestic starvation and disorder), both Rwanda in 1994 and what was then Zaire (now the Democratic Congo) in 1997, showed that Washington was not always moved to action by media coverage of human rights violations and humanitarian hardship. With regard to Kosovo, media pictures of trainloads of ethnic Albanians being forced from their homes, and other reports of refugee hardships, probably had something to do with western support for air strikes on Yugoslavia despite mistakes and collateral damage. But those pictures did not cause a public demand for ground troops and costly humanitarian intervention in terms of soldiers' lives.

Samantha Power has shown that throughout its modern history, when the USA has faced situations of genocide or near-genocide abroad, there has never been a powerful domestic push from public opinion or the Congress forcing the President into a decisive involvement. Presidents

---

[15] Aryeh Neier, "The New Double Standard," *Foreign Policy*, 105 (1996–1997), 91–102; and Ellen Dorsey, "US Foreign Policy and the Human Rights Movement," in Forsythe, *The United States and Human Rights*.

have felt free to pursue mostly realist policies of narrow self-interest, rather than liberal policies of protecting the rights of others.[16]

The matter of religious persecution abroad is instructive. The subject of religious freedom has a nice ring to it in American society, founded partly as it was to secure freedom from religious bigotry in Europe. In the 1990s, especially social conservatives pushed hard to elevate the subject of religious freedom in US foreign policy. But a number of pragmatic conservatives, as well as some international liberals, objected to the bills introduced in Congress. These bills called for automatic sanctions against countries engaging in, or tolerating, religious persecution. As such, these bills would have created sanctions on such US allies as Saudi Arabia, Israel, Greece, Pakistan, etc. Only when the bills were weakened so as to give the President considerable discretion in dealing with religious persecution abroad did a law finally pass. So there was more attention to religious freedom in US foreign policy, and a new office for such was created in the State Department. But there was also concern not to interfere very much with traditional US economic and strategic interests.[17] Some religious conservatives had teamed with some secular liberals to produce more attention to religious freedom and religious persecution, but traditional self interest in economic and security matters was hardly absent.[18]

President Clinton's rhetoric on foreign policy, although spasmodically delivered, was squarely within the activist tradition of American exceptionalism. Enlarging the global democratic community was supposedly one of the basic pillars of his foreign policy. The semantic emphasis was on personal freedom and democracy. He justified US troops in Bosnia by saying Washington must lead, must hold the feet of his European allies to the fire, must make a difference for a liberal democratic peace with human rights in the Balkans. The 1995 Dayton agreement was not just about peace, but about liberal democracy and human rights. There was strong Clinton talk in support of human rights: for universal rights at Vienna; for criminal prosecutions at The Hague in the International Criminal Tribunal for the Former Yugoslavia; for containment of repressive states like the Sudan, Iraq, and Iran; for sanctions on Burma/Myanmar. As long as one does not have to pay a high national price, in blood or treasure, to advance human rights, the USA is certainly for them – at least for the civil and political rights congruent with the American self-image. These were the rights stressed in Clinton's 1998 visit to China.

[16] Samantha Power, *"A Problem From Hell;" America and the Age of Genocide* (New York: Basic Books, 2002).

[17] See further Eric Schmitt, "Bill to Punish Nations Limiting Religious Beliefs Passes Senate," *New York Times*, October 10, 1998, A 3.

[18] See further Allen D. Hertzke, *Freeing God's Children: The Unlikely Alliance for Global Human Rights* (New York: Rowman & Littlefield, 2004).

Self-interested economic and strategic concerns were hardly absent from US foreign policy during the Clinton era. His first Assistant Secretary of State for human rights, John Shattuck, contemplated resigning several times in frustration over the lack of commitment to human rights.[19] Not only did the Clinton Administration not intervene to stop genocide in Rwanda in 1994, but also that Administration de-linked trading privileges from basic civil and political rights in China.

The difficulty of arriving at firm generalizations about the Clinton era and human rights is shown by Kosovo.[20] There the Clinton Administration and other NATO governments became involved in expensive air strikes over several months, and put the reputation of the United States and NATO on the line, for the primary reason of human rights. The controlling issues initially were liberal democracy in Europe and international action against minority oppression. More traditional geopolitical interests involved the stability of friendly states and the coherence of NATO. Complicating analysis was that US interest in stopping persecution could be seen as a self-interested desire to recover reputation. The USA, having been slow to act to stop abuses in Bosnia 1991–1994, was partly propelled to act in Kosovo in 1999 to regain the reputational high ground, which is a basis for the exercise of soft power.

President George W. Bush's foreign policy in general stressed American exceptionalism as its guiding principle. Rhetoric promoting American ideals – namely freedom and liberty – was omnipresent in his speeches, especially his second inaugural address. Despite the originally declared justifications for invading Iraq in 2003, which had little to do with human rights and much to do with national security, the president's post-war language was replete with references to democracy and personal freedom. Whereas during his first term George W. Bush paid hardly any discernible attention to the decline of democracy in Russia, during the second term Bush himself laid great public and private stress on precisely that topic. Increasingly George W. Bush went beyond Clinton's rhetorical but sporadic forays into the human rights domain. Increasingly the Republican Bush took on the political coloring of a Jimmy Carter or a Woodrow Wilson to stress the advancement of democracy, and its civil and political rights, as the central pillar of his foreign policy.

A year after the September 11 attacks, the Bush Administration presented its National Security Strategy statement, outlining a foreign policy

---

[19] John Shattuck, *Freedom On Fire: Human Rights Wars & America's Response* (Cambridge, MA: Harvard University Press, 2003).
[20] Clinton's memoirs provide little insight into the importance of various human rights, either for the man or for his Administration.

with much semantic attention to personal rights. "Human rights" was not a privileged phrase, but freedom and democracy were. While the first major section of the outline declared an intention to "Champion Aspirations for Human Dignity," it was also the strategy's shortest portion, other than its initial outline.[21] References to "human rights" can be found sparsely strung about the document, but even more apparent were references to "human dignity," a notion that seems to be replacing the language of human rights in American foreign policy. Throughout the document, "human rights" was offered as a vague matter to be dealt with by other states, while "human dignity" was outlined in substantial detail: "the rule of law; limits on the absolute power of the state; free speech; freedom of worship; equal justice; respect for women; religious and ethnic tolerance; and respect for private property."[22] Norms like free speech, freedom of worship, and respect for private property, are all values firmly embedded in American political discourse.

Further probing reveals two major soft spots in the contemporary US approach to human rights, regardless of changing Administrations. The first of these is that the USA, unlike its North Atlantic allies, refuses to accept cultural, economic, and social rights as real human rights. When the USA talks about its support for the Universal Declaration of Human Rights, it simply omits reference to those articles endorsing fundamental rights to adequate standards of food, clothing, shelter, health care, and social security. It has never ratified the International Covenant on Economic, Social, and Cultural Rights. Federal laws, and most internal state laws, do not provide for socio-economic fundamental entitlements, as compared with optional benefits. There is no recognized right to health care, much less a recognized right to adequate food, clothing, and shelter. The USA is one of the few states not to adhere to the UN Convention on the Rights of the Child. The Convention appears to make encroachments on family privacy, arguably protected by the US Constitution. The Clinton Administration did rhetorically accept the right to development at the Vienna conference, but this posture has been of no practical consequence.

The USA continues to exclusively emphasize civil and political rights, including the civil right to private property. But even on this subject the US support for international standards is highly qualified. The Senate has added many reservations, declarations, and understandings to its 1992 consent to the International Covenant on Civil and Political Rights (as well as failing to accept the Optional Protocol that would allow individual

---

[21] See "The National Security Strategy of the United States of America," http://www.whitehouse.gov/nsc/nss.html, accessed 2/18/05.

[22] See further Julie Mertus, *Bait and Switch: Human Rights and US Foreign Policy* (New York: Routledge, 2004), 59.

complaints about violations). It is clear the USA continues to emphasize a narrower national law rather than a broader international law of human rights. Even some of its international partners, like the Netherlands, have criticized this US orientation. It is well known that a number of Canadians view the US version of market democracy as unnecessarily harsh, overly individualized, and lacking in a sense of community.[23]

Second among the soft spots in US foreign policy on human rights is its undecided posture on authoritarian and otherwise illiberal development. Rhetorically, as noted, Washington supports development via liberal democracy. It has joined with other western states in the World Bank to occasionally manipulate loans in relation to human rights issues and democratic governance. Officially it provides economic assistance for democratic development in Russia and other formerly communist states in Europe, as well as in the Western Hemisphere. Political conditionality with a liberal flavor has been applied, in bilateral and multilateral channels, to states such as Cambodia, China, Croatia, Burma, Guatemala, Kenya, Malawi, and others. But where the USA has important economic or political interests, Washington has not sought to link human rights performance with either multilateral or bilateral economic transactions. This is clearly the case in current Sino-American relations, where Most Favored Nation trading status was de-linked from China's human rights record. It has always been the case that key oil-producing states like Saudi Arabia and Kuwait were exempt from US pressure on human rights. (Congressional elements did express concern about Kuwaiti repression after it was liberated in 1991.) Under its "democracy assistance" program, more funds have gone toward market restructuring and related economic and security concerns than toward support for civil and political rights.[24]

Whether the George W. Bush Administration can alter this pattern is not yet clear. On the one hand it talked about democratizing the Arab Middle East and did not exempt the oil-rich authoritarians from that discourse. On the other hand it continued to support various dictators, like Musharraf in Pakistan, and in 2005 concluded a deal to sell jet fighters to that government which had arrived in dictatorial power by way of an unconstitutional *coup d'état*.

Two factors generally account for this ambivalent and inconsistent US record on illiberal development. Much like the old Leninist notion of one

[23] Rhoda E. Howard, *Human Rights and the Search for Community* (Boulder: Westview, 1995).

[24] Thomas Carothers, *Assessing Democracy: The Case of Romania* (Washington: The Carnegie Endowment, 1996); and David P. Forsythe, Michelle Leonard, and Garry Baker, "US Foreign Policy, Democracy, and Migration," in Peter Bender and Aristide Zolberg, eds., *Global Migrants, Global Refugees* (Providence: Berghahn Books, 2000).

step back to make two steps forward, the USA can rationalize economic transactions with authoritarian states like China under the notion that modern, high-tech capitalism will force a further broadening and deepening of the rule of law, property rights, individual entrepreneurship, free flow of information, reduction of statism, and other developments necessarily leading to more civil and political rights. After all, in 2004 China wrote the protection of property rights into its new constitution (followed in 2005 by a further crackdown of any form of political dissent.) The second factor accounting for lack of consistent opposition to authoritarian development is the judgment that the pressures of today eliminate reasonable choice about the future. The monarchies in Saudi Arabia and Morocco are said to be too important in too many ways to allow human rights pressures. The old Kissinger argument about the Shah in Iran resurfaces. If one replaced the ruling family in Riyadh with another Khomeini, or produced another Algeria in Morocco, one would have advanced neither human rights nor US security and prosperity. Of course authoritarian governments play on this fear, telling Washington that the choice is between them or something worse. Mobutu did so in Zaire, and Kabila did the same in the Democratic Republic of the Congo. Musharraf does it in Pakistan.

There are three strong points to recent US foreign policy on rights abroad. First, as noted in chapter 3, the George H. W. Bush and Clinton Administrations both led in expanding the scope of Chapter VII of the UN Charter, involving matters on which the Council can take a binding decision. As a result of US policy in the UN Security Council when dealing with northern Iraq, Somalia, Bosnia, Haiti, Rwanda, Angola, etc., the Council has effectively decided that the security of persons inside states can constitute a threat to international peace and security, leading to authoritative protection attempts by the international community. Deployments of military force, limited combat, economic sanctions, and deeply intrusive diplomacy have all occurred in recent years in relation to human rights issues under Chapter VII. International law still provides no doctrine of humanitarian intervention, but the concept of international peace and security has been expanded to substitute for this lack. The USA has led in shrinking the domain of exclusive domestic jurisdiction, and in expanding the realm of authoritative decisions by the Council. This is a promising trend, at least in theory, for the international protection of human rights.

Second, also noted in chapter 3, the USA has also led in expanding the notion of peacekeeping so as to provide complex or second-generation peacekeeping with human rights dimensions. In places like Namibia, El Salvador, Cambodia, Guatemala, and Bosnia, and the Sudan, *inter alia*, the USA has encouraged UN and other field missions under Chapter VI of the Charter not simply to oversee a cease-fire or other military agreement, but more broadly to try to establish and consolidate a liberal democratic peace. As might be expected, the actual record of results is mixed. There has been more success in Namibia and El Salvador than in Cambodia and Bosnia. Nevertheless, Washington has been a leader in these developments particularly where the local protagonists show signs of good faith efforts to reach and implement international agreements.[25] The trend continued in 2005, with the US encouraging a UN security operation in the Sudan, long wracked by violence and instability and atrocities in the Darfur region, once it became clear that the African Union would not be able to decisively improve the situation. There was also a small UN security operation in the Democratic Republic of the Congo.

Third, as noted in chapter 4, the USA led in the resurrection of the idea of international criminal courts, dormant since the 1940s at Nuremberg and Tokyo. True, as we saw in an earlier chapter, when the US-led Security Council created the 1993 *ad hoc* court for former Yugoslavia and the 1995 *ad hoc* court for Rwanda, it was searching for action that would not entail costly military intervention. The two courts were as much the product of escape from responsibility as of commitment to legal justice for gross violations of human rights such as grave breaches of the laws of war, crimes against humanity, and genocide. Be that as it may, the USA has contributed more money and personnel to particularly the Yugoslav court than any other state. The State Department under Madeline Albright created a special office on "war crimes" headed by an Ambassador at Large (David Scheffer). The George W. Bush Administration did not disband this office (but placed Richard Prosper in charge).

US support for an independent and authoritative standing UN criminal court, however, is an entirely different matter. We traced the US opposition to the new international criminal court, approved at the 1998 Rome diplomatic conference, in an earlier chapter. This opposition continued during 1999 in the meetings of the preparatory commission that was working to create the court. In 2001, Congress passed the American Servicemembers' Protection Act, which precluded the USA from cooperating with the ICC and established a presidential prerogative to use "all means necessary" to protect US citizens and servicemembers from prosecution at the court. Since then, at least 18 states have signed documents

---

[25] See further David P. Forsythe, "Human Rights and International Security: United Nations Field Operations Redux," in M. Castermans, et al., eds., *The Role of the Nation State in the 21st Century* (Dordrecht: Kluwer, 1998), 265–276.

prohibiting extradition of Americans. Others have been threatened with withdrawal of US economic or military aid if similar agreements are not forged.[26]

Whereas President Clinton had signed the Rome Statute to keep the USA engaged in various negotiations about the ICC, President George W. Bush's opposition to the new court was so strong that he took the unprecedented step of "unsigning" that legal document. The Bush Administration, like the Reagan Administration before it, was very clear in its hostility to many international agreements, including human rights agreements. For the most part it was highly sceptical of supranational authority and international adjudication. Only on trade matters, centered on the WTO, did US governments allow an international organization to authoritatively review US policies. In 2005, however, the US did allow the UN Security Council to pass a resolution allowing the ICC Prosecutor to conduct investigations of individual criminal responsibility by Sudanese leaders for atrocities in the Darfur region. Rather then vetoing that resolution the USA abstained. This action suggested that Washington might tolerate the ICC as long as US nationals were exempted from its jurisdiction.

Unilateralism was a powerful force in the foreign policy of the Goldwater–Reagan–Bush wing of the Republican Party, buttressed by the self-righteous belief in American exceptionalism – and by primacy of putative hard power. These unilateralist views about not allowing international arrangements to seriously constrain a "benign hegemon" and force for good in the world were found not only in the Executive but in the Helms-Hatch wing of Congress, and in the Scalia school of the federal courts. In the latter case, Mr. Justice Scalia was scathing in his attacks on his judicial colleagues for introducing foreign and comparative legal standards into US Supreme Court judgments dealing with such matters as the execution of juvenile offenders. He did not want international human rights considerations to muddy the purity of strictly US norms of judicial interpretation, and a member of the US House of Representatives introduced a bill barring US courts from using most international and comparative sources of law.

So the Bush approach to foreign policy in general, and certainly to human rights issues in foreign policy, was highly unilateralist, affected by a genuine belief in American exceptionalism, and consequently dubious at best about what international norms and actors could bring to the subject of protection of human rights – both at home and abroad. As Condoleeza Rice accurately wrote in an article published in 2000, the

---

[26] See Nick Green, "Stonewalling Justice," *Harvard International Review* 26, 2 (2004): 34–37.

emphasis in the George W. Bush Administration would be on American, not international, values. Since American values were really universal, one could advance good things in the world by promoting American values.[27]

In the so-called US war on terrorism after 9/11/2001, the Bush Administration's rhetoric about democracy and freedom was accompanied by considerable abuse of enemy detainees. The fact of over two dozen deaths in US captivity across both Iraq and Afghanistan, and a large number of suicide attempts by prisoners at the US holding station in Guantanamo, Cuba (leased in perpetuity to the USA), plus the existence of a secret gulag of prisoner arrangements to which even the International Committee of the Red Cross did not have access, indicated the tip of the iceberg of an abusive policy. In 2004 the well publicized abuse of detainees at the US-run Abu Ghraib prison in Iraq indicated that high US officials had both authorized abusive interrogation at times, and failed to properly train for and supervise that interrogation process. It was very clear that high US officials in the White House and Department of Defense had tried to explain away traditional international legal protections for prisoners found in such instruments as the 1949 Geneva Conventions and additional Protocols, and the UN Convention against torture and degrading treatment. The USA was a party to both sets of laws, but tried unilateral interpretations to minimize their relevance to Guantanamo, Iraq, Afghanistan, and the US secret gulag.[28]

It was not clear whether a US crusade for democracy and personal freedom could be built on torture and other important violations of civil rights. After all, after dropping the atomic bomb on two Japanese cities, the USA led in transforming Japan into a stable democracy. Certainly Washington lost the moral high ground, and much soft power, by its detention policies after 9/11. These policies seemed not to disturb very much the US Congress and public opinion, but clearly did make relations with foreign parties – especially in the Arab and Islamic worlds – much more difficult.

Overall, US foreign policy on human rights after the Cold War reflects a number of paradoxes. The USA rhetorically supports universal human

---

[27] Condoleeza Rice, "Promoting the National Interest," *Foreign Affairs*, 79, 1 (January/February 2000), 45–62.

[28] Two key reports were Amnesty International, "United States of America–Human Dignity Denied: Torture and Accountability in the 'War on Terror,'" http://web.amnesty.org/library/print/ENGAMR511452004; and Human Rights Watch, "Getting Away with Torture?: Command Responsibility for the U.S. Abuse of Deteainees," HRW, April 2005, Vol. 17, No. 1(G). For an overview of US policy toward enemy detainees, and a documenting of intentional abuse, see David P. Forsythe, "US Policy toward Enemy Detainees," *Human Rights Quarterly*, forthcoming.

rights with great enthusiasm, but reserves to itself the practice of national particularism (elevation of national over international law, no socio-economic rights, rejection of the treaty on rights of the child which is virtually unanimously endorsed, relative lack of legal protections for minors and the mentally retarded in the criminal justice system, harsh prison conditions, forcible return of Haitian asylum seekers without due process, etc.).[29] Washington endorses development according to liberal democracy, but has extensive economic relations with numerous authoritarian and/or repressive states, from China to Kuwait, from Saudi Arabia to Pakistan. The USA led in creating new international criminal tribunals to respond to gross violations of human rights in certain states, but adamantly and actively opposes the standing criminal court as developed thus far, with the exception of tolerating ICC action in the Sudan. Washington led in expanding the notions of enforcement action under Chapter VII of the Charter and of complex peacekeeping under Chapter VI, but blocked any significant UN deployments of force to protect persons in both Rwanda and eastern Zaire/Democratic Congo. It then engaged in prolonged humanitarian intervention in Yugoslavia on behalf of Kosovar Albanians. US leaders spoke out against torture, even while engaging in abuse of prisoners that on occasion was tantamount to torture, and even while turning prisoners over to countries that had a long history of torture. Whether other states have compiled a better or more consistent record in their foreign policy on rights abroad is an interesting question.

Other liberal democracies

Virtually all other liberal democracies and polities that strive to be liberal democracies display increasingly active policies on international human rights. Like the USA, they take various initiatives on human rights abroad. Like the USA, they give a particular national slant to their policies. Like the USA, their general orientation to international human rights reflects their national political culture. Like the USA, most ascribe virtue to themselves in their orientation to internationally recognized human rights. Some, like Britain, are very similar to the USA in their rights policies abroad. Some, like Japan, are quite different. At the risk of superficiality, one can provide a brief summary of more thorough inquiries.

---

[29] See further Amnesty International, *United States of America: Rights for All* (London: Amnesty International Publications, 1998), and David P. Forsythe, "Human Rights Policy: Change and Continuity," in Randall B. Ripley and James M. Lindsay, eds., *US Foreign Policy After the Cold War* (Pittsburgh: University of Pittsburgh Press, 1997), 257–282.

The Netherlands, for example, likes to picture itself as highly international and cosmopolitan.[30] It was the home of Grotius, the father of international law; it was a great trading nation; it was and is a country interested in world peace, for normal trade requires peace; and now it prides itself as a country highly active on human rights. This last orientation is affected both by its protestant missionary tradition, and in some circles by a certain guilt about its colonial record and especially its handling of claims to independence by Indonesia in the 1940s. Both historical elements push the Dutch into activism on human rights. Thus Dutch governments engage in a friendly competition with like-minded states, perhaps especially Denmark and Norway, about who is the most progressive in foreign policy. The Dutch political classes see themselves as making a special contribution through their development assistance policies, perhaps because they know that the USA has one of the lowest ratios between gross domestic product and official development assistance of any western democracy (less than one-quarter of one per cent). During the Cold War, if the USA had to sacrifice some attention to human rights in order to lead on security issues, some in The Hague wanted to fill that gap.

Because of the Dutch self-image and considerable Dutch activism at the United Nations on both human rights and peacekeeping issues, the Dutch role in the Srebrenica massacre in the former Yugoslavia in July 1995 proved to be a national trauma – perhaps roughly similar to Canadian reactions to charges of human rights violations against some of their military forces in Somalia. A lightly armed Dutch contingent in UNPROFOR, supposedly guaranteeing Srebrenica as a "safe area," was withdrawn – after which a massacre by Serbian partisans of thousands of remaining Muslim males occurred.

Also problematic, but not so traumatic, was the Dutch effort to combine development assistance with protection of human rights – especially civil and political ones. The Netherlands was inclined to assist poorer countries, and regularly was among the leading countries in amount of the gross domestic product contributed to official development assistance. But aid was not offered to some countries because of human rights problems. To other countries aid was offered but suspended for a time, for the same reason. Indonesia has posed a special case for Dutch

---

[30] See further David Gillies, *Between Principle and Practice: Human Rights in North-South Relations* (Montreal: McGill-Queen's University Press, 1996); Peter R. Baehr, "The Netherlands and the United Nations: The Future Lies in the Past," in Chadwick F. Alger, Gene M. Lyons and John E. Trent, eds., *The United Nations System: The Policies of Member States* (Tokyo: United Nations University Press, 1995), 271–328; and Peter R. Baehr, "Problems of Aid Conditionality: The Netherlands and Indonesia," *Third World Quarterly*, 18, 2 (June 1997), 363–376.

governments, given the history involved and Jakarta's poor human rights record during times of authoritarian government. Certain Dutch statements led Indonesia in 1992 to indicate it would no longer receive foreign assistance from the Netherlands. So the aid relationship was terminated, leaving The Hague with no leverage on human rights developments in East Timor and other places controlled by Indonesia. Similar difficulties arose in relations with Suriname after a *coup* in that South American former colony, with the Dutch finally deciding to suspend assistance. Thus the Dutch, like the USA, have found it difficult to establish a consistent and principled policy on rights abroad, not only because of being entangled with other states via international organizations, but also because of wanting to pursue conflicting "public goods" – e.g., economic growth in poorer countries but with respect for civil and political rights.

British history, too, affects London's modern orientation to international human rights.[31] Political classes there strongly identify with civil and political rights and are proud of such early documents as the Magna Carta, the English Bill of Rights of 1689, laws on freedom of the press from 1695, etc. British leaders tend to see themselves as having generated great influence on subsequent developments for human rights in places like France and the USA, not to mention later developments in places like India and Zimbabwe. Like the USA, the UK prides itself on a strong legal culture emphasizing constitutionalism or limited government. Britain, like other colonial powers, tended to see its rule over foreign lands as benign and enlightening, rather than repressive and oppressive. Once it ended its colonial period, it became even more supportive of international human rights instruments – not having to be defensive about claims to national self-determination as a collective human right, or about the issue of individual petitions claiming rights violations in overseas territories.

Various British governments, unlike the USA, have not only accepted the full International Bill of Rights, along with European legal instruments, but also have undertaken concrete policies for specific situations – engaging in quiet diplomacy for the release of some Indonesian detainees, suspending foreign assistance to states like Chile and Uganda for human rights violations, supporting arms embargoes against South Africa and Chile, and so forth. It fought the Falklands/Malvinas war with Argentina with considerable attention to international humanitarian law. Like the USA, however, London has muted its criticism of some important states,

---

[31] See further *Human Rights in Foreign Policy*, Foreign Policy Document No. 268 (London: Foreign and Commonwealth Office, July, 1996); *Foreign Policy and Human Rights*, *Vol. 1*, House of Commons Sessions 1998–9, Foreign Affairs Committee (London: The Stationery Office, December 1998).

such as Saudi Arabia which provides the British with important arms sales. On the other hand, Britain did join the USA in trying to have the UN Human Rights Commission adopt a resolution critical of China in 1997. Some observers believe British governments are not as influenced by domestic human rights groups and media coverage as US policy, given the British tradition of parliamentary sovereignty but not necessarily popular sovereignty and radical interpretations of individual rights. Britain still does not have a written constitution or practice judicial review of parliamentary acts. On the other hand it has found its rights policies at home and abroad increasingly affected by its membership of the Council of Europe and the European Union. Britain has been far more affected by regional rights standards than the USA. These domestic and foreign factors interact to produce a foreign policy on rights somewhat similar to those of other European states – increasingly active and complicated, but inconsistent due to its variety of interests in international relations. In striking contrast to the USA, British governments support the ICC, even though Britain has sent its troops abroad in places like Iraq and Sierra Leone.

Japan, by contrast, readily admits that the concept of human rights was not indigenous but was introduced from the West in the nineteenth century.[32] Obviously in a country with a history of imperial and military government, and with an era of atrocities during the Second World War, the notion of human rights did not take firm hold until the modern constitution was imposed during a time of military defeat and foreign occupation. Even so, and despite the existence of some indigenous "liberal" groups, Japan has still struggled at home with issues of equality or fairness for women, other races, and various ethnic and national groups. Given this history, it is not so surprising that Japan during the Cold War was a liberal democracy aligned with the other western liberal democracies, but was more passive than active on international human rights issues. In 1992, long after the US Congress put human rights back on the foreign policy agenda in Washington in the mid-1970s, Japan issued a white paper saying that human rights and democracy could be factors that affected foreign assistance and investment. But in general, and certainly in dealings with Peru which had a president of Japanese descent, human rights considerations did not appear to be a major factor in Japanese foreign policy.

[32] See further John Peek, "Japan, the United Nations, and Human Rights," *Asian Survey*, 32, 3 (March 1992); Seiichiro Takagi, "Japan's Policy Towards China after Tiananmen," in James T.H. Tang, ed., *Human Rights and International Relations in the Asia Pacific* (London: Pinter, 1995); Yasuhiro Ueki, "Japan's New Diplomacy: Sources of Passivism and Activism," in Gerard Curtis, ed., *Japan's Foreign Policy After the Cold War: Coping with Change* (New York: M.E. Sharpe, 1997).

As Japan has sought to show the world that it deserves a permanent seat in the UN Security Council, that it is more than an appendage of the USA, and that it has put its darker past behind it, Tokyo has become more active on rights issues abroad. Japan played a leading role, a far larger role than Washington, in trying to produce a liberal democratic peace with human rights in Cambodia. But it remains much less active in general on rights abroad than most other western-style liberal democracies. Tokyo has not pressed the human rights issue in its economic relations with other Asian states in particular, although it did suspend economic dealings for a time with China after the Tiananmen Square massacre of 1989. Tokyo has been more reluctant than Washington to press the rights issues in Burma. Given the history of Japanese relations with the Asian mainland during the 1930s and 1940s, it would be quite difficult for Japan to play a leading role on rights matters. This history reinforces those public officials who would like to concentrate primarily on Japanese economic interests. Likewise, Japan has not been one of the members of the World Bank that seeks to link loans with human rights performance, including democratic governance. Japan has, however, mostly voted with the western group at the UN on various rights matters in such bodies as the General Assembly and the Human Rights Commission.

With regards to Japan's Official Development Assistance program, recent years have seen telling trends in Japanese policymaking. While human rights have not been inextricably linked to foreign assistance, they are far from absent. In 2003, Japan reformed its ODA charter, citing domestic and international debate over its development policies and practices. The reformed document declares that its bedrock objective is "to contribute to the peace and development of the international community, and thereby to help ensure Japan's own security and prosperity." It even goes so far as to list paying "adequate attention to . . . the situation regarding the protection of basic human rights and freedoms" as one of four ODA principles of implementation, albeit behind such principles as environmental conservation and attention to military expenditures and WMD.[33] Later, in March 2005, Japan announced its Initiative on Gender Development, a new push to integrate gender concerns with other ODA considerations.[34]

Japan pressed North Korea on nuclear proliferation, but also on its human rights record, particularly with regard to its involvement in the abduction of up to fifteen Japanese nationals during the 1970s and 1980s. Japan threatened to withdraw food aid, and even considered sanctions

---

[33] See "Overview: Circumstances Surrounding Japan's Official Development Assistance (ODA) and Revision of the ODA Charter," http://www.mofa.go.jp/policy/other/bluebook/2004/chap3-d.pdf.

[34] See http://www.mofa.go.jp/policy/oda/category/wid/gad.html.

against Kim Jong Il's regime.[35] It brought the issue to the United Nations Commission on Human Rights, helping to draft a resolution that dealt with North Korea's abduction of foreign nationals, among other human rights concerns.[36] But even as Japan sought to induce change in one of the world's most brutal regimes, it was forced to face its own tarnished past. While Tokyo was pressing Pyongyang to come clean on abductions, South Korea was demanding Japan follow Germany's example and apologize more completely for its wartime atrocities.[37]

Former European communist states like Hungary and Russia, to chose two almost at random, are now also active on international human rights issues.[38] Hungary strives to be like any other European state on these issues, although its relationship to ethnic Hungarians abroad generates clear differences. The Russian Federation is much more ambivalent about the place of human rights in foreign policy, although it too is propelled to considerable extent by concern for the protection of compatriots abroad. Both of these states stress minority rights in foreign policy much more than Washington.

Hungary presents an interesting situation in terms of foreign policy and human rights. Its history is mostly one of authoritarian rule, whether through empire or Soviet-imposed communism. Yet certain liberal tendencies were present, such as considerable respect for private property and a certain affinity for legal rules. Many politically active Hungarians considered themselves to be liberal and a part of the West. Considerable resistance to Leninist or Stalinist repression was much in evidence in the 1956 uprising, as was also the case at different times in what was then the German Democratic Republic, Poland, and what is now the Czech Republic. Many in these areas would have chosen western-style liberalism, had free choice been allowed. It was thus not very surprising that when the Soviet Union allowed Eastern Europe to go its own way in the late 1980s, Hungary embraced international human rights. This orientation came about not only because of a need to prove that it belonged in the Council of Europe, and perhaps the European Union and NATO, but also because of genuine domestic preferences.

---

[35] See Pilling, David and Jung a Song, "Tokyo Seeks Facts about Abducted Japanese." *Financial Times* (London), 9 November 2004, Asia ed.: Asia-Pacific, 2.

[36] See   http://documents-dds-ny.un.org/doc/UNDOC/GEN/G05/101/97/pdf/G0510197.pdf and http://www.mofa.go.jp/policy/other/bluebook/2004/chap3-c.pdf

[37] Parry, Richard Lloyd. "Seoul Searching for Japanese War Apology." *The Australian*, 3 March 2005, All-Around Country ed.: World 8.

[38] See further Bruce D. Porter and Carol R. Saivets, "The Once and Future Empire: Russia and the 'Near Abroad'," *The Washington Quarterly*, 17, 3 (1994), 75–76; Alexei Arbatov, "Russian Foreign Policy Thinking in Transition," in Vladimir Baranovsky, ed., *Russia and Europe: The Emerging Security Agenda* (Oxford: Oxford University Press, 1997); Istvan Pogany, ed., *Human Rights in Eastern Europe* (Aldershot: Edward Elgar, 1995).

Hungary has given special attention to minority rights in its foreign policy after the Cold War, given the number of ethnic Hungarians who reside in Romania, Slovakia, and Ukraine. Even while still officially communist, Hungary criticized its fellow communist neighbor, Romania, for its treatment of the Hungarian minority. Hungary thus broke the unwritten rule that European communist regimes did not criticize each other on human rights issues. Since adopting liberal democracy, Budapest has continued to make the relationship with ethnic Hungarians abroad the centerpiece of its foreign policy. This has led to periodic friction with especially Romania, which fears too much local autonomy, if not separatism, for that sizable minority. Budapest has found more satisfactory relations on this issue with Ukraine and Slovakia. On other human rights issues Hungary has generally behaved as any other European state, voting with the western group at the UN and accepting regional human rights obligations through the Council of Europe.

Russia presents a fascinating study of human rights and foreign policy. Whether as Russia or the Soviet Union, this area has long manifested a conflicted political culture. The dominant aspect was and is authoritarian, illiberal, Slavic, and suspicious of the West. The tradition of legal rights, especially individual rights, is very weak – especially in the *mir* as a rural, organic community in which law and individualism were insignificant. But at least from the time of Peter the Great there was a weaker, more liberal aspect to Russian culture. These liberal tendencies have been encouraged since the Gorbachev and Yeltsin eras, yet one does not change the dominant culture by simply issuing legal documents and making proclamations. Russian policies, for example, directed toward suppression of a separatist movement in Chechnya were clearly brutal.

There is a part of the Russian political class that longs for the Stalinist days of order and superpower status, and believes that human rights equates with pornography, criminality, and foreign religious sects. There is another part of the political class that is more sympathetic to human rights, but believes the West has not treated the new Russia with proper sensitivity and respect. In the view of this circle, Russia struggles to determine whether it should follow the US lead on certain human rights issues, align with a different European position, or strike out on its own. Like Hungary, Russia has given special attention to minority rights in foreign policy. Given the large number of ethnic Russians and Russian speakers in its "near abroad," and given its own problems with separatist movements, Russian foreign policy has been highly active on ethno-territorial-linguistic disputes in many former areas of Soviet control. Its still uncertain nationalism, reflecting a conflicted political culture, interacts with other factors such as an unsteady relationship with the powerful West to provide a most uncertain policy on rights abroad.

On human rights issues pertaining to the former Yugoslavia, Moscow tends to reflect the Slavic tendency of identifying as protector of the Serbs, but fears a further rejection by the West if it fully follows that course. It voted for the creation of the Yugoslav Criminal Court in the UN Security Council, but believes the Prosecutor's Office has been biased against the Serbs. At the Rome diplomatic conference in the summer of 1998, it aligned with the USA (and China, among a few others) in opposing a strong and independent UN standing criminal court. Likewise, it sought a relaxation of international pressure on dictatorial Iraq, believing that Baghdad had been punished enough (and wanting payment on existing commercial contracts), but again feared antagonizing the West, especially the USA, with that clear course of action. It wound up mediating the Kosovo crisis between NATO states and modern Yugoslavia. Russia was also not enthusiastic about UN sanctions on the government of Sudan for its policies in the Darfur regions, in part because it had a number of arms sales agreements with Khartoum.

Minority rights is not a moral sideshow for Moscow, any more than it is for Budapest. Minority rights in foreign policy is part of Russia's central effort to exercise influence in adjacent areas on the basis of nationalism. It does not necessarily want to encourage separatism, given its own problems in Chechnya and elsewhere. It may or may not want to encourage union – as in Belarus but without necessarily inheriting the problems involved. But it feels it cannot abandon Russians abroad. At the same time, it must be aware of how events are read in the West, lest foreign assistance and investment capital are restricted because of fears of Russian imperialism or illegal interference in another state's domestic affairs. So in Latvia Moscow thinks of sanctions to protect the interests of Russians there, but is cautioned by the western states about over-reaction. Russian foreign policy on rights is not well grounded domestically, and is quite uncertain in its applications abroad.

Russian president Vladimir Putin, a staunch ally in the US "war" on terrorism, was particularly vocal over the controversial results of the Ukrainian presidential election in 2004. The number of ethnic Russians living in Ukraine at the time was around 17%,[39] the largest minority population in the country. The two candidates championed different visions of Ukrainian alignment. Viktor Yushchenko, former prime minister and more pro-West than his opponent, espoused stronger ties with the European Union (and survived an attempt on his life by way of deadly poison),

---

[39] Figure from the CIA World Factbook, http://www.cia.gov/cia/publications/factbook/geos/up.html.

while his opponent, then-Prime Minister Viktor Yanukovich, stressed a more prominent relationship with Russia. Putin was heavily involved in the political conflict to preserve Russian soft power in former Soviet spheres of influence, but also to ensure Russia retains a hand in protecting Russian minorities abroad. In so doing, Putin aligned Russia with a Ukrainian political faction known for corruption and authoritarianism. This orientation brought criticism from Washington and others, even as Putin played fast and loose with human rights at home by reducing press freedoms, the independence and authority of parliament, and the power of other competing power centers. According to the NGO Freedom House, by 2005 Russia was only a partly free country.

One could look at any number of other liberal democracies – or would-be liberal democracies – and their foreign policies on human rights, from India to South Africa, from Canada to Costa Rica. Most such inquiries prove intriguing. France, origin of the 1789 Declaration on the Rights of Man and the state most like the USA in seeing itself as a universal model for human rights, presents a long history of support for corrupt and authoritarian rulers in Africa, not to mention a policy of torture and summary execution during the Algerian war of 1954–1962. Costa Rica, with some similarity to the USA, sees itself made up of an exceptionally good and peaceful people who therefore have a special and progressive role to play particularly in hemispheric affairs. However the moralizing of Oscar Arias, like that of Jimmy Carter, was not always well received by other Latin American heads of state.

India, the most populous democracy, has become much more defensive and low key about human rights abroad. In part this stems from an awareness of certain domestic problems. Also, the collapse of the Soviet Union, its major strategic partner, reduced its standing in international relations. Its foray into Sri Lankan ethnic struggles under Rajiv Gandhi, by way of an Indian "peacekeeping" force which itself engaged in atrocities, proved disastrous, both personally and politically speaking, contributing to the current Indian low profile. In general, India now tends to favor the principle of state sovereignty when in conflict with action for human rights, believing that the US-led Security Council has intervened too much in the affairs of the governments of the global south. The election of a clearly nationalistic government in 1998 intensified these trends. In 2005 it was still the case that India, given its colonial experience, was very sensitive about the USA or any other state engaging in public criticism of its human rights record.

Governments in South Africa emerging from all-race elections have identified strongly with international human rights, and – along with El Salvador – have pioneered official "truth commissions" to reveal the facts of past repression but without criminal prosecution for political crime. The Mandela government, however, was heavily involved in fairly disastrous gun-running in the Great Lakes Region of Africa, and also defied UN sanctions on dictatorial Libya in order to repay Libyan support for the anti-apartheid movement.

Canadian foreign policy has been generally progressive on rights abroad.[40] It is well known that Ottawa has long prided itself on its record especially in UN peacekeeping – including second-generation or complex peacekeeping that includes human rights dimensions. Canada, for example, joined the USA in practical efforts to bring liberal democracy to Haiti, no easy task given the history and impoverishment of that country. Canada has also been a leader in regard to a ban on anti-personnel landmines, and the creation of a UN criminal court. Limitations of space, however, compel us to move on.

Illiberal states

With due regard for gray areas and border-line cases, it can be said that liberal democracies are characterized by free and fair national elections based on broad suffrage, combined with protection of a wide variety of civil rights through independent courts and other mechanisms to provide fairness and tolerance. Limited government, or constitutionalism, is a key feature of liberal politics.[41] Whether or not a liberal democracy is also a social democracy depends on its commitment to socio-economic rights. Illiberal democracies may have reasonably free and fair national elections based on broad suffrage, but they do not counteract the tyranny of the majority with effective protections for ethnic and religious minorities or various types of dissenters. States like Croatia under Tjudman and Iran under the rule of the clerics exemplify illiberal democracies, in which the rights of political participation are exercised to deny certain civil rights protecting minorities and dissenters. Authoritarian states do not reach the threshold of free and fair national elections in which the winners actually govern.

Iran presents an interesting case study of human rights and foreign policy in an illiberal state.[42] The comparison with the USA, with its long tradition of formal separation of church and state, could not be more

---

[40] The standard work in this area is Robert O. Mathews and R. C. Pratt, eds., *Human Rights and Canadian Foreign Policy* (Montreal: McGill-Queen's Press, 1988).

[41] Fareed Zakaria, "The Rise of Illiberal Democracy," *Foreign Affairs*, 76, 6 (November–December, 1997), 22–43.

[42] See further Ali Mazrui, "Islamic and Western Values," *Foreign Affairs*, 76, 5 (Fall 1997), 118–132; Reza Afshari, "An Essay on Scholarship, Human Rights, and State Legitimacy: The Case of the Islamic Republic of Iran," *Human Rights Quarterly*, 18, 3 (Summer 1990), 544–593; and Anoushiravan Ehteshami, *After Khomeini: The Iranian Second Republic* (London: Routledge, 1995).

striking. Yet there are similarities. Each sees itself as a leader for a certain way of life or culture.

From the 1979 revolution, Iran instituted an Islamic theocracy which rejected the basic notion of secular and universal human rights as found in public international law. The clerics who wield ultimate authority in modern Iran believe that the Sharia, or fundamental Islamic law, has universal application for all Muslims. They do not accept the superiority of international human rights instruments. They just do not bother with the formalities of withdrawing Iran's adherence to international instruments on rights formally accepted by the previous government (and mostly ignored by the Shah in practice). Under the Sharia, as interpreted by contemporary Iranian leaders, the primary emphasis is on duties owed to the religious state, not individual rights that restrict the state. Individuals do not have human rights by virtue of being persons; they have those rights that Allah through the proper state provides them.

To a considerable extent, current Iranian rulers regard the international law of human rights, and related diplomacy in international organizations, as a product of the hated United States. That Iranian clerics might overstate the influence of the USA on international human rights developments does not mean that their critical beliefs are not firmly held. The Iranian leadership tends to dismiss foreign criticism on human rights issues, whether by the USA or other actors, including western-based NGOs, as being part of American neo-imperialism of a particularly evil nature. The fact that the USA employs double standards in its approach to human rights abroad, criticizing every defect in Iran vociferously, at least until a slight thaw in relations began in 1998, but remaining silent about major violations in Saudi Arabia and other allies, contributes to Iranian views.

Because Iran practices a type of cultural relativism with regard to human rights, its foreign policy on this subject is almost entirely defensive. It tries to reject foreign criticism, whether multilateral or bilateral, whether public or private, either by disputing facts or by claiming that a certain behavior is permitted under Islamic law. Iran tries to justify its discrimination against women on these latter grounds. Sometimes this defensive stance is difficult to make persuasive, for some Iranian policies fall short of Islamic as well as international law. This is apparently so, for example, concerning Teheran's vigorous persecution of the Iranian Ba'hai. The Sharia commands tolerance for minority religions as long as they are religions of the book – viz., Islam, Judaism, and Christianity. Only if one regards the Ba'hai as heretics from Islam, and not a branch of Islam, can one justify their severe persecution under Islamic law.

From 1997 the new Iranian President, Mohammed Khatami, addressed some of these domestic shortcomings dealing with persecution, censorship, and other violations of internationally recognized human rights. He even supported political pluralism. But he did so in the context of discussions on Islamic law. It is certainly possible that new interpretations of religious law might be forthcoming that would be more compatible with the international law of human rights. Other Muslim societies come up with different interpretations of the Sharia. At the end of 1997 an Egyptian court ruled against female genital mutilation. A continuing conflict between moderate and more fundamentalist interpretations of Islamic law was clearly in evidence in Iran during 1997 and 1998. All revolutions lose their radical zeal over time. This is beginning to happen in Iran. These domestic developments are intertwined with international ones – such as the desire of more moderate Iranian officials to reduce the country's status as international pariah, and in particular to take some steps toward repairing relations with the powerful USA. It is not inconceivable that Iranian policy on human rights might slowly evolve toward a less defensive posture, not exactly along the lines of the Tunisian or Indonesian or Jordanian model but in that general direction.

On the other hand, by 2005 it was reasonably clear that the moderates, centered in and around the President, had lost ground to the clerics determined to continue the values associated with Khomeiney. US heavy handed pressure on the question of nuclear weapons encouraged the clerics, who stood for national defiance against the "great Satan" and weakened the hand of those favoring some rapprochement with the West. Should the US, or even Israel, use the notion of preventive war to strike Iranian suspected nuclear weapons facilities, the cause of internationally recognized human rights, which were associated with western democracies, would certainly suffer in the short run.

Conclusions

During the era of the League of Nations, this chapter could not have been written. The League Covenant did not mention universal human rights, and states did not address human rights in their foreign policies. There was some international humanitarian law for armed conflicts, and states did sometimes display humanitarian policies dealing with refugees, the nature of rule in colonies (via the League Mandates Commission), and other social subjects. But as late as 1944 human rights remained essentially a national rather than international matter (with the exception of the Minority Treaties for some Central European states in the interwar years, and international law governing aliens).

Increasingly all states, whatever their political character, have to deal with internationally recognized human rights. International relations or world politics is not what it once was. Much of international law codifies liberal principles of human rights. But in addressing human rights, states bring with them their national history, character, self-image, and nationalism. These national traits cause states to be more or less active on human rights issues, more or less confident and assertive, more or less defensive. This history, plus their contemporary situation and interests, causes states to take different slants or emphases on rights in foreign policy. Fear and insecurity generally lead to realist foreign policies emphasizing narrow self-interest and military moves. Even when addressing human rights, the USA does not focus on socio-economic rights but rather on personal freedom. The Netherlands tries especially hard to link development assistance with rights behavior, and has a special focus on Indonesia. The Hungarians and Russians tend to emphasize minority rights for their ethnic and/or linguistic compatriots abroad. And so on.

It is significant that even states without a strong rights tradition or legal culture have been propelled to direct more attention to rights in foreign policy. This is true, for example, for both Japan and Russia. Even Iran, if it wishes to be accepted as a full or normal member of the international community, has found that it needs to respond to international pressures by addressing defects in Iranian society, even if it does so under the cover of a discussion of religious law rather than the secular law of international human rights.

Without downplaying the importance of international organizations, private non-profit groups, and even multinational corporations, it is still state foreign policy that plays a very large role in the promotion and protection of international human rights. So with regard to universal human rights and state foreign policy, it is both true and false to say: *la plus ça change, la plus c'est la même chose.* (the more things change, the more they remain the same). True, because despite the fact that we have change in favor of human rights norms in international relations, we still have to deal with nationalism and national interests. False, because we do have real changes in foreign policy concerning human rights; there is much more attention to international human rights in 2005 compared with the foreign policies of 1925 or 1905.

Discussion questions

– Is there a theoretical or otherwise systematic reason why different states come up with different emphases and interpretations of international human rights standards? Even among liberal democratic states of the

OECD, such as the United States, Britain, the Netherlands, and Japan there are major differences in their approaches to international human rights: why is this?

- In general, are states paying more or less attention to human rights through foreign policy? Why?
- Why is it that democracies like India and the United Kingdom take very different approaches to questions of international human rights?
- Why is it that countries like France and the United States, which have a long national history of attention to human rights, repeatedly find it so difficult to apply international standards to themselves – even though the West has had great influence on the evolution of international human rights, both regional and global?
- What is the probability that traditionally illiberal states in places such as the Middle East (e.g., Iran) and Asia (e.g., China) will adapt their foreign policies to international standards of human rights?.
- Is human rights in foreign policy primarily a matter of the executive branch, or do legislatures (and public opinion, with interest groups) play an important role?

Suggestions for further reading

Baehr, Peter and Monique Castermans-Holleman, *The Role of Human Rights in Foreign Policy* (New York: Palgrave Macmillan, 2004). Thorough text examining the various aspects of the role human rights plays in state foreign policy, with particular attention to US and Dutch foreign policy.

Carothers, Thomas, *Assessing Democracy: The Case of Romania* (Washington: The Carnegie Endowment, 1996). Shows how difficult it is to evaluate US foreign policy and democracy assistance, even in one country.

Curtis, Gerard, ed., *Japan's Foreign Policy After the Cold War: Coping with Change* (New York: M.E. Sharpe, 1997). Shows the changing nature of Japanese foreign policy, with some attention to human rights.

Egeland, Jan, *Impotent Large State – Potent Small State: Potentialities and Limitations of Human Rights Objectives in the Foreign Policies of the United States* (Oslo: Norwegian University Press, 1988). Argues that during the Cold War Norway had more room to maneuver for human rights in foreign policy than the United States, mainly because of US security obligations.

Forsythe, David, *The Humanitarians: The International Committee of the Red Cross* (Cambridge: Cambridge University Press, 2005). Contains a chapter on ICRC efforts to curtail US abuse of "enemy" prisoners.

Forsythe, David, et al., eds, *American Foreign Policy in a Globalized World* (New York: Routledge, 2006 forthcoming). Contains chapters on US democracy promotion in places like Afghanistan, Iraq, and the Middle East in general, as well as a chapter on US policy toward "enemy detainees."

Gillies, David, *Between Principle and Practice: Human Rights in North–South Relations* (Montreal: McGill-Queen's University Press, 1996). A good comparative study of the role of human rights in foreign policy among several developed countries, when dealing with certain less developed countries. Shows how difficult it is to construct a principled foreign policy when trying to blend human rights and support for development.

Greenbert, Karen J. and Joshua L. Dratel, eds., *The Torture Papers: The Road to Abu Ghraib* (Cambridge: Cambridge University Press, 2005). Shows the paper trail of how high US officials tried to vitiate the UN Convention against Torture, and the 1949 Geneva Conventions plus 1977 Additional Protocols, so as to give US interrogators a free hand in the treatment of "enemy" prisoners.

Hunt, Michael H., *Ideology and US Foreign Policy* (New Haven: Yale University Press, 1987). Argues that while the United States see itself as an exceptionally good nation, it has done a great deal of harm in the world through its racism and commitment to the *status quo*. Argues for a reduced US role in the world, even at the cost of less attention to liberal causes like international human rights.

Kissinger, Henry, *Diplomacy* (New York: Simon & Schuster, 1994). As in his other modern works, Kissinger is critical of liberal views of foreign policy and international relations, which he calls Wilsonianism, and argues that the United States must beware of liberal crusades that go beyond American power and wisdom. He is suspicious of the validity of universal standards pertaining to democracy and human rights, believing them to have evolved in special western circumstances.

Mathews, Robert O., and R.C. Pratt, eds., *Human Rights and Canadian Foreign Policy* (Montreal: McGill-Queen's Press, 1988). The definitive work for its time.

Mertus, Julie, *Bait and Switch: Human Rights and US Foreign Policy* (New York: Routledge, 2004). Based on interviews with numerous current and former US officials, the author finds that international human rights norms predispose Washington to talk about human rights, while human rights considerations remain frequently absent from US foreign policy.

Newsome, David, ed., *The Diplomacy of Human Rights* (Lanham, MD: University Press of America, 1986). A good collection showing how human rights can be blended into larger US foreign policy concerns, at least sometimes and to some extent.

Nolan, Cathal J., *Principled Diplomacy: Security and Rights in US Foreign Policy* (Westport: Greenwood, 1993). A realist makes a favorable assessment of how the USA tried to combine human rights and security concerns on two international issues: policy toward the United Nations, and toward the Soviet Union.

Pogany, Istvan, ed., *Human Rights in Eastern Europe* (Aldershot: Edward Elgar, 1995). Charts the many changes in the politics of Eastern Europe after the Cold War, with some attention to human rights in foreign policy.

Samantha Power, *"A Problem From Hell;" America and the Age of Genocide* (New York: Basic Books, 2002). Examines the United States' response to genocide throughout the 20th century, concluding that America's record has been consistently poor.

Sikkink, Kathryn, *Mixed Signals: U.S. Human Rights Policy and Latin America* (New York: Century Foundation, 2004). A scholarly overview of US human rights policy in most of the Western Hemisphere, stressing the mixed record emanating from Washington. Much rights talk is not always followed by consistent influence in behalf of that rhetoric.

Steinmetz, Sara, *Democratic Transition and Human Rights: Perspectives on US Foreign Policy* (Albany: SUNY Press, 1994). A study of human rights and US foreign policy toward certain states in transition. On the basis of studying Iran, Nicaragua, and the Philippines, the author reaches complex conclusions that support neither the "neo-conservatives" nor the "neo-realists."

Tang, James T.H., ed., *Human Rights and International Relations in the Asia Pacific* (London: Pinter, 1995). A good collection, with attention to diverse foreign policies and human rights in Asia.

Vogelgesang, Sandy, *American Dream, Global Nightmare: The Dilemma of US Human Rights Policy* (New York: Norton, 1980). One of the first studies of human rights and US foreign policy suggests the difficulty of establishing a foreign policy that is both principled and consistent.

Wiarda, Howard J., *Cracks in the Consensus* (Westport: Praeger, 1998). Tries to assess the impact of US foreign policy on democratic developments in certain countries in modern times.

Zakaria, Fareed, "The Rise of Illiberal Democracy," *Foreign Affairs*, 76, 6 (November–December 1997), 22–43. An important article noting the difference between liberal and illiberal democracy. Whereas the United States has in the past supported some illiberal elected governments, as in El Salvador, presumably the West now intends to enlarge the *liberal* democratic community.

7   Non-governmental organizations and human rights

By now it should be clear that states, acting frequently through international organizations and/or diplomatic conferences, produce the international law of human rights by concluding treaties and developing customary law. The resulting law obligates states, primarily. In chapter 6 we examined state foreign policy against the background of the international law of human rights. But private actors can be important at both ends of this process, affecting legislation and implementation.[1]

This chapter starts with an analysis of non-governmental organizations and their advocacy of human rights ideas, which is directed both to the creation and application of human rights norms. Probably the best known of these groups is Amnesty International. This analysis is eventually set within the confines of social movements. Such actors push for more liberalism in the form of human rights protection in international relations. The chapter then turns to those private groups that are mostly called relief or development agencies, or sometimes PVOs (private voluntary agencies) or VOLAGs (voluntary agencies). A classic example is Oxfam. These private actors are crucial especially for grassroots action that directly or indirectly attends to social and economic rights. Most can be said to be liberal or pragmatic-liberal actors, in that they emphasize policies for the betterment of individuals under legal norms, rather than emphasizing the collective national interests of states as pursued through the application of power. Chapter 8 addresses private for-profit actors, commonly called multinational or transnational corporations when they act across national borders.

Private advocacy for human rights

There are perhaps 250 private organizations consistently active across borders that take as their reason for being (*raison d'être*) the advocacy of

---

[1] For an introductory overview, see William Korey, *NGOs and the Universal Declaration of Human Rights: "A Curious Grapevine"* (New York: St. Martin's Press, 1998). See also Claude E. Welch, Jr., *NGOs and Human Rights: Promise and Performance* (Philadelphia: University of Pennsylvania Press, 2001).

some part of the international law of human rights and/or humanitarian affairs on a global basis.[2] From this group a handful have the requisite budget, contacts, expertise, and reputation to get the global media and major governments to pay them at least periodic attention across a range of issues and situations: Amnesty International, Human Rights Watch, the International Commission of Jurists, the International Federation for Human Rights, the International Committee of the Red Cross, Human Rights First, Lawyers Without Borders, Doctors Without Borders, Physicians for Human Rights, Anti-Slavery International, PEN (Poets, Essayists, Novelists), Article 19 (devoted to freedom of expression), etc. When there is an international meeting touching on human rights, private groups that identify themselves as working primarily for international law, peace, world order, and women's issues, etc. may swell the numbers of active advocacy groups to several hundred – 200 to 800 might be an expected range. The core advocacy groups are usually called NGOs or INGOS – non-governmental organizations or international non-governmental organizations. A related phenomenon is a governmentally created, quasi-private human rights organization, or GONGO. Some GONGOs have been surprisingly active and independent, as in Indonesia and Mexico.

The oldest and best-funded human rights NGOs are based in the west and concern themselves primarily with civil and political rights in peace time and international humanitarian law in war or similar situations. Western societies have manifested the civil rights, private wealth, leisure time and value structures that allow for the successful operation of major human rights NGOs. To advocate human rights via a truly independent and dynamic NGO, there must be respect for civil rights and a civic society to start with. With the spread of liberal democracy and more open societies after the Cold War, the number of NGOs at least spasmodically active on some human rights issues has greatly increased. But the percentage of human rights groups, relative to the total number of NGOs active in international relations, has remained rather stable.[3]

Many NGOs based in the global south manifest a different agenda from those based in the north or northwest. The former tend to emphasize the right to development and many socio-economic rights, without neglecting entirely civil and political rights. Some of the better known NGOs based in the richer countries, like AI and HRW, have adopted mission statements

---

[2] Jackie Smith and Ron Pagnucco with George A. Lopez, "Globalizing Human Rights: The Work of Transnational Human Rights NGOs in the 1990s," *Human Rights Quarterly*, 20, 2 (May 1998), 379–412.

[3] Margaret E. Keck and Kathryn Sikkink, *Activists beyond Borders: Advocacy Networks in International Politics* (Ithaca: Cornell University Press, 1998), 11.

that now pay some attention to socio-economic rights, on the argument that they do indeed impinge on civil and political rights. But for these latter, their emphasis remains on civil-political rights and humanitarian affairs (including humanitarian relief).[4]

Complicating the picture is the fact that other private groups that exist for secular or religious purposes may become international human rights actors at particular times and for particular causes. The Catholic Church in its various manifestations and the World Council of Churches, *inter alia*, are examples of religious groups that fit this mold.[5] Some faith based groups, for example, teamed with some secular human rights groups to help achieve greater attention to the right to religious freedom and the right to be free from religious discrimination in the recent past, at least in US foreign policy.[6] Labor unions that normally focus on domestic "bread and butter" issues, like the AFL-CIO in the United States, may – and increasingly do – have a private foreign policy on rights questions. Labor unions, in order to try to protect labor wages and benefits in their home country, may find it necessary to address labor rights in foreign countries. "Ethnic lobbies" such as "the Greek lobby" or "the China lobby" may and occasionally do take up human rights issues of concern. There are numerous national civil rights groups, such as the American Civil Liberties Union in the United States, that occasionally turn to international issues. Given the existence of transnational issues, or the penetration of international relations into domestic affairs, it is increasingly difficult to separate national from international human rights groups. A good example was the ACLU interest in US policy toward "enemy detainees" during the George W. Bush Administrations, leading to a focus on international humanitarian law among other concerns.

Increasingly this amalgam of private actors is referred to as civic actions groups, or as making up civil society. In global civil society, there

---

[4] For a discussion of the lack of effective lobbying by NGOs like HRW regarding socio-economic rights, see David P. Forsythe and Eric Heinze, "On the Margins of the Human Rights Discourse: International Welfare Rights and Foreign Policy," in Rhoda Howard Hassmann and Claude E. Welch, Jr., eds., *Economic Rights in Canada and the United States: Sleeping Under Bridges* (Philadelphia: University of Pennsylvania Press, 2006), forthcoming. Aryeh Neier, long time Executive Director of Human Rights Watch, was strongly opposed to broadening the focus of HRW so as to include socio-economic rights. See Aryeh Neier, *Taking Liberties: Four Decades in the Struggle for Rights* (New York: Public Affairs, 2003), introduction, xxx. For a discussion about NGOs and socio-economic rights, see the *Human Rights Quarterly*, 26, 4 (November, 2004), 866–881.

[5] See further Claude E. Welch, Jr., "Mobilizing Morality: The World Council of Churches and its Program to Combat Racism, 1969–1994," *Human Rights Quarterly*, 23, 4 (November 2001), 863–910.

[6] Allen D. Hertzke, *Freeing God's Children: The Unlikely Alliance for Global Human Rights* (London and New York: Rowman and Littlefield, 2004).

was a great variety of private, non-profit groups, some of them clearly opposed to internationally recognized human rights.[7] Some of these groups seemed to generate so much influence on certain issues that some observers saw a "power shift" in international relations, with governments becoming less important and private groups decidedly more important.[8]

Along with the growing numbers, salience, and maybe even influence of civil society organizations came growing criticism. If one wanted to contest the activism of Human Rights Watch, one might say that it was elitist, non-democratic, non-transparent, and unaccountable. It was true that aside from AI, most human rights NGOs were not mass-membership organizations and held no elections for their leaders. They were indeed self-appointed.

On the other hand, there was the view that arguments about democracy and accountability for governments were inappropriate for human rights NGOs.[9] Human rights NGOs might be perceived as legitimate, or playing a correct role, if they impartially and neutrally worked to advance norms that had been approved by states. And they might be considered accountable if they were transparent about the sources and uses of their funds, and how they reached their advocacy positions. It was illogical to argue that NGOs were illegitimate when they were approved to attend UN and other IGO meetings. The International Committee of the Red Cross, technically a private Swiss civic association, was even recognized – and given rights and duties – in the international humanitarian law approved by states.

Because traditional international human rights groups may indeed join with a variety of other actors to deal with particular human rights situations or issues, some prefer to speak of movements or coalitions rather than separate organizations.[10] Thus it was said that there was a movement to ban land-mines, or a movement in support of an international criminal court. According to Keck and Sikkink, such movements may include NGOs, local social movements, foundations, the media, churches, trade unions, consumer organizations, intellectuals, parts of inter-governmental organizations, and parts of national or sub-national

---

[7] See especially A. Florini, *The Third Force: The Rise of Transnational Civil Society* (Washington: Carnegie Endowment, 2000). And Michael Edwards, *Civil Society* (Cambridge, UK: Polity, 2004). In general, see the *Global Civil Society Yearbook*, published by the London School of Economics and Politics.

[8] Jessica Tuchman Mathews, "Power Shift," Foreign Affairs, 76, 1, (Jan.–Feb., 1997), 50–66.

[9] For background see M. Edwards, *NGO Rights and Responsibilities: A New Deal for Global Governance* (London: The Foreign Policy Center, 2000).

[10] See for example, Jackie Smith, Charles Chatfield, and Ron Pagnucco, eds., *Transnational Social Movements and Global Politics: Solidarity Beyond the State* (Syracuse: Syracuse University Press, 1997); and Keck and Sikkink, *Activists beyond Borders*.

governments.[11] Hence it was said sometimes that the movement in support of a UN criminal court was made up of "like-minded states" plus over 200 human rights NGOs plus elements of the communications media, along with individuals. The foreign minister of Canada, in his efforts to achieve a strong International Criminal Court, wrote in 1998: "With lessons learned from the successful campaign for a treaty banning land mines, we are engaging not only political leaders but also nongovernmental organizations, media and citizens around the world."[12] Such movements or coalitions were indeed made up of diverse partners.[13]

Increasingly individuals or organizations that operate web sites on the Internet may be part of a coalition active on one or more human rights issues. The collection and spreading of information about human rights on the Internet was a relatively new development in the 1990s that had the potential for considerable impact. For example, the International Monitor Institute started documenting human rights violations in the Balkans, moved to providing information on war crimes trials from the former Yugoslavia, and then created the Rwanda Archive.[14] This and other relevant electronic activity fed into the Rome Diplomatic Conference of July 1998 that approved a statute for an international criminal court.

The process

If we focus on the advocacy of traditional human rights organizations, either as separate entities or part of a movement, it is reasonably clear what these groups do.[15] First, the bedrock of all their activity is the collection of accurate information and its timely dissemination. For a group to generate influence on governments and other public authorities like the UN Human Rights Commission, it must manifest a reputation for accurate reporting and dissemination of information. States do not exist primarily to report the truth. They exist primarily to exercise power on

[11] On the important but little studied matter of funding of NGOs by charitable foundations, see Jay Ovsiovitch, "Feeding the Watchdogs: Philanthropic Support for Human Rights NGOs," *Buffalo Human Rights Law Review*, 4 (1998), 341–364.

[12] Lloyd Axworthy, "Without Justice, No Security for Ordinary People," *International Herald Tribune*, June 16, 1998, 6.

[13] See further Henry J. Steiner, *Diverse Partners: Non Governmental Organizations and the Human Rights Movement* (Cambridge, MA: Harvard Law College, 1991, for the Harvard Law School Human Rights Program and the Human Rights Internet). See also Laurie Wiseberg, "Human Rights Non-Governmental Organizations," in *The Role of Non Governmental Organizations in the Promotion and Protection of Human Rights* (Leiden: Stichting NJCM-Boekerig, N.D. [1989?]). And Keck and Sikkink, *Activists beyond Borders*.

[14] http://www.imisite.org.

[15] For a different approach see Howard J. Tolley, Jr., *The International Commission of Jurists: Global Advocates for Human Rights* (Philadelphia: University of Pennsylvania Press, 1994).

behalf of national interests as they see them. Relevant is the old maxim about the role of ambassadors: they are sent abroad to lie for their country. Private human rights groups, on the other hand, do not fare very well if they do not develop a reputation for accurate reporting of human rights information.

Amnesty International (AI) has developed a general reputation since its founding in 1961 for accurate reporting primarily about prisoners of conscience – those imprisoned for their political and social views expressed mostly non-violently – and about torture and the death penalty, *inter alia*. It has a research staff in London of about 320 persons (plus about 100 volunteers) that is much larger than the staff of the UN Human Rights Centre in Geneva.[16] AI's record is not perfect regarding accuracy, and in several instances it has had to retract public statements and reports, as when it got caught up in Kuwaiti propaganda in 1990 and erroneously repeated the story that invading Iraqi forces had torn incubators from premature Iraqi babies. But in general, AI is known for reliable reporting. One study found that AI's reporting was affected not just by the severity of human rights violations in a nation, but also by such factors as: the nation's links to US military assistance and prominence in the global media; and AI's opportunities to maximize advocacy, chance to shape norms, desire to raise its own profile, and other factors.[17]

The International Committee of the Red Cross (ICRC) has built up a reputation since 1863 for meticulously careful statements about prisoners of war and other victims of armed conflict and complex emergencies. Its staff of some 800 in Geneva, plus another 1,200 or so in the field (including those seconded from National Red Cross/Red Crescent Societies but not counting those hired locally), is extremely hesitant to comment unless its delegates in the field can directly verify what has transpired.[18] In its long history, this author could find no example of false public statements about factual conditions.[19]

While various actors may disagree with some of the policies that human rights NGOs advocate, very few scholars and responsible public officials challenge the record of accurate reporting over time by the most salient NGOs. The actors that do attack their veracity usually have something to

---

[16] For details about AI, see its News Service Release 108/99, March 1999.

[17] James Ron, et al., "Transnational Information Politics: NGO Human Rights Reporting, 1986–2000," *International Studies Quarterly*, 49, 3, (September 2005), 557–588. Some of the findings pertain to HRW as well as to AI.

[18] Details are available in the ICRC Annual Reports.

[19] See further David P. Forsythe, *The Humanitarians: The International Committee of the Red Cross*, (Cambridge: Cambridge University Press, 2005). This is not to say that the ICRC was never involved in controversy about public statements, only that its public statements were never shown to be at variance with facts "on the ground."

hide. This was true of the Reagan Administration in the 1980s, which supported gross violations of human rights by its clients in Central America while trying to roll back what it saw as communism in especially El Salvador and Nicaragua. Reagan officials therefore attacked the veracity of AI, when it reported on brutal US clients, precisely because they found its reports – which were eventually proved accurate – irritating and embarrassing.[20] The George W. Bush Administration attacked the veracity and impartiality of AI when the latter criticized US politics toward enemy detainees, but at the same time used AI reports to try to highlight the brutality of Saddam Hussein in Iraq.

Second, the human rights advocacy NGOs, on the basis of their analysis and dissemination of information, try to persuade public authorities to adopt new human rights standards or apply those already adopted. This activity can fairly be termed lobbying, but in order to preserve their non-political and tax-free status in most western societies, the groups tend to refer to this action as education.[21] The techniques are well known to students of politics. One can organize letter-writing campaigns, meet face-to-face with officials, arrange briefing sessions for staff assistants, submit editorials or "op ed" pieces to the print media, become a "talking head" on television, and so forth. A mass organization like AI will frequently combine a letter-writing campaign with elite contact. An organization like Human Rights Watch or the International Commission of Jurists, lacking a mass membership, eschews grass roots letter writing and other grassroots lobbying and concentrates on contact by the professional staff with public officials. The point is to press one's point of view, and of course its reasonableness under law, until it becomes controlling policy.

According to one study that focused on basic civil rights called rights to personal integrity (made up of the right to life, to freedom from forced disappearances and summary execution, and freedom from torture and inhumane treatment), international NGOs worked with domestic groups

---

[20] See further David P. Forsythe, "Human Rights and US Foreign Policy: Two Levels, Two Worlds," in David Beetham, ed., *Politics and Human Rights* (Oxford: Blackwell, 1995), 111–130, especially 120.

[21] Claude E. Welch, Jr. makes the argument that human rights NGOs are not interest groups because they are altruistic rather than self-centered actors seeking interests for themselves. This is not persuasive. There are public interest groups, like Common Cause in the USA, that are similar to the international human rights NGOs. They lobby in traditional ways for values that benefit society in general, and particular persons or groups of persons along the way. Common Cause is a public interest group, and so is Amnesty International. They are both interest groups. Compare Welch, *Protecting Human Rights in Africa: Strategies and Roles of Non Governmental Organizations* (Philadelphia: University of Pennsylvania Press, 1995), 44 and *passim.*

both to protect the space for action of the domestic groups and to bring about change in the policy of the target government.[22]

A danger for human rights NGOs is that in their single-minded pursuit of the issue of human rights, and with a concern for moral consistency, they may come across to public officials as moralistic, rigid, and politically naïve.[23] Top foreign policy officials are challenged to manage the contradictions inherent in the effort to blend security, economic, ecological, and human rights concerns into one overall policy.[24] We noted in chapter 6 how difficult it was for any state with multiple goals and interests, which means all of them, to present a consistent record on human rights issues. An NGO quest for perfect moral consistency may strike many foreign policy professionals as utopian. Only 11 per cent of surveyed NGOs reported success in achieving policy change in favor of the human rights positions they advocated.[25]

The other side of the coin, however, is that many movements that seemed moralistic and utopian at the outset achieved changed policies and situations over time. Slavery, jousting, foot-binding, denial of the vote to women, and many other ideas were firmly institutionalized in many societies in the past. Being ideas, they were all subject to change, and all did change under relentless pressure over time.[26] What was utopian became practical. What was firmly entrenched, even central, became anachronistic. In the 1980s there were not many foreign policy officials, or human rights advocates for that matter, who thought a standing international criminal court was likely. By 1998–2002, it became a reality, although its future was uncertain.

Even agreement between governments and NGOs on general or long-term goals may lead to disputes about immediate tactics. In the 1990s, many human rights NGOs pressed for immediate action to arrest those indicted for gross violations of human rights in former Yugoslavia. Many US officials, supportive of international criminal prosecution in principle, but concerned about neo-isolationistic impulses within the public and

---

[22] Thomas Risse, et al., *The Power of Human Rights* (Cambridge: Cambridge University Press, 1999).

[23] See the debate in *Foreign Policy*, 105 (Winter 1996–1997), 91–106, between Aryeh Neier, formerly of Human Rights Watch, who stresses the importance of moral consistency for human rights NGOs ("The New Double Standard"), and Jeffrey Garten, a former US official, who stresses the many roads to progress and the necessity for flexible judgment in context – and by implication the tolerance of inconsistency ("Comment: The Need for Pragmatism"). This debate was covered in detail in ch. 4.

[24] On foreign policy as the inherent management of contradictions, see Stanley Hoffmann, "The Hell of Good Intentions," *Foreign Policy*, 29 (Winter 1977–1978), 3–26.

[25] Smith, et al., "Globalizing Human Rights," 392.

[26] On the role of ideas in international relations see especially John Mueller, *Quiet Cataclysm: Reflections on the Recent Transformation of World Politics* (New York: Basic Books, 1995); and Judith Goldstein and Robert O. Keohane, eds., *Ideas and Foreign Policy: Beliefs, Institutions, and Political Change* (Ithaca: Cornell University Press, 1993).

Congress should there be US casualties, chose a policy on arrest that was more cautious than most human rights NGOs desired. Likewise during the 1990s, many human rights NGOs pressed for immediate sanctions on China in the context of continued systematic repression. Many US officials, desiring China's cooperation on a range of security, economic, and ecological issues, chose a policy on human rights in China that was more cautious and long term than many human rights NGOs desired. The broad responsibilities of top state officials guaranteed that from time to time their views of the "right" course of action would differ from those of human rights NGOs.

During 1999 AI bitterly denounced the brief and *pro forma* meeting that had been called to discuss the application of the Fourth Geneva Convention of 1949 to the territories occupied through war by Israel in the Middle East.[27] AI wanted a longer and more substantive meeting to deal with such questions as interrogation methods used by Israel on Palestinian detainees. But the Palestinian Authority, the United States, Israel, and finally most other participants decided that after the election of the Barak government in Israel, restarting a general peace process took precedence over criticizing Israel about issues in the territories. AI emphasized human rights issues in Israeli-controlled areas, whereas the key public authorities thought that peace and stable relations between the Israelis and Palestinians constituted the top priority, after which one could make better progress on other issues.

Traditional human rights NGOs cannot utilize two basic resources of many successful interest groups when dealing with public officials, because human rights NGOs possess neither the large or concentrated membership to threaten electoral punishment, nor the budgets to threaten the withholding of significant financial contributions. In the absence of these two resources, these NGOs fall back on accurate information and energetic lobbying by whatever name. These are combined with knowledge of the timing of key public policy decisions (easier in the legislative rather than the executive process of decision making), and the development of access to key policy makers and media outlets.

Third, traditional human rights NGOs publish information in the hopes of long-term education. This blends with the objective of influencing policy in the short term through dissemination. Today's education may become the context for tomorrow's policy making. Those educated today may be the policy makers of tomorrow. Virtually all of the traditional human rights NGOs manifest an active and extensive publishing program. Human Rights Watch has a publishing agreement with Yale

---

[27] News Service Release 135/99, July 15, 1999.

University Press. Most of the human rights NGOs have a line in their budget for publishing books, brochures, reports, etc. They all make use of the Internet to disseminate their information. They wish to raise the consciousness of both policy makers and the attentive public, so as to provide a better environment for their lobbying efforts.

The issue of publication to create and maintain a supportive political environment for human rights policy is crucial, whether one pictures it as part of grassroots lobbying or long-term education. We know that in the USA in the 1990s, American public opinion in general tended to support pragmatic internationalism but not so much moral internationalism.[28] That is to say, American public opinion was supportive of an active foreign policy on trade and other issues such as interdicting illegal drugs from abroad, as long as some direct connection could be shown to the betterment of American society. But where projected foreign policies seemed to be based on morality divorced from self-interest, as was the case with ending starvation in Somalia, American public opinion was not so supportive if perceived national interests had to be sacrificed – e.g., the deaths of American soldiers. In this type of political environment, private human rights groups regularly bemoaned their lack of ability to significantly and consistently influence foreign policy and international relations.[29] This type of pragmatic environment worked to the advantage of those business and labor organizations that advocated business as usual and the downgrading of human rights concerns to the extent that they interfered with international trade. Self interest being the strong factor that it was, the Executive Director of AI-USA wrote a book about why American citizens should be concerned about human rights in other countries. He based his arguments on American self-interest, not transnational morality.[30]

Symptomatic of the situation in the USA, the one remaining superpower, was a growing consensus in both the executive and legislative branches that unilateral economic sanctions interfered with trade objectives, caused friction with allies, and were not very effective.[31] Economic

---

[28] Ole Holsti, "Public Opinion and Human Rights in American Foreign Policy," in David P. Forsythe, ed., *The United States and Human Rights: Looking Inward and Outward* (Lincoln: University of Nebraska Press, 1999), ch. 7. This point was covered in ch. 6 of the present volume.

[29] In addition to Neier, "The New Double Standard," see Ellen Dorsey, "US Foreign Policy and the Human Rights Movement: New Strategies for a Global Era," in Forsythe, *The United States and Human Rights*, ch. 8.

[30] William F. Schulz, *In Our Own Best Interest: How Defending Human Rights Benefits Us All* (Boston: Beacon Press, 2001).

[31] Eric Schmitt, "US Backs Off Sanctions, Seeing Poor Effect Abroad," *New York Times*, July 31, 1998, 1. But in 1999 the Clinton Administration announced unilateral economic sanctions against the Taliban government in Afghanistan, primarily in reaction to alleged state-supported terrorism, but also because of discrimination against women. The Congress and American public quietly deferred.

sanctions in support of human rights goals were not very popular. Policy makers in Washington knew that they would not be subjected to mass public pressure in support of most human rights situations abroad. They knew that if foreign policy exceeded a certain permissive range and began to incur costs divorced from evident self-interest, that policy would be in trouble – as in Somalia from late fall 1993. This attitudinal environment helps explain the NATO policy of relatively high altitude air strikes on Yugoslavia in 1999 and the reluctance to commit ground troops in Kosovo. This general political environment, in which many citizens in many countries were unwilling to sacrifice for the rights of others, undercut much effort by private human rights groups. Samantha Power has shown that the American public has never generated strong pressure on any American President to respond decisively to even genocide abroad, or punished a President for having failed to do so.[32]

A pragmatic rather than moralistic political culture, as a general political environment, did not mean that no advances could be made on behalf of internationally recognized human rights. Some private human rights groups teamed up with the Black Caucus in Congress to successfully direct attention to the situation in repressive Haiti in the mid-1990s. The Clinton Administration, which had from its beginnings manifested some officials also interested in doing something about repressive rule in Haiti, was able to undertake a military operation in support of democracy there and essentially end Haitian illegal emigration to the USA – but only as long as "significant" amounts of American blood and treasure were not sacrificed. Had Clinton's Haitian policy incurred the same costs as that in Somalia, namely the combat deaths of a dozen or so soldiers, it is highly likely the Haitian policy would have resulted in the same fate as the US's Somali policy – the withdrawal of congressional and public support. The same analysis could be applied to the deployment of US troops in Bosnia and their arrest of indicted war criminals. The executive could advance human rights abroad as long as no costs arose that important political circles might deem "significant." But if perceived major costs arose, especially human costs, the public would expect the executive to show a direct connection to expediential US concerns. (All of the examples noted above involve congressional influence, as much as NGO influence, along with the influence of the media.) Whether NGO human rights education could make transnational political culture more sensitive to, and supportive of, human rights concerns was an important question.[33]

---

[32] Samantha Power, *"A Problem from Hell:" America and the Age of Genocide* (New York: Perennial, 2002.)

[33] NGO human rights education was joined by formal human rights education at all levels of learning, and by human rights education in professional associations. See

At least in the USA after the terrorist attacks of September 11, 2001, if one wanted to do something about violations of human rights and lack of democracy in a state like Somalia, one was more likely to get a sympathetic hearing in Congress and the public if one stressed US self-interests in closing down a safe haven for terrorists, rather than stressing the need for better rights for foreigners.

Fourth and finally, some human rights advocacy groups also provide direct services to those victimized by human rights violations. They may engage in "judicial lobbying" or legal advocacy by participating in court cases. They may advise litigants or submit friendly briefs (*amicus curiae* briefs) in an effort to get courts to make rulings favorable to human rights standards. They may advise asylum seekers about how to present their claims to refugee status under international law. They may observe trials in the hopes of deterring a miscarriage of justice. A unique (*sui generis*) organization like the ICRC engages both in detention visits to help ensure humanitarian conditions of detention (and sometimes the release of the detainee on humanitarian grounds), and in multifaceted relief efforts for both prisoners and other victims of war and political conflict.

In sum to this point, the number of advocacy groups for various human rights causes grew dramatically in the last quarter of the twentieth century, even if the core group with a global focus and a link strictly to the international law of human rights and humanitarian affairs has remained relatively small. At the 1993 UN Conference on Human Rights at Vienna, the UN officially reported that 841 NGOs attended.[34] Particularly remarkable has been the number of groups advocating greater attention to women's rights as human rights. Their presence was felt both at Vienna and at the 1991 UN Conference on Women at Beijing. These and other UN conferences were sometimes criticized as nothing more than talking shops or debating societies. Hardly ever did states drastically change their policies immediately after these meetings. But the conferences provided focal points for NGO organizing and networking. And at least for a time they raised the world's consciousness about human rights in general or particular rights questions.[35] In the early twenty-first century there were more private reports being issued on more human rights

further George J. Andreopoulos and Richard Pierre Claude, eds., *Human Rights Education for the Twenty-First Century* (Philadelphia: University of Pennsylvania Press, 1997); and Sia Spiliopoulou Akermark, *Human Rights Education: Achievements and Challenges* (Turku/Abo, Finland: Institute for Human Rights, Abo Akademi University, 1998).

[34] UN Doc.: A/conf.157/24 (Report of the World Conference on Human Rights), 13 October 1993, Part I, 9.

[35] In general see Michael Schechter, *UN Global Conferences*, (London and New York: Routledge, 2005).

topics than ever before in world history. Women's rights, children's rights, prisoner's rights, etc. all drew extensive NGO attention. True, biases continued. Social and economic rights continued to be the step-children or illegitimate offspring of the human rights movement, especially on the part of NGOs based in the West. Nevertheless, an international civic society was emerging in which human rights advocacy groups and their allies were highly active.

Influence?

The most important question was not so much what the human rights groups did, and how; that was reasonably clear to close observers. Rather, the challenging question was how to specify, then generalize about, their influence.[36] It had long proved difficult to precisely analyze the influence of any interest group or coalition in any political system over time.[37] Why was it that in the USA the "tobacco lobby" seemed so powerful, only to suddenly be placed on the defensive in the 1990s and lose a series of votes in the US Congress that might produce tougher laws on tobacco advertising and use? Why was it that the "Israeli lobby," generally thought to be one of the more powerful in American politics, seemed to weaken in the 1990s and was certainly unable to block a whole series of arms sales to Arab states? Why was the "China lobby," presumably strong in Washington during the Cold War, unable to block a rapprochement between Washington and Beijing? These and other questions about the influence of lobbies in general, or in relation to foreign policy, are not easy to answer. It was often said that "special interests" dominated modern politics, but proving the precise influence of these "special interests" became more difficult the more one probed into specifics.

A pervasive difficulty in analyzing NGO influence centered around the concept of success. If one or more NGOs succeeded in helping a UN Security Council resolution creating a criminal court for Rwanda to be adopted, but the *ad hoc* court turned out to have little impact on the Great Lakes Region of Africa, could that be considered a success for NGO influence? But if later the *ad hoc* court contributed to the creation of a standing international criminal court at the UN, would the criteria for

---

[36] See further Don Hubert, "Inferring Influence: Gauging the Impact of NGOs," in Charlotte Ku and Thomas G. Weiss, eds., *Toward Understanding Global Governance: The International Law and International Relations Toolbox* (Providence, RI: ACUNS Reports and Papers, No. 2, 1998), 27–54.

[37] Bernard C. Cohen, *The Public's Impact on Foreign Policy* (Boston: Little, Brown, 1973). In general see David P. Forsythe, *Human Rights and World Politics*, 2nd edn (Lincoln: University of Nebraska Press, 1989), ch. 6.

success change? If Amnesty International or the International Committee of the Red Cross prevented some instances of torture, how would one prove that success since the violation of human rights never occurred? If NGOs in Bosnia helped reduce political rape and murder, but in so doing, by moving vulnerable civilians out of the path of enemy forces, they thereby contributed to ethnic cleansing and the basic political objective of a fighting party, was that a success?

In dealing with the sometimes elusive notion of success or achievement, sometimes it helped to distinguish among the following: success in getting an item or subject on the agenda for discussion, success in achieving serious discussion, success in getting procedural or institutional change, and finally success in achieving substantive policy change that clearly ameliorated or eliminated the problem. In the early stages of campaigns against slavery or female genital mutilation, it could be considered remarkable success just to get high state officials to think about the subject as an important problem.[38] In addressing gay rights in Muslim nations, it might be a mark of success just to get reasonable public debate.

Relatedly, one of the most helpful contributions that a human rights NGO or movement could obtain was the supportive finding of an epistemic community. Epistemic communities are networks of scientists or "thinkers" who deal in "truth" as demonstrated by cause and effect. To the extent that there is widespread agreement on scientific truth, public policy tends to follow accordingly – albeit with a time lag during which advocacy or lobbying comes into play. If the scientific evidence of the harmful effects of "second-hand smoke" had been stronger sooner, those campaigning against smoking in public and indoor places would have an easier time of it. When medical personnel can show conclusively that female genital mutilation presents clear risks to those undergoing this ritual cutting in much of Africa and other places, the reporting and dissemination of this scientific truth aided those human rights groups trying to eliminate the practice.[39] Unfortunately, most decisions in support of international human rights involved political and moral choice rather than scientific truth.

The greatest obstacle to proving the influence of human rights NGOs was that in most situations their influence was merged with the influence of public officials in the context of other factors such as media coverage.

---

[38] Keck and Sikkink, *Activists beyond Borders.*

[39] See further Ernst Haas, *When Knowledge is Power: Three Models of Change in International Organizations* (Berkeley: University of California Press, 1990); and Peter Haas, "Introduction: Epistemic Communities and International Policy Coordination," *International Organization*, 46, 3 (Winter 1992), 1–36.

Private human rights groups had long urged the creation of a United Nations High Commissioner for Human Rights, and the post was voted into being in 1993. Many private groups wanted to claim credit, but many governments had also been active in support of this cause. The UN Vienna Conference, made up of governments, had approved the plan. Salient personalities like former President Carter had campaigned vigorously for the creation of the post. And frequently media coverage is at work as well.

Likewise human rights NGOs like Helsinki Watch certainly pressured the European communists during the Cold War, acting in tandem with private individuals and groups inside those communist states. But western states were also active on human rights issues through the CSCE process. When European communism fell, it was impossible to say scientifically what was the exact impact of the human rights NGOs compared with state pressures, or for that matter compared with the economic difficulties of the European communists themselves (as noted in chapter 4).

Most events have multiple causes, and it is often impossible to factor out in a precise way the exact impact of a human rights NGO or even a movement or coalition. In 1975 a relatively unknown member of the lower house of the US Congress, Donald Fraser, decided to hold hearings on human rights in US foreign policy. As chair of a sub-committee in the House of Representatives, Fraser had the authority to take such a decision by himself.[40] The Fraser hearings led to the reintroduction of the issue of human rights into US foreign policy after an absence of some two decades. But NGOs had some impact on these events in three ways.

Various anti-war NGOs and movements, which were the forerunners of several human rights NGOs in the USA, helped set the stage for the Fraser hearings.[41] It was growing domestic opposition to US policies in Vietnam, and a growing sense that US foreign policy had become amoral if not immoral, that contributed to the political climate in the USA in which Fraser acted. NGOs and social movements helped create that climate of opinion. Second, once scheduled, the Fraser hearings were the scene of testimony on human rights issues by AI-USA and other human rights NGOs. Third, Fraser's principal staff person on foreign policy, John Salzburg, had worked for an NGO and still shared the values of a number of those in the NGO community in Washington. So although there is no clear evidence that NGOs pressed Fraser to take the momentous course

[40] See further Donald M. Fraser, "Freedom and Foreign Policy," *Foreign Policy*, 26 (Spring 1977), 140–156; and John Salzburg, "A View from the Hill: US Legislation and Human Rights," in David D. Newsom, ed., *The Diplomacy of Human Rights* (Lanham: University Press of America, 1986), 13–20.

[41] Lowell W. Livezey, *Non Governmental Organizations and the Idea of Human Rights* (Princeton: Princeton University Center for International Studies, 1988).

of action he did, NGOs did have some influence, probably of rather high significance, in combining with Fraser and other public officials to emphasize human rights in US foreign policy.

Nial McDermot, an experienced staff member of the International Commission of Jurists, wrote accurately: "NGOs create the conditions in which governmental pressure can be effective."[42] It is in the synergy or interplay of public and private action that one normally understands the full role of human rights NGOs and their coalitions. Thus influence by private human rights groups is normally exercised in a quasi-private, quasi-public way. Just as much policy making is now transnational or inter-domestic, involving both international and domestic players, so that policy making is also both public and private at one and the same time. Public officials may join with NGOs and the media, etc. to effectuate change. This is precisely why a focus on movements or coalitions or networks has come into vogue, although it is still challenging to try to determine which actor in the movement exercised crucial influence at crucial times.

In some situations it is relatively clear that human rights NGOs, or a coalition of them and their allies, have had direct impact on what might be termed a human rights decision. Several authors have shown that one can trace the release of one or more prisoners of conscience to action by AI.[43] One can also show that NGOs made significant contributions to the negotiation of human rights standards in certain treaties.[44] A strong case can be made that human rights NGOs, in combination with other actors such as media representatives *inter alia*, have helped transform the political culture of Mexico, Argentina, and other states in the Western Hemisphere which now show more sensitivity to human rights issues.[45] Many if not most of the UN monitoring mechanisms, from review committees to special rapporteurs, rely on NGO information in conducting their activities. When critical questions are raised, or critical conclusions

---

[42] N. McDermot, "The Role of NGOs in the Promotion and Protection of Human Rights," in *The Role of Non Governmental Organizations*, 45–52.

[43] Jonathan Power, *Amnesty International: The Human Rights Story* (New York: McGraw-Hill, 1981); Egon Larsen, *A Flame in Barbed Wire: The Story of Amnesty International* (London: F. Muller, 1978). See also Jane Connors, "Amnesty International at the United Nations," in Peter Willetts, ed., *"The Conscience of the World": The Influence of Non-Governmental Organizations in the UN System* (Washington: Brookings, 1996).

[44] Peter R. Baehr, "The General Assembly: Negotiating the Convention on Torture," in David P. Forsythe, ed., *The United Nations in the World Political Economy* (London: Macmillan, 1989), 36–53; Lawrence J. LeBlanc, *The Convention on the Rights of the Child: United Nations Lawmaking on Human Rights* (Lincoln: University of Nebraska Press, 1995), ch. 2.

[45] Keck and Sikkink, *Activists beyond Borders*, 3.

reached, it is frequently on the basis, at least in part, of NGO information. The reduction of state funding for certain UN activities has increased the impact of NGOs in the human rights domain; the UN offices lack the resources to conduct their own extensive inquiries, and thus fall back on information from the human rights NGOs.[46]

From time to time certain states have tried to block some human rights NGOs from receiving or renewing their consultative status with the UN system. This is a status that allows NGOs to circulate documents and speak in certain UN meetings. If NGOs had no influence, and never proved irritating to states, the latter would not be so interested in blocking the activities of the former. State opposition to, and criticism of, NGOs is a reasonably clear indication that states, meaning the governments that speak for them, pay some attention to human rights NGOs and worry about what they say. It is obvious that most states care about their reputations in international relations, and go to great efforts to try to counter critical commentary.[47]

During 1999, the UN Committee on Non-Governmental Organizations, which reports to ECOSOC, withdrew consultative status for Christian Solidarity International, based in Zurich. That controversial NGO had antagonized the government of the Sudan in several ways. Likewise the committee refused to approve the credentials of Human Rights in China, based in New York, which had offended the government in Beijing.[48] So even after the Cold War, and despite the immense influence of western states in the UN system, mainly the states of the global south continued to try to limit the role of some human rights advocacy groups in UN proceedings.

It cannot be scientifically proved, but a null hypothesis is certainly interesting: if human rights NGOs had not existed during the past thirty-five years, human rights would have a much less salient position in international relations. Serious, even grave, human rights violations in Cambodia in the 1970s and Mexico in the late 1960s did not lead to international attention and pressure because local and international NGOs were not

---

[46] P.H. Kooijmans, "The Non Governmental Organizations and the Monitoring Activities of the United Nations in the Field of Human Rights," in *The Role of Non Governmental Organizations*, 15–22. Peter R. Baehr and Leon Gordenker, *United Nations University Public Forum on Human Rights and Non Governmental Organizations* (Tokyo: United Nations University Lectures, September 14, 15, 18, 1996).

[47] A classic case in point is the effort by the Argentine Junta in the 1980s to try to block criticism of its human rights record in the UN Human Rights Commission, as recorded by Iain Guest in *Behind the Disappearances: Argentina's Dirty War Against Human Rights and the United Nations* (Philadelphia: University of Pennsylvania Press, 1990).

[48] Paul Lewis, "UN Committee, Under Pressure, Limits Rights Groups," *New York Times*, June 22, 1999, A3.

in place to report on and act against those violations.[49] More positively, what began as action by the Anti-Slavery Society in London in the early nineteenth century triggered a successful movement against slavery and the slave trade over about a century. It is quite clear as well that since 1863, what is now called the International Committee of the Red Cross has advanced the cause of international humanitarian law, or the law of human rights in armed conflict. These are clear examples of NGOs that have had a broad impact on international relations, even if they frequently acted, or act today, in conjunction with public authorities. Public officials may take the decision to adopt human rights standards or seek certain forms of implementation. But they may act in an environment created to a considerable extent by human rights NGOs or human rights coalitions. Much of this influence is amorphous and remains difficult to specify. In the future it might prove possible to further elaborate the conditions under which a human rights NGO or movement might expect to be successful – e.g., where leaders of a state targeted for pressure are on record as favoring human rights in principle, where such leaders do not regard the human rights violation as crucial to their hold on power or to the security of their state, where a target state is not a pivotal or vital state to others in strategic or economic terms, etc.

In the meantime, human rights NGOs have helped create a climate of opinion in international relations generally sympathetic to human rights. In this regard these NGOs have helped restrict and thus transform the idea of state sovereignty. It can be stated in general that the responsible exercise of state sovereignty entails respect for internationally recognized human rights. States, like Saddam Hussein's Iraq, that engage in gross and systematic violation of the most elemental human rights are not afforded the normal prerogatives that stem from the principle of sovereignty. During the 1990s Iraq was put into *de facto* receivership under United Nations supervision. This was because of the misuse of sovereignty via violations of human rights in Iraq and Kuwait, combined with aggression against Kuwait. A similar analysis could be made about Milosevic in Yugoslavia. It is still valid to say, as Francis Fukuyama wrote, that in dominant international political theory, the most fully legitimate state is the liberal democratic state that respects civil and political rights.[50]

---

[49] On Mexico see Keck and Sikkink, *Activists beyond Borders*. On Cambodia, I refer to genocide on a massive scale after most foreign observers had been kicked out by the Khmer Rouge.

[50] Francis Fukuyama, *The End of History and the Last Man* (New York: The Free Press, 1992). Of course there is a gap between the political theory of legitimate states and the practice of international relations. In practice, persons and public authorities may grant legitimacy, meaning a sense of correct rule, on the basis of tradition, alliances, and/or effective exercise of power, and not just human rights performance. See

Advocacy groups for human rights play the basic role of reminding everyone of human rights performance, and particularly when gross and systematic violations occur that call into existence the basic right of a government to act for the state.

Private action for relief and development

As we have seen, the International Bill of Rights contains economic and social rights such as the rights to adequate food, clothing, shelter, and medical care in peace time. International humanitarian law contains non-combatant rights to emergency assistance – referring to similar food, clothing, shelter, and medical care – in armed conflict.[51] United Nations resolutions have extended these same rights to "complex emergencies," an imprecise term meant to cover situations in which the relevant authority denies that there is an armed conflict covered by international humanitarian law, but in which civilians are in need and public order disrupted. In a tradition that defies legal logic, private groups working to implement these socio-economic rights in peace and war are not normally referred to as human rights groups but as relief (or humanitarian) and development agencies. This semantic tradition may exist because many agencies were working for relief and development before the discourse on human rights became so salient.

Whatever the semantic traditions, there are complicated international systems for both relief and development, and neither would function without private agencies. At the same time, the private groups are frequently supported by state donations of one type or another, and frequently act in conjunction with inter-governmental organizations. As with advocacy groups, so with relief and development agencies, the resulting process is both private and public at the same time. In both relief and development, the United States and the states of the European Union provide most of the resources.[52] In both, UN agencies are heavily involved – UNICEF, the WHO, the World Food Program, the UN Development Program, etc. But in both, private grassroots action is, to a very great extent, essential to whether persons on the ground get the food, clothing, shelter, and

David P. Forsythe, *Human Rights and Peace: International and National Views* (Lincoln: University of Nebraska Press, 1993), ch. 3. Compare Jack Donnelly, "Human Rights: A New Standard of Civilization?," *International Affairs*, 74, 1 (1998), 1–24.

[51] Legal obligations in this regard under the 1949 Geneva Conventions, and 1977 Additional Protocols, for victims of armed conflicts have been analyzed by numerous commentators, including Monika Sandvik-Nylund, *Caught in Conflicts: Civilian Victims, Humanitarian Assistance and International Law* (Oturku/Abo, Finland: Institute for Human Rights of Abo Akademi University, 1998).

[52] See further Alexander Natsios, *US Foreign Policy and the Four Horsemen of the Apocalypse: Humanitarian Relief in Complex Emergencies* (Westport: Praeger, 1997).

medical care which international law guarantees on paper. It is the private groups that turn the law on the books into the law in action. It is the private groups that condition and sometimes transform the operation of state sovereignty.

Relief

Because of international humanitarian law, the relief system in armed conflict and complex emergencies is somewhat different from that in peace time. The norms supposedly guiding action are different, and some of the actors are different. For reasons of space, only relief in wars and complex emergencies is covered here.[53]

In so-called "man-made" disasters, the private International Committee of the Red Cross usually plays a central role because of its long association with victims of war and international humanitarian law. It was ultimately, for example, the best-positioned relief actor in Somalia in the early 1990s, and remained so even after the arrival of tens of thousands of US military personnel. The ICRC does not monopolize relief in these situations, however. In Bosnia in the first half of the 1990s, it was the Office of the UN High Commissioner for Refugees that ran the largest civilian relief program, followed by the ICRC. In Cambodia in the late 1980s, UNHCR and the ICRC were essentially co-lead agencies for international relief. In the Sudan during the 1970s and 1980s, UNICEF and the ICRC carried out important roles. But in these and similar situations, numerous private agencies are active in relief: World Vision, Church World Service, Caritas, Oxfam, Save the Children, Doctors Without Borders, etc. It is not unusual to find several hundred private relief agencies active in a conflict situation like Rwanda and its environs in the mid-1990s.

Relief: process

One can summarize the challenges facing all these private relief agencies (aka socio-economic human rights groups).[54]

1. *They must negotiate access to those in need.* One may speak of guaranteed rights, even a right to assistance. And in the 1990s there was much discussion about a right to humanitarian intervention. But as a practical matter, one must reach agreement with those who have the guns on

---

[53] Relief in natural disasters such as floods, earthquakes, typhoons, volcanic eruptions, etc. is analyzed in many sources, including by the late expert Frederick Cuny in *Disasters and Development* (New York: Oxford University Press, 1983).

[54] The following is drawn from David P. Forsythe, "The International Committee of the Red Cross and Humanitarian Assistance – A Policy Analysis," *International Review of the Red Cross*, 314 (September–October, 1997), 512–531.

the ground in order to provide relief/assistance in armed conflict and complex emergencies. Even if there is some general agreement between public authorities (*de jure and de facto*) and relief agencies on providing relief, specifics have to be agreed upon for particular times and places. Negotiating conditions of access can be a tricky business, as fighting parties may seek to divert relief for military and political objectives, even as relief agencies may insist on impartiality and neutrality. With numerous relief agencies vying for a piece of the action, machiavellian political actors may play one off against another. Some of the smaller, less-experienced agencies have proved themselves subject to political manipulation.

2. *Relief agencies must provide an accurate assessment of need.* Relief must be tailored to local conditions, and there should be control for redundant or unneeded goods and services. The use of systematic rape as a weapon of war, terror, and ethnic cleansing has meant the need for gynecological and psychiatric services for many women.

3. *The private groups must mobilize relief in a timely and effective way.* Here the ICRC has certain advantages, as it is well known and respected by most western states, and has links to national Red Cross or Red Crescent societies in over 180 states. But other private agencies have their own means of mobilization, being able to tap into well-established religious or secular networks.

4. *Of obvious importance is the ability of a private group to actually deliver the assistance in a timely and cost-effective way.* Here again the ICRC presents certain advantages, as it is smaller and less bureaucratic than some UN bodies, has regional, country and intra-country offices in many places around the world (in addition to the national Red Cross/Red Crescent societies), and since the 1970s has built up experience in the delivery of relief in ongoing conflicts and occupied territory. Its reputation for effectiveness on the ground was particularly outstanding in Somalia in the early 1990s. But other agencies, particularly the UNHCR, have been accumulating experience as well. And often the sheer size of a relief problem can be too great for the ICRC. In Rwanda in 1994 and thereafter, where as many as two million persons fled genocidal ethnic conflict and civil war, the ICRC concentrated its activities inside Rwanda and left to other actors the matter of relief in neighboring countries.

5. *All relief agencies have to engage in evaluation of past action and planning for the future.* All of the major relief players do this, but some of the smaller, less-experienced, and more ad hoc groups do not.

The international system, movement, or coalition for relief in man-made disasters faces no shortage of pressing issues.

1. *Should there be more coordination?* There has been much talk about more coordination, but none of the major players wants to be dominated by any other actor. Legally speaking, the ICRC is a Swiss private agency whose statutes give policy-making authority to an all-Swiss assembly that co-opts members from Swiss society only. It resists control by any United Nations body, any other Red Cross agency, or any state. Also, the UNHCR, UNICEF, the WHO, and the WFP all have independent budgets, executive heads, governing bodies, and mandates. Each resists control by any UN principal organ or by the UN Emergency Relief Coordinator (now the Under Secretary-General for Humanitarian Assistance) who reports to the Secretary-General. The latter UN office lacked the legal, political, and budgetary clout to bring the other actors under its control. Politically speaking, the major donors, the USA and the EU, have not insisted on more formal coordination. There are advantages to the present system. UNHCR may be best positioned in one conflict, UNICEF or the ICRC in another. And there was *de facto* cooperation among many of the relief actors much of the time, with processes for coordination both in New York and Geneva. More importantly, there was considerable cooperation among agencies in the field. Yet duplication and conflicts occurred with regularity; there was certainly room for improvement.

2. *Should one try to separate politics from humanitarian action?* Particularly the ICRC argued in favor of strict adherence to the principles of impartiality and neutrality, and preferred to keep its distance from "political" decisions which involved coercion or any official preference for one side over another in armed conflict and complex emergencies. But even the ICRC had to operate under military protection in Somalia to deliver relief effectively (and had to accept military protection for released prisoners on occasion in Bosnia). In Bosnia, much of the fighting was about civilians – their location and sustenance. The UNHCR's relief program became "politicized" in the sense of intertwined with carrots and sticks provided in relation to diplomacy and peacemaking. There was disagreement about the wisdom of this course of action. But it was clear that once the UN authorized use of force in places like Bosnia to coerce a change in Serbian policy, then UN civilian (and military) personnel on the ground became subject to hostage-taking by antagonized Serb combatants. It was clear that the idea of a neutral Red Cross or UN presence for relief purposes was not widely respected in almost all of the armed conflicts and

complex emergencies after the Cold War. Relief workers from various organizations were killed in places like Chechnya, Bosnia, Rwanda, Burundi, Liberia, Somalia, etc. Other relief workers were taken hostage for ransom. Sometimes armed relief, even "humanitarian war," seemed the only feasible option, but others disagreed.[55]

3. *Could one change the situation through new legislation and/or better dissemination of norms?* It was evident from the Soviet Union to communist Yugoslavia, to take just two clear examples, that former states had not taken fully seriously their obligation to teach international humanitarian law to military personnel, despite the strictures of especially the 1949 Geneva Conventions and additional 1977 Protocols for the protection of victims of war. After especially the French failed to have codified new laws on humanitarian intervention in the 1990s, action turned to international criminal justice and the creation of international tribunals to try those individuals accused of war crimes, genocide, and crimes against humanity. NGOs lobbied vigorously for these new norms and agencies to enforce them, as we have already noted. But much violence was carried out by private armies such as rebel or secessionist groups, clans and organized mobs. Relief workers more than once faced child soldiers on drugs armed with automatic weapons. How to make international norms, whether new or old, effective on such combatants was a tough nut to crack. It was said of Somalia, only in slight exaggeration, that no one with a weapon had ever heard of the Geneva Conventions.[56] At least many of the relief agencies agreed on a code of conduct for themselves, which approximated but did not exactly replicate the core principles of the Geneva Conventions.

Relief: influence?

There is no question but that private actors have considerable if amorphous influence or impact in the matter of international relief in "manmade" conflicts. The ICRC was a major player in Somalia 1991–1995, the UNHCR and its private partners were a major player in Bosnia 1992–1995. The UNHCR does not so much deliver relief itself as contract with private agencies for that task. UNHCR manages, supervises,

---

[55] Adam Roberts, "Humanitarian War: Military Intervention and Human Rights," *International Affairs*, 69, 3 (July, 1993), 429f. See further Jonathan Moore, ed., *Hard Choices: Moral Dilemmas in Humanitarian Intervention* (Lanham: Rowman and Littlefield, 1998); and Thomas G. Weiss, "The Humanitarian Identity Crisis," in *Ethics & International Affairs*, 13 (1999), 1–22, with associated commentary.

[56] Jennifer Learning, "When the System Doesn't Work: Somalia, 1992," in Kevin M. Cahill, ed., *Framework for Survival: Health, Human Rights, and Humanitarian Assistance in Conflicts and Disasters* (New York: Basic Books, for the Council on Foreign Relations, 1993), 112.

and coordinates, but private actors like Doctors Without Borders do much of the grassroots relief. To use a negative example of influence, if several private groups disagree with a policy decision taken by the UNHCR and decide to operate differently, the UNHCR is constrained in what it can do. The same is even more true for the World Food Program, which has a very limited capacity to operate in the field by itself. The ICRC, as should be clear by now, is a private actor whose norms and accomplishments often affect the other players, directly or indirectly.

Having noted this NGO independent position, one must still recognize that states and inter-governmental organizations are the major sources for material resources directed to humanitarian assistance in wars and complex emergencies. It is states, directly or through IGOs, that provide the physical security that relief NGOs need for their grassroots operations. (These NGOs may prefer to rely on their own reputation for security of operations, but if that fails, they have to rely on the hard power of states.) Influence is a complex two-way street. Public authorities need the NGOs, which opens up possibilities for subtle influence on the part of the latter. But the NGOs need the support and cooperation of the public authorities. If NGOs pull out of a relief operation and develop the image of unreasonable non-cooperation, they will cut themselves out of operations that constitute their reason for being, get bad publicity, and make it more difficult to raise money. Once again, as with traditional advocacy for human rights, we find that the movement to provide relief is both private and public at the same time, and that influence among the disparate elements is difficult to pinpoint in general.

The challenge facing relief/humanitarian agencies is probably even greater than that facing more traditional human rights advocacy groups. The former are dealing with states and other primary protagonists that have resorted to violence in pursuit of their goals. The issues at stake have already been deemed worth fighting over. In this context of armed conflict or complex emergency, it is exceedingly difficult to get the protagonists to elevate assistance to civilians to a rank of the first order. Moreover, in all too many conflicts, especially after the Cold War, intentional attacks on civilians, and their brutal manipulation otherwise, became part of the grand strategy of one or more of the fighting parties. It was therefore difficult if not impossible to fully neutralize and humanize civilian relief.

Development: process

As in relief, the development process on an international scale presents a mixture of public and private actors. If we focus just on the PVOs based in the North Atlantic area we find they are exceedingly numerous – perhaps now up to about 5,000 in number – and quite varied in their orientations.[57] While some of these PVOs or VOLAGs reject state funding to protect their independence, and consequently wind up frequently on the margins of the development process, most act otherwise and serve as conduits for public monies and public policies. PVOs themselves provide only about 10 per cent of development assistance in a typical year.

Private development agencies, like Oxfam, that cooperate with public authorities and operate consistently across international borders are a crucial part of the public–private development process. These development NGOs provide values and services often lacking in the public sector: "smallness, good contacts at the local level, freedom from political manipulation, a labor- rather than capital-intensive orientation, innovativeness, and flexibility in administration."[58]

The OECD states find "mainstream" NGOs useful in implementing their goals while reducing suspicions of neo-imperialism or other unwanted intrusions in the affairs of developing states. Other public authorities seem to be coming around to this same view. Major intergovernmental actors are the World Bank (officially the International Bank for Reconstruction and Development), other development banks on a regional basis, and the United Nations Development Program (UNDP). The International Monetary Fund (IMF) is not, strictly speaking, a development institution. It frequently functions, however, in conjunction with the World Bank in making loans (affording drawing rights) to stabilize currency transaction.

Increasingly the World Bank officially endorses the participation of NGOs and community-based organizations (CBOs) in establishing development programs.[59] Theory and practice are not always the same, and historically relations between the Bank and development NGOs have been less than perfectly smooth. Many development NGOs have criticized the Bank for being insensitive to the needs of especially the rural poor, and within that group especially indigenous peoples, who did not benefit so clearly from the past industrial schemes of the Bank, and who may have been forced out of their traditional homes by development projects funded by the Bank.

The UNDP also officially endorses the bringing together of NGOs and CBOs to provide grassroots participation in development projects.

[57] *Directory of Non-Governmental Organisations Active in Sustainable Development* (Paris: OECD, 1996).

[58] Brian H. Smith, *More than Altruism: The Politics of Private Foreign Aid* (Princeton: Princeton University Press, 1990), 6.

[59] See further David P. Forsythe, "The United Nations, Human Rights, and Development," *Human Rights Quarterly*, 19, 2 (May 1997), 334–349.

If practiced seriously, this type of micro- or economic democracy would combine *de facto* attention to civil and political rights, as the rights of participation, with social and economic rights. Endorsement of NGO and CBO participation in the development process by the Bank, UNDP, and OECD states comprised part of the mantra of "sustainable human development" at the turn of the century. As theory, it was an improvement over the top-down massive infrastructure projects devised in Washington and New York in the 1960s and 1970s.

Development: influence?

Private development agencies faced no lack of problems in trying to help achieve sustainable human development in keeping with internationally recognized human rights. A new barrier in the 1990s was that the prevalence of ethnic conflict and other forms of internal armed conflict and political instability caused public authorities to channel vast amounts of resources into relief. Consequently, fewer funds and less attention went to development.

A historical problem was that PVOs and VOLAGs did not always think of development in relation to human rights,[60] although with time there was a shift toward focusing on empowerment – which was a synonym for participatory rights.[61] This shift was certainly welcomed by those development NGOs that had long expressed concern about authoritarian rather than democratic development.[62] We noted above how the theory of the World Bank, UNDP, and OECD states all accepted participation in decision making by NGOs and CBOs. There was also a considerable shift toward integrating women's rights with development strategies.[63] Much less pronounced was any shift toward emphasizing socio-economic rights in the development process. But since "southern" NGOs tended toward this emphasis, and since they had growing contacts with "northern" NGOs, it was possible that more practical and not just rhetorical attention would be given to these "second-generation" rights.

Development NGOs, much like traditional advocacy NGOs for human rights, had trouble in precisely specifying their influence in the

---

[60] Theo Van Boven, "Human Rights and Development: The UN Experience," in David P. Forsythe, ed., *Human Rights and Development: International Views* (London: Macmillan, 1989), 121–135.

[61] Julie Fisher, *Non-Governments: NGOs and the Political Development of the Third World* (West Hartford: Kumarian Press, 1998).

[62] Smith, *More than Altruism*, 72.

[63] See, for example, Sue Ellen M. Charlton and Jana Everett, eds., *NGOs and Grassroots in Development Work in South India: Elizabeth Moen Mathiot* (Lanham: University Press of America, 1998).

development process *vis-à-vis* other actors.[64] As with the advocacy groups, many leaders of development NGOs were active out of moral commitment and would continue with their ideas and objectives whether or not they were able to change public programs to their liking. As with advocacy groups, the real influence of development NGOs was to be found in their amorphous contribution to a wider movement, network, or coalition interested in sustainable *human* development. While true that public authorities provide most of the capital for development projects, some influence flows from the NGOs back toward public authorities – especially through the give and take over different approaches to development. Public authorities have no monopoly over ideas related to development, and some of the ideas that prove controlling over time originate with NGOs.

Conclusion

NGOs that advocate human rights ideas, that implement the right to humanitarian assistance for those in dire straits, and that contribute to the human rights inherent in sustainable human development have impacted both public authorities and private individuals in numerous ways. They have advanced some form of liberalism in international relations through their emphasis on individuals and law, as compared with state interests and power. Advocacy groups provide much of the information that allows the rights agencies of international organizations to function, while challenging or validating the facts and policies put forward by states. It is difficult to believe the making and implementing of human rights standards would operate in the same way without these advocacy groups. The international relief system would simply not be able to get humanitarian assistance to those in need in most situations without the private relief agencies. The development process would be seriously hampered without the private development organizations to serve as intermediaries between the public authorities that provide most of the resources and the individuals and indigenous groups that implement, and benefit from, the development programs at the grassroots level.

States and their inter-governmental organizations are thus dependent on these NGOs. States share the stage of international relations with these NGOs, which is to say that state sovereignty is at times restricted by the activity of these NGOs that work for civil and political, social and economic rights. A restricted sovereignty is a transformed sovereignty, no longer absolute.

[64] Michael Edwards and David Hulme, eds., *Beyond the Magic Bullet: NGO Performance and Accountability in the Post-Cold War World* (West Hartford: Kumarian Press, in cooperation with Save the Children Fund, 1996).

As much as NGOs need states – to arrest war criminals, to provide food and tents and sometimes physical protection for relief, to provide capital and cooperation for development – states need NGOs for a variety of ideas and services. Thus the stage is set for the subtle interplay of influence between the two types of actors on behalf of human rights, relief, and sustainable *human* development.

Discussion questions

- Is it more helpful for understanding to focus on separate or distinct private human rights organizations, or to focus on networks or movements? Can one understand a movement without understanding the precise actors that make up that movement? Can public officials be part of a human rights or humanitarian movement?
- Are western-based private human rights organizations part of western cultural imperialism? To what extent does an organization like Amnesty International have broad support in the non-western world?
- Are the better-known private human rights organizations moralistic and legalistic, in that they fail to consistently understand and appreciate the political context within which governments take decisions that impact human rights? Do they unreasonably discount other values and policies that governments and their publics consider legitimate – such as peace, security, economic growth? Or are the private groups absolutely vital to shaking governments and mass public opinion out of their set ways regarding the death penalty, gay rights, the continuing prevalence of torture, excessive spending on the military compared with basic human needs, etc.?
- What practical steps can be taken to improve the delivery of food, clothing, shelter, and medical care to civilians in armed conflicts and complex emergencies? Do these steps involve private actors such as the International Committee of the Red Cross, Doctors Without Borders, etc.? Given that a number of fighting parties *intentionally* attack and abuse civilians, should humanitarian action be left to NATO or the US Department of Defense in place of private relief organizations? After all, national military establishments (at least the major ones) have tremendous logistical capacity. Paradoxes aside, should humanitarian action be nationalized and militarized?
- Is the global pursuit of "development" sufficiently attentive to "sustainable *human* development" and human rights? How important is the role of private actors like Oxfam in this development process? Do public authorities like the World Bank, the UN Development Program and the US Agency for International Development approve of a large role for private organizations and human-oriented development? Is

this orientation perhaps theory and not practice? How would practical policies change if human rights were genuinely incorporated into the "development" process?

Suggestions for further reading

Cahill, Kevin M., ed., *Framework for Survival: Health, Human Rights, and Humanitarian Assistance in Conflicts and Disasters* (New York: Basic Books for the Council on Foreign Relations, 1993). A good stock-taking of problems early in the post-Cold War period. Much attention to private actors.

Edwards, Michael, and David Hulme, eds., *Beyond the Magic Bullet: NGO Performance and Accountability in the Post-Cold War World* (West Hartford: Kumarian Press, in corporation with Save the Children Fund, 1996). Deals with the central question of how democratic, accountable and open NGOs really are, even though they claim to represent "the people."

Florini, A., *The Third Force: The Rise of Transnational Civil Society* (Washington: Carnegie Endowment, 2000). An excellent overview of the global spread of NGOs in all their variety.

Fisher, Julie, *Non-Governments: NGOs and the Political Development of the Third World* (West Hartford: Kumarian Press, 1998). A critical look at the impact of human rights and development NGOs in the global south.

Haas, Ernst, *When Knowledge is Power: Three Models of Change in International Organizations* (Berkeley: University of California Press, 1990). A complicated model of why international organizations develop the policies that they do, stressing the role of private scientific communities in that process. Considerable attention to human rights.

Keck, Margaret E., and Kathryn Sikkink, *Activists beyond Borders: Advocacy Networks in International Politics* (Ithaca: Cornell Unniversity Press, 1998). An outstanding example of using the concept of "movement" to try to analyze essentially private action for human rights, although the authors conceive of certain public officials as part of a movement.

Korey, William, *NGOs and the Universal Declaration of Human Rights: "A Curious Grapevine,"* (New York: St. Martin's Press, 1998). A personalized and disjointed account, but containing much useful information for introductory purposes. Places great weight on NGO action, especially by Jewish groups, in the evolution of modern human rights.

Livezey, Lowell W., *Non Governmental Organizations and the Idea of Human Rights* (Princeton: Princeton Center for International Studies, 1988). A thoughtful if somewhat dated overview.

Mathews, Jessica Tuchman, "Power Shift," *Foreign Affairs*, 76, 1 (January–February 1997), 50–66. A sweeping argument and highly optimistic view about the growing influence of all sorts of NGOs in international relations. The other side of her coin is the declining influence of the territorial state.

Moore, Jonathan, ed., *Hard Choices: Moral Dilemmas in Humanitarian Intervention* (Lanham: Rowman and Littlefield, 1998). A good collection by practitioners and theorists about different views toward, and experiences with, humanitarian assistance.

Natsios, Alexander, *US Foreign Policy and the Four Horsemen of the Apocalypse: Humanitarian Relief in Complex Emergencies* (Westport: Praeger, 1997). The author, who was at different times both a US official and a key player for World Vision, a church-related private relief organization, focuses on the USA but stresses the interactions of governments, international organizations, and private actors like the ICRC.

Power, Jonathan, *Amnesty International: The Human Rights Story* (New York: McGraw-Hill, 1981). A solid if somewhat dated overview.

Smith, Brian H., *More than Altruism: The Politics of Private Foreign Aid* (Princeton: Princeton University Press, 1990). A sharp look at private development and relief organizations.

Smith, Jackie, and Ron Pagnucco, with George A. Lopez, "Globalizing Human Rights: The Work of Transnational Human Rights NGOs in the 1990s," *Human Rights Quarterly*, 20, 2 (May 1998), 379–412. An essential if largely descriptive overview.

Smith, Jackie, Charles Chatfield, and Ron Pagnucco, eds., *Transnational Social Movements and Global Politics: Solidarity Beyond the State* (Syracuse: Syracuse University Press, 1997). A good collection of case studies featuring private networks and their impact on human rights.

Steiner, Henry J., *Diverse Partners: Non Governmental Organizations and the Human Rights Movement* (Cambridge, MA: Harvard Law College, 1991, for the Harvard Law School Human Rights Program and the Human Rights Internet). A short analysis of the different types of private actors working on human rights issues.

Tolley, Howard J., Jr., *The International Commission of Jurists: Global Advocates for Human Rights* (Philadelphia: University of Pennsylvania Press, 1994). A careful look at a well-known, Geneva-based human rights NGO with a legal focus. Also an attempt to blend political history with social science theory.

Weiss, Thomas G., "The Humanitarian Identity Crisis," in *Ethics & International Affairs*, 13 (1999), 1–22. A leading scholar of humanitarian affairs nicely summarizes much debate, while advocating major changes in international action. Accompanied by other views on the same topic in the same journal.

Weiss, Thomas G. and Leon Gordenker, eds., *NGOs, The UN, & Global Governance* (Boulder: Lynne Rienner, 1996). An examination of how private actors intersect with UN bodies, with attention to human rights, humanitarian affairs, women's rights.

Welch, Claude E., *Protecting Human Rights in Africa: Strategies and Roles of Non Governmental Organizations* (Philadelphia: University of Pennsylvania Press, 1995). A good overview of this subject, with a generally favorable view of African NGOs and their impact over time, despite a hostile environment.

Welch, *NGOs and Human Rights: Promise and Performance* (Philadelphia: University of Pennsylvania Press, 2001). A solid overview.

Willetts, Peter, ed., *"The Conscience of the World": The Influence of Non-Governmental Organizations in the UN System* (Washington: Brookings, 1996). An excellent collection with a very good chapter on Amnesty International and human rights by Jane Connors.

8   Transnational corporations and human rights

We saw in chapter 7 that the international law of human rights was directed mainly to public authorities like states and their governments, but that private non-profit actors like human rights advocacy groups helped shape the rights discourse and action. In this chapter we will show that for-profit private actors like transnational corporations have a tremendous effect on persons in the modern world, for good or ill. For the first fifty years after the adoption of the United Nations Charter and Universal Declaration of Human Rights, these business enterprises mostly fell outside the mainstream debate about the promotion and protection of internationally recognized human rights. This was so despite the fact that the leaders of the German firm I.G. Farben had faced legal justice at the Nuremberg Trials for their role in the Holocaust. This general situation was changing in the early twenty-first century. Attention to transnational corporations and human rights constitutes a new frontier in the international discourse on human rights.[1] Non-profit human rights groups, along with the media and particularly consumer organizations and movements, are targeting the corporations. The result is renewed pressure on public authorities, especially states, to adopt norms and policies ensuring that business practices contribute to, rather than contradict, internationally recognized human rights. The corporations themselves are under considerable pressure to pay attention to human rights, although there remain formidable structural obstacles to a broad corporate social responsibility that includes human rights.[2]

---

[1] Jedrzej George Frynas and Scott Pegg, eds., *Transnational Corporations and Human Rights* (London: Palgrave Macmillan, 2003); Michael K. Addo, *Human Rights Standards and the Responsibility of Transnational Corporations* (The Hague: Kluwer Law International, 1999); S. Rees, ed., *Human Rights, Corporate Responsibility: A Dialogue* (Sydney: Allen and Unwin, 2000).

[2] See Mahmood Monshipouri, Claude E. Welch, Jr., and Evan T. Kennedy, "Multinational Corporations and the Ethics of Global Responsibility: Problems and Possibilities," *Human Rights Quarterly*, 25, 4 (November 2004), 965–989. They argue against MNC self-policing and for some combination of external pressures.

Enormous impact

It has been long recognized that business enterprises that operate across national boundaries have an enormous impact on the modern world. If we compare the revenues of the twenty-five largest transnational corporations (TNCs) with revenues of states, as in table 8.1, we see that economic significance.

The world's 200 largest TNCs are incorporated in just ten states, as shown in table 8.2, above all in the United States and Japan. This means, of course, that if one could affect the national policies of these TNCs in this small number of states, one could greatly affect TNCs' global impact.

Beyond macro-statistics, it is clear that with regard to the internationally recognized right to health, and if we take the case of the HIV/AIDS pandemic in Africa and other places, the role of drug companies (often claiming intellectual property rights) is central. The willingness of these companies, under pressure of course, to contribute to managing the crisis through such policies as helping with lower-priced generic drugs is highly important.[3]

Debate continues as to whether TNCs, because of their enormous economic power, which can sometimes be translated into political power, are beyond the effective control of national governments. A classic study concluded that TNCs were not, in general, beyond the reach of the "sovereign" state.[4] At the same time, however, most observers today agree that it is difficult for a given state to effectively regulate "its" corporations abroad for a variety of reasons. Business enterprises move resources, especially capital, rapidly around the globe, and it is only with some difficulty and a time lag that national governments know what TNCs are doing. Also, TNCs normally have considerable influence in national political systems, especially through pro-business political parties and personalities. This, of course, makes regulation of business difficult to achieve.

Moreover, it is difficult for one state to act alone in this regard. International law has not historically encouraged states to try to project extra-territorial jurisdiction in economic matters.[5] And if the state did so, it might restrict "its" corporations in global competition so that the state received fewer economic benefits and competitors more. When in 1977

---

[3] See, for example, Nana K. Polu and Alan Whiteside, eds., *Political Economy of AIDS in Africa* (Aldershot, UK: Ashgate, 2004).

[4] Raymond Vernon, *Sovereignty at Bay: The Multinational Spread of US Enterprises* (New York: Basic Books, 1971).

[5] But see Mark Gibney and David R. Emerick, "The Extraterritorial Application of United States Law and the Protection of Human Rights: Holding Multinational Corporations to Domestic and International Standards," *Temple International and Comparative Law Journal*, 10, 1 (Spring 1996), 123–145.

Table 8.1. *States and TNCs compared*

State/TNC	Revenues	Year
US	$1.782 trillion	2003
Japan	$1.327 trillion	2003
Germany	$1.079 trillion	2003
France	$882.8 billion	2003
United Kingdom	$688.9 billion	2003
Italy	$668 billion	2003
Canada	$348.2 billion	2003
Spain	$330.7 billion	2003
China	$265.8 billion	2003
WAL MART	$263 billion	2003
Netherlands	$237.1 billion	2003
BP	$232.6 billion	2003
EXXON MOBIL	$222.9 billion	2003
ROYAL DUTCH/SHELL GROUP	$201.7 billion	2003
GENERAL MOTORS	$195.3 billion	2003
Australia	$185 billion	2003
Sweden	$177.7 billion	2003
FORD MOTOR	$164.5 billion	2003
DAIMLERCHRYSLER	$156.6 billion	2003
TOYOTA MOTOR	$153.1 billion	2003
Brazil	$147.2 billion	2003
S. Korea	$135.5 billion	2003
GENERAL ELECTRIC	$134.2 billion	2003
Switzerland	$123.2 billion	2003
Denmark	$118.5 billion	2003
TOTAL	$118.4 billion	2003
ALLIANZ	$115 billion	2003
CHEVRONTEXACO	$112.9 billion	2003
AXA	$111.9 billion	2003
CONOCOPHILLIPS	$99.5 billion	2003
VOLKSWAGEN	$98.6 billion	2003
NIPPON TELEGRAPH & TELEPONE	$98.2 billion	2003
ING GROUP	$95.9 billion	2003
CITIGROUP	$94.7 billion	2003
INTERNATIONAL BUSINESS MACHINES	$89.1 billion	2003
India	$86.69 billion	2003
AMERICAN INTERNATIONAL GROUP	$81.3 billion	2003

Data on Corporations: WORLD'S LARGEST CORPORATIONS, Fortune, 7/26/2004, Vol. 150, Issue 2
Data on State Revenues: The World Factbook as posted on the World Wide Web.

Table 8.2. *The world's largest TNCs: home country, revenues and profits*

Country	Number of firms	Annual revenues	Annual profits	Global revenues %	Global profit %
Japan	62	3,196	46.0	40.7	18.3
United States	53	1,998	98.0	25.4	39.2
Germany	23	786	24.5	10.0	9.8
France	19	572	16.0	7.3	6.3
United Kingdom	11	275	20.0	3.5	8.0
Switzerland	8	244	9.7	3.1	3.9
South Korea	6	183	3.5	2.3	1.4
Italy	5	171	6.0	2.2	2.5
UK/Netherlands	2	159	9.0	2.0	3.7
Netherlands	4	118	5.0	1.5	2.0
Venezuela	1	26	3.0	0.3	1.2
Sweden	1	24	1.3	0.3	0.5
Belgium/Netherlands	1	22	0.8	0.3	0.3
Mexico	1	22	1.5	0.3	0.6
China	1	19	0.8	0.2	0.3
Brazil	1	18	4.3	0.2	1.7
Canada	1	17	0.5	0.2	0.2
Total	200	7,850	251.0	100.0	100.0
World GNP		25,223			
200 TNC Revenues as % of World GNP				31.2	

Source: *Le Monde Diplomatique*, April 1997, 16.

Data for 1995; revenue and profit figures in US$ billions.

the USA passed anti-corruption legislation (the Foreign Corrupt Practices Act) making it illegal for corporations registered in the country to pay bribes to get contracts from foreign parties, this put those firms at a competitive disadvantage in global competition. It was only in 1998 that the USA could persuade its partners in the Organization for Economic Cooperation and Development to level the playing field by adopting a multilateral convention, implemented through national legislation, on the subject.[6] The logic of cooperation under conditions of anarchy, or in this case relatively unregulated market competition, is an important subject. Particularly social regulation is weak – viz., regulation for social rather than economic purposes.

The central question is not so much the power of TNCs, or the difficulty of their regulation. Both points are readily agreed to. The more complex question is what, on balance, the impact of TNCs is on persons

[6] AP, "Congress Passes Bill to Curb International Business Bribery," *New York Times*, October 22, 1998, A5.

and their human rights in the modern world. On this there is considerable debate. It follows that there is also a lively exchange on whether there should be more public regulation of TNCs in the name of human rights.

A critical view

Few persons other than Social Darwinists look with favor on the early stages of the capitalist industrial revolution. There was a certain national economic advance that was achieved via basically unregulated capitalism, and certainly the property owners benefited. But now there is almost universal rejection of the human conditions (not to mention environmental damage) of that early industrial capitalism, illustrated by the novels of Charles Dickens. No western market democracy, and no capitalist state in any developed country, now endorses pure *laissez-faire* economics.

A first basic point is that a sophisticated view of modern markets recognizes they are a social construct, with deep governmental intrusion.[7] Markets are actually created by governments, and extensively regulated by them, for reasons of economic effectiveness. Markets have rules and supervisors to promote investor confidence and minimize inhibiting factors like corruption, fraud, and theft. Modern national markets do not exist in nature, as it were, but as the result of governmental action. Even so-called laissez-faire economics results from governmental action, not a state of nature.

A second basic point is that in contemporary market democracies, even so-called political conservatives such as Ronald Reagan and Margaret Thatcher endorsed certain aspects of regulated or welfare state capitalism (Thatcher was a strong defender, for example, of the British National Health Service). Socially responsible pro-business persons recognize that capitalism is a harsh system, that not all persons benefit, that some persons require the protection of the state for a life with dignity under an economic system based on the right to private property.[8] It has never proved persuasive to argue that both the poor and the rich have the same freedom to sleep under the bridges as they wish.[9] And so all modern market democracies regulate national markets for social as well as economic reasons. All use tax and other policies to limit the harshness of crude

---

[7] See especially Cass Sunstein, *The Second Bill of Rights: FDR's Unfinished Revolution and Why We need It More Than Ever* (New York: Basic Books, 2004), especially ch. 2.

[8] See Michael Novak and Leslie Lenkowsky, "Economic Growth Won't End Poverty," *New York Times*, July 24, 1985, A19. The authors were associated with the American Enterprise Institute, a conservative, pro-business think tank in Washington.

[9] See further Rhoda Howard-Hassmann and Claude E. Welch, Jr., eds., *Economic Rights Policies in Canada and The United States: Sleeping Under Bridges* (Philadelphia: University of Pennsylvania Press, 2006), forthcoming.

capitalism. At the national level, all western democratic polities try in different ways to create capitalism with a human face.[10]

This brief reference to historical patterns and basic realities is an important critique of unregulated business. If left to itself, even in western countries that manifested so much concern for the individual that they evolved into liberal and/or social democracies, unregulated business has often exploited, crushed, de-humanized, and affronted human dignity. Once the bonds of community, found in rural and agricultural settings, were replaced by the urban and more impersonal conditions of industrial capitalism, the have-nots were clearly in need of protection from the power of the haves. Whatever the difficulties of the political process, relatively humane national regulation of the for-profit system was achieved (at least relative to Dickens' England). The intervention of the state was used to limit the enormous power of the Henry Fords and Andrew Carnegies and the other "robber barons" of early industrial capitalism.[11] One of the great problems immediately after the Cold War in places like Russia and Albania, *inter alia*, was that this regulation of the robber barons had yet to be made effective. This is why the successful financier, investor, and philanthropist George Soros has written that the greatest threat to democracy in the former communist lands of the Soviet Union and Eastern Europe is precisely capitalism.[12] As one who understands capitalism well, Soros knows that crude capitalism is so harsh and unfair that it is not sustainable when citizens have the freedom to accept or reject it.

What has not been tolerated in the national political economies of the West for about a century, namely unregulated capitalism, has been allowed to proceed in international relations – at least until recently. And while one can chart growing international law in the domain of economics, most of that regulation is designed to encourage free trade and commercial activity, certainly not to restrict it in the name of human rights. That regulation is for economic, not social, reasons. The General Agreement on Tariffs and Trade (GATT) and the World Trade

---

[10] Those unfamiliar with the history of the Cold War may not fully appreciate this irony of semantics. In events leading up to 1968, particularly reform communists in what was then Czechoslovakia tried to create what was called communism with a human face. The attempt was to create a communism that was less harsh and repressive, that blended a new socialism with certain civil and political rights. This move was endorsed by western market democracies, even as it was crushed by a pre-Gorbachev Soviet Union. In the early 21st century it was the western-led economic globalization that was often said to be in need of a human face.

[11] On the political system as a counterweight to business power in the West, see especially E.E. Schattschneider, *The Semi-Sovereign People: A Realist's View of Democracy in America* (New York: Holt, Rinehart and Winston, 1960).

[12] George Soros, "The Capitalist Threat," *Atlantic Monthly*, 279, 2 (February 1997), 45 and *passim*.

Organization (WTO) are primarily designed to encourage international capitalism, not regulate it according to social values. This was also the main thrust of NAFTA (North American Free Trade Agreement), with provisions on ecology and labor rights added only as afterthoughts when demanded by American unions and others. There is a disconnect between much of the normative framework for *national* capitalism (to prevent gross exploitation) and the main concern of regulation of *international* capitalism (to stabilize capitalism regardless of exploitation).

In the national political economy, at least from the view of nationality and with class considerations aside, we are all "us." In the international political economy, there is an "in" group – us – and an "out" group – them. Nationalism being what it is, as long as the benefits flow to "us," the moral imperative to show concern for "them" is reduced. The World Development Report, produced by the United Nations Development Program, regularly chronicles the large and growing gap between the wealthy global north and the impoverished global south. As one would expect in a situation of mostly unregulated international economics where a sense of global community is weak, the elites with property rights and capital prosper, and many of the have-nots live a life on the margins of human dignity. Dickens would not be surprised.

Against this background, one can easily find horror stories of unprincipled TNCs making handsome profits at the expense of clearly exploited employees and bystanders. Authors from Stephen Hymer to David Korten have chronicled the record.[13] Economic globalization is partly the story of sweatshops, child labor, dangerous work, low pay, forced and slave labor, opposition to unions, and in extreme cases crimes against humanity and genocide. IBM and other outside companies were complicit in the German Holocaust.[14] As early as 1938, before Nazi Germany had invaded Poland and before Swiss leaders had reasonable concern about a Nazi invasion of Switzerland, some Swiss banks were stealing the property of Austrian Jews and turning it over to well paying Germans.[15] More recently, Union Carbide has been less than exemplary in ensuring that those killed and hurt by the poisonous gas leak at its plant in

---

[13] Stephen Hymer, "The Multinational Corporation and the Law of Uneven Development," in J.W. Bhagwati, ed., *Economics and World Order* (New York: Macmillan, 1971), 113–140; David Korten, *When Corporations Rule the World* (West Hartford: Kumarian Press, 1995). See also Richard J. Barnet and John Cavanagh, *Global Dreams: Imperial Corporations and the New World Order* (New York: Simon & Schuster, 1994).

[14] See further Edwin Black, *IBM and the Holocaust: The Strategic Alliance Between Nazi Germany and America's Most Powerful Corporation* (New York: Random House, Crown, 2001). In general, however, on the role of business in the German Holocaust, see the scholarship of Peter Hayes, including a critical book review of Black's *IBM and the Holocaust*.

[15] William Glaberson, "Huge Award Details How Bank Aided Nazis," *International Herald Tribune*, April 14, 2005, www.iht.com/articles/2005/04/13/news/austria.html.

Bhopal, India in 1984 have had their minimal rights to fair compensation respected.[16]

Debora L. Spar of the Harvard Business School believes that the social record of TNCs engaged in the extraction of natural resources in foreign countries has been especially poor.[17] On the one hand the TNC must have cozy relations with the (all-too-often reactionary) government that controls access to the resource. The TNC and local government share an interest in a docile and compliant labor force. On the other hand, the TNC has little interest in other aspects of the local population. The resource is mostly sold abroad, with a certain amount of the profits going to the governmental elite. If that elite does not act progressively to reinvest the profit into infrastructures that improve the lot of the local population, such as education, health care, and ecological protection, the TNC has seen little short-term economic interest in the situation.

It is reasonably clear that Royal Dutch Shell in Nigeria cooperated closely with military governments in suppressing local resistance to prevailing policies centering on extraction of oil in Ogoniland. Not only did Shell make it possible, at company expense, for the Abacha government to violently suppress those objecting to environmental degradation by Shell in Ogoniland. But also Shell refused to intercede with the government to object to the execution of Ken Saro-Wiwa, one of the most outspoken leaders of the Ogoni people in Nigeria. In reaction to considerable criticism, Shell took a number of steps to elevate the discourse about human rights as related to its business operations. But on balance the facts to date indicate that Shell has been less than fully socially responsible in its operations in Nigeria.

The most fundamental *raison d'être* of the TNC is precisely economic self-interest, not to be a human rights actor. At least that has been the historical situation. "Investors and executives tended to see human rights as a matter for government officials and diplomats to implement, and resisted pressures to have their businesses used as tools for political reform ... The globalization of the economy and the globalization of human rights concerns, both important phenomena in the second half of this century, developed separately from each other."[18]

Some TNCs went beyond cooperation with, and active support for, a reactionary elite. United Fruit in Guatemala (1954) and ITT in Chile

---

[16] Saritha Rai, "Bhopal Victims Not Fully Paid, Rights Group Says," *New York Times*, November 30, 2004, W3.

[17] Debora L. Spar, "Multinationals and Human Rights: A Case of Strange Bedfellows," in *Human Rights Interest Group Newsletter*, American Society of International Law, 8, 1 (Winter 1998), 13–16.

[18] Lance Compa and Tashia Hinchliffe-Darricarrere, "Enforcing International Rights through Corporate Codes of Conduct," *Columbia Journal of Transnational Law*, 33 (1995), 665.

(1973) actively cooperated with the US government in helping to over-throw politicians (Arbenz in Guatemala and Allende in Chile) who were champions especially of labor rights for their nationals.[19] Various TNCs, from United Fruit to Coca-Cola, actively opposed progressive govern-ments and laws designed to advance labor rights and other human rights.

There are powerful economic and political forces pushing corpora-tions into exploitative and otherwise abusive policies. Economically there is the bottom line: companies must make a profit to stay in business. If the competition uses cheap labor, then it is difficult if not impossi-ble for a company to use unionized, well paid labor. The history of Levi Straus demonstrates this clearly.[20] This San Francisco based company, with a reputation for treating its labor force properly, has basically stopped manufacturing in the USA, and has felt compelled to outsource its pro-duction to foreign countries like China with poor human rights records, all because of pursuit of the bottom line. Within countries like the USA, when labor organized in northern cities like Detroit, management moved production to places like South Carolina and Alabama where labor was cheap and unions weak. The same process now characterizes business on a transnational or global scale. In this sense economic globalization does reflect a race to the bottom.[21]

Politically, when corporations deal with repressive governments and/or those known to violate international standards on human rights and humanitarian affairs, to get the business, companies tend to defer to governmental policies. This is true not just of IBM in Nazi Germany. The Caterpillar Company, when urged by certain human rights groups to not allow its bulldozers to be used by Israel in ways that violated international humanitarian law in the West Bank (collective punishments through destruction of houses alleged to be linked to "terrorists"), said it was a matter for the Israeli government.[22] Had Caterpillar withdrawn, it is likely that Israel would have continued the policy through a different company. When the USA prohibited its oil companies from doing busi-ness in the Sudan, because of major human rights violations principally

[19] On Arbenz and Guatemala, see especially Piero Gleijeses, *Shattered Hope: The Guatemalan Revolution and the United States 1944–1954* (Princeton: Princeton University Press, 1991). On Allende and Chile, see especially Richard Z. Israel, *Politics and Ideology in Allende's Chile* (Tempe: Arizona State University Press, 1989).

[20] See Karl Schoenberger, *Levi's Children: Coming To Terms With Human Rights In The Global Marketplace* (New York: Atlantic Monthly Press, 2000).

[21] See further Kimberly Ann Elliiott and Richard B. Freeman, *Can Labor Standards Improve Under Globalization?* (Washington: Institute of International Economics, 2003).

[22] See Human Rights Watch, "Israel: Caterpillar Should Suspend Bulldozer Sales," hrw.org/English/docs/2004/11/22/isrlpa9711_txt.htm.

in the Darfur region, other oil companies took the business, especially those from China.

The economic "laws" of competition, of supply and demand, tend to produce major human rights violations when markets are unregulated for social reasons.

A more positive view

At the same time that Professor Spar, as noted above, believes that extractive TNCs in particular have a poor social record, she observes that there are other types of TNCS: consumer products firms, manufacturing firms, service and information firms. Some of these, she argues, are engaged in business that is compatible with several human rights. She goes so far as to argue that TNCs sometimes export human rights values.[23] According to her research, some TNCs are interested in not just cheap labor but a good labor force that is highly educated and exists in the context of stable democracy. Thus Intel chose Costa Rica for one of its foreign plants. Firms intending to sell in foreign markets have an interest in a well-paid labor force with disposable income to buy their products.

Above all, Spar argues, all firms have an economic interest in avoiding negative publicity that might damage their sales. Thus TNCs do not want to face consumer boycotts and negative publicity because of the harsh, exploitive conditions in their foreign plants, or cooperation with pariah regimes. She cites a number of firms that have altered their policies, especially to establish codes of conduct for business practices and to allow independent monitoring of labor conditions, in relation to widespread criticism: Starbucks Coffee, the Gap clothiers, Nike, Reebok, Toys R Us, Avon, etc. She notes that a number of firms have pulled out of Burma, where a highly repressive military government has been internationally condemned: Levi Strauss, Macy's, Liz Claiborne, Eddie Bauer, Heineken, etc. She cites as especially effective the international campaign against child labor in the making of soccer balls, which led major TNC sporting firms to certify that no child or slave labor was used in the making of the balls. After all, one might add, if it is common practice to certify that tuna are not caught with nets that endanger dolphins, why not certify that consumer products are not made with processes that violate human rights?

[23] In addition to her views already noted, see her article "The Spotlight and the Bottom Line: How Multinationals Export Human Rights," *Foreign Affairs*, 77, 2 (March–April 1998), 7–12. See further Kenneth A. Rodman, "Think Globally, Punish Locally: Non-State Actors, Multinational Corporations, and Human Rights Sanctions," *Ethics & International Affairs*, 12 (1998), 19–42.

Moreover, beyond reacting to negative publicity that might hurt the firms' bottom line on their economic books, some observers note that TNCs export standard operating procedures that are sometimes an improvement over those previously existing in a developing country. TNC plants in the global south may provide infirmaries for health care, or improved safety conditions. TNCs, even while paying wages below standards in the global north, may pay wages in developing countries that permit growth, savings, and investment over time.

After all, the Asian Tigers like Taiwan made remarkable economic progress from the mid-1950s to the mid-1990s on the basis of an economy open to TNCs. Countries like South Korea and Taiwan not only became more prosperous over time, with a skilled work force, but also became liberal and social democracies, at least relative to their past. Thus, it is argued, there is nothing inherent in the operations of TNCs that requires that they block beneficial change in host countries or that they oppose human rights standards. While they have certainly done so in the past on occasion, an emerging world of liberal market democracies, or even social democracies, would be perfectly compatible with a bottom line in the black for TNCs.

After all, the major trading partners of the USA are other market democracies like Canada and the states of the European Union. After all, most West European states, like The Netherlands, vigorously protect a wide range of human rights, including a right to health care and extensive unemployment and social security entitlements, while maintaining an economy that does very well over time. After all, some social science research finds a positive correlation between foreign economic penetration, or direct foreign investment, and the respect for a wide range of human rights.[24]

Another study has found similarly that the presence of TNCs and direct foreign investment is positively correlated with the practice of civil and political rights in developing countries. Those same civil and political rights were also positively correlated with higher GNP, US foreign assistance, and higher debt. Direct foreign investment was also positively correlated with the Physical Quality of Life Index, measuring longevity, nutrition, and education. Hence the author of this study concluded that in the modern world TNCs were engines of progressive development, associated with both improved civil-political and socio-economic rights.[25]

---

[24] David L. Richards, et.al., "Money with a Mean Streak?: Foreign Economic Penetration and Government Respect for Human Rights in Developing Countries," *International Studies Quarterly*, 45, 2 (June 2001), 219–240.

[25] William H. Meyer, "Human Rights and Multi-National Corporations: Theory v. Quantitative Analysis," *Human Rights Quarterly*, 18, 2 (Spring 1996), 368–397; and his book

There are other optimistic accounts of the social and political workings of capitalism over time.[26]

One does not need gross exploitation to make capitalism work, Marxist analysis notwithstanding. But one may need global social regulation to level the playing field, so that corporations are not tempted to move from rights protective polities to oppressive ones.

A balance sheet

Two overviews of the effects of economic globalization on individuals and their human rights point in the same direction. Rhoda Howard Hassmann concludes that global capitalism will be good for many individuals in the grand scheme of things over time, but that there will be the danger of many human rights abuses along the way.[27] The challenge is to leap over the human rights abuses that characterized the development of national capitalism, so that the workings of global capitalism are more humane. Pietra Rivoli concludes likewise that capitalism works to the benefit of many, but that there are usually large numbers of individuals who are negatively affected either through exploitation or loss of jobs. She too sees an important role for public authorities in constructing a global capitalism with a more human face.[28]

It follows that if left unregulated, many TNCs will opt for short-term profits at the expense of human dignity for many persons affected directly and indirectly by their practices. It seems there must be countervailing power, either from public authorities, or from human rights organizations and movements, if TNC practices are to be made basically compatible with the International Bill of Rights. Given what we have noted before, namely that many parties are not enthusiastic about the IBR, effective human rights are usually wrestled from below in a tough struggle.[29] The clear experience of the global north is that unregulated capitalism is injurious to human dignity and social justice. Just as limitations on crude capitalism were achieved in western market democracies through tough struggle, sometimes bloody, so globalized economics is

making the same points, *Human Rights and International Political Economy in Third World Nations: Multinational Corporations, Foreign Aid, and Repression* (Westport, CT: Praeger, 1998). There followed a debate about his methods and conclusions.

[26] Max Singer and Aaron Wildavsky, *The Real World Order: Zones of Peace, Zones of Turmoil,* rev. edn (Chatham, NJ: Chatham House Publishers, 1996).

[27] "The Second Great Transformation: Human Rights Leapfrogging in the Era of Globalization," *Human Rights Quarterly,* 27, 1 (February 2005), 1–40.

[28] *The Travels of a T-Shirt in the Global Economy: An Economist Examines the Markets, Power, and Politics of World Trade* (New York: Wiley, 2005).

[29] See further, for example, Rhoda Howard, *Human Rights in Commonwealth Africa* (Totowa, NJ: Rowman & Littlefield, 1986).

likely to be changed only in a similar process. Protests against the WTO in particular and economic globalization in general reflect this historical pattern.

Events in Indonesia during 1998 fit this larger pattern. The authoritarian Suharto government, with the support of many TNCs, clung to the *status quo* under the general banner of "Asian values" – meaning for present purposes that authoritarian Asian states had found a model of successful economics that did not require broad political participation, independent labor unions, and other manifestations of internationally recognized human rights. There was a pattern of impressive economic growth, but the continuation of much poverty – exactly as predicted by Novak and Lenkowsky.[30] But the "Asian flu" of economic recession caused a re-evaluation of "crony capitalism," led by students, labor groups, and others demanding more attention to human rights. Suharto stepped down, the succeeding government ceased to be a champion of "Asian values," and numerous changes occurred. Parts of the elite took reform measures, under popular pressures, which was precisely the pattern that had obtained in the West during earlier periods.

Relevant also was the history of Nike and Reebok in Asia. Both companies had sub-contracted the production of athletic shoes and soccer balls, *inter alia*, to firms that operated sweatshops, employed child labor, and otherwise violated internationally recognized labor rights. Negative publicity caused both companies to alter certain policies, and at one point Nike hired a prominent American public figure, Andrew Young, to examine some of its Asian operations. But a debate continued over whether the companies were engaged primarily in public relations and damage control, or in substantive change in keeping with human rights standards. (As noted in chapter 3, certain labor rights such as freedom from slavery, freedom to bargain collectively, freedom of association, etc. are considered to be part of basic human rights.) The controversy was especially troubling to Reebok, which had pioneered certain policies related to human rights such as sponsoring rock concerts to benefit Amnesty International and making an annual human rights award. These two companies and others did participate in a program designed to guarantee that child labor was not used in the manufacture of soccer balls carrying their brand name (small fingers had proved useful in sewing).[31] By 2005 Nike,

---

[30] Cf. Novak and Lenkowsky, "Economic Growth".

[31] As with Shell in Nigeria, so with particularly Nike in Asia, there is a small library on the subject. See further, for example, Philip Segal, "Nike Hones Its Image on Rights in Asia," *New York Times*, June 26, 1998, 1. In 1998 alone, the *New York Times* and other members of the global media carried numerous stories on this subject.

under considerable pressure, had promised to disclose the location of all of its manufacturing, presumably to enhance transparency and convince consumers and others that it was not operating sweatshops.

Regulation for human rights?

Three points are noteworthy about TNCs and international regulation in the name of human rights:

1. the weakness of current international law, especially as developed through the United Nations system, in regulating the social effects of international business;
2. the growing importance of private activism, including law suits and consumer and other social movements, plus the communications media, in providing critiques of for-profit behavior; and
3. the facilitative actions of some states, especially the USA during the Clinton Administration, but not Japan in general or the George W. Bush Administration, in trying to close the gap between much TNC practice and human rights standards.

Weakness of international law

As noted earlier in this chapter, international law has had little to say about the social effects of TNC action. International law is directed mostly to states. States are held responsible for human rights conditions within their jurisdiction. The basic rule of international law is that TNCs are not subjects of that law, but only objects through the intermediary role of the state where they are incorporated.[32] Thus, TNCs are not directly responsible to international law, and TNCs – outside of the EU framework – have mostly escaped direct regulation under international law.

The example of the Convention on the Rights of All Migrant Workers and Members of their Families was instructive. Those bound by this multilateral treaty were states. The twenty-one ratifying states needed to bring the treaty into legal force was achieved in 2003. But no industrialized country ratified, and it is these countries that serve as hosts to most migrant workers. It was the sending states that tended to ratify (e.g., Bosnia, Mexico, the Philippines, Uganda, etc.) So despite the treaty, most migrant workers and the companies that employed them remained outside the legal protections of the treaty, because the industrialized states refused to obligate their corporations under this part of international law.[33]

[32] See further the Barcelona Traction case, *International Court of Justice Reports*, 1970, 3.
[33] See Human Rights Watch, "Migrant Workers Need Protection," July 1, 2003, www.hrw.org.press/2003/06/mwc063003.htm.

UN narrowly defined

During the 1970s when the United Nations was the scene of debates about a New International Economic Order (NIEO), there were demands from the global south, supported by the communist East, for a binding code of conduct on TNCs. Like the NIEO itself, this binding code for TNCs never came to fruition, due to blocking action by the capital exporting states whose primary concern was to protect the freedom of "their" corporations to make profits. (The OECD, made up of the westernized democracies, approved a non-binding code, but it has generated little influence.) A code of conduct for TNCs was negotiated in UNCTAD (UN Conference on Trade and Development) but never formally approved. A series of statements from UNCTAD, controlled by the developing countries, has been generally critical of the TNC record, but these statements were muted during the 1980s and thereafter. Attracting direct foreign investment via TNCs, not scaring it away, became the name of the game, especially after the demise of European communism.

For a time one could find a series of critical statements about TNCs from the UN Human Rights Sub-Commission. A typical statement was issued by a special rapporteur in August 1998. El Hadji Guisse of Senegal called for criminal penalties in the national law of home states to regulate TNC actions that violated internationally recognized social and economic rights.[34] By 2003 the Sub-Commission, comprised of independent experts rather than state representatives, had adopted a set of "Norms on the Responsibilities of Transnational Corporations and Other Business Enterprises with Regard to Human Rights."[35] Arguing that all corporations and business have an "obligation" (moral?, legal?) to protect the human rights recognized in national and international law, this UN document then goes on to elaborate such basic principles as equality and non-discrimination, personal security, labor rights, and so on.

In 2005, the UN Human Rights Commission itself appointed an individual to make a study of business and human rights. This move was opposed by the governments of Australia and the USA.

All of this effort directed to non-binding codes and further studies at the UN fit with the creation of the Global Compact, an initiative of Secretary-General Kofi Annan to get TNCs to endorse a set of nine principles dealing mainly with human rights but also with ecological protection. The approach was positive in the sense of asking business to police itself and accept certain standards of social responsibility. Whether all

---

[34] Inter press service, "Human Rights: Holding Transnationals in Check," Global Policy Forum, http://www.igc.apc.org/globalpolicy/socecon/tncs/humrig.htm.

[35] UN Doc: E/CN.4/Sub.2/2003/12/Rev.2 (2003).

of this standard setting and "social pressure light" would prove more effective than the various non-binding codes of conduct in the past remained to be seen. It is possible that assertive pressure from civil society might cause corporations to take these UN norms at least somewhat seriously.[36]

UN broadly defined

The International Labor Organization has not played a highly effective role in efforts after the Cold War to target abusive practices by TNCs. In part this was because national business associations made up one-third of the membership of the ILO. Another reason was that some western states, chiefly the USA, did not favor channeling their major concerns through the ILO. During the Cold War the ILO had fallen out of favor with Washington due to various political battles. By the turn of the century the ILO had not recovered from these bruising struggles and had not proved to be a dynamic organization capable of achieving striking developments in defense of labor rights. The ILO had a role to play in long term socialization. Its basic standards fed into other developments at the UN Human Rights Commission and the Global Compact. But its record of decisive, short-run improvements was not striking.

The ILO was old and distinguished, and it has long manifested a human rights program in relation to labor rights. As we noted in chapter 3, since 1919 it had developed a series of reasonable – if sometimes vague – standards about international labor rights pertaining to a safe and healthy work environment, non-discrimination, fair wages, working hours, child labor, convict or forced labor, freedom of association, the right to organize, and the right to collective bargaining. But despite an elaborate system for reviewing and supervising its conventions, the ILO was unable to achieve very much "support in international practice – at least in the sense of universal compliance by multinational corporations with these standards."[37] The ILO Tripartite Declaration of Principles Concerning Multinational Enterprises and Social Policy (1977) also failed to affect the practice of TNCs. In theory during the Cold War, labor rights should have been an area for cooperation between East and West, if not north and south. But the ILO was able to produce little progressive change

---

[36] See further Sean D. Murphy, "Taking Multinational Corporate Codes of Conduct to the Next Level," *Columbia Journal of Transnational Law Association*, 43 (2005), starting at 389.

[37] Diane F. Orentlicher and Timothy A. Gelatt, "Public Law, Private Actors: The Impact of Human Rights on Business Investors in China," *Northwestern Journal of International Law and Business*, 14 (1993), 116 and *passim*.

during the Cold War,[38] as after. The abstract norms might remain valid. The principles underlying the basic conventions might have entered into customary law and become binding even on non-parties that were members of the ILO. The question was how to develop a political process that paid them some concrete attention.

A bright spot in the global picture after the Cold War was the growing attention to child labor.[39] The International Convention on the Rights of the Child was almost universally accepted – only the USA and Somalia refused to ratify.[40] This law obligated states to protect child workers against forced and unsafe labor, *inter alia*.[41] UNICEF, the UN's premier agency dealing with children, was increasingly linking itself to this treaty and was seeing itself as much an actor for human rights as for relief and development. At a global conference in 1997 UNICEF expressed some optimism that the worst forms of exploitation of the 250 million working children could be successfully challenged, as had proved true with regard to much child labor in the garment industry.[42]

One needed to be careful, however, about a negative approach to the subject that insisted on a simple ban on child labor. This approach alone condemned children and their families to continued poverty and a denial of the recognized right to an adequate standard of living. What was required was a ban combined with positive developments. The source of child labor was under-development. Small steps like providing the funds for better meals in schools could get children out of the fields and sweatshops. Overall development would have the same effect. Just removing children from the production of soccer balls in Pakistan did little but to guarantee continued grinding poverty for them and their families, plus a boost for machine-made soccer balls in the sweatshops of China.[43]

---

[38] Ernst A. Haas, *Human Rights and International Action* (Stanford: Stanford University Press, 1970).

[39] Burns H. Weston, ed., *Child Labor and Human Rights: Making Children Matter* (Boulder: Lynne Rienner, 2005).

[40] Important circles in the USA championed parental and privacy rights and were skeptical of the intrusion of public authority into this domain, whether national or international. While some of the American opposition to this Convention was irrational, it remained strong. Fears about the introduction of abortion rights or the undermining of parental authority in matters of religion might be misguided, but they were held intensely by some.

[41] Especially Article 32.

[42] Reuters, "Child Labor Conference Ends on Hopeful Note," http://www.yahoo.com/ headlines/970227/international/stories/children_1.html.

[43] See further Mahmood Monshipoori, "Human Rights and Child Labor in South Asia," in David P. Forsythe and Patrice C. McMahon, eds., *Human Rights and Diversity: Area Studies Revisited* (Lincoln: University of Nebraska Press, 2003). See also a series of articles on this subject in the *New York Times* by Nicholas D. Kristof, as in "The Fuss over Child Labor is Misguided," April 6, 2004.

Trade law

On the other side of the coin, embryonic trade law might not prove so supportive of growing attention to human rights. As noted earlier in this book, there was some fear that dispute panels under the new World Trade Organization would strike down national and sub-national legislation designed to curtail TNC activity in repressive states like Burma. Observers had been fearful that human rights legislation, such as from the state of Massachusetts, would be struck down in the WTO as an impermissible restraint on free trade. But the US Supreme Court made this particular point moot. Massachusetts had adopted a state law specifying that any company doing business in repressive Burma/Myanmar could not contract for services with Massachusetts. But the highest US Court ruled unanimously that such internal state legislation was unconstitutional, as the US Federal government had pre-empted legislation pertaining to Burma. Thus the Court held that Massachusetts was unconstitutionally interfering with the foreign policy power of the Federal government.[44] (In the past, other internal legislation on human rights in foreign states, as in the Republic of South Africa under white minority rule, had been allowed, as the Federal government had not tried to pre-empt internal state and local action.)

At the time of writing, efforts to interject stronger provisions into the WTO regarding human rights, and especially labor rights, had not been successful.

In fact, the WTO continued to strongly endorse business prerogatives especially when buttressed by TRIPS – the agreement linked to the WTO protecting trade related intellectual property rights. Among other issues, the TRIPS protected the right of transnational drug companies under patent law to ensure the sale of their higher priced drugs, and to block the sale of cheaper generic drugs that might impinge on those patents. But in places like sub-Sahara Africa, where HIV/AIDS was rampant, many human rights organizations pressured the drug companies to put people ahead of profits, to cooperate with the use of the cheaper generic drugs despite intellectual property rights. After much controversy the TNC pharmaceuticals did yield on a number of points, while making their own point that protection of patents was necessary to ensure some profitable return on investments, it being those investments in costly research that led to new drugs. There were several barriers to an adequate response to the African HIVS/AIDS pandemic, a situation that might repeat itself

---

[44] For an analysis of *National Foreign Trade Council v. Crosby*, see Peter J. Spiro, "U.S. Supreme Court Knocks Down State Burma Law," *ASIL Insights*, American Society of International Law, June 2000, www.asil.org/insights/insigh46.htm.

in parts of Asia as well. The arrangements for Africa showed both the clash of different human rights – to private property and to adequate health – as well as the prevalence of negotiated arrangements rather than legal solutions.[45] The pharmaceuticals were concerned about damage to their brand names by a full and absolute insistence on their recognized property rights.

There is also regional trade law. In the North American Free Trade Agreement (NAFTA), unlike the WTO, there is a "side agreement" on labor rights (as well as on ecological protection). This reference to labor is relatively weak, at least in the view of Human Rights Watch and many other unions and human rights NGOs.[46] But one labor expert took a more positive view, arguing that NAFTA's labor provisions had legit-imized the linkage between trade and human rights, while advancing a number of important principles as well as some regional cooperation on labor rights.[47] The same general situation characterizes the Central American Free Trade Agreement (CAFTA): there is some mention of labor rights, but the supervising and adjudicatory measures are weak. Given the influence of the Republican Party, the party of big business in US politics, it was difficult to get strong labor provisions in these regional arrangements in the Western Hemisphere. Even in the USA, a member of both CAFTA and NAFTA, and with its own Federal and internal state legislation, there were significant labor abuses. In the state of Florida, for example, a number of agricultural workers existed in conditions of virtual forced labor and slavery, not to mention poor working conditions, lack of health care, and low wages.[48]

The only relatively strong protections for labor rights at the regional level are to be found in the European Union (EU).[49] Within the EU, treaty law and the case law of the European Court of Justice (ECJ) pro-tect the free movement of workers within the EU without discrimination on grounds of nationality. ECJ cases also stipulate equal pay for men

[45] For one view see Susan K. Sell and Aseem Prakash, "Using Ideas Strategically: The Contest Between Business and NGO Networks in Intellectual Property Rights," *The International Studies Quarterly*, 48, 1 (March 2004), 143–175.

[46] Human Rights Watch, "Nafta Labor Accord Ineffective," April 16, 2001, http://hrw.org/English/docs/2001/04/16/global179.htm. See also the criticism in David Bacon, *The Children of NAFTA: Labor Wars on the U.S./Mexico Border* (Berkeley: University of California Press, 2004).

[47] Lance Compa, "A Glass Half Full: The NAFTA Labor Agreement and Cross-Border Labor Action," in George J. Andreopoulos, ed., *Concepts and Strategies in International Human Rights* (New York: Peter Lang, 2003).

[48] See further Human Rights Watch, "Human Rights of Florida's Farm Workers are under Serious Threat," March 2, 2005, http://hrw.org/english/docs/2005/03/02/usdom10284_txt.htm.

[49] See further Paul Craig and Grainne de Burca, *EU Law: Text Cases & Materials* (Oxford: Oxford University Press, 2003), 3rd ed., chapters 17 and 20.

and women, and that such standards are directed not just to the goal of economic prosperity but to advancing the rights of individuals as part of the pursuit of social progress. Directives by the EU Council of Ministers endorse not only equal pay for equal work, but also equality in pension benefits and equal parental leave. Not just state members of the EU but corporations operating within the EU are obligated to follow these standards.

An ICC role?

The first prosecutor of the International Criminal Court suggested in several venues that he might be inclined to bring indictments against business leaders who are complicit in genocide, or crimes against humanity, or major war crimes.[50] There has been considerable discussion of the relevance of this possibility in situations like the Democratic Republic of the Congo. There, where public authority is weak and in some areas virtually non-existant, as in the Ituri district, a number of corporations are involved in extracting the abundant and valuable natural resources of the country – such as diamonds, gold, coltran (used in cell phones), and timber. The industries involved hire security firms to protect their operations, and allegedly these militia are some of the actors engaging in the atrocities often reported in various sources.[51] The long-running conflict in the DRC is the most disruptive and deadly in any country since the Second World War. The size and complexity of the problem makes it very difficult to find outside parties that want to seriously engage in order to manage the situation. There is little prospect of "humanitarian intervention" by states, and the IGOs controlled by states, like the UN or African Union, are only engaged in marginal ways. In this situation, where one finds "resource wars" and "blood diamonds," prosecution of corporate leaders under international criminal law might be one of the few promising avenues for doing something about systematic abuse including murder, rape, persecution, and forced displacement.

Indictment of business leaders in the ICC, however, is not likely to encourage the USA to support or tolerate the court, at least as long as the Republican Party, with its reluctance to link business and human rights, controls or substantially influences US foreign policy. On the other hand, some corporations are supportive of international action against those benefiting from these resource wars. The De Beers diamond

---

[50] James Podgers, "Corporations In The Line Of Fire," *ABA Journal*, January 2004, 13.

[51] See for example Julia Graff, "Corporate War Criminals and the International Criminal Court: Blood and Profits in the Democratic Republic of Congo," *Human Rights Brief*, 11, 2 (Winter 2004), 23–26.

company wants to shut off the flow of black market diamonds from places like Angola and Sierra Leone, in order to protect its market share. De Beers, with the support of Belgium, a traditional center for the diamond trade, would be only too happy to see the curtailment of black market diamonds.[52]

Non-profit dynamism

Chapter 7 charted the growth of an international civic society in which various non-profit organizations and movements, including human rights groups, were increasingly active on public policy issues. This chapter follows up by showing that numerous organizations and movements have begun to focus on TNC practices in the light of human rights standards. One may use the broad phrase "social responsibility" in reference to TNCs, but human rights values are part of that concern (which also includes anti-bribery and anti-corruption measures, along with ecological matters).[53] As far back as 1972 the International Chamber of Commerce adopted a non-binding code of conduct for TNCs. Some business executives formed the Caux Round Table, which promotes TNC social responsibility, including "a commitment to human dignity, [and] political and economic freedoms."[54] Standard human rights organizations like Human Rights Watch and Amnesty International began to pay more attention to TNCs.[55] Groups that had long tracked business practices in the interests of consumers, such as Ralph Nader's Global Trade Watch in Washington, began to focus more on human rights issues. Labor unions like the AFL-CIO were highly active on transnational labor issues. An important internet site was the Business and Human Rights Resource Center, created by AI and a number of other private groups, that provided broad monitoring of business and human rights issues (www.business-humanrights.org). There were other important web sites run by NGOs as well, such as by Social Accountability International (www.cepaa.org).

---

[52] Alan Cowell, "De Beers Plans Guarantee: Diamonds Not From Rebels," *International Herald Tribune*, March 1, 2000, 15.

[53] See further Lance A. Compa and Stephen F. Diamond, eds., *Human Rights, Labor Rights, and International Trade* (Philadelphia: University of Pennsylvania Press, 1996); John W. Houck and Oliver F. Willaims, *Is the Good Corporation Dead: Social Responsibility in a Global Economy* (Lanham, MD: Rowman & Littlefield, 1996); and Lee Tavis, *Power and Responsibility* (Notre Dame: Notre Dame Press, 1997).

[54] http://www.cauxroundtable.org/.

[55] On this point see especially the chapter by David P. Forsythe and Eric Heinze, "On the Margins of the Human Rights Discourse: Foreign Policy and International Welfare Rights," in Hassmann and Welch, *Human Rights Policies in Canada and the U.S.: Sleeping Under Bridges* (Philadelphia: University of Pennsylvania Press, 2006), forthcoming. One has only to observe the web sites or publication lists of these NGOs. See for example http://www.hrw.org/about/initiatives/corp.html.

In some cases of private pressure there has been undeniable success. In response to a citizen boycott of its operations in south Florida over the treatment of immigrant workers picking tomatoes, Taco Bell agreed in 2005 to raise the wages of affected workers and imposed a tough code of conduct pertaining to its suppliers.[56] The "Sullivan Principles" at least directed attention to the effects of apartheid on working conditions in the Republic of South Africa under white minority rule, even if Reverend Sullivan of Philadelphia eventually concluded that his code – intended to affect investments – was inadequate for achieving major improvements in an integrated work force in South Africa. The "McBride Principles" directed attention to sectarian discrimination in employment practices in Northern Ireland, as any number of investors in that British province tied their investments to these principles designed to reduce prejudice against Catholics or Protestants. As noted, other firms have been shamed into altering their policies in the light of human rights values. Starbucks Coffee opened its foreign operations to human rights monitors, Heineken withdrew from doing business in Burma, and Levi Strauss withdrew from manufacturing in China for a time.

In the fall of 1998, a group of companies in the apparel and footwear industries, including Liz Claiborne, Nike, Reebok, and others, agreed to open their overseas operations to independent human rights monitors under formal agreement. The "Apparel Industry Partnership" or "Fair Labor Association" provided for periodic inspection by the Lawyers Committee for Human Rights, now renamed Human Rights First, based in New York, and other respected human rights NGOs under detailed provisions.[57] The deal was brokered by the Clinton Administration, which had worked for over two years to get such an agreement. While arrangements were criticized by various American labor groups, some American university students, and others as not going far enough, this development was hailed by its supporters as a major advance in providing specific attention to labor rights on a transnational basis.[58] About twenty major American universities with well-known sports programs and popular sports apparel, like Michigan, Notre Dame, and Nebraska, among others, joined this arrangement.[59]

When, for example, the University of Nebraska in 2005 concluded a new contract with Adidas for the provision of sports apparel, the contract

[56] Eric Schlosser, "A Side Order of Human Rights," *New York Times,* April 6, 2005, p. A29.
[57] For one summary see http://www.lchr.org/sweatshop.summary.htm.
[58] Steven Greenhouse, "Groups Reach Agreement For Curtailing Sweatshops," *New York Times,* November 5, 1998, A18.
[59] Steven Greenhouse, "17 Top Colleges Enter Alliance on Sweatshops," *New York Times,* March 16, 1999, A15.

contained a human rights clause that required the company and its sub-contractors to meet certain standards pertaining to freedom of associ-ation and collective bargaining, limitations on working hours, women's equality, prohibition of discrimination and harassment, etc. – a clause that would be independently supervised. The wording, however, did not address explicitly and specifically a fair or living wage.

Under the AIP/FLA, reports on companies are made public, allow-ing consumers to take whatever action they want on the basis of the reports. The reports focus on a workplace code, detailed in the agree-ment, and are based on a selected percentage of the companies' oper-ating facilities. Analysis of wages are pegged to a US Department of Labor study regarding employee basic needs in the country at issue. There is also a procedure for filing complaints against the company. A "no sweat" label can be added to products made in compliance with this agreement.

Also in 1998, a number of companies including Toys R Us and Avon created the Council on Economic Priorities. This CEP deals with the usual labor rights in foreign subsidiaries or sub-contractors, but also with what constitutes a "living wage" in different countries. On this latter point, according to a specific formula, one calculates the cost of basic human need in caloric terms. This is done in a way that allows spe-cific numbers to be provided country by country. The formula has been generally regarded as appropriate. But the CEP terms were sufficiently demanding for some business groups and commentators to endorse the AIP/FLA as indicated above, on the grounds that a specific "living wage" standard would curtail some foreign investment leading to loss of jobs in the global south.[60] After all, certain governments as in Malaysia have been very explicit about low wages constituting one of their important comparative advantages in global markets.

Still other companies created the American Apparel Manufacturers Association. While this arrangement provided monitoring of labor rights, the standards were so low that it was generally discredited by most human rights groups, unions, attentive university students, and other observers outside the apparel industry.

Still further, some students and union leaders created the Worker Rights Consortium (WRC). This movement, excluding business lead-ers in the formulation of its plans, pushed for unannounced inspections of plants and factories as well as for a tough "living wage" for workers. Its approach was abrasive enough for Nike to break off arrangements with

[60] Aaron Bernstein, "Sweatshop Reform: How to Solve the Standoff," *Business Week*, May 3, 1999, 186–190.

several major American universities, like Michigan, when they accepted WRC terms.[61] Later, however, Nike, while still not agreeing to WRC terms, did promise to open all of its foreign operations to public disclosure and did admit that a certain number of labor problems existed in its various facilities.[62]

A summary analysis of private action intended to make TNCs more sensitive to human rights standards is elusive. As noted already, Shell Oil was not forced out of Nigeria, nor into providing clearly different policies in Ogoniland where Shell operations had allegedly damaged the environment, nor into saving the life of Ken Saro-Wiwa and his Ogoni compatriots who had protested against Shell policies. At best Shell was forced into paying more attention to public relations and fending off calls for major boycotts and sanctions. Yet the story about Shell and Nigeria is not over, and it remains to be seen whether relations between this TNC and post-Abacha governments in Lagos remain the same as in the past. Private advocacy for better TNC policies may yet prove at least somewhat influential in this case. In chapter 7 we noted the elusive nature of "success" for human rights groups and movements, as well as noting the importance of long-term, informal education in changing views over time.

Finally in this section we should note that some private actors have brought law suits in national courts against TNCs and their global operations. For example, in the USA, the Alien Tort Statute of 1789 allows civil suits against private parties where a violation of the law of nations is involved, regardless of the nationality of the parties. Most of the case law under this statute has concerned torture.[63] But in the 1990s certain individuals sought to sue the Unocal oil firm, based in California, for engaging in – or allowing sub-contractors to engage in – forced labor and other human rights violations in its operations in Burma. The US district court in question, in a jurisdictional ruling of considerable importance, allowed the case to proceed. In the merits phase, however, the court held that plaintiffs had not proven legal culpability by Unocal. Despite this ruling, while the case was still under appeal, Unocal agreed to settle with the plaintiffs, thus giving the impression that litigation in US courts against TNCs for human rights violations might be effective in producing progressive settlements.[64]

---

[61] Mark Asher and Josh Barr, "Nike Pulls Funds From Campus Critics," *International Herald Tribune,* May 6–7, 2000, 9.

[62] Rukmini Callimachi, "Nike Reveals Overseas Factories," AP report, carried in the *Lincoln Journal Star,* April 14, 2005, C1.

[63] Beth Stevens and Steven R. Ratner, *International Human Rights Litigation in US Courts* (Irvington-on-Hudson, NY: Transnational Publishers, 1996).

[64] For a good review of this general subject, see Beth Stephens, "Upsetting Checks and Balances," *Harvard Human Rights Journal* 17 (Spring 2004), 169–205.

Complicating matters, however, was the fact that as private citizens, human rights groups, and their lawyers sought to use the Alien Tort Statute to go after businesses for violating international human rights standards, the George W. Bush Administration tried to get US courts to narrow the scope of application of that Statute.[65] The Bush Administration, reflecting the pro-business and free-enterprise philosophy of the Republican Party, was not happy when businesses were made defendants in US courts regarding international human rights issues. And in March 2004, the US Supreme Court did try to narrow the application of the Alien Tort Statute.[66] Thereafter, in November 2004, a Federal district court in New York threw out a suit against several major American corporations (e.g., General Electric, General Motors, etc.) for being complicit in the human rights violations in South Africa during the apartheid era.[67]

It bears noting that it was the threat (promise?) of legal action that caused Swiss banks to reach an out of court settlement about claims pertaining primarily to Jewish account holders arising from the Holocaust era.[68] Likewise it was the prospect of similar legal action that caused Volkswagen and other German corporations also to reach an out of court settlement that provided a fund to compensate forced and slave laborers whose rights were violated in that same era.

Nation state action

In the 1970s, as already noted, western or home state governments tried to fend off demands for new international law to regulate TNCs as part of the NIEO. By the 1990s this situation had partially changed, as a number of governments – including some that were pro-business and right of center – in westernized democracies advocated at least codes of conduct and other non-binding measures designed to advance social responsibility, including attention to human rights, in the activities of TNCs. The German government of Helmut Kohl underwrote the "Rugmark campaign," designed to ensure that Asian rugs were not made with child

---

[65] See Daphne Eviatar, "A Big Win for Human Rights," *The Nation*, May 9, 2005, www.thenation.com/20050509&s=eviatar. But see also Human Rights Watch, "US: Ashcroft Attacks Human Rights Law," May 15, 2003, www.hrw.org/press/2003/05/us051503.htm.

[66] For a readable analysis of the Alvarez-Marchain case, see Warren Richey, "Ruling Makes it Harder for Foreigners to Sue in US Courts," *Christian Science Monitor*, June 30, 2004, http://0-web.lexis-nexis.com.library.unl.edu/universe/document?_m=77a8f707d45981ecda.

[67] For a readable analysis of the South African case, see Julia Preston, "Judge Dismisses Big Rights Suit On Apartheid," *New York Times*, November 30, 2004, A6.

[68] See Stuart E. Eizenstat, *Imperfect Justice: Looted Assets, Slave Labor, and the Unfinished Business of World War II* (New York, Public Affairs, 2003).

labor. The Chretian government in Canada also began to address the issue of child labor abroad. The Clinton Administration brokered the AIP/FLA arrangement discussed above, while trying to pressure Shell because of its policies in Nigeria. European governments, through the European Parliament, tried to embarrass British Petroleum over its policies in Colombia which allegedly led to the repression of labor rights through brutal actions by the army in constructing a BP pipeline. On the other hand we have noted the opposition of the George W. Bush Administration to linking TNCs to international human rights standards, an opposition which included voting against a measure which passed in the UN Human Rights Commission in the spring of 2005 calling for further attention to this subject.

In general it can still be said that home state governments remain reluctant to firmly and effectively use public law to regulate TNCs in the name of international human rights. The real shift that is underway is for national governments to prod "their" corporations to regulate themselves, under non-binding codes and now increasingly NGO monitoring. The sanction at work is that of negative publicity and consumer sanctions. This has proved somewhat effective for those companies that sell directly to individual consumers, as Heineken and Nike, *inter alia*, will attest.

A review of US foreign policy and TNC action for human rights, however, is an example that indicates more vague rhetoric than concrete examples of effective action – certainly beyond the AIP/FLA agreement.[69] The United States, especially under Republican administrations, is still wary of "statism" that would intrude deeply into the marketplace.

In 1996 the US Department of Commerce advanced a code called The Model Business Principles linked to universal human rights. The code referred to a safe and healthy workplace, fair employment practices, and free expression and opposition to political coercion in the workplace, along with environmental and anti-corruption concerns. But aside from the AIP/FLA agreement, it seems that nothing much has come about in the wake of this code. The Department of Commerce is normally pro-business, and was notably so in the Clinton Administration by comparison with the Labor Department under Robert Reich. As in most governments, there was tension between competing elements.

It is said that the State Department, the Office of the US Trade Representative, and other US bodies take up labor concerns in foreign countries. It is true that the Annual Country Human Rights Reports, compiled by the State Department's Bureau of Democracy, Human Rights, and Labor, consider labor issues. But it is well known that there has

---

[69] See http://www.state.gov/www/global/human_rights/business_principles.html.

been a persistent gap between the recording of violations of internationally recognized human rights in these reports, which has been done fairly conscientiously since 1976, and any effective follow-up steps by the USA. Washington's trade statutes include language that allows trade to be made conditional on human rights behavior.[70] But as in EU relations with non-European trade partners, this conditionality is rarely if ever invoked in practice.

It is also true that US foreign policy officials make speeches on behalf of labor rights and corporate social responsibility, but concrete action by the USA in opposing certain TNC practices is not always easy to demonstrate. The United States has been more active, for a longer period of time, in opposing TNC bribery than in opposing child labor and other violations of labor rights.

It can be noted, however, that the USA joined a number of other actors like UNICEF in providing funds to allow underage children to return to school rather than work in Asian sweatshops. The Departments of Commerce and Labor do publish information on child labor abroad, and provide a list of codes of conduct and possible monitoring organizations for TNC use if they so choose. And the United States continues to support certain ILO programs, even if these have not always proved very effective.

Conclusions

Whereas not so long ago TNCs were urged not to get involved in the domestic affairs of host states, now there has been a considerable shift in expectations; TNCs are frequently urged by citizens and their governments to undertake a more active commitment to international human rights.[71] As a *New York Times* editorial noted: "A quarter-century ago, business argued that protecting the environment was not their job. Few American companies would say so today. A similar change may be developing in corporate attitudes about human rights. Companies are increasingly recognizing that their actions can affect human rights, and that respecting rights can be in their business interest."[72]

---

[70] Compa and Hinchliffe-Darricarrere, "Enforcing International Rights," 667.

[71] The Dutch Sections of Amnesty International and Pax Christi International, *Multinational Enterprises and Human Rights* (no place: AI and PCI, no date), 22–23. See further Thomas Donaldson, "Moral Minimums for Multinationals," in Joel H. Rosenthal, ed., *Ethics and International Affairs: A Reader*, 2nd edn (Washington: Georgetown University Press, 1999), 455–480.

[72] Quoted in "Human Rights and Business: Profiting from Observing Human Rights," *Ethics in Economics*, 1998 (nos. 1 & 2), 2, 125 E. Broad St., Columbus, Ohio, www.businessethics.org.

Despite the fact that most public international law, and so far international criminal law, does not apply thus far to TNCs, there are ways to reorient private corporations to public standards of human rights. Non-binding codes of conduct, devoid of monitoring mechanisms, have proved uniformly weak in the 1970s and 1980s, whether originating from the International Chamber of Commerce, the OECD, the ILO, the US government, or in draft form from UNCTAD. But private codes, in the form of negotiated agreements, accompanied by independent monitoring and public reporting, hold some promise for changing corporate behavior. This is especially so when such agreements have the backing of governments which can be expected to assist in implementation. Recall that the AIP/FLA is underwritten by the US government, whose Department of Labor carries out studies, *inter alia*, to promote compliance. Recall that the Rugmark campaign was underwritten by the German government.

It is in this a-legal gray area of public and private action that one is most likely to see progress in the near future in getting TNCs to pay more attention to human rights standards. The pressure will come mostly from the non-profit side, in the context of media exposure, with the threat of consumer or citizen action that endangers the corporation's profit margin. But socially responsible partners will exist within some corporations and governments. The process is likely to remain quasi-legal and extrajudicial, although national court cases making TNCs liable for civil penalties for human rights violations could be a factor of great significance.

All of this is part of a new psychological environment in which TNCs are expected by many to engage in socially responsible policies. Many of these policies center on international standards of human rights. It was in this context that the JPMorgan Bank apologized for its role in supporting slavery in the past in the USA, and then set up a five million dollar program in Louisiana (where several of its acquired banks had operated) for African-American students to pursue higher education.[73]

Discussion questions

- Are transnational corporations too large and powerful for control by public authorities? To what extent are international authorities, compared with national authorities, important for the regulation of TNCs?
- What is the experience in OECD countries with regard to private, for-profit corporations and their impact on labor at home? Has the lesson of this experience been properly applied to international relations?

[73] Associated Press, "JPMorgan: Banks had links to slavery," *Lincoln Journal Star*, January 21, 2005, A9.

- Are human rights considerations, when applied to TNCs, actually a form of western imperialism in that the application of human rights standards to protect workers actually impedes economic growth and prosperity in the global south?
- If you are a stockholder in a TNC, do you really want "your" company to pay attention to human rights as labor rights if it reduces the return on your investment? What if you are both an owner and a consumer at the same time: does this change any important equation in your thinking? Why should we expect American and European owners or consumers to be concerned about Asian, African or Latin American workers?
- Are companies like Nike and Reebok engaged in public relations maneuvers by joining a-legal codes of conduct like AIP/FLA, or do they show a real commitment to the human dignity of the workers in their Asian sub-contractors? Is there any real difference between Nike and Royal Dutch Shell when it comes to social issues in foreign countries?
- Can TNCs be effectively counter-balanced on sweatshop issues by a movement featuring primarily university students, unions, human rights groups, and the media? Is it necessary for governments to lend their support to such a movement? Can private a-legal codes of conduct be effective on TNC policies?
- Given that the ILO has been around since about 1920, why does so much action on labor rights take place outside the procedures of this organization? Can one make more progress on labor rights by circumventing international law and organization? Conversely, should we make TNCs directly accountable under international law, instead of indirectly accountable through nation states? Is politics more important than law?
- Was the George W. Bush administration correct in arguing that the Alien Tort Statute of 1789 was not intended to cover civil suits for violations of international human rights in the twenty-first century? Regardless of the original intent of those who drafted and passed that statute, was it proper policy for that administration to try to narrow the application of that law so as to exclude attempts to protect against corporate abuses?

Suggestions for further reading

Barnet, Richard J., and John Cavanagh, *Global Dreams: Imperial Corporations and the New World Order* (New York: Simon & Schuster, 1994). A hard look at TNCs and public policy from left of center.

Compa, Lance A., and Stephen F. Diamond, eds., *Human Rights, Labor Rights, and International Trade* (Philadelphia: University of Pennsylvania Press, 1996). A good collection that provides a solid overview.

Donaldson, Thomas, "Moral Minimums for Multinationals," in Joel H. Rosenthal, ed., *Ethics and International Affairs: A Reader*, 2nd edn (Washington: Georgetown University Press, 1999), 455–480. A good, short treatment of ethical conduct in the world of TNCs.

Frynas, Jedrzeg George, and Scott Pegg, eds., *Transnational Corporations and Human Rights* (London: Palgrave Macmillan, 2004). Useful short studies of private activism, codes of conduct, conflict situations, oil companies in Nigeria, mining in Papua New Guinea, the coffee industry, labor in South East Asia, community-corporate partnerships in Canada.

Gilpin, Robert, *The Political Economy of International Relations* (Princeton: Princeton University Press, 1987). A classic study. Chapter 6 deals with TNCs. Not much explicitly on human rights, but lots on TNC behavior in broad political perspective.

Haas, Ernst A., *Human Rights and International Action* (Stanford: Stanford University Press, 1970). Concludes that the ILO during the Cold War was not able to improve labor rights in the communist bloc.

Howard Hassmann, Rhoda, "The Second Great Transformation: Leapfrogging in the Era of Globalization," *Human Rights Quarterly*, 27, 1 (February 2005), 1–40. A broad argument about the place of human rights in the transformation from national industrial capitalism to global technocratic capitalism.

Houck, John W., and Oliver F. Williams, *Is the Good Corporation Dead: Social Responsibility in a Global Economy* (Lanham, MD: Rowman & Littlefield, 1996). A thorough examination of the concept of social responsibility in relation to corporate behavior.

Hymer, Stephen, "Multinational Corporations and the Law of Uneven Development," in J. W. Bhagwati, ed., *Economics and World Order* (New York: Macmillan, 1971), 113–140. A classic study of the evils TNCs can do.

Korten, David, *When Corporations Rule the World* (West Hartford: Kumarian Press, 1995). Another critical look, some would say hyper-critical, at TNCs and the damage they can do.

Meyer, William H., *Human Rights and International Political Economy in Third World Nations: Multinational Corporations, Foreign Aid, and Repression* (Westport, CT: Praeger, 1998). A quantitative study finding positive correlations, in general, between the presence of TNCs in the global south and lots of good things. The author's methodology has been questioned by other scholars.

Rivoli, Pietra, *The Travels of a T-Shirt in the Global Economy: An Economist Examines the Markets, Power, and Politics of World Trade* (New York: Wiley, 2005). A broad and readable view of how global economics works, with attention to both benefits and problems – including why certain individuals will not benefit under free trade and the WTO.

Rodman, Kenneth A., "Think Globally, Punish Locally: Non-State Actors, Multinational Corporations, and Human Rights," *Ethics and International Affairs*, 12 (1998), 19–42. Notes the growing pressure on corporations to better respect labor rights, principally from human rights organizations and consumer movements.

Schlesinger, Stephen C., and Stephen Kinzer, *Bitter Fruit: The Untold Story of the American Coup in Guatemala* (Garden City, NY: Doubleday, 1982). American corporations team with the US government to overthrow the Arbenz government in Guatemala, ushering in several decades of brutal repression.

Soros, George, "The Capitalist Threat," *Atlantic Monthly*, 279, 2 (February 1997), 47 and *passim*. The successful Hungarian financier and philanthropist warns of the dangers of unregulated capitalism in Eastern Europe and the former Soviet Union.

Spar, Deborah, "The Spotlight and the Bottom Line: How Multinationals Export Human Rights," *Foreign Affairs*, 77, 2 (March–April 1998), 7–12. A short essay that is basically positive about the role of regulated or pressured corporations. The author notes that some corporations have a very poor record on human rights.

Tavis, Lee, *Power and Responsibility* (Notre Dame: Notre Dame Press, 1997). Another useful look at social responsibility and corporate behavior.

Vernon, Raymond, *Sovereignty at Bay: The Multinational Spread of US Enterprises* (New York: Basic Books, 1971). A classic study arguing that TNCs have not escaped control by the modern state.

Part III

Conclusion

9   The politics of liberalism in a realist world

This book has clearly shown the extent to which human rights has become a routine part of international relations. Michael Ignatieff has captured the trend succinctly but brilliantly: "We are scarcely aware of the extent to which our moral imagination has been transformed since 1945 by the growth of a language and practice of moral universalism, expressed above all in a shared human rights culture."[1] The language and practice of universal human rights, and of its first cousin, regional human rights, has been a redeeming feature of a very bloody and harsh twentieth century.

But the journalist David Rieff reminds us of a more skeptical interpretation of universal human rights. "The universalizing impulse is an old tradition in the West, and, for all the condemnations that it routinely incurs today, particularly in the universities, it has probably done at least as much good as harm. But universalism easily declines into sentimentalism, into a tortured but useless distance from the particulars of human affairs."[2] Or, to drive the same point home with a more concrete example, whereas virtually all states formally endorse the abstract principles of human rights in peace and war, "Combatants are as likely to know as much about the laws of war as they do about quantum mechanics."[3]

The international law of human rights is based on liberalism, but the practice of human rights all too often reflects a realist world. State interests rather than personal rights often prevail, interpersonal equality often gives way to disrespect for – if not hatred of – "others," violent conflict is persistent, and weak international institutions are easily demonstrated.[4]

---

[1] Michael Ignatieff, *The Warrior's Honor: Ethnic War and the Modern Conscience* (New York: Metropolitan, 1997), 8.

[2] David Rieff, "The Humanitarian Illusion," *The New Republic*, March 16, 1998, 28.

[3] David Scheffer, "The Clear and Present Danger of War Crimes," Address, University of Oklahoma College of Law, February 24, 1998, unpublished.

[4] To expand on notions of realism discussed in chapter 1, see further among many sources Jack Donnelly, *Realism in International Relations* (Cambridge: Cambridge University Press, 2000). On the difference between human and national interests in international relations, see especially Robert C. Johansen, *The National Interest and the Human Interest: An Analysis of US Foreign Policy* (Princeton: Princeton University Press, 1980).

It is a type of liberal progress in keeping with Ignatieff's view that we now recognize the enslavement and other exploitation of the persons in the Congo river basin between about 1460 and 1960 as a violation of their human rights.[5] It is a testament to the continuing explanatory power of David Rieff's realism that we note the lack of effective or decisive international response to the massacres and other gross violations of human rights in the Congo river basin after 1960, whether one speaks of Zaire or the Democratic Republic of Congo.

We recognize rights, but often we do not act to protect them. This provides one good answer to the frequently heard lament: "How could the rhetoric of human rights be so globally pervasive while the politics of human rights is so utterly weak?"[6]

To review

Given the ground covered in this work thus far, a brief review of main points is in order. Dichotomies and paradoxes characterize the turbulent international relations of the turn of the century in 2000, as we noted in chapter 1. International human rights are here to stay, but so is state sovereignty. The latter notion is being transformed by the actions, *inter alia*, of intergovernmental and transnational non-governmental organizations. But state consent still usually matters legally, and state policy and power still count for much in human affairs. One historian – tongue in cheek – quotes a British diplomat to the effect that we need an additional article in the UN Charter: "Nothing in the present Charter should be allowed to foster the illusion that [state] power is no longer of any consequence."[7] Our moral imagination has been expanded by the language of universal rights, but we live in a world in which nationalism and the nation-state and national interests are frequently powerful barriers to effective action in the name of international human rights. Trade-offs and compromises between liberal and realist principles are legion, as human rights values are contextualized in a modified nation-state system of international relations.[8]

As covered in chapter 2, the International Bill of Rights and supplemental standards give us the modern international law of global human rights. For all of its defects, noted in various critiques covered below, it is

---

[5] Adam Hochschild, *King Leopold's Ghost: A Story of Greed, Terror, and Heroism in Colonial Africa* (Boston: Houghton Mifflin, 1998).

[6] Kenneth Cmiel, "The Recent History of Human Rights," *American Historical Review*, 109, 1 (February 2004), 117–135, at 118.

[7] Geoffrey Best, Book Review, *Los Angeles Times*, August 16, 1998, 8.

[8] See further Rein Mullerson, *Human Rights Diplomacy* (London: Routledge, 1997).

far more developed (meaning specified and structured) than some other parts of international law pertaining to such subject matter as ecology.

Like all law it is the result of a political process, frequently contentious. Surely it comes as no surprise that transnational standards pertaining to the right to life or to the right of freedom of religion or to freedom from discrimination, *inter alia*, should prove controversial. The existence of international human rights law owes much to the western-style democracies – their liberal values and their hard power (the liberal values themselves can be a type of soft power). Still, internationally recognized human rights were also affected by the old communist coalition, and certainly by the newly independent states of the global south after about 1960.

It cannot be stressed too much that whereas certainly the practice of politics on the basis of respect for the notion of human rights was extensively developed in certain western states, the idea of human rights is a defense against abuse of power everywhere.[9] Wherever the bicycle was invented, its utility is not limited to that historical and geographical situation. So it is also with the idea and practice of human rights.

The human dignity of especially those without great power and wealth normally benefits from the barriers to injurious acts of commission and omission provided by human rights standards. Intentional mass murder and neglectful mass misery are equal affronts to any conception of human dignity. Mass misery no less than mass murder can be changed by human endeavor, and is thus grist for the mill of human rights discourse. As often noted, there is no material or moral reason for world hunger, save for the way we choose to organize ourselves as inhabitants of the planet earth.[10] We create territorial states whose governments are sometimes said to have responsibility only to their citizens; foster a type of nationalism that tends to restrict morality to within national borders; and internationally endorse a harsh form of *laissez-faire* economics despite its rejection on moral grounds at home. The idea of universal human rights seeks to change those mind sets.

But human dignity itself, and human rights as a means to that end, are contested constructs whose meaning must be established in a never-ceasing process of moral, political, and legal debate and review. Beyond mass murder and mass misery, the dividing line between fundamental personal rights and myriad optional legal rights is a matter of considerable controversy.

[9] See further Thomas M. Franck, "Is Personal Freedom a Western Value?," *American Journal of International Law*, 91, 4 (October 1997), 593–627.
[10] Thomas Pogge, *World Poverty and Human Rights: Cosmopolitan Responsibilities and Reforms* (Cambridge: Polity, 2002).

In chapter 3 we saw that the UN has moved beyond the setting of human rights standards toward the systematic supervision of state behavior. This is a very broad and accelerating development, unfortunately partially undermined not only by a paucity of resources that states allow the overall UN human rights program, but also by the disjointed nature of the beast. The sum total of the diplomacy of shaming, or the politics of embarrassment, certainly has had an educative effect over time, even if the calculated violation continued in the short term.

At least at first glance it was encouraging that the United Nations Security Council after the Cold War should pay so much attention to human rights issues in the guise of threats to international peace and security. The Council's deployment of field missions under the idea of second-generation or complex peacekeeping, mostly directed to producing a liberal democratic order out of failed states, showed a willingness to deal with many of the root causes of human rights violations – as long as the principal parties gave their consent to the UN presence. Such missions clearly were on the progressive side of history in places like El Salvador, Namibia and Mozambique. The trend continued in places like Bosnia, Kosovo, East Timor, and Cambodia.

It was also noteworthy that the Council should authorize enforcement actions on behalf of democratic governance and other humane values in places like Haiti and Somalia, even if the job had to be contracted out to one or more member states, and even if the follow-up left something to be desired. Unfortunately the Council was heavily dependent on the one remaining superpower, the United States, to make its enforcement actions effective. The result was a very spotty record of UN accomplishments, especially where the USA saw few traditional national interests to sustain a complicated involvement. In the Kosovo crisis of 1999 the United States tried to enforce human rights protections via NATO, but without Security Council authorization and through a highly controversial military strategy.

On balance the UN was paying more attention to human rights, not less. It was being creative in the interpretation of Chapters VI and VII of the Charter, in calling emergency sessions of the Human Rights Commission, in expanding the authority of its monitoring mechanisms, in creating the office of the High Commissioner for Human Rights, in utilizing NGO information, and in other ways.

Some of this UN creativity had to do with the establishment of the two *ad hoc* international criminal courts by the Security Council, as we saw in chapter 4. The new standing international criminal court, whose statute was overwhelmingly approved in 1998, and which began to function during 2002–2003, was to be loosely associated with the UN. This renewed foray into international criminal justice was a noteworthy development after a hiatus of some fifty years. It triggered a new round of debate about peace v. justice, and about what was central to peace as compared with a moral sideshow. Ignatieff is again brilliantly concise when he writes, "Justice in itself is not a problematic objective, but whether the attainment of [criminal] justice always contributes to reconciliation is anything but evident."[11] New efforts at international criminal justice also caused national policy makers to calculate carefully about how vigorously to go after those indicted for war crimes, crimes against humanity, and genocide, for fear of undermining larger objectives or incurring human costs difficult to justify according to traditional notions of national interest.

The permanent court particularly was bitterly opposed by conservative circles in the USA, who saw the projected infringements on state sovereignty, if such they were, as completely unacceptable.[12] There was nothing more frightening to them than an effective international law that would really circumscribe their freedom of national decision making. That the USA should be actively pushing a new special criminal tribunal for Cambodia at the same time that it was fending off the new permanent court that might (but probably would not) wind up exercising jurisdiction over Americans was a double standard too blatant to ignore. That the USA was in favor of criminal justice for those in the former Yugoslavia and the Great Lakes Region of Africa, but not as applied to itself, was – smokescreen arguments aside – a position which undermined US attempts to present itself as a human rights model for others. Moreover, when the USA reduced military assistance to about a dozen states in the Western Hemisphere in order to pressure them to sign agreements exempting Americans from the ICC, this action hurt US attempts to work with these same militaries in curtailing the drug trade and other common objectives.[13]

What started out in 1993 as mostly a public relations ploy, namely to create an *ad hoc* tribunal to appear to be doing something about human rights violations in Bosnia without major risk, by 2005 had become an important global movement for international criminal justice formally accepted by about 100 states. Such were the unexpected outcomes of a series of "accidental" or *ad hoc* decisions, as states muddled their way through complex calculations of media coverage, popular pressure,

---

[11] Ignatieff, *The Warrior's Honor*, 170.
[12] See for example John Bolton (former US Assistant Secretary of State for International Organizations and later US representative to the UN), "The Global Prosecutors: Hunting War Criminals in the Name of Utopia," *Foreign Affairs*, 78, 1 (January/February 1999), 157–164.
[13] Juan Forero, "Bush's Aid Cuts on Court Issue Roil Neighbors," *New York Times*, August 19, 2005, A1.

traditional national interests, and state power. Private armies might commit many of the violations of human rights, and private human rights groups might be players in the legislative process, but ultimately it was states that decided. Even the normally cynical British and French split with the USA over the issue of a permanent court, endorsing its establishment.

This might have been the case in part because, as we saw in chapter 5, the British and the French and most other European states had become accustomed to having supranational courts make judgments on human rights in both the Council of Europe and the European Union. French policy in particular had undergone a considerable change. Like the USA, France long considered its record on human rights beyond the need for the type of international review provided by individual petitions and a supranational regional court. But France – and Turkey – shifted over time, providing at least a glimmer of hope that eventually US nationalism might prove more accommodating to multilateral human rights developments.[14]

Be that latter point as it may, European protections of civil and political rights remained a beacon of rationality and effectiveness in a troubled world. The Council of Europe and the European Union proved that liberal principles of human rights could indeed be effectively combined with realist principles of the state system. Of course European developments transformed the regional state system in important ways, as states used their sovereignty to restrict their independence of policy making. Yet states continued to exist in meaningful ways, as did their views of their national interests. But an international view on protecting human rights also mattered in very important ways, mostly through the judgments of the supranational courts existing in Strasburg and Luxemburg.

In less striking, more diplomatic (as compared with legal) ways the Organization for Security and Cooperation in Europe mattered regarding especially the diplomatic protection of national minorities. That NATO should be used to try to protect Albanian Kosovar rights in 1999 was indicative not only of the importance of regional organizations, but also of the importance of international action for human rights in Europe. It was not hyperbole to say that commitment to human rights was the touchstone of being European. Beyond Europe, the human rights agencies associated with the Organization of American States, especially the InterAmerican Commission on Human Rights, at least generated some impact sometimes on some issues. While the short-term view regarding African regional developments for human rights was even less encouraging, it was at least possible that the Banjul Charter and the African

---

[14] In *Of Paradise and Power: America and Europe in the New World Order* (New York: Vintage, 2003, 2004), Robert Kagan argues that Europeans are much more committed to international law and organization as essential public goods than is the USA.

Commission on Human Rights were laying the foundations for long-term progress. After all, both the European Commission and Court had mostly undistinguished records during their first decade of operation, although both operated in an environment more conducive to real regional protection compared with Africa (and historically the Western Hemisphere). At least for Latin American states (but not so much the English speaking states of the Western Hemisphere), there were more states (not less) accepting the jurisdiction of the InterAmerican Court of Human Rights, and that court was handing down more (not less) judgments.

Permeating all these international developments on human rights was state foreign policy, as we saw in chapter 6. It is states that take the most important decisions in most inter-governmental organizations, and it is states that are the primary targets of lobbying activities by traditional advocacy groups. State sovereignty is being transformed by transnational interests and movements, but states and their conceptions of sovereignty remain an important – indeed essential – aspect of world affairs at the turn of the century.

Contrary to some realist principles, rational states do not always adopt similar foreign policies despite their existing in anarchic international relations. Because of history, culture, ideology, and self-image, some states do strongly identify with international human rights. They may take different slants and emphases when incorporating human rights into their foreign policies. But increasingly many states wish to stand for something besides independent existence and power. States certainly have not abandoned self-interest and pursuit of advantage, but more so than in the past they often seek to combine these traditional expediential concerns with concern for the human rights of others. The liberal framework of international relations, embedded in international law and organization, pushes them in that direction.

To be sure the result is usually inconsistent foreign policies that fall short of the goals demanded by the human rights advocacy groups. But in empirical and relative terms, there is now more attention to human rights in foreign policy than was the case in the League of Nations era. In a shrinking world, states that profess humane values at home find it difficult to completely ignore questions of human rights and dignity beyond their borders. Their self-image, their political culture, mandates that linkage. States that initially seek to bypass issues of individual human rights, like China and Iran, find themselves drawn into a process in which they at least endorse, perhaps in initially vague ways, human rights standards.

Traditional human rights advocacy groups have been active concerning both legislation and implementation of norms, as we traced in chapter 7. Basing their actions mostly on accurate information, they have followed a self-defined moral imperative to try to "educate" public authorities into elevating their concerns for internationally recognized human rights. Frequently coalescing into movements or networks entailing diverse partners, they have engaged in soft lobbying (viz., lobbying that bypasses electoral and financial threat). Mostly relying on the politics of embarrassment or shaming, they have sought to use reason and publicity to bring about progressive change.

It has usually been difficult to factor out the general but singular influence of this or that human rights NGO, or even this or that movement. Nevertheless, given the flood of information they produce and the persistent dynamism the major groups like Amnesty International exhibit, it is difficult to believe that the same evolution concerning international human rights would have occurred over the past thirty years without their efforts. In some cases and situations NGO influence can indeed be documented. It is certainly true that the international system for provision of emergency relief in armed conflict and complex emergencies would not be the same without private groups such as the International Committee of the Red Cross. Likewise, there are numerous groups active for "development," or social and economic rights, like Oxfam, Save the Children, etc., and they often provide an important link between the donor agencies and the persons who presumably benefit from "development."

Increasingly it is necessary to look beyond not only states and their inter-governmental organizations, but also beyond the private groups active for human rights, relief, and development for an understanding of the fate of human rights in the modern world. We especially need to look at transnational corporations, as we did in chapter 8. Given their enormous and growing power in international economics, and given the dynamics of capitalism, it is small wonder that their labor practices have come under closer scrutiny. It may be states that formally make and mostly enforce human rights norms. But it is private corporations, frequently acting under pressure from private groups and movements, that can have a great impact on the reality of human rights – especially in the workplace. Sometimes states are rather like mediators or facilitators, channeling concern from private advocacy groups and movements into arrangements that corporations come to accept.[15] Such was the case with the US government concerning labor standards in the apparel industry, and with the German government concerning child labor in the international rug industry.

One of the more interesting developments concerning international human rights at the close of the twentieth century was the linkage between student activism and labor standards at many universities in

---

[15] See further B. Hocking, *Catalytic Diplomacy* (Leicester: Centre for Diplomatic Studies, 1996).

the global north. This merger resulted in growing pressure on particularly the apparel industry to end the use of not only child labor but sweatshops by their foreign sub-contractors. But progressive developments were not limited to that one industry, as corporations selling coffee and other products felt the need to protect their brand name and bottom line by opening their foreign facilities to international inspection under international labor standards. It was not so much muscular international law and established inter-governmental relations that brought about new developments. Rather it was a movement made up of consumer groups, unions, the communications media, student movements, churches, and traditional advocacy groups that brought about codes of conduct with inspections and public reports.[16]

Still, one should not be Pollyannaish. Many of the corporations dealing in extraction of natural resources had compiled a record quite different from at least some TNCs in the American-based apparel industry. And many companies seemed more interested in public relations than in genuine commitment to either human rights or other means to human dignity.

Toward the future

The future of international human rights is not easy to predict with any specificity. One might agree with the statement attributed to the Danish philosopher Kierkegaard: life is lived forward but understood backward. Or one might agree with a statement from Vaclav Havel, first President of the Czech Republic: "That life is unfathomable is part of its dramatic beauty and its charm."[17] Nevertheless, one point is clear about human rights in international relations. We will not lack for controversy.

Human rights has indeed been institutionalized in international relations, but that discourse will remain controversial. This is paradoxical but true. Debate is inherent in the concept of human rights. I do not refer now to the effort by philosophers to find an ultimate metaphysical source of, or justification for, the notion of human rights. Rather I refer to debates by policy makers and others interested in practical action in interpersonal relations. There is debate both by liberals of various sorts who believe in the positive contributions of human rights, and by non-liberals such as realists and Marxists.

---

[16] For example, the Presbyterian Church USA considered divesting from certain corporations providing military equipment to Israel, such was that church's concern about Isreaeli policies in the occupied territories. See Laurie Goodstein, "Threat to Divest Is Church Tool In Israeli Fight," *New York Times*, August 6, 2005, A1.

[17] Vaclav Havel, *Summer Meditations* (New York: Vintage, 1993), 102.

Controversies in liberalism

Enduring questions

Even for those who believe that international human rights constitute on balance a good thing, there are no clear and fixed, much less scientific, answers to a series of questions. What defines universal human dignity? What are the proper moral human rights, as means, to that dignity? Which are truly fundamental, and which are optional? Which are so fundamental as to be absolutely non-violable, even in war and other situations threatening national security or the life of the nation, and thus constituting part of *jus cogens* in international law (legal rules from which no conflicting rules or derogation is permitted)? What crimes are so heinous that the notion of universal jurisdiction attaches to them? When moral rights are translated into legal rights, and when there is conflict among legal rights, who resolves the conflicts, and on what principle?

Traditional principles

If we focus on particular principles that are said to be human rights principles in contemporary international law, derived from liberalism, we still cannot avoid debate. Revisit, if you will, the principle discussed in chapter 2 and codified in Article 1 of the two International Covenants in the International Bill of Rights: the collective right of the self-determination of peoples. How do we define a people with such a right – the Kosovars, the Quebecois, the Basques, the Ibos, the Kurds, the Slovaks, the Chechens, the Ossetians? Who is authorized to pronounce on such definitional issues? If we could define such a people, what form or forms can self-determination take? And why have states in contemporary international relations been unable to specify authoritative rules under this general principle that would prove relevant and helpful to conflicts over self-determination? Why is the evidence so overwhelming that most of these disputes are settled by politics, and frequently on the basis of superior coercive power, rather than on the basis of legal rules about collective rights?

Even if we take the widely shared principle of freedom from torture, we cannot avoid controversy. The classic counter-example involves the hypothetical prisoner who has knowledge of an impending nuclear attack. Is it moral to observe the no-torture principle if it results in death or serious injury and sickness to millions? As we noted especially in chapter six, the USA from 2002 employed some coercive interrogation in its military detention centers, ran a secret detention system in which abusive interrogation was probably the norm (why else keep it secret), and "rendered" persons to other states where mistreatment and even torture were widely regarded as prevalent. Was all of this truly necessary for US homeland security? Could the same information have been extracted by more humane methods? If one did obtain some "actionable intelligence," but in the process engaged in a widely known abusive process that produced even more "terrorists" because of their outrage, how should one evaluate the overall security situation? How should one evaluate the experience of other countries that had employed mistreatment or torture, like France in the Algerian war, Britain in Nothern Ireland, and Israel between 1967 and 1999?[18]

Even if we take the widely shared principle about a right to religious freedom, we cannot escape controversy.[19] This is so even in countries that recognize the principle (and thus I exclude for the moment various controversies about Saudi Arabia and other states that reject the basic principle). What is a religion? The US government says that scientology is a religion, whereas the German government says it is a dangerous, perhaps neo-fascist cult. Do certain Native Americans in prison have a right to use marijuana as part of their arguably religious practices? Is religious belief a valid basis for refusal to serve in the military? Should religious freedom be elevated to those basic rights of the first order, as demanded at one point by the Republican-controlled Congress in the 1990s, and be made the object of special US concern? Or should religious freedom be considered one of many rights, and deserving of no automatic priority over other rights – for example, freedom from torture – in state foreign policy? The latter was the position of the Clinton Administration, although as noted it did respond to congressional pressures by creating a special office in the State Department to deal with religious freedom.

New claims

Certainly if we observe the demands for acknowledgment of a new, third generation of human rights in international relations, we cannot escape

---

[18] See further especially Joseph Lelyveld, "Interrogating Ourselves," *New York Times Magazine*, June 12, 2005, starting at p. 36. See also Michael Ignatieff, *The Lesser Evil: Political Ethics in an Age of Terror* (Princeton: Princeton University Press, 2005); and Richard Ashby Wilson, ed., *Human Rights in the "War on Terror"* (Cambridge: Cambridge University Press, 2005).

[19] See further Kevin Boyle and Juliet Sheen, eds., *Freedom of Religion and Belief: A World Report* (London: Routledge, 1997).

the reality of continuing controversy. Should the principle be recognized of a human right to a safe environment? If so, would the enumeration of specific rules under this principle provide anything new, as compared with a repetition of already recognized civil rights about freedom of information, speech, association, and non-discrimination? On the other hand, is it not wise to draw further attention to ecological dangers by recasting norms as human rights norms, even at the price of some redundancy? Then again, given that many states of the global north already have extensive legal regulations to protect the environment, why is it necessary to apply the concept of human rights to environmental law?[20] Do we not have a proliferation of human rights claims already?[21] Do we not need a moratorium on new claims about human rights, perhaps until those rights already recognized can be better enforced?[22]

Process priorities

As should be clear by now, classical and pragmatic liberals do not always agree on how to direct attention to human rights, how much emphasis to give, and what priorities to establish when desired goals do not mesh easily. The classical liberal places great faith in persistent emphasis on law, criminal justice, and other punishments for violation of the law. The neo-liberal argues for many avenues to the advancement of personal dignity and social justice, of which attention to legal rights, adjudication and sanctions is only one.

As a pragmatic liberal, I see no alternative to a case-by-case evaluation of when to stress human rights law and adjudication, hard law, that is, and when to opt for the priority of other liberal values through diplomacy. I believe, for example, that it was correct to pursue the Dayton accord in 1995 for increased peace in Bosnia, even if it meant at that time not indicting and arresting Slobodan Milosevic for his support for and encouragement of heinous acts. The persons of that area benefited

---

[20] See further Alan Boyle and Michael Anderson, eds., *Human Rights Approaches to Environmental Protection* (New York: Oxford University Press, 1996); Barbara Rose Johnston, ed., *Life and Death Matters: Human Rights and the Environment at the End of the Millennium* (Walnut Creek, CA: AltaMira Press, 1997).

[21] See further Carl Wellman, *The Proliferation of Rights: Moral Progress or Empty Rhetoric?* (Boulder: Westview, 1999).

[22] See further W. Paul Gormley, *Human Rights and The Environment: the Need for International Co-operation* (Leiden: W.W. Sijthoff, 1976); and Human Rights Watch, *Defending the Earth: Abuses of Human Rights and the Environment* (New York: Human Rights Watch, 1992). But see Philip Alston, who opposes the development of most new categories of human rights when the older categories are not well enforced, in "Conjuring Up New Human Rights: A Proposal for Quality Control," *American Journal of International Law*, 78, 3 (July 1984), 607–621.

from increased peace, decline of atrocities, and the attempt to establish liberal democracies in the region. I believe it was correct to go slow in the arrest of indicted persons in the Balkans, lest the United States and other western states incur casualties, as in Somalia in 1993, that would have undermined other needed international involvement, as in Rwanda in 1994.

I believe it was correct to emphasize truth commissions rather than criminal proceedings in places like El Salvador and South Africa, despite the gross violations of human rights under military rule in San Salvador and under apartheid in Pretoria. Long-term national reconciliation and stable liberal democracy are advancing in those two countries, whereas pursuit of criminal justice may have hardened animosities between the principal communities On the other hand, I think it a good idea to try to hold Augusto Pinochet legally accountable for crimes against humanity, including torture and disappearances, when he ruled Chile. His extradition from Britain and prosecution in Spain would make other tyrants more cautious about violating human rights.

Given the Chinese elite's preoccupation with national stability, in the light of their turbulent national history and the closely watched disintegration of the Soviet Union during Gorbachev's political reforms, I believe it is correct to take a long-term, diplomatic approach to the matter of improvement of human rights in China. I believe we should use the international law of human rights as a guide for diplomacy and a goal for China's evolution. But in the absence of another massacre as in Tiananmen Square in 1989, or some comparable gross violation of human rights, I believe that constructive engagement is the right general orientation.

None of these policy positions is offered as doctrinal truth. Many of them depend on the evolution of future events which are unknowable. All are offered as examples of policy choices that the typical pragmatic liberal might make, that are based on liberal commitment to the welfare of individuals over time regardless of nationality or gender or other distinguishing feature, and that sometimes avoid an emphasis on criminal justice and other forms of punishment in the immediate future.

The pragmatic liberal approach allows for a great deal of flexibility and guarantees a certain amount of inconsistency. The pragmatic-liberal may support criminal justice for human rights violations in one situation, e.g., Spain regarding Chile, but not in another, e.g., Cambodia regarding the Khmer Rouge. The pragmatic liberal might well regard major sanctions as mostly inadvisable for Chinese violations of human rights, but find them useful in dealing with Iraq, or Afghanistan, or Burma, or Yugoslavia – or maybe not.

What we are certainly going to continue to see, even among liberals, is considerable debate about policy choice.

Feminist perspectives

Even the most radical feminists do not reject the international law of human rights, in the last analysis,[23] and thus I list feminist perspectives as part of liberalism despite great variety among feminist publicists. Much of the feminist critique of extant human rights actually turns out to be gendered liberalism or pragmatic liberalism.[24]

The traditional feminist critique of human rights centers on the argument that those norms, being produced in a male-dominated legislative process, focus on the public rather than private domain.[25] The public arena is the man's world, while women have been confined to the home as sexual object, mother, unpaid domestic worker, etc. Thus it is said that international human rights fail to deal adequately with domestic abuse and oppression of women. International human rights have supposedly been gendered to the detriment of women, despite an active role for some women in the drafting of the Universal Declaration of Human Rights (as noted in chapter 3).

One feminist critique attacks one half of the International Bill of Rights as it exists today, preferring to emphasize supposedly feminist values like caring and responsibility.[26] Here the argument is that a rights-based approach can only lead to negative rights of the civil and political variety. If one wishes to move beyond them to adequate food, clothing, shelter,

---

[23] Eva Brems, "Enemies or Allies? Feminism and Cultural Relativism as Dissident Voices in the Human Rights Discourse," *Human Rights Quarterly*, 19, 1 (February 1997), 140–141.

[24] It can be noted in passing that one strand of feminism reflects a "post-modern" or "critical" or "essentialist" approach in that it argues that unless one is female, one cannot understand female human dignity and the rights (and perhaps other institutions) needed to protect it. Male observers and scholars, as well as policy makers, are simply incapable of comprehending either the problem or its solution. I myself would not consider this approach part of the liberal tradition, for liberalism stresses a common rationality and scientific method available to all without regard to gender. See further Christine Sylvester, "The Contributions of Feminist Theory to International Relations," in Steve Smith, Ken Booth and Marysia Zalewski, eds., *International Theory: Positivism and Beyond* (Cambridge: Cambridge University Press, 1996), 254–278.

[25] See further, from a growing literature, Rebecca J. Cook, ed., *Human Rights of Women: National and International Perspectives* (Philadelphia: University of Pennsylvania Press, 1994). See the extensive literature cited regarding women's rights on the Internet at www.law-lib.utoronto.ca/diana. See further the extensive citations to women's issues in international relations at www.umn.edu/humanrts/links/women/html.

[26] Fiona Robinson, "The Limits of a Rights Based Approach to International Ethics," in Tony Evans, ed., *Human Rights Fifty Years On: A Reappraisal* (Manchester: Manchester University Press, 1998), 58–76.

and health care, one needs a feminist ethics of care that stresses not rights but the morality of attentiveness, trust, and respect.

Parts of international human rights law are being revised to respond to the first critique. International and more specifically comparative refugee law now stipulates that private abuse can constitute persecution and that women can constitute a social group subject to persecution. Thus a woman, crossing an international border to flee such behavior as female genital mutilation, or a well-founded fear of such behavior, particularly when the home government does not exercise proper protection, is to be provided asylum and is not to be returned to such a situation. Canada and the United States have led the way in reading this new interpretation into refugee law, acting under advisory guidelines established by the Office of the UN High Commissioner for Refugees.[27]

As for the second critique, it should be repeated that the discourse on human rights does not capture the totality of ethics pertaining to interpersonal relations. No doubt an ethics of care and responsibility has its place. Whether such an ethics in international relations is particularly feminine, and whether it can be specified and encouraged to better effect than the human rights discourse, are interesting questions. It is by no means certain that a rights approach must be limited to negative rights, and cannot adequately lead to minimal floors for nutrition, clothing, shelter, and health care.[28]

The second feminist critique overlaps with parts of the pragmatic liberal argument in arguing the merits of at least supplementing legal rights with action not based on rights but still oriented to the welfare of individuals. Once again we find that much of the feminist critique of human rights reflects some form of liberalism, mostly gendered pragmatic liberalism. One needs the concept of human rights, if perhaps revised to take further account of special problems of dignity and justice that pertain to women, but one may also need to go beyond rights to extra-legal or a-legal programs that do not center on adjudication.

Still, a reason for legal rights is the reliability and efficacy of thinking in terms of entitlements that public authority must respect. That is why Henry Dunant and then the ICRC started with the notion of charity toward those wounded in war, but quickly moved to trying to make medical assistance to the wounded a legal obligation in international law.

---

[27] In general see Stephen H. Legomsky, *Immigration and Refugee Law and Policy*, 2nd edn (New York: The Foundation Press, 1997). See also Connie M. Ericson, "In Re Kasinga: An Expansion of the Grounds for Asylum for Women," *Houston Journal of International Law*, 20, 3 (1998), 671–694.

[28] Paul Hunt, *Reclaiming Social Rights: International and Comparative Perspectives* (Aldershot: Dartmouth, 1996).

Controversies beyond liberalism

When considering the future of human rights, I have tried to indicate the tip of the iceberg of controversy even when one accepts the concept of human rights as a beneficial part of international relations. But there is controversy of a different order, based on a more profound critique of human rights as that notion has evolved in international relations. This second type of controversy, which takes different forms or schools of thought, is based on the shared view that individual human rights based on liberal philosophy is misguided as a means to human dignity. The dominant critique, at least for western liberals, has been by realists. But we should also note, at least in passing, the views of Marxists.[29]

Realism

Realism in its various versions has historically captured some prevalent features of traditional international relations. Its strong point has been its emphasis on collective egoism, as numerous political leaders, claiming to speak for a nation, have indeed acted frequently on the basis of their view of narrow self-interest. It has also been accurate in emphasizing calculations of power and balance – or more precisely distribution – of power, however elusive the objective perception of power and its distribution might prove. Such calculations have indeed been a prevalent feature of international relations. In being state-centric, realism captures much of the real strength of nationalism and national identity.

The central weakness of realism has always been its inability to specify what comprises the objective national interest, and therefore its inability to say what is the rational pursuit of that interest based on power calculations. Realism assumes the permanence of a certain nineteenth-century view of international relations in which the dominant principles are state sovereignty understood to mean independence, non-intervention in the domestic affairs of states, and the inevitability of interstate power struggles cumulating in war.

---

[29] It should be stressed that there are numerous approaches to understanding international relations, and the place of human rights therein. A short introductory overview such as this one cannot be expected to be comprehensive. See further Scott Burchill and Andrew Linklater, eds., *Theories of International Relations* (New York: St. Martin's Press, 1996). As noted in chapter 1, Michael Doyle has shown that one can gain many insights by concentrating on liberalism, realism, and Marxism/socialism. The present book follows that approach. Some authors stress not liberalism versus realism but liberalism versus communitarianism – the idea that the community, not the individual, is the proper dominant concern. All liberal orders have to deal with individual rights and autonomy versus the rights and needs of the larger community. We have covered part of this controversy when discussing "Asian values."

Realism discounts the possibility that states would see their real security and other national interests advanced by *losing* considerable independence – e.g., by joining supranational organizations. Realism discounts the possibility of the rise of important transnational interests so that the distinction between domestic structure and issues and international relations loses much of its meaning. Realism discounts the possibility of a decline if not elimination of hegemonic global war among the great powers, and thus does not contemplate the irrationality of saving one's major preoccupations for a war that will not occur – perhaps at all and certainly without great frequency.

Realism discounts the emergence of values such as real commitment to universal human rights and instead posits, in the face of considerable contradictory evidence, that states will always prefer separateness and independent policy making over advancement of human rights (or for that matter over quest for greater wealth through regulated trade or better environmental protection). Realists are prepared to look away when gross violations of human rights are committed inside states; morality and state obligation tend to stop at national frontiers – and anyway the game of correction is not worth the candle. To realists, international liberalism, and the international human rights to which it gives rise, is a utopian snare left over from the European enlightenment with its excessive belief in human rationality, common standards, and capacity for progress.

In situations *not* characterized by intense fear, suspicion, and the classic security dilemma, however, realism misses much of the real stuff of international politics. Where states and governments do not perceive threats to the life of the nation as they have known it, they behave in ways that realism cannot anticipate or explain. Realism is largely irrelevant to international integration in Europe through the Council of Europe and European Union. Realism has no explanation for NATO's unified commitment to a democratic Europe, and hence to its intervention in Federal Yugoslavia to protect Kosovars, save for the argument that the entire policy of intervention is irrational. Realism cannot explain international human rights developments over the past fifty years, except to suggest that most of the states of the world have been either hypocritical or sentimental in approving human rights norms and creating extensive diplomatic machinery for their supervision. Realists like Kissinger were out of touch with important developments in international relations when he opposed the human rights and humanitarian aspects of the 1975 Helsinki Accord, and when he came to accept those principles only as a useful bargaining tool with, and weapon against, the European communists. Even then, he was more comfortable with traditional security matters as Metternich and other nineteenth century diplomats would have understood them.

In some types of international politics realists are relevant, but in other types they are anachronistic.[30] Realists well understand the prevalent negative correlation between war and protection of most human rights. Insecurity does indeed breed human rights violations. On the other hand, much of international relations cannot be properly understood by simple reference to "prisoner's dilemma," in which fear of insecurity is the only attitude, explaining all policies. Some states will pursue human rights abroad only when such action can be made to fit with traditional national interests. But some states in some situations will pursue human rights through international action even at the expense of certain traditional interests, such as independence in policy making, hence the Council of Europe and European Union. At least sometimes they will incur some costs for the rights of others, as NATO did over Kosovo, as the British did in Sierra Leone, etc. Realists do not understand that some states, like some natural persons, wish to stand for something besides independent power, obtained and used in other than a machiavellian process.

Marxists

The Marxist critique of international human rights merits a separate book. But it is accurate to say here, albeit briefly, that Marxists consider individual legal rights a sham in the context of economic forces and structures that prevent the effective exercise of human rights. Legal human rights on paper are supposedly negated by exploitative capitalism that leads to the accumulation of profit rather than the betterment of human beings. When large parts of the world manifest persons earning less than one dollar per day, extensive human rights in legal form are meaningless. In this view international human rights have been used more since 1945 to legitimate international capitalism than to protect human beings from predatory capitalistic states and corporations.[31]

For a classical Marxist, "the contradictions that characterize human rights reflect the conflicts inherent in capitalist society, lead to pervasive violations of those rights, and make respect for them impossible, particularly in this era of global capitalism."[32] Thus, material conditions control, exercising rights depends on having wealth, corporate for-profit rights trump individual fundamental rights, and the Universal Declaration of

---

[30] See further Robert O. Keohane and Joseph H. Nye, *Power and Interdependence: World Politics in Transition* (Boston: Little, Brown, 1977). In their view, realism is not very relevant to that type of international relations called complex interdependence.

[31] See, for example, Norman Lewis, "Human Rights, Law, and Democracy in an Unfree World," in Evans, ed., *Human Rights Fifty Years On*, 77–104.

[32] Gary Teeple, *The Riddle of Human Rights* (Amherst, NY: Humanity Books, 2005).

Rights cannot be realized as long as international relations reflects global capitalism.

There is some overlap between Marxists and pragmatic liberals. Both would agree that the international financial institutions such as the World Bank and the International Monetary Fund need to consider further the human hardship caused by their structural adjustment programs. Both argue the futility of seeing and dealing with human rights apart from their socio-economic context. Pragmatic liberals differ from Marxists in believing that regulated capitalism, and its primary global agent the transnational corporation, can be a force for progress and is not irredeemably exploitative. Pragmatic liberals also differ from Marxists in seeing in western history an effort to combine political freedom, economic freedom, and checks on gross abuses of human dignity, and not a record of unrelenting exploitation.

In summary of these two illiberal critiques, one can say that realism has been the most important historically. Realism has been the dominant prism in the powerful western world for understanding international relations. It has argued that national liberals, if rational, would not be liberal in anarchical international relations, or if they understood the evil "nature of man." Nowhere has the *practice* of Marxism led to an attractive model of human development entailing an acceptable degree of personal freedom.[33] Marxism, perhaps in the form of democratic socialism, however, would seem to have continuing relevance by reminding us of the exploitative tendencies of unregulated capitalism, and of the weakness of legal rights when divorced from certain social and economic facts – e.g., minimal achievements in education and income.

In the final analysis even most of the critics of what I have termed classical political liberalism at the close of the twentieth century do not reject entirely the concept of universal human rights. They argue for its validity, but stress various cautions, reforms, and refinements. Even Kissinger and most other realists tolerate international human rights, although they do not give them high priority and they are unwilling to greatly complicate traditional diplomacy with much attention to them.

Fukuyama may yet be proved correct, however, in that no theory save some type of liberalism offers much prospect of a better world in the twenty-first century. A caution bears repeating. If Fukuyama is read to mean support for libertarianism and minimal governance, instability is the likely result. Libertarian liberalism wants to emphasize private property as a civil right, and to elevate it to a central and absolute position in its

---

[33] See further Zbigniew Brzezinski, *The Grand Failure: The Birth and Death of Communism in the Twentieth Century* (New York: Scribner, 1989).

view of the good life. But the result of this view is Dickens' England, or the USA in the era of Henry Ford. There are definitely liberal interpretations that are injurious to human dignity, as recalled particularly in chapter 8 where the misdeeds of certain private corporations were reviewed. It is no small task to combine property rights featuring "economic freedom" with other rights and freedoms so as to produce a widely shared view of social justice or human dignity.

The Big Picture

Are there important and enduring patterns and correlations on the subject of human rights in international relations? The answer is yes, with awareness of limitations and constant modification through new research.[34] If we focus on rights of personal integrity such as freedom from torture, forced disappearances, summary execution, and the like, we find that the protection of these rights is positively correlated with: democracy, economic development, peace, former status as British colony, and small population size. In other words, individuals are most at risk for torture and other violations of personal integrity in populous, authoritarian, poor states, facing international or internal armed conflict, and without the restraining traditions of British heritage.

If we inquire more carefully into why democracy seems to generally reduce violations of personal integrity, research by Bruce Bueno De Mesquita and others suggests that: full democracy through the form of multiparty competitive elections is necessary to get this effect; more limited forms of democracy short of multi-party elections do not produce the same effect; and the notion of real accountability to the electorate seems to be the key to the process.[35]

Such general trends are then cross cut by others. For example, economic development in Arab-Islamic states does not have a positive correlation with protection of women's rights. Particular cultural factors intervene to block the normally beneficial impact of economic development.

Can we say for sure what produces democracy, with its civil and political rights? No, but there are some correlations between economic wealth and sustaining democracy. According to Adam Przeworski and Fernando Limongi, democracy does not last very long in the face of economic

---

[34] For an overview see David P. Forsythe and Patrice C. McMahon, eds., *Human Rights and Diversity: Area Studies Revisited* (Lincoln: University of Nebraska Press, 2003), especially chapters 1 and 2, and the conclusion.

[35] "Thinking Inside the Box: A Closer Look at Democracy and Human Rights," *International Studies Quarterly*, 49, 3 (September 2005), from 439.

adversity.[36] During the Cold War more or less, a democratic state with a per-capita income of $1,500 lasted eight years or less; a per-capita income up to $3,000 increased the longevity of a democratic state to an average of 18 years; above a per-capita income of $6,000, democratic sustainability was largely assured. Against this background, it made complete sense that in 2004 citizens in relatively poor states like Russia or several states in the Western Hemisphere expressed considerable sympathy for a return to authoritarian government, given that existing democratic (or partially democratic) governments had compiled a poor record on increasing per-capita income.[37]

One could group states in different ways, and inquire into correlations about different rights and types of rights, but it was clear that some insights into the fate of rights could be obtained through careful research.[38] One of the most persistent conclusions out of this type of research was that it was futile to focus on civil and political rights without regard to their socio-economic and cultural context. From the time of Weimar Germany in the 1920s and 1930s to Afghanistan after the Taliban, holding elections would only mean so much over time. Without attention to economic development and equitable distribution of the fruits of that development, and without attention to cultural factors impeding equity if not equality, elections would not contribute to sustained human dignity.

One might recall at this point that the UN General Assembly has repeatedly endorsed the notion that civil, political, economic, social, and cultural rights are interdependent and equally important.

Final thoughts

In the early 1980s the conclusion to one overview of human rights in international relations started with a discussion of Stalinism in the Soviet Union and finished with a discussion of apartheid in South Africa.[39] In the late 1990s neither the Soviet Union nor legally segregated South Africa existed. Things do change, and sometimes in progressive fashion.[40] That is one reason for a guarded optimism about the future of human rights.

Both European Stalinism and white racism in southern Africa are spent forces. Each yielded to persistent criticism over many decades. Along the

---

[36] "Modernization: Theories and Facts," *World Politics*, 49, 2 (January 1997), 155–183.

[37] Warren Hoge, "Latin Americans are Nostalgic for Strongman Rule," *International Herald Tribune*, April 21, 2004.

[38] See Forsythe and McMahon, op.cit., especially the chapter by David L. Richards.

[39] David P. Forsythe, *Human Rights and World Politics* (Lincoln: University of Nebraska Press, 1983), ch. 6.

[40] See further especially Paul Gordon Lauren, *The Evolution of International Human Rights: Visions Seen* (Philadelphia: University of Pennsylvania Press, 1998).

way elites in Moscow and Pretoria were staunchly committed to gross violations of human rights, albeit rationalized in the name of some "higher good." In the case of communism it was the quest for a classless utopia. In the case of apartheid it was betterment through separate development. Prospects for radical change often seemed bleak. And yet a historical perspective shows a certain progress.

But in areas of both former European communism and former white racism in southern Africa, violations of human rights remain. Far too many in both areas lack adequate food, clothing, shelter, and health care mandated by internationally recognized human rights. Corrupt judges and police officers make a mockery of many civil rights, as does rampant crime – much of it organized transnationally. In some areas the right to political participation is not secure. Nor are minorities.

And so the quest for better protection of individual and collective human rights continues. All human rights victories are partial, since the perfectly rights-protective society has yet to appear. The end of Stalinism in the Czech Republic seems to have done little to change discrimination against the Roma in that country. Some human rights victories are pyrrhic, since the *ancien régime* can look relatively good in historical perspective. Tito's Yugoslavia did not implement anything close to the full range of internationally recognized civil and political rights. But it did not engage in mass murder, mass misery, ethnic cleansing, and systematic rape as a weapon of war. These things did appear, however, in both Bosnia and Kosovo in the 1990s.

The various levels of action for human rights – whether global, regional, national, or sub-national – were not likely to wither away because of lack of human rights violations with which to deal. Pursuing liberalism in a realist world is no simple task.

Discussion questions

- Do the past fifty years show that serious concern for personal rights can indeed improve the human condition in the state system of international relations?
- If one compares the Congo during King Leopold's time with the Democratic Congo (formerly Zaire) today, has anything changed about the human condition?
- When is it appropriate, if ever, to grant immunity for past violations of human rights, and otherwise to avoid legal proceedings about human rights violations, for the sake of improving the human condition?
- Are the demands for a third-generation of human rights to peace, development, and a healthy environment well considered?

- Do internationally recognized human rights require radical change so as to properly protect women's dignity?
- Even after the political demise of European Marxism, are Marxists correct that capitalism and the transnational corporation are inherently exploitative of labor? What social values can markets advance (e.g., efficiency?), and what social values can they not advance (e.g., equity?)?
- Should one be optimistic or pessimistic about the future of human rights in international relations?

Suggestions for further reading

Alston, Philip, "Conjuring Up New Human Rights: A Proposal for Quality Control," *American Journal of International Law*, 78, 3 (July 1984), 607–621. A plea for a moratorium on more human rights until protection improves for those already recognized.

Boyle, Kevin, and Juliet Sheen, eds., *Freedom of Religion and Belief: A World Report* (London: Routledge, 1997). An encyclopedia on the subject.

Brzezinski, Zbigniew, *The Grand Failure: The Birth and Death of Communism in the Twentieth Century* (New York: Scribner, 1989). An overview of what went wrong particularly with European communism, written in engaging style by the National Security Advisor to President Carter.

Cook, Rebecca J., ed., *Human Rights of Women: National and International Perspectives* (Philadelphia: University of Pennsylvania Press, 1994). A good and broad coverage of feminist perspectives on human rights.

Forsythe, David P. and Patrice C. McMahon, *Human Rights and Diversity: Area Studies Revisited* (Lincoln: University of Nebraska Press, 2003). A collection of essays studying the interplay of universal rights and global trends with factors particular to certain areas and regions.

Franck, Thomas M., "Is Personal Freedom a Western Value?," *American Journal of International Law*, 91, 4 (October 1997), 593–627. Suggests that the West has no monopoly on the desire for personal freedom.

Gormley, W. Paul, *Human Rights and the Environment: The Need for International Co-operation* (Leiden: W.W. Sijthoff, 1976). An early study based on the premise that we need a third-generation human right to a healthy environment.

Hochschild, Adam, *King Leopold's Ghost: A Story of Greed, Terror, and Heroism in Colonial Africa* (Boston: Houghton Mifflin, 1998). A gripping history of the lack of human rights in Central Africa when the Congo was the personal fiefdom of the King of Belgium.

Hocking, B., *Catalytic Diplomacy* (Leicester: Centre for Diplomatic Studies, 1996). Argues that in the modern world what governments frequently do is organize others for agreement and action, rather than establish a foreign policy completely independent from other actors.

Ignatieff, Michael, *The Warrior's Honor: Ethnic War and the Modern Conscience* (New York: Metropolitan, 1997). A cosmopolitan and Renaissance man reflects on whether humane limits can be applied to ethnic war, arguing for the importance of traditional conceptions such as military honor.

Ignatieff, *The Lesser Evil: Political Ethics in an Age of Terrorism* (Princeton: Princeton University Press, 2005). A leading thinker on human rights contemplates the effects of confronting Al Qaida after September 11, 2001.

Johansen, Robert C., *The National Interest and the Human Interest: An Analysis of US Foreign Policy* (Princeton: Princeton University Press, 1980). Shows clearly that if one starts with realist principles of state interest, one winds up with different policies than if one starts with liberal principles of human interest.

Kagan, Robert, *Of Paradise and Power: America and Europe in the New World Order* (New York: Vintage, 2004). Supposedly the Europeans are interested in human rights and international law and organization, while the USA is interested in the use of power to protect national security in a hostile world.

Keohane, Robert O., and Joseph H. Nye, *Power and Interdependence: World Politics in Transition* (Boston: Little, Brown, 1977). A major study arguing that there are different types of international relations. Realism may be appropriate to some, liberalism or pragmatic-liberalism to others. Argues that realism is less and less appropriate to contemporary international relations.

Pogge, Thomas, *World Poverty and Human Rights: Cosmopolitan Responsibilities and Reforms* (Cambridge: Polity, 2002). A leading philosopher reflects on, and provides data about, poverty, hunger, and human rights.

Slaughter, Anne-Marie, *A New World Order* (Princeton: Princeton University Press, 2005). The Dean of the Princeton Woodrow Wilson School argues that national authorities are cooperating with international courts in a way that is already producing considerable transnational protection of certain human rights.

Teeple, Gary, *The Riddle of Human Rights* (Amherst, NY: Humanity Books, 2005). A clearly argued Marxist analysis.

Index